GRIEF, DYING, AND DEATH

Clinical Interventions
for Caregivers

THERESE A. RANDO

Foreword by J. William Worden

RESEARCH PRESS
2612 NORTH MATTIS AVENUE
CHAMPAIGN, ILLINOIS 61822
www.researchpress.com

Advisory Editor, Frederick H. Kanfer

Cover design by Jack W. Davis
Composition by Graphic World

ISBN 0-87822-232-4
Library of Congress Catalog Card Number: 84-60903

This book is lovingly dedicated to my family of origin:

to my parents,
Thomas A. and Letitia G. Rando,
whose lives taught me about love
and
whose deaths taught me about grief

and to my siblings,
Beth and Randy,
who went through it all with me.

Contents

Foreword

Nearly 20 years ago Colin Parkes and his colleagues were conducting the Harvard Bereavement Study at the Massachusetts Mental Health Center and Phyllis Silverman was launching her pioneering work with Widow-to-Widow programs. Across Boston, at the Massachusetts General Hospital, Avery Weisman and I began the Omega Project studying various aspects of life-threatening illness and behavior. At that time research interest in dying and bereavement was just beginning to increase, and the literature on these subjects was still manageable. However, over these 20 years there has been an explosion of research, discussion, and writing in these areas. Much of the important material from this period is collected in this book, to which Dr. Rando has added her own observations as a researcher and clinician.

In 1974 Elisabeth Ross and I asked 6,000 health care providers if working with the dying presented any difficulties for them. Of the 98% who experienced difficulty, many said it was because the dying patient confronted them with their own mortality. I believe this same phenomena exists today. To develop skills in terminal illness care without addressing the issue of personal death awareness is to miss an important dimension, and Dr. Rando has recognized this. Therefore the book opens by addressing our society's attitude toward death and the issue of our own personal death awareness, which can make working with the dying and bereaved difficult.

Early chapters of this book address the issue of bereavement, why it is necessary and how to work with individuals and families who are hurting from a loss. The latter half of the book looks at the issue of terminal illness care. Dr. Rando presents a sensitive but realistic approach to the difficult issues to be faced in the dying process. She offers many practical suggestions for the caregiver who is working with both individuals and families.

One of the best chapters in this book is the one on funeral

practices. Here Dr. Rando examines the case for funerals and funeral rituals from both a psychological and sociological perspective. A reader who has not thought through the importance of the funeral would do well to study this chapter, for there is some very convincing evidence presented here.

Another change that has occurred during the last 20 years is the emergence of the Hospice Movement in the U.S. and other parts of the world. This movement is bringing together all types of people to care for the dying and the bereaved. It both excites and frightens me that there are so many people out there willing to help. I can only hope that this bodes well for the future, but training and knowledge can help assure the best outcome. The exercises found in this book give the reader an opportunity to respond personally to the material, and can be useful in the training of hospice personnel.

This book is full of material. I would encourage the reader to read the book carefully and to try to integrate the information with his own clinical experience. Research need not only be done formally and on a large scale; it can also be done by the individual clinician. By keeping systematic observations of his own experience, a clinician can help expand the horizons of our understanding of bereavement and dying.

I would also encourage the reader to question the concepts presented in any book on bereavement and death, judging the evidence on which the information is based. In any emerging field it is easy for folk beliefs to arise and to become dogma, so we need to continually question these beliefs and to be open to evidence that both supports and challenges them. This book provides a great deal of well-chosen material for the reader to consider.

In the final analysis there is no one right way to work with the dying or the bereaved. We would do well to heed the admonition of Professor Gordon Allport, who would tell those of us studying psychology with him at Harvard, "Remember, each man is like all other men, each man is like some other men, and it is also true that each man is like no other man." In the end death is still a very personal and individual event. Avery Weisman's concept of "appropriate death" reminds us that a fitting death will be different for each person. We as caregivers need to keep this in mind, and Dr. Rando gives us much to draw on as we try to find the best approach for a particular patient or family.

Harvard Medical School   J. William Worden, PhD
Massachusetts General Hospital
Boston, Massachusetts

Acknowledgments

One's knowledge of grief, dying, and death can come from a variety of sources. There are a number of people who have been especially influential to my work in these areas and who have indirectly contributed to many of the ideas in this book. Although it is prohibitive to name all of these individuals here, I would like to take the opportunity to acknowledge some very special people.

Appreciation must go to my patients, who have continually proved to me that, although nothing can be in pain as much as the human heart, there is nothing as indomitable as the human spirit.

The members of Thanatology Associates of Rhode Island, Inc., have served as professional and personal resources for me since 1975. They include Esther D'Orsi; J. Eugene Knott, PhD; N. Claire Kowalski, MSW; A. J. Nookie, MWW; Reverend Duane Parker, PhD; Ralph Redding, MD; Michael E. Scala, MD; Reverend Kenneth Wentzel; and Barbara Wright, RN, BS. Another member, Marion A. Humphrey, RN, MA, has been significantly helpful by sharing with me her vast clinical experience and her unparalleled expertise and sensitivity in working with the dying.

I have been fortunate to have been gifted with two superb mentors, one in clinical psychology and one in thanatology. In the field of clinical psychology I am indebted to Lawrence C. Grebstein, PhD, who has provided years of instruction, supervision, and insight into the art and science of the profession. The individual who has been most responsible for guiding and supporting my work in the field of thanatology has been J. Eugene Knott, PhD. He has been uniquely instrumental in the unfolding of my career. His encouragement and understanding have been pivotal, both personally and professionally.

Patricia Sammann and Ann Wendel of Research Press receive my deep gratitude, not only for their professional guidance, but also for their warm support and understanding throughout the longer-than-expected process of writing this book.

My administrative assistant, Barbara Tremaine Vargas, deserves particular mention. Without her help, and that provided by her able associate, Manrique, this book would have been impossible.

And the most special acknowledgment of all goes to my best friend, Anthony.

Introduction

This book has a dual purpose. It is first meant to provide pertinent clinical interventions to front-line caregivers, based on relevant research on grief and dying. Second, it presents primary sources from the thanatological literature. At a time when students of thanatology are reading texts that are summaries of summaries of summaries, it seemed important to offer the original material from both the classic works and the newest research. Consequently, this book presents practical, specific intervention strategies through material taken from primary sources.

The approach taken in this book emphasizes several points:

- Loss is stressed as the central theme of both terminal illness and bereavement, with the dying experience viewed as a specific example of the grief process. The basic course and tasks of grief and mourning are clearly delineated in terms of the therapeutic issues that need to be addressed in each loss situation.
- Ongoing assessment of each individual's unique situation within a psychological, sociological, physiological/medical, and socioeconomic framework is encouraged. This assessment includes consideration of not only universal types of reactions, but also developmental life span issues and the individual's idiosyncratic concerns in grief and dying. This is done in the hope of dispelling the notion that all patients or grievers undergo similar reactions in a set pattern.
- The caregiver's personal and professional feelings, fears, and expectations are viewed as significant factors affecting patient care that must be examined. A realistic perspective for caregivers is proposed, one designed to facilitate the most therapeutic interactions with the dying and bereaved.
- A series of recent social, technological, and medical changes are recognized as having dramatically complicated the dying and grieving process for individuals in Western society, thus

making these experiences increasingly difficult to undergo. Specific interventions designed to ameliorate these effects are suggested.

Exercises and case examples are included to connect theory with practical applications and to assist readers in confronting personal concerns, thoughts, and feelings affecting their work with the dying and bereaved.

The term *caregiver* was chosen purposely for use throughout this book. It reflects the fact that many different types of professionals are involved in the care of the dying and the bereaved— nurses, physicians, mental health professionals, social workers, physical and recreational therapists, clergy, hospice volunteers, and funeral directors, to name but a few. Educators and health care administrators have an impact as well, albeit in different ways. However, the term *caregiver* also encompasses nonprofessionals, for it is not only professionals who can give care. A caregiver can be a friend, a concerned loved one, a confidant. This book has been written for all those who wish to interact with the dying and bereaved in a caring manner.

Throughout the book, the use of masculine and feminine pronouns has been alternated. This was done to acknowledge the fact that both men and women can be caregivers or in need of care.

The book starts with a self-examination of our own personal feelings about death, as individuals and as part of American society. It then moves to a discussion of grief, beginning with a clarification of the grief process in Chapter 2, a consideration of the factors affecting individuals' grief reactions in Chapter 3, and an examination of the forms and causes of unresolved grief in Chapter 4. Specific interventions for the bereaved are explained in Chapter 5. In Chapter 6, four different bereavement situations and their unique intervention strategies are described: grief after the death of a child; grief after the death of a spouse; grief after suicide; and children's grief. Chapter 7 focuses on the benefits of funerals and how they can be adapted to suit the needs of mourners. The dying patient is first considered in Chapter 8, which covers the patient's experience of the living-dying interval. Chapter 9 is devoted to the dying patient's reactions to the approach of death; Chapter 10 addresses the coping mechanisms that can be used to handle this threat. Guidelines for working with dying patients are contained in Chapter 11, including attitudes towards patients, communication with patients, selection of interventions, treatment of pain, and the roles of clergy and ancillary personnel. The effects of terminal illness on the entire family system is the topic of Chapter 12, and Chapter 13 considers the special stresses created when the dying family member is a child. The final chapter, Chapter 14, takes up ethical issues and decision making, and the caregiver's stress from working with the dying and bereaved.

CHAPTER 1

Our Attitudes Towards Death

SELF-MORTALITY

Throughout history, humanity has been concerned with mortality. Philosophy, religion, and science have all been employed in an attempt to understand and control death. However, death continues to be inevitable, and this knowledge determines much of how we look at life.

Life as we know it is inconceivable without the tacit assumption that it must end. Such things as reproduction, emotion, competition, and ambition would be pointless if there were never any death (Verwoerdt, 1966). The very fact that we are finite and have only limited time makes life all the more poignant and meaningful. If we were immortal there would be no reason for aspiring, hoping, striving, and attempting to make meaning out of life; our experiences would pale in intensity if there were an endless supply of tomorrows with limitless opportunities.

Death affects our perceptions of life in many beneficial ways (Koestenbaum, 1976):

- It helps us savor life.
- It provides an opposite by which to judge being alive.
- It gives us a sense of a real, individual existence.
- It gives meaning to courage and integrity, allowing us to effectively express our convictions.
- It provides us with the strength to make major decisions.
- It reveals the importance of intimacy in our lives.
- It helps us ascribe meaning to our lives retroactively, which is especially useful for older people.
- It shows us the importance of ego-transcending achievements.
- It allows us to see our achievements as having significance.

1

However, death also threatens us with the negation of ourselves and all that we value. We are future-oriented; to conceive of a time in which there will be no future arouses anxiety. Even events associated with death, such as separation, loss, sleep, illness, loss of control, or saying good-bye can bring out this feeling. Each of us is continuously subject to the threat of death; thus, each of us (unless severely organic) must find a way to cope with this threat. There are many possibilities, as attitudes towards death may range from complete denial to complete and existential acceptance. Nevertheless, as therapists and philosophers have noted, the particular attitude adopted will be sure to influence our lives significantly.

For instance, one person may choose to deny his mortality. Because of this, he will avoid talking about death with anyone. His children's questions about the topic will be ignored or rejected. Wakes and funerals will be missed. He may postpone the necessity of making a will or getting a yearly physical exam. Separations and losses will be minimized. Another person might try to counter death by defying it. He might be a daredevil, consciously taking on dangerous situations; or he might ignore the physician's instructions about a serious medical problem. Such a person needs to prove that he has control over death and will be the master of his fate. Someone else will put his faith in a life after death. Through religion, he can believe that his life here is merely a prelude to the afterlife. Thus, he may deny the importance of worldly striving and seek to follow his religion's teachings. Still others may use a combination of these, or shift from one to another.

The fact that we, at some future time, will "not be" has innumerable ramifications and reactions in the "now." The responses will be diverse: from the individual who denies death and has his body cryonically frozen to be brought back at a future time, to the person who accepts the finitude of life but establishes immortality through the reproduction of offspring or the creation of artistic works, to the existentialist who endeavors to create meaning in the present with disregard for the future. In an infinite number of ways we all react to the knowledge of the fact that we will die, and this reaction is extremely crucial in determining how we choose to live and die.

PERSONAL FEELINGS ABOUT DEATH

In the 70s, a superb book by Robert Kavanaugh was published entitled *Facing Death* (1974). In it is a chapter called "Confronting Death-Related Feelings" in which Kavanaugh legitimizes our having a variety of personal gut-level responses towards death. His unique contribution is that he notes that these responses do not preclude our doing effective work with the dying and the bereaved *if* we are aware of them. He explains that it is normal and natural to have less-than-positive feelings about death.

Most Americans have no more than shadowy indications of their true feelings about death. Ask friends how they feel about dying or death, and you will hear how they would like to feel or how they think they ought to feel. . . . It became clear to me that an honest and humane approach to death can begin only when we allow ourselves to get in touch with our visceral *feelings*. Otherwise, any stance we adopt toward death will be no more than another form of blocking and avoiding honest confrontation. It is not the dying or the dead we fear as much as the unknown and untested *feelings* they evoke within ourselves. . . .

We assume a variety of masks to pretend we are objective when we only mean we are controlled. . . . Society recognizes that there are times when every human being needs to don a mask. . . . Human limitations require that we invest only so much of self in the loss and grief of others. No man can rightfully tell another how far to push himself. . . .

Honest recognition of our latent feelings about human mortality enables us to be free enough to make some choices. Only when we know our feelings can we respect our unique reactions. No longer need we pummel and even smash our emotional selves behind artificial defenses. Once free, we can choose the masks we want or need, even sometimes going maskless, instead of compulsively avoiding the reality of all death and grief because we lack the humility and courage to be any other way.

Most people I observe don their masks compulsively. Some of our masks are cruel, demeaning, inflammatory or actually harmful to patients and families, reflecting a coldness we do not feel, a curtness, an indifference, a sense of being too busy. Once we become aware of our rigid, compulsive behavior, we may start to find some freedom of choice, and alternative stances are possible. Professionals and laymen can select a shield that fits the situation, respecting personal needs and limitations and the needs of folks they visit. It helps immensely for professionals to inspect the mask they wear, encouraging honest feedback from patients or families. Those who believe their traditional stance is one of objectivity may soon learn how narrow the line is between objectivity and coldness. . . .

No books or conferences, no movies or discussions, will be effective, ultimately, in helping us master the art of peace and graciousness near death, until we permit our feelings to be honestly and fully felt, and admit it is alright to feel as we do. Until then, newly acquired skills will be no more than fresh evasions.

Only some uneasiness and fear will disappear when we succeed in opening up. Much will remain as part of our cultural heritage. We will not grow instantly brave, only gradually less fearful of being human, of owning up to the reality of self. What is so wrong with feeling a modicum of fear and uneasiness without running to hide? Such feelings are as normal and natural as death. . . . For practiced and unpracticed alike, it is normal to feel uneasy around death. And it is not abnormal to admit or show it. . . .

Let me reassure you it is okay to feel uneasy or afraid. It is okay to want to run, to send floral wreaths or mass cards instead of self. It is okay to feel eerie or unduly tense, to hide and cry, to want to swear or scream or lash out at easy targets. It is okay to feel relieved and even happy when someone dies. It is okay to feel whatever is real. Feelings have no morality. They are neither good nor bad, always ethically neutral. (pp. 22-27, 39)

Kavanaugh continues his encouragement to seek out and identify our fears about death. He suggests that we focus on early experiences that possibly formed our present attitudes towards death. As a second approach he urges us to carefully reflect on the death fears admitted by others, since any list of such fears would be sure to contain concerns and trepidations of our own. And what does he suggest that we do once we have explored our death-related feelings?

Once we discover the nature and extent of our visceral feelings, it helps to counter-attack. It facilitates growth to experience what we fear without trying so hard to mask our reactions. Uneasy in the presence of the dying? Visit them and stay longer than needed. Fearful of open tears? Visit grief-stricken friends. Uncomfortable at wakes and funerals? Go! And soon we will find that others can accept our clumsiness whenever we can. In fact, the clumsiness of professionals and friends grants to patients and their families permission to exhibit tears and awkwardness they never dared display before.

I would prefer the clammy or trembling hand of someone than no hand at all. In fact, I would never know if the moisture and shakes were theirs or mine. I would prefer a doctor who stuttered and lost some dignity in tears than to be continually chilled by professional aloofness. I would rather a friend came and dumped his own fears than to grieve alone or with too fearless a friend. I could gain far more from a mortician with a real tear in his eye and a real quiver in his voice than from one with impeccable control and modulated emotions. Humaneness triggers humaneness. Warmth generates warmth. (p. 27)

Exercise I at the end of this chapter provides an opportunity to consider and evaluate our own early experiences with death.

AMERICAN SOCIO-CULTURAL ATTITUDES TOWARDS DEATH

In order to appreciate our own and others' responses to loss and death, we need to have an understanding of the socio-cultural context within which they occur. Because death is universal, each culture has had to develop its own beliefs, mores, norms, standards, and restrictions. Appropriate ways to respond in one culture may be punished in another. Each society dictates the standards to be followed, supporting or prohibiting certain behaviors and determining the repertoire of responses from which mourners can choose. Any work with people in the areas of loss and death must take into account their social, cultural, religious/philosophical, and ethnic backgrounds.

Only a brief overview of the dominant American attitude towards death will be presented here, as it would be impossible to discuss the many rich and varied differences found across the world. Even within our own culture, though, there will be many differences among individuals depending upon their ethnic, social, and religious backgrounds.

Each society's response to death is a function of how death fits into its teleological view of life. For all societies there seem to be three general patterns of response: *death-accepting, death-defying,* or *death-denying.*

Primitive, nontechnological societies, such as those of the Fiji Islanders and Trobrianders, are usually death-accepting. The people in these societies view death as an inevitable and natural part of the life cycle. Dying and attendant behaviors are integrated into the everyday patterns of living.

Death-defying societies are those such as in early Egypt. Here the populace refused to believe that death would take anything away. Hence, pyramids were built to contain all the Pharoah's wives and money and possessions for the world after death. Death itself would not deprive the Pharoah; he would vanquish it.

The United States today is an example of a death-denying culture. There is widespread refusal to confront death. There are fewer rituals for recognizing it, replaced by contrivances for coping with it. The attitude is that death is antithetical to living and that it is not a natural part of human existence.

Many Americans go to great lengths to shield themselves from the realities of death. Take for example the fact that the vast majority of Americans no longer die in their own homes, but are sent to nursing homes and hospitals to die, away from their own familiar home, family, and friends. It is true that because of this family members need not be made uncomfortable by watching their loved one die; but for the dying individual death becomes lonely, mechanical, and dehumanized. At the very moment that people most need the comfort of human companionship and sentiment they are isolated in a hospital room to await death alone and unassisted.

Kübler-Ross paints a classic picture of a more natural death in her book *On Death and Dying* (1969):

> I remember as a child the death of a farmer. He fell from a tree and was not expected to live. He asked simply to die at home, a wish that was granted without questioning. He called his daughters into the bedroom and spoke with each one of them alone for a few minutes. He arranged his affairs quietly, though he was in great pain, and distributed his belongings and his land, none of which was to be split until his wife should follow him in death. He also asked each of his children to share in the work, duties, and tasks that he had carried on until the time of the accident. He asked his friends to visit him once more, to bid good-bye to them. Although I was a small child at the time, he did not exclude me or my siblings. We were allowed to share in the preparations of the family just as we were permitted to grieve with them until he died. When he did die, he was left at home, in his own beloved home which he had built, and among his friends and neighbors who went to take a last look at him where he lay in the midst of flowers in the place he had lived in and loved so much. In that country today there is still no make-believe slumber room, no embalming, no false makeup to pretend sleep. Only the signs of very disfiguring illnesses are covered up with bandages and only infectious cases are removed from the home prior to the burial.
>
> Why do I describe such "old-fashioned" customs? I think they are an indication of our acceptance of a fatal outcome, and they help the dying patient as well as his family to accept the loss of a loved one. If a patient is allowed to terminate his life in the familiar and beloved environment, it requires less adjustment. . . . The fact that children are allowed to stay at home where a fatality has stricken and are included in the talk, discussions, and fears gives them the feeling that they are not alone in the grief and gives them the comfort of shared responsibility and shared mourning. It prepares them gradually and helps them view death as part of life. (pp. 5-6)

Kübler-Ross is attempting to stress the importance of treating death as a natural part of life. But the death of the farmer in Switzerland she describes would be all too foreign in America. While there has been some progress in recent years in discussing death more openly, for the most part Americans still take great pains to avoid the fact of death. The dying are sent away to institutions at the end of their lives. The dead person resides in the "slumber room." Phrases like "pass on" and "at rest" are used, and there is little open communication about the death. Funerals and mourning rituals are decried as unnecessary and barbaric. In effect, the fact that the individual has died is denied to a large extent. Worse still, that denial is perpetuated in the young by sending them away because they are "too young to understand" or by telling lies such as "Mommy has gone to sleep." Many Americans will go to practically any extreme to avoid accepting death for what it is—a cessation of life, a natural part of the life cycle.

Herman Feifel, in his essay "The Meaning of Death in American Society: Implications for Education" (1971), traces some of the reasons why it is so difficult for Americans today to accept death. He contrasts today with the Middle Ages, when death was viewed as the emergence into a new life. The Christian idea of death as a continuation of life, albeit changed from before, was prevalent. Death was the reunification with the Creator; death would carry one to a final reward. Today, with the disintegration of family ties and other supportive group interactions, plus the upsurge in technology and its resulting depersonalization and alienation, there is a "waning of providential faith, death no longer signals atonement and redemption as much as man's loneliness and a threat to his pursuit of happiness. Fear of death reveals less concern with judgment, and more with total annihilation and loss of identity" (p. 4). Americans no longer have the sense of continuity or relationship with others that might help them transcend death in a meaningful way, leaving them with existential anxiety.

Lifton, in *Death in Life: Survivors of Hiroshima* (1968), has come to some of the same conclusions as Feifel in delineating what has led Americans to have increased difficulty in dealing with death. He describes six variables:

- *Urbanization.* Individuals are increasingly removed from nature and witnessing of the life/death cycle. They also have less of a sense of community with others, and have few common rituals to express feelings and guide behavior.
- *Exclusion of the aged and dying.* These people are segregated away from the general populace into nursing homes and hospitals, making death a foreign experience that elicits the fear of being alone.
- *Movement towards the nuclear family.* With the absence of the extended family comes increased vulnerability to devastation and loss of support following the death of a loved one. There also is no opportunity to see aged relatives die and to experience death as a natural part of the life cycle.
- *Secularization from religion.* Religion used to minimize the impact of physical death by focusing on the hereafter, endow death with a special meaning and purpose, and provide for a future and immortality. With the decline in religion there has been a marked loss of these coping mechanisms.
- *Advances in medical technology.* These have given humanity more of a sense of control. There is less of a need for systems of thought that make death meaningful, such as philosophy or religion. Technology has promised immortality through cryonics; however, it also has created torturous bioethical

quandaries (e.g., the definition of death, euthanasia). As life can be extended, deaths become more infrequent occurrences, and terminal illnesses become chronic. All of these advances have compromised the ability to understand death as a natural part of human life.

- *Mass death.* Previously if someone contemplated her own death she could assume that it would cause a ripple in humanity signifying some degree of importance. With today's constant threat of mass death and nuclear destruction, however, this is absent. What good will it do to leave something behind if there is no world left to be aware of it? Additionally, peoples' sensitivities have become blunted to individual death. People learned to feel "good" that only 15 men died in Viet Nam instead of 30 on a particular day. In the past just one death would have been more horrifying.

Although advances and changes in Western culture have compounded Americans' struggle to cope with death, there are some systems that can offer comfort in dealing with death and that provide some form of immortality. Lifton (1973) suggests five modes:

- *The biological mode.* We extend ourselves into the future through our children. Our very genes and memories will be carried on in the projection of ourselves through our heirs.
- *The social mode.* Our lives have direction and meaning if we can leave something worthwhile behind us. This usually comes about through our work or creative endeavors.
- *The religious mode.* Religion provides a clear future in an immortal hereafter.
- *The natural mode.* We are part of nature. The decomposition of our bodies will nourish further growth in nature; we will not forever be destroyed because of our spot in the cycle of the chain of life.
- *The experiential transcendence mode.* There are psychological states that are so intense that there is a feeling of being beyond the confines of ordinary daily life. Time and death disappear. They can occur in religious or secular mysticism, in song, dance, battle, sexual love, or in the contemplation of artistic or intellectual creations; there is an extraordinary psychic unity and perceptual intensity in which there is no longer a restriction of the senses, including the awareness of mortality.

Some of us may find meaning and solace in one or more of these modes; others may seek alternative ways of coping with natural death anxiety, such as hedonism, existential philosophy, or beliefs in reincarnation.

Consideration of all these variables will provide a more complete understanding of the social and cultural framework out of which most patients and their families will operate. An appreciation of this is important because of the strong influence that society and culture will have upon their responses, as well as our own. In Exercise II at the end of this chapter, personal, social, and cultural attitudes towards death can be explored.

EXERCISE I

Early Experiences
Influencing Reactions to Loss and Death

Our early experiences with loss and death leave us with messages, feelings, fears, and attitudes we will carry throughout life. To prevent our being controlled by our unconscious and conscious reactions to past experiences, it is important to recognize and state explicitly how these experiences have influenced us and our lifestyles.

Think about your earliest death-related experience:
When did it occur? Where was it? Who was involved? What happened?

What were your reactions, positive and negative?

What were you advised to do, and what did you do, to cope with the experience?

What did you learn about death and loss as a result of this experience?

Of the things you learned then, what makes you feel fearful or anxious now?

Of the things you learned then, what makes it easier for you to cope with death now?

Consider your next death-related experience:
When did it occur? Where was it? Who was involved? What happened?

What were your reactions, positive and negative?

What were you advised to do, and what did you do, to cope with the experience?

What did you learn about death and loss as a result of this experience?

Of the things you learned then, what makes you feel fearful or anxious now?

Of the things you learned then, what makes it easier for you to cope with death now?

Taking together both of these early death-related experiences, what ideas or feelings appear repeatedly?

Think of your own feelings about death and the attitudes you maintain about it *currently*. Write down these feelings and attitudes.

The feelings and attitudes we have about death influence how we live all aspects of our lives. In what ways do your feelings and attitudes about death influence your own lifestyle and experience? (Do you defy death by being a daredevil? Do you deny death by avoiding wakes and funerals? Do you lessen the importance of death by espousing a religion promising eternal life? Do you attempt to accept death by being fatalistic?)

How do these feelings and attitudes about death affect how you currently cope with loss experiences, positively and negatively?

How does your interest in working with dying patients and the bereaved fit in with your issues related to death?

EXERCISE II

Your Socio-Cultural, Ethnic, and Religious/Philosophical Attitudes Towards Death

Reflect on your upbringing and socialization. Think about areas such as afterlife; burial rites, expected attitudes of loved ones towards the dying person before and after death; expected attitude of the dying person; expected differences in reactions to death due to age or gender; meaning of death to life; attitude towards caregivers; or attitude towards telling children about death. Then note those attitudes held towards death by your social group, cultural group, ethnic group, and religious/philosophical group.

Which norms, mores, beliefs, sanctions, and attitudes have you internalized about death from these groups?

How do these ideas affect the ways in which you work with the terminally ill and the bereaved, positively and negatively?

CHAPTER 2

Grief:
The Reaction to Loss

The terms *grief, mourning,* and *bereavement* are employed continuously when discussing loss. At some times they have been assigned specific meanings in the literature, while at other times they have been used interchangeably. As used in this text, they mean the following:

GRIEF: The process of psychological, social, and somatic reactions to the perception of loss. This implies that grief is (a) manifested in each of the psychological, social, and somatic realms; (b) a continuing development involving many changes; (c) a natural, expectable reaction (in fact, the absence of it is abnormal in most cases); (d) the reaction to the experience of many kinds of loss, not necessarily death alone; and (e) based upon the unique, individualistic perception of loss by the griever, that is, it is not necessary to have the loss recognized or validated by others for the person to experience grief. It is also hypothesized that grief is a product of biological evolution that has adaptive value (Averill, 1968). By making separation from the group or from its members an extremely stressful event, it helps assure group cohesiveness. This is important for those species in which the maintenance of social bonds is necessary for survival and those bonds are based upon individual recognition and attachment.

MOURNING: This term has historically had two meanings. The first, derived from psychoanalytic theory, is a wide array of intrapsychic processes, conscious and unconscious, that are prompted by loss (Bowlby, 1980). The second meaning is the cultural response to grief. This implies that there is no one style of grief, but that it is a reaction that, like other reactions, is socially and culturally influenced. As used in this text, the term *mourning* recognizes both meanings, but will be used interchangeably with grief because of its connotation of the same role and experience in that role for the griever. Grief may be conceptualized as a transitional phase in the overarching process of mourning (Knott, Note 1).

BEREAVEMENT: The state of having suffered a loss.

Grief is the normal reaction to loss, a universal experience repeatedly encountered. Loss is a natural part of existence: children lose baby teeth and childhood naivete; a pet kitten dies; a child graduates from high school; a lover is abandoned; a friend fails to achieve a goal; a brother moves away; a wife succumbs to cancer; retirement occurs.

Losses may be of two kinds: *physical* (tangible) or *symbolic* (psychosocial). Examples of a physical (tangible) loss include losing a desired possession or having a friend die; examples of a symbolic (psychosocial) loss include getting a divorce or losing status because of a job demotion. Usually a symbolic loss is not identified as a loss per se, so we may not realize we need to take the time to grieve and deal .with our feelings about it. Nevertheless, it will initiate a process of grief just as a physical loss will.

Loss always results in a deprivation of some kind. There are many losses that are clearly perceived as unpleasant deprivations, such as the loss of a spouse or the theft of valued jewelry. However, there are losses that are less clearly recognized as losses, and that do not necessarily result from negative events. These losses occur in response to normal change and growth. For example, when a couple has a child they automatically lose a relative amount of independence and freedom from responsibility. Some losses are competency-based. For example, terminating therapy, graduating from college, or having achieved a long-worked-for goal are experiences that result in the loss of striving. They also involve changes, which constitute a loss of the status quo. All these losses create deprivations, but they may not be recognized as losses, especially those that are associated with positive events. Consequently, these losses are not grieved. Such situations often cause the grievers of these kinds of losses to wonder why they feel sad after experiencing a normally happy event. This is why, for example, an executive may be so surprised when he finds himself feeling less than happily ecstatic after finally receiving a long-awaited promotion.

Over and over we must confront issues of loss. To a greater or lesser degree the process of grief occurs in reaction to each of these losses. The nature, intensity, and length of the grief process will be influenced by a number of variables (to be discussed in the next chapter); however, some response will always occur, even if it is merely an "Oh, I wish that hadn't happened!" after a teenager breaks her longest fingernail. The very same process also initiates the full-blown acute grief response to the death of a loved one. Grief is the process that allows us to let go of that which was and be ready for that which is to come.

If we think about it, it becomes apparent that many of the situations that have been difficult for us in our lives have entailed our having to experience some kind of loss, whether it be physical or symbolic. Neither one is necessarily any easier to cope with than the other. For a more personal understanding of this, complete Exercise III at the end of this chapter.

After having done this exercise, most people find that their most difficult experiences in life have involved a loss of some kind. This is why it is crucially important to recognize that grief is *not* only relegated to a reaction subsequent to the physical death of a loved one. For many of you, if the difficult situations you described had been interpreted as "symbolic deaths" (e.g., a divorce, an argument with a colleague, the breakup of a love relationship, a move to another city), you would have seen that your intense reactions were part of a grief process that you were unaware you were experiencing. This understanding might have enabled you to cope better at that time. In fact, in all of the different forms of therapy, one of the main ways in which the therapist helps the client is by assisting that client to recognize that a loss has occurred and that the client must now grieve for it, or by pointing out that the client's symptoms themselves are a form of grief reaction over the loss. It is critical that we as caregivers help identify symbolic losses for those we work with, for when those losses are not identified, individuals often fail to grieve appropriately, or do not recognize or understand the reactions they are undergoing and may suffer more as a consequence.

It is very common for a physical loss to result in a number of symbolic losses. For example, take the case of a patient hospitalized for a mastectomy necessitated by cancer. The loss of the breast is a physical loss; however, other symbolic losses ensue. Just being in a hospital setting entails the loss of the familiar home environment. Being sick and dependent upon others for care also causes a loss of independence and control for the individual, who is now in a patient role. The illness of cancer may bring with it a number of attendant physical and symbolic losses: loss of autonomy, loss of predictability, loss of bodily functions, loss of body parts, loss of identity, loss of intimacy, loss of social contact, loss of self-esteem, and loss of mobility. Each loss has an impact upon the individual and prompts some form of its own grief reaction. The loss of the breast is not necessarily perceived by the patient as any more or less of a loss than the loss of social contact. The meaning and extent of the loss will differ for each person according to that person's individual personality and characteristics. As caregivers, we should remember several things:

- An illness involves numerous losses that are both physical and symbolic in nature.
- Each of the specific losses must be identified.
- Each of these losses prompts and requires its own grief response.
- The importance of a loss will vary according to its meaning to the specific individual.

BASIC TASKS OF GRIEF

To completely understand the experience of the grief process it is necessary to know the basic tasks of grief. Lindemann offered his conceptualization in 1944, and it is still valid, as shown by its incorporation into contemporary researchers' definitions of the grief process (Parkes & Weiss, 1983; Worden, 1982). Three tasks constitute what Lindemann called *grief work*. They are discussed here in relation to the loss of a loved one, but can be equally applied to other types of losses.

- Emancipation from the bondage of the deceased
- Readjustment to the environment in which the deceased is missing
- Formation of new relationships

Emancipation From the Bondage of the Deceased

When an individual cares about someone, he emotionally invests part of himself in that person. In psychoanalytic terms this is called *cathexis*. There is an emotional bond between the person and whoever he cares about that develops as that individual invests his psychic and emotional energy in the loved one. To conceptualize this visually, picture your two hands clasped together with intertwined fingers, almost as if your hands were folded for prayer. When two people love each other, they are intertwined emotionally as represented by your two hands. The interlocking fingers represent the bonds of emotional ties to one another. When one of the people dies, the remaining person has to withdraw the emotional energy that was invested in the person who is no longer alive. He has to relinquish his attachments to that person and develop new ones based on the altered status of the loved one. This is what Irion (1976) meant when he said there would have to be "movement along a continuum from a relationship of presence (i.e., living,

interactive, responsive relationship) to a relationship of memory"
(p. 32).

The single most crucial task in grief is "untying the ties that
bind" the griever to the deceased individual. This does not mean
that the deceased is forgotten or not loved; rather, it means that
the emotional energy that the mourner had invested in the deceased is modified to allow the mourner to turn it towards others
for emotional satisfaction. In the analogy just given, this would be
portrayed by disentangling and unclasping your hands and fingers.
The hand that represented the griever will then be free to someday
clasp another hand. This is termed *decathexis*, detaching and modifying emotional ties so that new relationships can be established
and the mourner is not tied nontherapeutically to someone who is
no longer alive. (See "Cognitive and Intrapsychic Processes of
Grief" in Chapter 5 for more on this topic.) It is not an easy or
simple process. Human beings understandably want to resist it,
yet cannot avoid it if they want to successfully resolve their loss
and the pain it arouses.

It must be stressed again that this does not mean that the
deceased is forgotten or betrayed. The relationship is altered to be
sure, but it still exists in a very special way in the heart and mind
of the griever. What is changed is the griever's ongoing investment
in and attachment to the deceased as a living person who could
return the investment. The energy that previously went into keeping the relationship with the deceased alive now must be channeled
elsewhere, where it can be returned.

Readjustment to the Environment in Which
the Deceased is Missing

The task here is for the griever to accommodate to the world
without the presence of the deceased. He may have to adopt new
roles and skills to compensate for those functions that once were
performed by the loved one. His own identity must be redefined
so it reflects the reality of the loss and its consequences. For example,
a husband whose wife has died must shift from thinking of himself
as part of a couple, "we," to a single individual, "I," and from his
role as "husband" to one of "widower." Many distressing feelings
accompany this adjustment as the survivor struggles to bear the
pain of separation and become accustomed to the loved one's absence. The loss affects the survivor emotionally, physically, socially, and financially in many ways.

Formation of New Relationships

The emotional energy that is withdrawn from the previous
relationship has to be reinvested in someone or something else.
For example, a widow may start to date again or become involved

in volunteer work where she can give her love to handicapped children. The time it takes before the griever can reinvest in someone or something else after a death or serious loss will depend on a host of factors; however, at some point the griever should be able to take the energy that had been used to keep the previous relationship alive and redirect it towards establishing and maintaining rewarding investments in other people and things. This will not necessarily be a substitute for the lost person. However, it will constitute a different attachment and reinvestment of emotional energy.

The three tasks of grief are quite similar to the three stages of a rite of passage (van Gennep, 1960): separation from a former state, transition into a new state, and incorporation into that new state. (See "Functions of Funerals" in Chapter 7 for more on this topic.) Thus, the process of grief work is not only an end in itself, but also is an important rite of passage that the mourner must experience and traverse in order to completely become reintegrated back into the world.

GRIEF AS WORK

Lindemann's term *grief work* is an apt one, for grief requires the expenditure of both physical and emotional energy. It is not less strenuous or arduous a task than digging a ditch. Yet grief is not commonly perceived as work, and this often causes difficulties for the bereaved. They fail to anticipate the physical toll the grief process exacts. They usually are not prepared for the intensity of their own emotional reactions and/or do not fully understand the importance of accepting and expressing them. Since others are similarly unaware, they frequently do not provide the social or emotional support necessary to sustain the bereaved during their grief work and mourning. In fact, society's unrealistic expectations and inappropriate responses to the griever's normal grief reactions often make the grief experience much worse than it has to be. For instance, if grievers were not told by society to "be brave," they would have fewer conflicts about expressing their grief.

The work of grieving entails not only grieving for the actual person that is lost, but also for all of the hopes, dreams, fantasies, and unfulfilled expectations the griever held for that person and their relationship. It is rarely recognized that these constitute significant symbolic losses, which also must be identified and grieved for. For example, many people fail to understand that a woman who suffers a miscarriage has a critical grief process to complete. They erroneously think that because there was never an actual baby to love the loss is minimal. However, from the moment a woman is aware she is pregnant, she starts to develop feelings about the future child and a host of dreams and expectations for it. When she sustains a miscarriage, she has to grieve for all of the dreams and expectations that will go unmet, despite the fact that she never had personal experiences with the child itself. The same is true whenever any relationship is severed: the griever must identify not only what has been lost in the present, but also what has been lost in the future. It is no less of a loss and it must also be grieved for.

Another major complicating factor in accomplishing grief work is that loss resurrects old issues and conflicts for the mourner. The pain, emptiness, and sorrow of the separation from the loved one often reawakens the earliest and most repressed feelings of anxiety and helplessness associated with separation from the mother figure in the first year of life. The terror and power of these reawakened preverbal memories can be overwhelming. Conflicts around childhood dependency, ambivalence, parent-child relations, and security, to name but a few, also are stirred by the experience of loss and may militate against the easy resolution of grief. It is unfortunate, but these past issues tend to arise at the moment when the griever is struggling to confront a current loss, adding to the burden of the grief process.

ORIGINS OF GRIEF

In 1961 Bowlby described the processes of mourning, dividing them into three phases: the urge to recover the lost object; disorganization and despair; and reorganization. (See "Descriptions of the Grief Process" later in this chapter for his revised schema.) These phases are derived from attachment theory, a theory that suggests that there are fundamental reasons for the ways humans react to grief (Bowlby, 1969, 1973, 1980; Parkes, 1974).

During the course of healthy development humans instinctively develop attachments, initially between child and parent and later between adult and adult. As with other forms of instinctive behavior, attachment behavior is mediated by homeostatic systems that are goal directed. The goal of attachment behavior is to maintain certain degrees of proximity to or communication with the person to whom the individual is attached. Attachment behavior is characteristic of many species because it contributes to the organism's survival by keeping the organism in touch with its caretakers, reducing the risk of harm.

Since the goal of attachment behavior is to maintain an affectional bond, any situation that appears to endanger that bond will elicit action to preserve it. The greater the perceived threat of loss, the more intense and varied the actions will be to prevent it.

This behavior pattern is actually quite adaptive. At first the organism cries. This is adaptive because usually when a young creature cries the mother returns to him. After crying, he becomes angry. In temporary separations this is useful because it can help him overcome obstacles to reunion and punish the one responsible for the termination, making a subsequent separation less likely. Problems arise, however, when the loss is permanent. Anger and aggressive behavior are then less adaptive. Nevertheless, they consistently appear as responses to loss and they reveal that early in bereavement the organism has not truly recognized the permanence of the loss and still hopes for a reunion. The constructive purpose of expressing anger may explain why the bereaved often accuse and reproach themselves, the deceased, and those who try to offer them comfort. Clinical observation has shown that grievers who maintain intense anger over the loss often appear to receive some gratification from it. It suggests that they have not truly accepted the permanence of the loss, that the anger keeps them from having to face it, and that they can make the deceased seem alive and close through this intense stimulation of affect.

Parkes (1974) has discussed the phenomenon of searching that occurs during this angry phase. It is part of the "urge to recover the lost object" described by Bowlby. Implicit in the act of searching is a disregard of the permanence of the loss. However, the unrewarded searching actually assists the griever in "unlearning" his attachment to a person who has died. It makes the loss become more real.

Searching contains motor, perceptual, and ideational components.

- The griever moves about restlessly, physically searching for the deceased.
- The griever is preoccupied with thoughts of the lost person and the events and places associated with the loss. Maintaining a clear visual memory of the deceased would facilitate the search for the lost loved one if that person could in fact be found.
- The griever develops a perceptual "set" to perceive and pay attention to stimuli that suggest the presence of the deceased and ignore those that don't. Occasionally ambiguous sensory data will fit the image of the lost person and the griever will think he has seen the lost loved one. As well as having the illusion of seeing the person, the griever may also feel a comforting sense of the presence of the deceased or have to restrain impulses to speak to or do things for the absent person.
- The griever directs his attention to those parts of the environment in which the deceased would have been likely to be. He may feel drawn towards places or objects associated with the deceased.

- The griever calls for the lost person, directly addressing the person and crying. The memory of the deceased seems to be critical in eliciting crying.
- The griever recognizes the urge to search for the lost person. An adult griever is often well aware that searching for the deceased is irrational, and therefore will resist the suggestion that this is what he wants to do. Children, psychotics, and those who recognize the irrational components of their behavior may not find the idea as upsetting.

All of these are symptoms of the unconscious, and sometimes conscious, desire of the griever to search for and recover the lost loved one. It is only by the repeated frustration of these intense longings for the deceased that the finality of the death is made real.

Following the phase of yearning and searching comes that of disorganization and despair. This phase is also adaptive and necessary for proceeding to the final phase of reorganization. The depression that is seen in mourning arises as a result of the disorganization of behavior patterns between the deceased and the griever. If new patterns are ever to emerge, the old ones must be broken down, even though this brings on depression. Anxiety is also a major aspect of this phase, as it is frightening to cope with such large dislocations. There will necessarily be a redefinition of self and situation. It is painful, for it means finally relinquishing all hope that the deceased can be recovered and the old situation reestablished. (See "Formation of a New Identity" in Chapter 5 for more on this topic.)

In the final phase of reorganization, the bereaved individual resumes social contacts. He starts to adopt new roles, learn new skills, and make new attachments.

DESCRIPTIONS OF THE GRIEF PROCESS

In 1917 Sigmund Freud published his classic paper "Mourning and Melancholia" in which he undertook to define the normal process of grief. He wrote that mourning is

the reaction to the loss of a loved person, or to the loss of some abstraction which has taken the place of one, such as one's country, liberty, an ideal, and so on. . . . It is also well worth notice that, although mourning involves grave departures from the normal attitude to life, it never occurs to us to regard it as a pathological condition and to refer it to medical treatment. We rely on its being overcome after a certain lapse of time, and we look upon any interference with it as useless or even harmful. (Freud, 1957, pp. 243-244)

This reinforces several of the important aspects about normal grief. It asserts that grief is prompted by loss and that this loss need not only involve a death; it notes that grief is a normal and expectable process; and it implies a self-healing aspect to grief that, under normal conditions, will occur without intervention. Freud's four "grave departures from the normal attitude to life" constitute the major characteristics normally associated with grief:

- A profoundly painful dejection
- Cessation of interest in the outside world (insofar as it does not recall the lost loved one)
- Loss of capacity to love
- Inhibition of activity by withdrawal from any activity not connected with thoughts of the lost person

In his landmark study after the tragedy of the Cocoanut Grove Fire in Boston in 1944, Erich Lindemann, the pioneer in grief investigation, wrote about acute grief as a normal reaction to a distressing situation. It was mentioned as being often cited among alleged psychological factors in psychosomatic disorders. The reaction was marked by a definite syndrome with psychological and somatic symptomatology. Five characteristics of grief were noted:

- Somatic distress
- Preoccupation with the image of the deceased
- Guilt
- Hostile reactions
- Loss of patterns of conduct

A sixth characteristic was evidenced by people who appeared to border on having pathological reactions—the appearance of traits of the deceased in the behavior of the bereaved, especially the symptoms shown during the last illness.

Lindemann described three stages of grief:

- Shock and disbelief, which is recognizable by the inability to accept the loss and occasionally the absolute denial that the loss has occurred.
- Acute mourning, characterized by acceptance of the loss, disinterest in daily affairs, weeping, feelings of loneliness, insomnia, and loss of appetite. There is an intense preoccupation with the image of the deceased.
- Resolution of the grief process, with a gradual reentry into the activities of daily life and a reduction in preoccupation with the image of the deceased.

As mentioned earlier, Bowlby presented a theory of grief in 1961 that differentiated three main phases: the urge to recover the lost object; disorganization and despair; and reorganization. Later Parkes (1974) revealed that Bowlby had recognized that a brief but important first phase had been omitted: numbing. This was later acknowledged by Bowlby in 1980. Currently both men endorse the following schema of the grief process:

- *Phase of Numbness.* This is a stage of being stunned. Varying degrees of denial of the loss are usually present.
- *Phase of Yearning and Searching.* The bereaved show manifestations of the strong urge to find, recover, and reunite with the lost person. Anger at the loss and the fruitlessness of the search is visible in the restlessness and irritability directed towards the self or others. Disbelief, tension, tearfulness, and the tendency to want to keep a clear visual memory of the deceased may be apparent.
- *Phase of Disorganization and Despair.* This phase is characterized by giving up the searching attempts to recover the deceased. There is depression and a disinclination to look to the future or to see any purpose in life.
- *Phase of Reorganization.* In this phase the bereaved breaks down attachments to the lost loved one and starts to establish new ties to others. There is a gradual return of interests and appetites.

In 1964 Engel identified five characteristic features of grief:
- Interruption of automatic, taken-for-granted aspects of living, for instance, awareness of the innumerable ways in which the deceased supported and gratified the mourner
- Attempts to refute, deny, and dispute the reality of the death
- Transmittal of various behavioral cries for help to solicit the response of others and express feelings of impotence, loss, and helplessness
- Attempts to construct a mental representation of the deceased to replace the physical presence
- Personal, social, and institutionalized experiences of grief that serve to detach the mourner from the dead and restore him to his place as a member of the social community

Engel saw grief as a healing process that can be interfered with by unsound intervention, suboptimal conditions for healing, or a lack of individual coping resources. He described the normal sequence of grief as follows:

- *Shock and disbelief.* The mourner is stunned and incredulous. He attempts to protect himself against the effects of the overwhelming stress by being numb, and tries to block out recognition of the loss and painful feelings.
- *Developing awareness.* The reality of the death and its meaning starts to penetrate consciousness in the form of an acute and increasing awareness of the anguish of the loss. Anger, guilt, impulsive acting-out or self-destructive behavior may occur. Crying

is typical and involves both the acknowledgment of the loss and regression to a more helpless state. Crying is an important communication for soliciting support from the social group. Inability to cry is a serious matter likely to occur when the relationship with the deceased has been highly ambivalent or when the survivor experiences much guilt and shame. This is to be distinguished from the voluntary suppression of crying because of environmental or cultural demands or the lack of it due to the absence of close ties with the deceased.

• *Restitution.* This is the work of mourning in terms of the various rituals of the funeral that help to initiate the recovery process. These rituals involve social support, emphasize the reality of death, stimulate the expression of feelings, and prompt a process of identification with the deceased, helping the mourner to cope with the loss. Individual religious and spiritual beliefs may offer expectations of reunion after death, expiation of guilt, and meaning to help the mourner cope with the loss.

• *Resolving the loss.* In this phase the mourner attempts to deal with the painful void left by the absence of the deceased, which may be felt as a loss of intactness and wholeness in self. There is often an increased awareness of bodily sensations, which may be identical with the symptoms experienced by the deceased. The mourner's thoughts are almost exclusively preoccupied with the deceased, first with the emphasis on the personal experience of the loss and later with emphasis on the person who died. Review of the relationship and discussion of it, along with ventilation of the feelings that are engendered, occurs repeatedly. The mourner erects in his mind an image of the deceased practically devoid of all negative or undesirable features.

• *Idealization.* All negative and hostile feelings towards the deceased are repressed. The repression may lead to fluctuating feelings of guilt or remorse for past acts or fantasies of unkindness to the deceased. Recollection of some of them may be exaggerated. There may be a sense of responsibility for the death. The recurring thoughts and reminiscences about the deceased serve to establish and to foster identification through the conscious and unconscious taking on of the deceased's qualities and attributes. Over time the preoccupation with the deceased progressively lessens. Fewer reminders evoke feelings of sadness, ambivalent memories can be tolerated with less guilt, yearnings to be with the deceased are replaced by movements towards life, and the identification with the lost loved one's ideals and aspirations provides an impetus to continue on in life. An interest in new relationships begins as the psychic dependence on the deceased diminishes.

• *The outcome.* Successful mourning takes a year or more, with successful healing being evident in the ability to remember comfortably and realistically both the pleasures and disappointments of the lost relationship.

Kübler-Ross (1969) outlined five stages an individual undergoes when coping with imminent death. These have also been used to identify the grief of individuals after a loss.

- Denial and Isolation, a period of shock that functions as a buffer against the overwhelming reality of the situation and then gradually gives way to less radical defenses
- Anger
- Bargaining, in which pleas are made to God or the doctor to forestall the loss or behaviors are undertaken to avoid grieving over it after it has occurred
- Depression
- Acceptance

Worden (1982) believes that mourning involves four tasks:
- To accept the reality of the loss
- To experience the pain of grief
- To adjust to an environment in which the deceased is missing
- To withdraw emotional energy and reinvest it in another relationship

Parkes and Weiss (1983) believe that three tasks must be accomplished in order for recovery from grief to take place:

- *Intellectual recognition and explanation of the loss.* Bereaved individuals must develop an explanation of how the loss happened that answers all their questions, identifying an inevitable cause of the death. Without such explanation, the bereaved will never relax their vigilance against the threat of new loss and will continue to feel anxious.

- *Emotional acceptance of the loss.* Grievers finally reach a point where they no longer find the reminders of the loss too painful to face. This only happens after repeated confrontations with every element of the loss through obsessive review of thoughts, memories, and feelings, with gradual changes in emphasis and focus. Such a review may be avoided early in grief, not as a true denial, but as a form of distancing to gain respite from the pain. The obsessive review and denial only become problems when they are continued too long.

- *Assumption of a new identity.* Mourners gradually develop new identities that reflect their new circumstances. The process begins as mourners become uncomfortably aware of the discrepancy between the world that is now and the world that was.

The amputee has to learn not to step on a foot that is not there, the nearly blind must learn that it is useless to look toward the source of a noise, and, in like manner, the bereaved must stop including the dead person in their plans, thoughts, and conversations. This process of learning is inevitably painful and time consuming. Time and again the amputee gets out of bed in the morning only to find himself sprawling on the floor, the blind person repeatedly peers through sightless eyes, and the widow or widower again and again forgets that the dead partner is gone forever.

Each time a mistake of this kind is made (and they are very common at first), the person is brought up short. A pang of grief is experienced, a stab of frustration, a sense of alarm—for if we cannot rely on our assumptions about the world, what can we rely on? For a while it feels as if time is out of joint; there is a rent in the fabric of reality; nothing makes sense anymore. Lacking a clear understanding of what has been lost and what assumptions have got to change, the person in transition loses confidence in his or her grasp of reality. . . . The new widow or widower . . . repeatedly encounters empty space where security once was. (pp. 70-71)

Movement towards a new identity is slow and halting, and there may be times when mourners "forget" their new status or act as if the deceased is still present, but the speed of the progress is not important as long as progress is being made.

PSYCHOLOGICAL MANIFESTATIONS OF GRIEF

There are numerous other conceptualizations of the process of grief, describing such populations as dying patients, divorcing individuals, patients coping with amputation, and survivors of natural disasters. The theories and conceptualizations may have different names and focus on different topics, but they all entail loss. They all cover the same basic feelings; only the labels differ.

Because of this, it is helpful to consider the psychological reactions to normal grief as fitting within three broad categories: *Avoidance*, in which there is shock, denial, and disbelief; *Confrontation*, a highly emotional state wherein the grief is most intense and the psychological reactions to the loss are felt most acutely; and *Reestablishment*, in which there is a gradual decline of the grief and the beginning of an emotional and social reentry back into the everyday world. Any theory of the symptomatology of grief can be collapsed into these three broad phases.

Before continuing further it is important to address the issue of "stages." There has been much controversy in recent years about stage theories, mainly due to the fact that the word stage implies the existence of an invariant and sequential process. Some caregivers who have believed stages to be invariant have responded to the dying or mourners in terms of the stages they were supposed to be in rather than their individual needs at that point in time. They have tried to fit the individual to the theory instead of using the theory to gain a better understanding of the individual. Not all people will have the same experience, need the same interventions, or follow the same clinical course. To use the Kübler-Ross schema as an example, to try to push patients through the stage of Depression in order to try to get them to Acceptance is doing them the grossest misservice, since their individual needs are not being attended to; it is also a misinterpretation of the purpose of the theory, which is to provide a general pattern, but not suggest a static, necessary, or absolute course.

For this reason, the schema presented here is discussed in terms of reactions rather than stages. These reactions are colored by both the individual characteristics of each person and pertinent social and psychological factors. (See Chapter 3 for more on this topic.) The reactions do not form rigid phases and the griever will probably move back and forth among them. All individuals will not experience all reactions presented; these are only some of the possible responses to a loss.

The Avoidance Phase

During this phase there is a desire to avoid the terrible acknowledgment that that which was loved is now lost. The world is shaken and the individual is overwhelmed by the impact. Just as the human body goes into shock after a large enough insult, so too does the human psyche go into shock when confronted with an important loss. It is the natural reaction to the impact of such a blow. During this period the individual may be confused and dazed, unable to comprehend what has happened. A feeling of numbness is quite common.

As recognition starts to seep in and shock starts slowly wearing off, denial immediately crops up. It is only natural that the individual would want or need to deny that such a terrible event has occurred. At this time denial is therapeutic. It functions as a buffer by allowing the individual to absorb the reality of the loss a little at a time, preventing her from being completely overwhelmed by it. It is an "emotional anesthesia" that serves as a protective mechanism for those who have suddenly been confronted with the destruction of the world they used to know.

Disbelief and a need to know why the death occurred may appear at this time. There may be an explosion from the more outgoing, or withdrawal or depersonalization from a more introverted mourner. Confusion and disorganization are also both common at this time.

Occasionally the initial response will be an intellectualized acceptance of the death, followed by initiation of seemingly appropriate activities such as comforting of others or making funeral arrangements. In such a case the loss is recognized, but the emotional response to it is denied. This example illustrates what may be seen later on in grief as well—the denial of the emotions generated by the death. It will be important to differentiate between when the mourner is denying the death (ultimately an unhealthy response) and when he is denying the emotions stimulated by the death (not quite as pathological, although requiring therapeutic intervention).

The Confrontation Phase
During this phase grief is experienced most intensely. The individual has recognized that there has been a loss and the shock has worn off to a great degree. Denial and disbelief may still occur, but a whole host of new reactions arise that spring from the individual's confrontation with the loss and its implications. It has been characterized as a time of "angry sadness."

Extremes of emotion are felt. For some, these emotions will be readily expressed, while others will have conflict about giving vent to them at all. Still others will want to express them, but find they are not able to do so. The remainder will have a mixture of ability and inability to express these reactions.

The perception of new reactions in itself may prompt fear and anxiety in the griever. The recognition that he is behaving and feeling differently than normal is especially unsettling and makes the experience more frightening and painful. For example, a person who is usually a concerned and loving individual may be shocked to find that he feels indifferent to others. This is one reason why it is critical to assure the mourner that his feelings are normal and legitimate.

A sense of panic or generalized anxiety also may be experienced by the griever, either intermittently or chronically during this phase. It stems from apprehension of the unknown and unfamiliar. It is frequently experienced by the griever when he awakens in the morning and remembers he must face another day without the loved one. Concerns about going it alone, fright arising from the sense of vulnerability caused by the loss, distress associated with memories of earlier losses and separations, heightened emotional and physical arousal that exacerbates feelings of tension and uneasiness—all serve to intensify the experience.

There are two emotions common to grief that cause problems because of society's attitudes towards them—anger and guilt. Anger is always to be expected to some degree following a significant loss, as a natural consequence of being deprived of something desired. It also reflects a biological predisposition to attempt to find and recover the lost loved one and ensure that no further separations occur (see the "Origins of Grief" section of this chapter). Unfortunately, our society does not accept this anger well. Therefore, both the mourner and those trying to console the mourner may have difficulty acknowledging and coping with this very natural and expected emotion.

Many times the anger is displaced onto other people, frequently without the griever's conscious knowledge or intent. This anger may be vented at God, the doctors, the person who died, others who have not sustained the loss, and the bereaved person himself. Self-hatred may also be the result of guilt, loss of control, or frustration. Anger at the deceased for dying and "abandoning" the griever is not uncommon. This may be very difficult for the griever to admit since it is not socially appropriate to speak ill of the dead or to blame the deceased for the death (except in cases of suicide). The griever may become very bitter. He may be easily hurt and have an exaggerated sensitivity to real or imagined slights. He also may feel intense envy towards those unaffected by death.

Anger may also be the result of a loss of faith in God or a philosophy. The death precipitates a quest for meaning to make sense out of such a loss. Many grievers have a profound sense of injustice and disillusionment, feeling that they have played life by the rules but lost the game. The values and beliefs that once were comforting are now useless. Some grievers alienate others with their bitterness when their value systems fail them. In time they may be able to put the loss into a perspective that lends it some meaning. However, some never recover their trust of value systems and are chronically angry towards religion or authority figures.

Guilt reactions in grief are not limited to those who tend to feel guilty normally, such as those who are anxious. They are a normal and expectable aspect of the grief experience. Because human relationships always contain some measure of ambivalence, a mixture of negative and positive feelings, and because our relationships, as ourselves, are not perfect, guilt will be a natural concomitant to the loss of another. It is a cruel trick of human nature, but in the early phases of experiencing a loss, people tend to recall everything that was negative in their relationship with the deceased while failing to remember the positives as well.

There are other sources of guilt too. The griever may feel guilty that he is still alive while the loved one has died (also known as "survival guilt"). He may have inappropriate expectations of himself and consequently experience guilt when he fails to live up to such unrealistic standards. For example, the daughter who feels she should never be upset with her mother may suffer from guilt after the mother's death when recalling how her mother irritated her at times. The griever may feel responsible for failure to protect the loved one from death. This is especially prevalent in parents whose children die. The many diverse emotions of grief themselves may prompt guilt feelings. For example, an individual may feel guilty for having a normal sense of anger at the deceased for having died and left him, for having longed for the end of a lengthy illness, or for feeling a sense of relief over the termination of his responsibilities for the deceased. Crying over the loss may be enough to resurrect guilt for some if they interpret it as a loss of control. (See "Maintain a Therapeutic and Realistic Perspective" in Chapter 5 for more on this topic.)

Some of the reactions associated with guilt, and often seen in bereavement, are self-reproach and a sense of worthlessness. When extreme, they signify pathological grief reactions. However, in mild and moderate amounts, they are not uncommon in acute grief. They may not only be a form of self-punishment to expiate guilt, but also be an expression of anger towards others that has been directed inward or a reaction to the loss of a primary support figure.

Other responses at this time typically include acute feelings of separation, deprivation, anguish, sadness, yearning, and longing. The intensity of these reactions usually surprises and shocks the griever.

Depression and despair are common reactions to important losses. Many writers feel that it is precisely an important loss that gives rise to any psychological depression. Whether or not this is true, there are numerous symptoms of depression that also are usual manifestations of grief: withdrawal, anhedonia, apathy, feelings of meaninglessness, decreased energy, decreased sexual desire; regression, dependency, feelings of helplessness; loneliness, sadness, feelings of hopelessness or abandonment; ambivalence, shame; feelings of being out of control, depersonalization; disorganization, lack of concentration; somatic problems.

The depressed mourner's inability to concentrate or process information should not be underestimated. He often feels he is losing control because he feels so confused and lacks the decision-making abilities and incisiveness he once had. He may be nonassertive. This lack of clarity and certainty only heightens the anxiety and unreality of the situation. In many cases, the bereaved individual becomes very angry at himself for not being able to see things more clearly, so it is important for him to know that such responses are natural and will appear in all areas of life (e.g., difficulty working, confusion about social arrangements).

The combination of depression and changes in normal capabilities often causes the mourner to feel childlike, helpless, and dependent on others. These intense regressive feelings can bring out latent negative self-images (Horowitz, Wilner, Marmar, & Krupnick, 1980). Mourners need support in acknowledging their regressive feelings and coping with them without becoming hostile or internalizing these feelings as permanent characteristics.

Accompanying depression may be a lack of concern for the self. When moderate, it appears as a disregard for personal matters due to preoccupation with the deceased. Self-care may be permitted only as it benefits others, for example, "If it weren't for the children, I would have ended it all myself." When taken to an extreme, this lack of concern is manifested in self-destructive behaviors, even suicide. While many bereaved individuals have fleeting thoughts of suicide as a means of reuniting with the lost one and escaping the pain of grief, most do not act on them. However, suicide threats should be taken seriously and be evaluated, especially with the following high-risk groups: those who have previously attempted suicide; those with past or present psychological disorders, especially problems with impulse control or acting-out personalities; those who have difficulty dealing with anger; those who feel hopeless; those who are overly dependent; those who feel they lack the resources they need to cope or who lack social support; those who are deeply depressed; and those who have made concrete plans for suicide.

Several common reactions are a combination of depression and anger. These include irritability, anxiety, and tension. There is heightened psychological arousal. It is common for the bereaved to be very restless, to wander anxiously, or to feel a sense that something is going to happen. This is part of the searching behavior that normally goes on during grief.

Another common reaction about which a great many bereaved individuals talk is a feeling of "mutilation." They express their loss in physical terms. This not only reflects their sense of separation from one to whom they felt so close, but reveals their own awareness of the loss of parts of their identities that had been validated by or in relationship to the deceased. For example, the husband who loses his life's companion in the death of his wife also loses that part of himself that played the role of husband opposite his spouse's role of wife. This role has been irretrievably taken away. Even if he should remarry, that part of him that existed in the special and unique relationship he had in interaction with his first wife is no more. In this sense, part of the griever himself dies, in addition to the deceased, making some of the grief for the griever, as well as the lost loved one.

A natural response to loss is preoccupation with the deceased. It occurs both as a wish to undo the loss and a reflection of the internal grief work being done in which the griever is focusing attention on the deceased as he begins to detach emotionally from her in order to be free for new attachments in the future. It is akin to hugging someone and holding her tightly before saying good- bye and letting her go. This preoccupation with the deceased is often manifested in obsessive rumination about the deceased, dreaming about the deceased, thinking the loved one has been seen, actively searching for her. There will be intense yearning, an aching and pining for what has been taken away. This is the single most typical feature of grief (Parkes & Weiss, 1983). Sometimes this is even experienced physically as well as psychologically—a gut-wrenching, gnawing emptiness that needs to be filled, or sharp, intense pangs of grief that cut into the heart. A significant proportion of mourners actually experiences some type of visual or auditory hallucination of the deceased, or feels an intuitive, overwhelming sense of her presence.

In an effort to attempt to gain some control and understanding over what appears to be a meaningless, unmanageable event, the bereaved often engage in an obsessional review of the circumstances of the death. Additionally they may attempt to cognitively restructure the situation so that it seems that they had some inkling that it would happen. This provides them with a sense of control and predictability in the midst of what seems to be chaos.

One relatively common type of experience that causes great concern to the griever is the "grief attack." This is an acute upsurge in grief that occurs suddenly and often when least expected, interrupting ongoing activities and temporarily leaving the person out of control. At times such feelings may not be experienced as an attack but as waves or pangs that produce painful emotional and physical sensations. While normal for some time after the death, grievers must stop their activities and deal with their feelings until they are in control again, or else risk possible injury to themselves or others. Such grief attacks have contributed to automobile accidents, occupational injuries, and countless other types of mishaps. A grief attack is an extreme example of distractibility and confusion. The griever may find himself lost in a fog, stopping at green lights or arriving at a destination and not recalling how he got there.

Individuals may have some identification with the deceased. In appropriate amounts this is not harmful and serves as a way of holding onto parts of the lost loved one. A son might pick up his dead father's hobby of stamp collecting or take over his household chores. A widow might make a decision based on what she thin her husband would have done. However, if the identification oc too intensely, the griever may lose his own sense of personal tity or may seriously impede the grief process by failing t thect from the deceased.

The intensity of these and other grief reactions oft mourners wonder if they are going crazy. People are so adequately prepared for the type and strength of gr they sustain. These reactions are so different, unco expected, and intense that some mourners believ tually lost touch with reality. In truth, if someon same symptomatology as a griever but had no loss, that person would be considered psych and probably would be hospitalized. Grief is a "craziness," but grievers are usually not crazy.

An additional difficulty for the griever is that there are few models or culturally prescribed roles for mourners in our society. This makes it difficult for the mourner to know how he should act or feel. With the absence of such guidelines there is an increase in ambiguity. This ambiguity fosters more stress in a situation that is already overburdened by it, contributing further to the mourner's feelings of losing control and "going crazy."

A comment needs to be made about the sense of relief that some grievers experience (and most feel guilty over). The griever may be relieved when the end finally comes, especially when the deceased has been suffering or there has been a long drawn-out illness. It is not a statement about the feelings or lack of feelings for the deceased, but more a reflection of the griever's response to the alleviation of suffering and the termination of responsibilities. Grievers may also feel relief simply because they themselves are not dying, or because their relationship with the deceased was marked by a great deal of conflict or oppression.

Denial is still possible in this phase, and it may range from slight distortion to full-blown delusion. Dorpat (1973) described three possible forms. There is denial of the fact of the loss, as when the mourner refuses to believe that the person has died and acts accordingly. Then there is a denial of the meaning of the loss, in which the griever may minimize the importance of the relationship severed, taking away the need to grieve. Finally there is denial of the irreversibility of the loss, for example, when the mourner maintains a chronic expectation that the deceased will return or that there can be some sort of a reunion with the person, as through a medium. This is harmful when it precludes acceptance of the reality of the death and progression through grief work. A fourth form is a denial of the feelings of grief, sometimes in an attempt to avoid the pain of loss.

The Reestablishment Phase

This phase constitutes a gradual decline of grief and marks the beginning of the emotional and social reentry back into the everyday world. Although the old adage "Once bereaved, always bereaved" is unquestionable, the mourner learns to live with the loss as emotional energy is reinvested in new persons, things, and ideas. The loss is not forgotten, but merely put in a special place which, while allowing it to be remembered, also frees the mourner to go on to new attachments without being pathologically tied to the old ones.

This phase, like the others, is not an all-or-nothing phase. Rather, it waxes and wanes during the latter part of the Confrontation phase and continues slowly thereafter. It never arrives all at once and for some time it coexists with many of the previous reactions.

Guilt often accompanies the beginning efforts at reestablishment as the mourner copes with the fact that she continues to live and experience in spite of the loss. This is a particularly thorny issue, as the mourner may erroneously feel that she is betraying the deceased if she enjoys life without that person.

SOCIAL MANIFESTATIONS OF GRIEF

The experience of grief appears socially in a loss of normal patterns of conduct (Lindemann, 1944) including the following:
- Restlessness and the inability to sit still
- A painful lack of ability to initiate and maintain organized patterns of activity
- Social withdrawal behavior that is antithetical to the establishment of new relations and the alleviation of stress

Although the griever's great need for comfort attracts the consolation of others, the griever herself is so intent on the impossibility of regaining the lost loved one that she devalues the help offered. Thus, many potential supporters are driven away. The focus on the lost relationship also causes the griever to neglect other relationships. The pain of seeing others with their loved ones further encourages the griever to withdraw from others.

PHYSIOLOGICAL MANIFESTATIONS OF GRIEF

There are a number of physiological reactions that accompany the emotional reactions to loss. These have been documented most notably by Lindemann (1944) and Parkes (1964, 1970, 1972). The following is a list of some of the more common physiological symptoms that occur in normal grief:
- Anorexia and other gastrointestinal disturbances
- Loss of weight
- Inability to sleep
- Crying
- Tendency to sigh
- Lack of strength
- Physical exhaustion
- Feelings of emptiness and heaviness
- Feelings of "something stuck in the throat"
- Heart palpitations and other indications of anxiety
- Nervousness and tension
- Loss of sexual desire or hypersexuality
- Lack of energy and psychomotor retardation
- Restlessness and searching for something to do
- Shortness of breath

The important thing to remember is that althou
ally conceived of as a psychological reaction, in fac
ways somatic reactions as well. Frequently somatic *is usu-*
the only overt indications that grief still remains unre *al-*
presence is often the sole reason that individuals with *are*
grief are referred for therapy.

Exercise IV at the end of this chapter can help deve
personal understanding of the psychological, social, a
logical manifestations of grief.

ANTICIPATORY GRIEF

In the anticipation of a future loss a form of normal gr
occur. It is termed *anticipatory grief*, and it includes many o.
symptoms and processes of grief following a loss. Dying patien.
do experience anticipatory grief (see Chapter 9 for more on this
topic), but the term is most often used when discussing the families
of the terminally ill.

Fulton and Fulton (1971) delineated four aspects of anticipatory grief:

- Depression
- Heightened concern for the terminally ill person
- Rehearsal of the death
- Attempts to adjust to the consequences of the death

Anticipatory grief also allows for:

- Absorbing the reality of the loss gradually over time
- Finishing unfinished business with the dying person, e.g.,
  expressing feelings, resolving past conflicts
- Beginning to change assumptions about life and identity
- Making plans for the future so that they will not be felt as
  betrayals of the deceased after death

While the threat of loss usually elicits separation anxiety, struggling to accept the reality before the death occurs is ultimately
easier than trying to cope with it afterward when the death is
unexpected.

Anticipatory grief may occur in advance of losses other than
death. In 1958, Janis noted how the "work of worry" prior to surgery, a form of anticipatory grief, was associated with better
psychological and physical outcomes. The beneficial effects of anticipatory grief have prompted caregivers to help patients anticipate future losses so that when such losses occur they will be more
prepared for them. For example, the patient who is to have a leg
amputation is often encouraged to speak with others who have had
such an operation and have found ways of coping with it.

In 1972, Futterman, Hoffman, and Sabshin published their ex-

dy on parental anticipatory grief. Their findings are ap-
to anticipatory grief in general. They conceptualized an-
y grief as a series of five functionally related aspects:

1. *Acknowledgment:* Becoming progressively convinced that
the child's death is inevitable.

2. *Grieving:* Experiencing and expressing the emotional impact of the anticipated loss and the physical, psychological, and
interpersonal turmoil associated with it.

3. *Reconciliation:* Developing perspectives on the child's expected death which preserve a sense of confidence in the worth
of the child's life and in the worth of life in general.

4. *Detachment:* Withdrawing emotional investment from the
child as a growing being with a real future.

5. *Memorialization:* Developing a relatively fixed conscious
mental representation of the dying child which will endure beyond his death. (p. 252)

Futterman et al. reported that grief becomes more differentiated and focused with time: the acute emotional pain characteristic of the early reactions becomes a more tempered melancholy,
accompanied by articulation and evaluation of the impending loss.
This mellowing of grief occurs simultaneously with an increase in
reconciliation, detachment, and memorialization. At the time of
actual death there is a deepened sense of loss with a brief upsurge
of acute grief, followed by further reconciliation.

Presence of grieving at this time testified to the significant emotional investment in the child that had been maintained through
the entire illness, while the limited intensity and duration of post-
bereavement turmoil testified to the work accomplished in anticipatory mourning. (p. 267)

It was maintained that although the task of mourning was well
advanced at the time of death, the mourning was rarely completed
and significant work remained to be accomplished. They also reported that in retrospect, although behavioral signs of detachment
were evident, parents maintained care of their child's physical and
emotional needs, thus integrating both anticipatory grief and the
care of their child. The parents' detachment was not so much a
detachment from the child herself, but from their image of the
child "as a growing being with a real future."

Although the preparation afforded in anticipatory grief has
been found to be therapeutic, there are some concerns about the
deleterious effects of too much anticipatory grief. Some researchers
are concerned that too much of it will predispose the mourner to
prematurely detach from the dying patient. Excess amounts of it,
like insufficient amounts, have been associated in one study with
less participation with the hospitalized terminally ill child and

higher anger and hostility and loss of control indices after the death (Rando, 1983). Despite this, parental preparation at the time of death and subsequent adjustment to the child's death were shown to be positively related to anticipatory grief. Increased anticipatory grief also was related to a decrease in abnormal grief.

In some instances, if the expected loss does not occur, the grievers have already mourned in anticipation to such an extent that they have emotionally detached themselves from the individual. This was evidenced by the high divorce rates in the marriages of POW soldiers who returned home after the Viet Nam War. Their families had apparently grieved their absence to such an extent that when they did return the emotional investment was no longer present. It is also manifested in family members of terminally ill patients who experience the *Lazarus syndrome*. This occurs when a patient is expected to die, the family members' potential losses are as resolved as possible prior to death, and the patient goes into remission. In this case the family members may be unable to reinvest in the patient and may feel frustration, anger, and resentment that will require working through and normalization.

Fulton and Fulton (1971) noted that a period of anticipation may reduce the amount of public mourning grievers display. This may put them in a difficult situation, as they are expected to show emotions that have already been worked through during the anticipatory grief process. This can cause guilt or shame on the part of the mourners, stimulated by their own reactions to their less-than-expected feelings and the disapproval of others. The anticipatory grief also may make them feel that funeral rituals are unnecessary, taking away the opportunity to experience the social confirmation and support such rituals afford. Anticipatory grief can be less than therapeutic for the dying patient as well, who may be responded to negatively, if at all, by those who have decathected from her.

Anticipatory grief is currently the subject of much concern. There are numerous research investigations to prove both its relevance and its insignificance. However, all findings must be subject to careful scrutiny, since frequently anticipatory grief has been confused with forewarning of loss (Fulton & Gottesman, 1980). It is erroneous to assume that people who have been informed of a diagnosis will understand it, react to it, or actually commence anticipatory grieving (Clayton, Halikas, Maurice, & Robbins, 1973; Parkes & Weiss, 1983). Nevertheless, several research studies have dispelled some myths about anticipatory grief. They have demonstrated that grief following anticipated loss is no less painful than unanticipated loss; however, the preparation of anticipatory grief allows for less of an assault on the mourner's adaptive capacities (Clayton et al., 1973; Glick, Weiss, & Parkes, 1974; Parkes

& Weiss, 1983). The postdeath reaction may be more abbreviated, although this will vary with individual cases.

Anticipatory grief does *not* necessarily entail a complete decathexis from the dying patient, as was once thought. While it is definitely a danger when there is too much anticipatory grief, it is not a necessary consequence of the experience. Indeed, as noted by Parkes and Weiss (1983), the interval of anticipatory grief during terminal illness may actually draw people closer together and result in a more intimate and involved relationship than previously. This heightened attachment may preclude the mourning that would help the grievers prepare for death.

Anticipatory grief also can stir up ambivalent feelings that will lead to more problematic grief after the death. This ambivalence is one of the significant differences between anticipatory and postdeath grief noted by Aldrich (1974). He has observed that a long period of anticipation increases the possibility of hostility developing as well as the opportunity for working through the loss. Aldrich believes that the impact of ambivalence on anticipatory grief is significantly different than that on conventional postdeath grief because the target of the ambivalent feelings is not only still alive, but is potentially vulnerable, balanced between life and death. This vulnerability makes any death wish on the part of the mourner particularly potent and dangerous, and may contribute to the clinically observed impression that anticipatory grief is more readily denied than postdeath grief.

Clearly, depending on its length and the situation, anticipatory grief can be either helpful or harmful to grievers. It is important that anticipatory grief be recognized as a legitimate phenomenon for intervention. Interventions made at this point can prevent problems in mourning from developing; later interventions can only try to remedy difficulties that already have occurred. (See Chapter 12 for more on this topic.)

EXERCISE III

Your Responses to Difficult Situations

Write down the three most difficult situations you have had to deal with in your life. Have any of these involved a physical or a symbolic loss? If so, which ones? Make a list of some of your reactions at the time when you were faced with the situations.

Note your reactions after you dealt with the situations and since that time.

EXERCISE IV

Finding Out You Have Grieved Before

Take a moment now and compare the manifestations of grief just discussed with the personal reactions you noted in Exercise III to the most difficult situations you had experienced in your own life. Note how many of them are exactly the same. This illustrates that we all have *some* experience with grief that we can draw on to assist us in helping the bereaved, even if we have not lost a close loved one through death.

CHAPTER 3

Factors Influencing the Grief Reaction

For interventions to be effective they need to be individually tailored to specific grief reactions. Each person's grief will be idiosyncratic, determined by a unique combination of psychological, social, and physiological factors.

PSYCHOLOGICAL FACTORS

The unique nature and meaning of the loss sustained or the relationship severed. Not everyone responds in a similar way to the same loss. To be told that for medical reasons running must be restricted to 2 miles a day might be a small disappointment for many of us, but it would be a major traumatic loss to someone who aspired to be a marathon runner. It is not enough to use solely our own standards to determine the impact of a loss on another human being; instead, we must view the loss from that person's frame of reference.

We need to appreciate the idiosyncratic meaning a particular loss has for a given individual in order to understand that person's grief. The loss of a pet may be painful to many people, but it may be exceptionally devastating to the elderly person to whom it has meant company and security. That person may grieve more over the loss of the pet than over the loss of a sibling, if the pet has been more important and meant more to the individual. The death of a grandparent may carry more impact than the death of a parent if the griever has had a more intimate relationship with the grandparent. It cannot be automatically assumed that a parent's death will bring more grief or a grandparent's loss bring less.

The individual qualities of the relationship lost. The psychological nature of the relationship severed, and the strength of the

43

attachment, will always influence the mourner's capacity to complete grief work. For example, a relationship characterized by extreme ambivalence is more difficult to resolve than one that is not as conflicted. If there is a small degree of attachment in a relationship, it will be relatively easier to cope with the grief for it than for a closer relationship where more is felt to be lost. Those who are strongly dependent upon an individual who dies often have more problems than others as they try to part with the lost relationship and establish new ones. They often evidence intense yearning and insecurity in the absence of the loved one, and are predisposed to pathological chronic grief reactions.

It is important to differentiate between *role-loss* and *object-loss*. A role-loss entails a loss of status or function (a symbolic loss), while an object-loss involves the loss of a particular person or object (a physical loss). For example, if a woman becomes widowed she loses her husband (object-loss), as well as her status and function of being a wife (role-loss). In many situations the role-loss, with its attendant alterations in status and function, may be more important than the actual object-loss. For instance, some people become quite depressed after their last child gets married. Usually in these cases it is the loss of being able to parent, to nurture, and to feel needed that causes the grief, and not necessarily the physical loss of the child, since that child is still alive and well. When people grieve and there is no object-loss, they may in fact be reacting to a role-loss.

The roles that the deceased occupied in the family or social system of the griever. While this discussion will address the loss of a family member, similar dynamics occur when a significant other in the griever's social system outside the family dies. In such a case it is the social system that responds, and not the family.

Each family members plays a variety of roles within a family unit and the losses resulting from these unoccupied roles must be identified and grieved for. The complexity of this multi-role phenomenon was noted by Parkes (1972):

> Even bereavement by death is not as simple a stress as it might, at first sight, appear to be. In any bereavement it is seldom clear exactly what is lost. A loss of a husband, for instance, may or may not mean the loss of a sexual partner, companion, accountant, gardener, baby-minder, audience, bed-warmer, and so on, depending upon the particular roles normally performed by this husband. (p. 7)

All families are like systems—they require ongoing support of each individual component to keep the system operating in balance. When an element is added or taken away, the system becomes unbalanced and there is a struggle to reach homeostasis again.

This is exactly what happens psychologically within families (Bowen, 1976; Goldberg, 1973).

When a family member cannot function anymore in the roles usually assigned to that member (e g., due to an illness or death), new roles are assigned to and new demands are put on the remaining family members. Consequently, a bereaved family member may not have to cope solely with the complexities of the grief process itself, but also with an altered, out-of-balance system and new role responsibilities and demands as a result of the role reorganization due to the absence of the deceased. A number of secondary losses, that is, losses that develop out of the intial loss of the loved one through death (e.g., loss of income, loss of intimacy, loss of previous lifestyle), may accrue. When these are combined with the new role responsibilities generated by death, they will necessarily affect the grief process of the mourner by increasing the demand for adaptation. Therefore, the roles played in the family by the deceased, and the new roles and responsibilities subsequently thrust upon the griever, along with the additional stress of a family struggling to regain its balance, are variables that will profoundly influence the individual's grief experience. (See Chapter 12 for more on this topic.)

The individual's coping behaviors, personality, and mental health. These psychological attributes will influence the response to grief just as they influence all other responses in life. If a person has consistently coped with crises by running away, chances are that the same behavior will occur in the grief situation. If she tends to approach crises in a healthy, straightforward manner, she will typically have a positive approach to grief work. Obviously people can sometimes change; however, most will cope with grief using the responses they have become familiar with. The mourner will tend to grieve (and the dying patient will tend to die) in much the same manner in which the rest of her life has been conducted. This is why it is crucial to have an assessment of the griever's past coping behaviors in order to be prepared to support the ones that are the most healthy and offer alternatives for those that are nontherapeutic. This information also helps establish realistic expectations for a particular individual's grief experience.

Some of the more usual methods for coping with grief follow (Shuchter, 1984). They represent conscious and unconscious efforts to deal with the pain of loss and avoid being overwhelmed by affect.

- *Avoidance of painful stimuli.* This includes not talking about the deceased, hiding pictures or mementos of him, and avoiding contact with people who may have known him.
- *Distraction.* Preoccupation with activities such as work,

school, or social organizations precludes thoughts and feelings about the deceased. Such distraction often becomes difficult when the person is home alone. At these times reading, listening to music, and watching television may serve the purpose of taking the bereaved's mind off the loss.

- *Drugs, alcohol, or food.* These may be a means of self-gratification, "filling up" the emptiness of the loss, or blocking out reality.
- *Obsessional rumination.* Preoccupation with the cognitive details of the loss allows the griever to escape his painful feelings.
- *Impulsive behavior or escape.* This is another form of distraction. It is often seen as a rash decision involving a major change, e.g., selling a home or becoming deeply involved with a new person.
- *Prayer.* It provides an outlet for the expression of feelings, offers hope, allows for relief of feelings of guilt and other suffering, and gives a sense of protection and caring. Additionally it indicates a continued relationship with God which can mitigate the sense of loss. The formal or informal ritualization of prayer can lend some meaning and structure to the individual's response to the loss.
- *Rationalization and intellectualization.* These put the loss into a less painful perspective.
- *Contact with people.* This often mitigates the intense feelings of loss, loneliness, and despair that can erupt in mourners.

In moderate amounts these coping mechanisms help grievers deal with their intense feelings. Overuse may prevent the bereaved from experiencing grief; underuse will leave them without relief from the pain of loss.

Many aspects of the personality also affect the individual's response: self-esteem, conscious and unconscious conflicts, emotions, beliefs, attitudes, values, desires, needs, strengths. The relationships the individual has will also partially be determined by her personality. All these factors require assessment, not only in order to form accurate expectations, but also to predict areas of difficulty in the grief process and to develop individualized, appropriate support strategies.

Additionally, the person's current and past state of mental health and ego strength will affect that person's response to the loss, since they influence the person's perceptions, reactions, and coping mechanisms. A past history of depressive illness or borderline pathology is usually associated with poorer grief resolution.

The individual's level of maturity and intelligence. These additional personality attributes have a direct influence on the type

of relationship the person had with the deceased, the degree of
cognitive understanding of the meaning and implications of death,
and the type of coping resources available. Maturity and intelligence have been found to be consistently and positively correlated
with effective coping skills and with favorable resolution of loss.

The individual's past experiences with loss and death. Past
experiences will not only set up expectations, but will also influence
the coping strategies and/or defense mechanisms used by the griever. As with anything else, if a similar situation has been experienced
previously, it will be slightly easier to cope with, since it will not
be as strange as it was at first. By the same token, previous negative
experiences can affect a griever in a harmful way. Someone who
has learned through previous deaths that intense grief will diminish if properly attended to will be more willing to yield to the grief
process than someone who has learned to deny loss in an effort to
avoid pain.

Previous unresolved losses generally hinder effective grief resolution. The issues that were not dealt with tend to arise and complicate the current situation. A desire to avoid confronting previous
losses may prevent resolution of the current loss, especially when
a pattern of avoidance has become firmly entrenched.

If an individual has experienced too many deaths, she can suffer
bereavement overload (Kastenbaum, 1969). Although originally used
to describe the serial loss of social contacts experienced by the
elderly, the term can be applied equally as well to the griever who
sustains many bereavements either at one time (e.g., the loss of
multiple family members from a disaster) or serially. In either case,
these past experiences with death may leave the griever depleted
emotionally and unable to adequately address the current loss.

**The individual's social, cultural, ethnic, and religious/philo-
sophical backgrounds.** As noted in Chapter 1, the individual's responses to loss and death generally reflect the norms, mores, and
sanctions of the socio-cultural environment. The religious/philo-
sophical training to which the individual has been exposed also
will significantly affect the beliefs, meanings, and values that person holds for life, death, and life after death. If we fail to appreciate
these significant influences on an individual's grief response, we run
the risk of misunderstanding the experience of the griever and/or
incorrectly assessing the grief response itself.

Case Example: Roberta was a 60-year-old English widow referred for therapy because of chronic diarrhea that kept her
socially isolated. She was overly intellectualized and evidenced little affect. In therapy it became apparent that she
suffered from inhibited grief, and the therapist was quite successful in having Roberta confront her loss and begin dealing

with her grief. However, this therapist had underestimated her own effectiveness with regard to this patient. She erroneously thought that she had not helped Roberta get in touch with her grief because Roberta failed to do much crying in the session. All the therapist could get from Roberta were two big tears sliding silently down her cheeks.

Coming from an ethnic group where grievers are much more expressive, and crying and wailing are the norm, the therapist had unrealistic expectations for this reserved, intellectual Englishwoman. The two tears rolling down her cheeks constituted as intense a grief response for her as hours of mournful sobbing would have for someone from the therapist's own ethnic background.

The individual's sex-role conditioning. In Western cultures males traditionally are conditioned to be controlled and to avoid the expression of feelings. Although there are fewer constraints on the expression of anger or hostile feelings, emotions such as sadness, loss, depression, or loneliness are expected to be restrained. Crying or requesting assistance is poorly tolerated. Consequently, when a male is grieving he may experience conflict, as the expression of feelings necessary for resolution of the grief is often contrary to previous sex-role conditioning. When doing therapy with males, therapists frequently have to work through the societal and cultural dictates of stereotypical sex-role conditioning before the loss can be addressed. If these are not worked through, they will interfere with the adequate processing of grief and prevent mourning. It should be noted that it is not the function of the therapist to "de-condition" the client, but to make the client just comfortable enough with the necessary responses to grief that the grief work can be resolved.

Traditionally women have experienced less conflict between their sex-role conditioning and requirements for successful resolution of their grief. The feelings and behaviors most often prompted in response to a loss are well tolerated in females. Where women tend to have relatively more difficulty is with anger and with assuming control and decision making, since typically women are poorly trained to handle these issues.

These generalizations obviously are based on stereotypes, and as society becomes more androgenous, there will probably be more exceptions. The critical point is that an individual's sex-role conditioning, like his social, cultural, ethnic, and religious/philosophical backgrounds, must be recognized as a strong determinant of any grief response. If this is not taken into account when an individual's grief reaction is evaluated, there cannot be an adequate assessment of its status or normality.

The individual's age. The age of the bereaved is associated with other factors relating to the loss, such as past experiences with loss and death and level of maturity and intelligence. If the bereaved is a child rather than an adult, there will be differences in the level of understanding, maturity of emotional coping mechanisms, and access to resources. However, even among adults, there appear to be some age-related differences. One of the trends that has been found in bereaved mortality studies is that the loss effect is strongest in the younger widowed and weakens with increasing age (Maddison & Walker, 1967; Stroebe, Stroebe, Gergen, & Gergen, 1981-82). Widows and widowers under 40 appear to be at greater risk for poor bereavement outcome than older widows and widowers when both groups are compared to still married age-mates (Parkes & Weiss, 1983).

The characteristics of the deceased. The characteristics of the relationship severed and the functions the deceased performed in the mourner's life have been identified as critical variables in the determination of the mourner's grief experience. The particular interactional role that the deceased occupied in relationship to the mourner will also influence the grief response. For example, it has been said that to lose your parents you lose your past; to lose your spouse you lose your present; and to lose your children you lose your future. Of course these responses will be mediated by the meaning of that particular relationship to the griever; but there is some empirical evidence in the literature to support, for example, the idea that the death of one's child, irrespective of age, provokes more intense grief reactions than the death of a spouse or parent (Clayton, Desmarais, & Winokur. 1968; Gorer, 1965; Sanders, 1979-80; Schwab, Chalmers, Conroy, Farris, & Markush, 1975). (See "Grief After the Death of a Child" in Chapter 6 for more on this topic.)

The age of the deceased and the type of person he was also will play a large part in the type of reaction the mourner will have. In our society, the death of the young is viewed as a worse loss than the death of the elderly, so grief is usually more intense subsequent to the loss of an adolescent than to the loss of his grandparent. There are exceptions to this, but in general our society (correctly or not) tends to expect a decreasing intensity of grief with increasing age of the deceased. This expectation should be applied cautiously, since it would be incorrect to minimize the intensity of a mourner's grief merely because his loved one was elderly. It makes little difference to a man of 80 that his 78-year-old wife has died and that she should constitute a "low grief loss." Age is irrelevant to him—he has lost his life's companion.

There is also a tendency for our society to approve of grief for those who are good and worthwhile but not for those who are "bad." The death of a criminal in the midst of a robbery does not arouse much social concern, but it will still be significant to the criminal's family, and they will need to grieve accordingly.

The amount of unfinished business between the griever and the deceased. *Unfinished business* refers to those issues that were never addressed or lacked successful closure in the relationship. While it also refers to practical matters such as setting up estates or tying up loose ends in business, the term as used here primarily focuses on psychosocial issues between the griever and the deceased. Were they able to express the things they needed or wanted to express to one another? Did they come to some closure about their mutual relationship? Were there any loose ends in the relationship that were not addressed? (Could one finally explain to the other why he had been so hurt and angry at a specific point in time? Were past conflicts resolved? Were regrets and thank you's stated? Did they get to say good-bye to each other?)

Unfinished business remains just that—unfinished. This lack of completion is anxiety-provoking, and may cause a griever to restlessly search for an opportunity to come to closure with the deceased. Some grievers feel they cannot relinquish their grief, and so fail to grieve, until they have brought some ending to that which was unfinished. The griever may seek to find some way to say the never-said "I love you," "I needed you," or "I'm sorry." The less unfinished business between the griever and the lost one, the better, for it means that there is less emotional baggage for the griever to cope with subsequent to the death.

The individual's perception of the deceased's fulfillment in life. The more the mourner perceives the deceased as having had a fulfilling life, the more readily can the death be accepted and the grief work be done. This is an additional reason why the death of the young is so difficult to comprehend and accept, since they have not had the opportunity to have had a fulfilling life.

The death surround. The term *death surround* refers to the immediate circumstances of the death. It includes the location, type of death, reason for the death, and degree of preparation for it. Ideally the mourner will feel that the circumstances are appropriate: the deceased had had a fulfilled life, was older, and died in familiar surroundings from an illness that had received the best medical attention possible; the mourner had had the opportunity and time to prepare for the loss and to finish unfinished business with the dying person.

To the extent that the death surround can be accepted by the griever, the grief will be more amenable to management and resolution. But the circumstances of the loss may also make grief harder to resolve. For example, it may be more difficult to cope with a loved one's death by decapitation in a car accident than a death from illness that occurred at home, with family and friends present at the time of death.

The timeliness of the death. Related in part to the death surround, timeliness also refers to the psychological acceptability of death for this person at this time. The death of the young in our society is always viewed as untimely. However, even among older individuals whose deaths would be viewed as more timely, the mourner's perception of the acceptability of the death at this point in time may depend less on social stereotype and more on what is happening in the relationship at the time of the death. For example, it seems especially unfair when a man dies immediately following the retirement for which he had worked for so long. Although he may be in the age group where such deaths are not entirely unexpected, the fact that he had only just begun to enjoy the fruits of his labors makes the death untimely for the ones left behind. Of course, for many, there would never be an acceptable or appropriate time for their loved one to die, but what is referred to here is the mourner's feelings about the specific timing of the loss. Other circumstances prior to the death, such as recent conflict or reconciliation with the deceased, or the deceased's having just turned over a new leaf or finally achieved a long-desired goal, may make it more difficult for the mourner to accept the fact that the death occurred when it did.

The individual's perception of preventability. A perception of a death as preventable appears to affect the duration and severity of grief (Bugen, 1979). Sometimes this is based on a realistic appraisal of what in fact could have been done; at other times it derives from unrealistic expectations the griever holds for himself. It is very often seen in parents whose children die. Indefinite blame and guilt can have severe consequences for the griever. In the normal process of grief, in which the individual recalls all his guilty feelings over negative acts and things he neglected to do or unfavorable thoughts and feelings that inevitably arose from the ambivalence in the relationship, the preventability issue will always be raised. If it is unclear whether or not the death could have been prevented, or if the griever assumes responsibility for having had the power to prevent it but failed to do so, grief will be greater and more guilt will probably arise to further complicate the mourning process.

The sudden versus expected death. Much of the literature points to the adaptational value of having some advanced warning prior to the actual death (Fulton & Fulton, 1971; Glick et al., 1974; Parkes, 1972, 1975; Parkes & Weiss, 1983). Traditionally it has been felt that such forewarning allows time for the experiences of anticipatory grief—finishing unfinished business, preparing for the consequences of loss, and absorbing the reality of the loss gradually

over time. These were felt to account for the more positive bereavement outcomes of those who suffered loss from expected
deaths, rather than sudden ones. However, although these experiences definitely are therapeutic, more recent writings on the topic
have indicated that it is not that anticipatory grief lessens the grief,
but that unexpected loss overwhelms people and so severely reduces their functioning that recovery becomes very difficult (Glick
et al., 1974; Parkes & Weiss, 1983). In fact, the experiences of anticipatory grief are being interpreted by researchers as being therapeutic because they permit certain kinds of anticipatory preparation that help to keep the loss from being unexpected and make
it seem the result of an understood, although hated, process (Parkes
& Weiss, 1983).

The impact of sudden death on the bereaved can be illustrated
by a study by Glick et al. (1974), who found that widows without
time for anticipatory grief failed to move towards remarriage, in
contrast to those who had experienced anticipated deaths. They
appeared to be unwilling to risk future unanticipated loss for themselves or their children. However, there was no difference in the
depth of grief between both groups. Clearly, unexpected loss "can
overwhelm a person's existing ability to cope with stress and trigger reactions that will lead to lasting problems" (Parkes & Weiss,
1983, p. 239). There is less likelihood of regaining full capacity for
functioning, happiness, and security.

At least when a death has been anticipated, even though it puts
tremendous emotional demands on the individuals involved, coping capacities are directed toward an expectable end. When the
loss occurs, it has been prepared for. When this preparation is
lacking, and the loss comes from out of the blue, grievers are
shocked. They painfully learn that major catastrophic events can
occur without warning. As a result, they develop a chronic apprehension that something unpleasant may happen at any time. It is
this lack of security, along with the experience of being overwhelmed and unable to grasp the situation, that accounts for the
relatively severe postdeath bereavement complications that occur
in cases of sudden death.

The length of the illness prior to death. Despite the importance
of a period of preparation prior to a death, there is some evidence
that too long a period of forewarning can also predispose grievers
to poorer bereavement outcomes (Gerber, Rusalem, Hannon, Battin, & Arkin, 1975; Hamovitch, 1964; Maddison, 1968; Schwab et
al., 1975; Schwab, Farris, Conroy, & Markush, 1976). There are a
number of reasons why a prolonged period of illness would exacerbate the problems of the bereaved afterwards. Caring for the
dying patient requires large amounts of time, causing progressively
more social isolation. The responsibilities associated with care-
taking may lead to physical debilitation that can cause physical

and emotional problems. The emotional stresses are so intense and prolonged that they may lead to emotional exhaustion. When there are cycles of remission-relapse, ambivalence or anger towards the dying person may develop, with such resentments or death wishes later causing the bereaved to feel guilty. And an illness filled with remissions may even give rise to denial of the ultimate death, since death was always successfully avoided earlier in the illness, and this may result in a lack of preparation for the death and disturbed reactions following it. (See Chapter 12 for more on the problems faced by families during a terminal illness.)

Two recent studies have found that there appears to be an optimum length of time below and above which adjustment to bereavement is compromised. In investigating parents whose children had died from cancer, Rando (1983) found that those parents whose children's illnesses were less than 6 months or longer than 18 reported being the least prepared for death and having the least adjustment following the death. The longer the illness, the angrier the parents became, and the more atypical grief responses they evidenced after the death. These conclusions were supported by Sanders (1982-83), who discovered that grievers of a death from a short-term chronic illness (less than 6 months in duration) fared better than those from either a sudden death or a long-term chronic illness.

Anticipatory grief and involvement with the dying patient. Research suggests that anticipatory grief will affect the amount of involvement grievers have with the dying patient during the dying period. (See "Anticipatory Grief" in Chapter 2 for more on this topic.) It may bring them closer to the patient or cause them to decathect from him before death, depending upon the length of the grief and situational factors. Whatever the experience is, it will color the bereavement period following death.

The number, type, and quality of secondary losses. Those losses that develop as a consequence of the death of the loved one are known as *secondary losses*. For example, depending on the roles the deceased filled, the mourner may have to suffer a change of environment, loss of status, alteration of relationships with other family members, and other losses because the deceased is gone. At times these secondary losses cause more problems for the griever than the initial loss of the death of the loved one.

> *Case Example:* John was 20 when his father died. He was in college studying engineering at the time. After the death John was forced to abandon his dream of becoming an engineer in order to take over the family grocery store his father had owned and operated. Without this there would have been insufficient income for John's mother and three siblings.
>
> John not only lost his father; he also lost his vocation, his

independence (he had to move back home), his girlfriend (after John's withdrawal from the university she found someone else who was near enough to spend more time with her), and his role as a happy-go-lucky young adult (he now assumed his father's role in the family as eldest male and chief provider). Until John could identify and grieve over these secondary losses, his grief could not be resolved. Ironically, he could cope better with the loss of his father, which he had been gradually preparing for, than with the other losses that his father's death brought about.

Existing and potential secondary losses must be identified and predicted for the mourner so these losses also can be prepared for and grieved. The more there are, the greater amount of grief work mandated for the mourner.

The presence of concurrent stresses or crises. The griever may be confronted with ongoing stresses unrelated to the death that may add to the vicissitudes of the bereavement experience. For example, the individual who is unemployed, physically ill, getting a divorce, or struggling with a developmental crisis will have a relatively more difficult time coping with grief because of the additional burdens. Research has indicated that the presence of concurrent life crises is associated with poorer bereavement outcomes (Parkes, 1975; Raphael & Maddison, 1976).

SOCIAL FACTORS

The individual's social support system and the acceptance and assistance of its members. The type of support the griever will receive will be based on how the griever and the deceased are valued by members of the social system and the manner and circumstances of the death (e.g., grievers of a suicide are often left alone). However, when the griever does not receive the nonjudgmental compassion and support of concerned others, she loses a vital aid to handling the difficult confrontations demanded in grief work. The tasks of grief work require the encouragement, empathy, and sustenance gained from positive relationships. Lack of support usually leads to difficulty in the successful resolution of grief (Maddison, 1968; Maddison & Walker, 1967; Parkes, 1972; Raphael, 1977; Sheldon, Cochrane, Vachon, Lyall, Rogers, & Freeman, 1981; Vachon, Sheldon, Lancee, Lyall, Rogers, & Freeman, 1982). Problems may also occur as a result of inappropriate expectations from others.

The timing of social support is crucial. Parkes and Weiss (1983) and Vachon, Lyall, Rogers, Freedman-Letofsky, and Freeman (1980) found that the presence of supportive relationships, while valuable at the time of bereavement, had no significant association with later recovery. What seemed to be most important in fostering recovery was not whether social support was initially available, but whether it was available and utilized as time went on. Of course, this required the active reaching out or reciprocation of the bereaved individual as well as of the supporters. It is not all that uncommon for grievers to not utilize the support that is offered to them and to isolate themselves despite the presence of a concerned social group.

The individual's socio-cultural, ethnic, and religious/philosophical backgrounds. Differing socio-cultural, ethnic, and religious/philosophical groups maintain dissimilar attitudes towards the expression of grief. For example, in terms of cultural stereotypes, people from Latin cultures express their grief much differently than those from Eastern European cultures. Traditionally Latins are more emotive and tend to overtly express their grief, while Eastern Europeans are more stoic and repressive of their feelings. This is clearly an overgeneralization, but it illustrates the possible cultural differences in expression of grief. Differences due to culture, ethnic group, or religion/philosophy may help or hinder grief work as the individual tries to resolve the loss.

The educational, economic, and occupational status of the bereaved. A lack of education, financial resources, or occupational skills will only magnify the stresses on the griever. They may compromise the griever's ability to sustain and replenish herself (literally and figuratively) after the death, especially in regard to gaining access to health care and remaining self-supporting. This is particularly problematic when a griever is confronted with a lower standard of living for the first time in her life due to the costs of long-term illness. It is a prime example of a secondary loss.

The funerary rituals. These can be especially helpful or harmful to the initiation and resolution of the individual's grief work. Those rituals that promote realization and confirmation of the loss, assist in the expression of affect and memories, and offer social support to the bereaved are truly therapeutic. The absence of these rituals, or their inappropriate use, can be detrimental to the grief process. (See Chapter 7 for more on this topic.)

PHYSIOLOGICAL FACTORS

Drugs and sedatives. The potential negative effects of these psychopharmacological agents may outweigh their usefulness in many cases. Drugs that are calming or anesthetizing are nontherapeutic in that they keep the griever from experiencing the pain and realizing the loss that ultimately has to be faced. Often the bereaved are drugged during the wake and funeral, the precise times at which they should be encouraged to give vent to their emotions. This leaves them to confront their loss later on, at times at which there may not be the social support that is usually available during the initial period following the death. The bereaved are already psychically "numb," so the immediate use of drugs to accomplish the same effect is questionable.

> *Case Example:* Nan was in her early 50s when her husband dropped dead suddenly from a heart attack. Because Nan was a very emotional woman, her doctor kept her quite sedated during the funeral rituals and for several weeks afterwards. While flying to visit her family in France 2 months later, Nan came out of her drug fog. The full realization of what had happened hit her with a jolt when she was in a plane full of strangers midway across the Atlantic Ocean. She was overwhelmed with acute grief and lack of support. She would have been expected to sustain such grief during the funeral, when she would have been able to have been comforted by close friends. Now, because her physician had sought to "spare her the pain," Nan was forced to experience it alone and without assistance.

This is not to imply that there is no point at which drugs are a useful tool for the bereaved. Although heavy sedation to block the mourning process is not wise, mild sedation to prevent exhaustion and severe insomnia, and disease resulting from them, may be quite therapeutic. Since the bereaved need energy for their grief work, such medication may be helpful. Complications of the mourning process (e.g., clinical depression that is agitated or retarded, psychosis, elation, phobic anxiety states) will require the skilled evaluation of a psychiatrist and may be reduced by psychopharmacological intervention, as may other indices of unresolved grief.

Nutrition. It is not uncommon for the bereaved to be anorexic or, if they do eat, to complain of the altered taste of food and impaired gastrointestinal functioning. Despite this, they must be encouraged to maintain adequate nutritional balance and eating habits, for inadequate nutrition will compromise their ability to cope with the loss, meet the continuing demands of daily life, and overcome the numerous physiological symptoms generated by the stress of grief.

Rest and sleep. Some degree of sleep disturbance is normally expected in the grief process. However, a lack of sufficient sleep may predispose the bereaved to mental and physical exhaustion, disease, and unresolved grief. If the requisite energy to undertake grief work is impaired, medication may be warranted.

Physical health. Grief assaults the body, just as it assaults the psyche. The individual's physical condition and the responsivity of her nervous system will influence how the stress of grief is handled by her body. A certain amount of physical disturbance is a normal component of grief; however, physical symptoms should be cared for to preserve the griever's energy for grief work and to reduce the potential for morbidity and mortality.

Exercise. Adequate exercise not only keeps the body in good physical condition, but also provides an outlet for the emotions of grief. It allows for a reduction of aggressive feelings, a release of tension and anxiety, and a relief of depression. These emotions are then less likely to be somatized as psychosomatic illnesses.

CHAPTER 4

Unresolved Grief

Given the multitude of factors that combine to determine people's unique grief responses, it is not surprising that there are a number of variants on the typical process of grief. These variants, which will be discussed in this chapter, are termed *unresolved* because there has been some disturbance of the normal progress towards resolution.

FORMS OF UNRESOLVED GRIEF

The following descriptions of forms of unresolved grief have been taken from the analyses of Averill (1968), Parkes and Weiss (1983), and Raphael (1983). Any of these forms may overlap. In each there are components of denial or repression of aspects of the loss or of the feelings generated, as well as an attempt to hold on to the lost relationship.

Absent grief. In this situation feelings of grief and mourning processes are totally absent. It is as if the death never occurred at all. It requires either that the mourner completely deny the death or that he remain in the stage of shock.

Inhibited grief. In this form there is a lasting inhibition of many of the manifestations of normal grief, with the appearance of other symptoms such as somatic complaints in their place. The mourner may be able to relinquish and mourn only certain aspects of the deceased and not others, for example, the positive aspects but not the negative ones.

> *Case Example:* Ruth came to therapy because her deteriorating physical condition suggested a significant depression. She was compliant and eager to please in treatment. Investigation revealed that her estranged husband had committed suicide several years earlier. She had attended to the tasks of the funeral and then resumed her life as if nothing had occurred.

There were no behavioral expressions of any grief and no internal processing of it. Shortly afterwards Ruth developed severe gastrointestinal difficulties and the next several years were devoted to focusing on her physical complaints.

Delayed grief. Normal or conflicted grief may be delayed for an extended period of time, up to years, especially if there are pressing responsibilities or the mourner feels he cannot deal with the process at that time. A full grief reaction may eventually be initiated by another loss or by some event related to the original loss. For instance, a pet's death can trigger a response for a loved one who died years earlier, but who had never been mourned because the griever felt he had to be strong to take care of other family members. Meanwhile, only an inhibited form of grief may be observed.

Case Example: Randi was a high-school senior when her mother died suddenly following a successful heart operation. Her father had also died unexpectedly the previous year. Randi was always the domestic one and she took over the task of managing the house and paying the bills for her two siblings and herself. She was also the "strong one" and never took time to grieve. Several years after the death of her mother Randi entered nursing school. One day she went to give a cardiac patient an injection, but instead of seeing the patient in the bed she "saw" her own mother. This initiated an acute grief reaction.

Conflicted grief. In this grief there is frequently an exaggeration or distortion of one or more of the manifestations of normal grief, while other aspects of the grief may be suppressed at the same time. Two common patterns are extreme anger and extreme guilt. This grief reaction can be abnormally prolonged and is often associated with a previously dependent or ambivalent relationship with the deceased.

Case Example: Felicia's 10-year-old son died from acute appendicitis 8 months prior to her referral for therapy. Felicia was an overemotional woman who for years had become hysterical whenever she had to contact the pediatrician about her son. She had strong ambivalent feelings towards her son because of his father's having deserted her when she discovered she was pregnant. At the time of the appendicitis attack, the pediatrician had heard Felicia exaggerate her son's symptoms once too often and consequently responded too slowly to save the child's life. Felicia's grief continued unabated as she constantly blamed herself for not convincing the pediatrician of the gravity of the illness, and she was filled with self-reproach for the resentment she frequently had felt for her son.

Chronic grief. In chronic grief the mourner continuously exhibits intense grief reactions that would be appropriate in the early stages of loss. Mourning fails to draw to its natural conclusion and it almost seems that the bereaved keeps the deceased alive with grief. Intense yearning, often associated with an intensely dependent relationship on the deceased fostered by the mourner's insecurity, is symptomatic of this grief. It is also evident after the loss of an irreplaceable relationship in which the bereaved had extraordinary, and possibly pathological, emotional investment.

> *Case Example:* Bill was a shy, insecure man who was devoted to his wife and built his entire emotional world around her. She handled all the family finances, organized their social schedule, and raised the children independently. Most of his social contacts with others were through her. After she died he was both deeply depressed and isolated. He went through only the minimum attempts at communicating with others, being fearful of them. He spent most of his time alone and arranged for a housekeeper to handle the domestic duties and take responsibility for the children. Six years later he had made no changes since she died.

Unanticipated grief. This is a form of grief reaction that only recently has been discussed in the literature (Glick et al., 1974; Parkes & Weiss, 1983). It occurs after a sudden, unanticipated loss and is so disruptive that recovery is usually complicated. In unanticipated grief, mourners are unable to grasp the full implications of the loss. Their adaptive capabilities are seriously assaulted and they suffer extreme feelings of bewilderment, anxiety, self-reproach, and depression that render them unable to function normally in any area of their lives. There is difficulty in accepting the loss, despite intellectual recognition of the death, and the death may continue to seem inexplicable. Grief symptomology persists much longer than usual.

> *Case Example:* Jane's husband was hit by a drunk driver after he had stopped to help a motorist change a tire. Jane was completely overwhelmed when informed of the accident, and this feeling stayed with her for almost a year. She could not believe that the death had actually occurred, and she frequently had to remind herself that her husband was not going to return. Many of her grief symptoms persisted for an abnormally long period of time. Although she was able to go through the motions of putting her life back together again, Jane became chronically anxious and apprehensive, always awaiting another trauma to befall her. Jane dated, but she was never able to make a commitment to another man for fear that he would be taken from her too.

Abbreviated grief. This reaction is often mistaken for unresolved grief. In fact, it is a short-lived but normal form of grief. It may occur because of the immediate replacement of the lost person (e.g., marrying a new spouse right after the first one dies) or an insufficient attachment to the lost person (e.g., the individual was never that attached to the person in the first place). Sometimes it occurs when a significant amount of anticipatory grief has been completed prior to a death. After the actual death occurs the individual grieves, but much of the grief work has been accomplished so that the postdeath bereavement period, while painful, may be relatively shorter.

> *Case Example:* Peter's wife succumbed to cancer after a long illness of several years. Peter had gone through a long process of anticipatory grief during the illness and consequently, after a short but intense grief reaction at the time of her death, was left with little to grieve for. He started dating within 10 weeks of his wife's death and evidenced no further symptoms of grief.

SYMPTOMS AND BEHAVIORS OF UNRESOLVED GRIEF

The following lists adopted from Lindemann (1944), Lazare (1979), and Worden (1982) enumerate some symptoms and behaviors indicative of unresolved grief. These individual symptoms may be unremarkable during the acute stage of grief. However, they are the major signs of incomplete grief work when they are manifested *beyond* the expected time for resolution of grief. The more of these symptoms the mourner has, the stronger the diagnosis of unresolved grief.

The following manifestations of unresolved grief reaction were put forth by Lindemann (1944):

- Overactivity without a sense of loss
- Acquisition of symptoms belonging to the last illness of the deceased
- Development of a psychosomatic medical illness
- Alteration in relationships with friends and relatives
- Furious hostility against specific persons somehow connected with the death (e.g., doctor, nurse)
- Wooden and formal conduct that masks hostile feelings and resembles a schizophrenic reaction in which there is a lack of emotion
- Lasting loss of patterns of social interaction
- Acts detrimental to one's own social and economic existence (e.g., giving away belongings, making foolish economic deals)
- Agitated depression with tension, agitation, insomnia, feel-

ings of worthlessness, bitter self-accusation, and obvious need for punishment, and even suicidal tendencies.

The following diagnostic criteria for unresolved grief were proposed by Lazare (1979). When one or more of these symptoms or behaviors transpires after a death and continues beyond 6 months to 1 year, he considers the diagnosis of unresolved grief. The greater the number of symptoms and behaviors, the greater the likelihood of unresolved grief.

- A depressive syndrome of varying degrees of severity since the time of the death, frequently a very mild, subclinical one often accompanied by persistent guilt and lowered self-esteem
- A history of delayed or prolonged grief, indicating that the person characteristically avoids or has difficulty with grief work
- Symptoms of guilt and self-reproach, panic attacks, and somatic expressions of fear such as choking sensations and shortness of breath
- Somatic symptoms representing identification with the deceased, often the symptoms of the terminal illness
- Physical distress under the upper half of the sternum, accompanied by expressions such as "There is something stuck inside" or "I feel there is a demon inside of me"
- Searching that continues over time, with a great deal of random behavior, restlessness, and moving around
- Recurrence of symptoms of depression and searching behavior on specific dates, such as anniversaries of the death, birthdays of the deceased, achieving the age of the deceased, and holidays (especially Christmas), that are more extreme than those anniversary reactions normally expected
- A feeling that the death occurred yesterday, even though the loss took place months or years ago
- Unwillingness to move the material possessions of the deceased after a reasonable amount of time has passed
- Changes in relationships following the death
- Diminished participation in religious and ritual activities that are part of the mourner's culture, including avoidance of visiting the grave or taking part in funerary rituals
- An inability to discuss the deceased without crying or having the voice crack, particularly when the death occurred over a year ago
- Themes of loss

These additional symptoms of unresolved grief were suggested by Worden (1982):

- A relatively minor event triggering major grief reactions

- False euphoria subsequent to the death
- Overidentification with the deceased leading to a compulsion to imitate the dead person, particularly if it is unconscious and the mourner lacks the competence for the same behavior
- Self-destructive impulses
- Radical changes in lifestyle
- Exclusion of friends, family members, or activities associated with the deceased
- Phobias about illness or death

These lists are not all-inclusive. Mourners can be expected to manifest widely varying symptoms of unresolved grief, and caregivers will place varying amounts of importance on the presence or absence of specific symptoms depending upon the norms they develop over time as they work with the bereaved.

Three primary variables demarcate unresolved grief: absence of a normal grief reaction, prolongation of a normal grief reaction, and distortion of a normal grief reaction (Siggins, 1966). To make a determination of unresolved grief it is necessary to know the full range of normal grief against which the behavior in question is being compared and the psychological, social, and physiological variables that would influence the individual's grief reaction. Without an understanding of and appreciation for these variables and how they affect a particular individual's grief experience, *no* judgments can be made about the person's grief response.

REASONS FOR UNRESOLVED GRIEF

Jackson (1957) feels that two conditions may provoke difficulties in accomplishing grief work and thus predispose the mourner to unresolved grief. In the first condition, the mourner is unable to tolerate the emotional distress of grief and resists dealing with the necessary tasks and feelings of grief. The second condition occurs when the mourner has an excessive need to maintain interaction with the deceased. In this case the mourner denies the loss and fails to appropriately decathect from the deceased, thereby failing in the requisite tasks of grief work. Of course, all of the factors noted in Chapter 3 have the potential to interfere with the completion of grief.

Lazare (1979) has given a number of psychological and social reasons for failure to grieve. The following factors are adapted from his work.

Psychological Factors in Unresolved Grief

Guilt. Unresolved grief may occur when mourners are afraid to grieve because reviewing their relationship with the deceased would bring up negative acts or feelings they had directed towards her, or things they had neglected to do, making them feel guilty. This concern usually develops in people with harsh superegos whose feelings towards the deceased are highly ambivalent. Guilt resulting from other factors can also block the grief process if mourners feel unable to confront the guilt. (See "The Confrontation Phase" in Chapter 2 for more on this topic.)

Loss of an extension of the self. Some people may be so dependent upon, or place such a high value on, the deceased that they will not grieve in order to avoid the reality of the loss. In this case, the deceased had been perceived as an extension of the bereaved and to recognize the loss and grief would constitute a severe narcissistic loss to the self. One mourner said, "Mother was my other half. I cannot be complete without her. She cannot be dead."

Reawakening of an old loss. In some cases individuals are reluctant to grieve because the current loss reawakens a more profound and painful loss that has not yet been resolved. An example of this would be the man who cannot grieve for his divorce because it resurrects the memory of the death of his mother, for whom he never appropriately grieved.

Multiple loss. Those who experience multiple losses, such as the death of an entire family or a number of sequential losses within a relatively short period of time, sometimes have difficulty grieving because the losses are too overwhelming to contemplate and deal with. Essentially they are suffering from "bereavement overload" (Kastenbaum, 1969). In the case of losing family members it is additionally complicated because those who would normally support the griever no longer exist.

Inadequate ego development. To mourn appropriately the individual needs to have achieved the state of object constancy and to have realized an adequate integration of a number of basic ego functions. Without these prerequisites, the individual responds to loss and separation with serious ego regression. Consequently, people with severe ego impairments (e.g., borderline personalities) are often unable to adequately complete the grief process because they cannot meet the necessary intrapsychic tasks. Instead, they frequently experience feelings of intense hopelessness, rage, frustration, depression, anxiety, and despair that they cannot defend against. Often psychotic behavior results when their primitive defense mechanisms fail. Such individuals are not psychologically able to successfully master the tasks of grief. For instance, one borderline patient could never complete grieving over the death of his father because he was incapable of maintaining a consistent mental image of his father from which to decathect.

Idiosyncratic resistances to mourning. There are individuals who do not permit themselves to grieve because of specific psychological issues that interfere with the process. For example, some people will not grieve for fear of losing control or appearing weak to themselves and others. Others have expressed the concern that if they start to cry the tears will never stop. Still other grievers are afraid to give up the pain, since it binds them closely to the deceased. Any individual fear, conflict, issue, or conditioned response that interferes with the mourner's yielding to the normal process of grief will constitute a resistance to mourning and may have to be interpreted and addressed with the help of a therapist if it cannot be successfully worked through by the individual.

Social Factors in Unresolved Grief

Social negation of a loss. In this situation the loss is not socially defined as a loss, e.g., an abortion, a miscarriage, an infant given up for adoption. Although grief work is necessary, the social support for it is inadequate or nonexistent. This is what occurs in many cases involving symbolic psychosocial losses.

Socially unspeakable loss. In this case the loss is so "unspeakable" that members of the social system cannot be of any assistance to the bereaved. They tend to shy away out of ignorance of what to say to help or moral repugnance. Examples of such a loss include death by an overdose of morphine, murder, suicide, or the death of an illicit lover.

Social isolation and/or geographic distance from social support. In this instance the individual is either away from her social supports at the time of mourning or there are no existing social supports available for assistance. Geographical distance from support is becoming increasingly common as individuals are becoming more and more mobile. In addition, deaths may occur in places or at times when people may be unable to travel conveniently or quickly. The difficulties inherent in this type of situation are seen in the dilemma of the 20-year-old college student whose mother did not inform her that her father had died until after she returned from school following final examinations. By that time the family had already dealt with a great deal of their own grief and provided her with little support in her own initial stages of grief. People also fail to grieve when they have no social support in the first place. The breakdown of the nuclear family, the decline in primary group interactions with consequent depersonalization and alienation, and the diminished importance of religious institutions all account for this lack of support.

Assumption of the role of the strong one. In some situations there are certain people who are designated to be the "strong one" by those around them. They must make all the funeral arrangements, bolster the morale of others, and not show any emotion. Sometimes their very occupations or roles require this, as with priests or Army captains. Often these individuals miss the opportunity to deal with their own grief due to the roles they attempt to maintain.

Uncertainty over the loss. In cases where the loss is uncertain, such as when a boater is lost at sea or a child is kidnapped, the grievers and their social systems are often unable to commence grieving until they know the precise status of the lost person. This is why so much time, money, and effort is spent searching to recover missing bodies and confirm deaths.

BEREAVEMENT PROBLEMS CAUSED BY SOCIAL ROLES

Volkart (1976) has put forth the notion that the grieving person has social roles to perform and that this may contribute to some of the mental health problems that develop in bereavement.

> The formulation, for example, opens up the possibility that some bereavement problems may be occasioned not by severe loss but by an awareness of one's inability to play the bereaved role properly. If we assume that one of the role obligations is to express grief and loss and that these sentiments are imputed to the bereaved by others, the bereaved person who lacks these sentiments may be in a painfully dangerous situation as a result of guilty fear. (p. 252)

In American culture the social role of the bereaved appears to center around loss and the desirability of expressing feelings of loss and grief. However, problems develop when this type of role expectation is not psychologically congruent with the experience of the bereaved person. For example, the socially conditioned sex role of the male in American culture is contrary to the emotional expression of loss that is expected of a bereaved person.

There are other problems that develop as a consequence of the social role expectations regarding grief expression. Volkart notes that while there is a concentration on the feeling and expression of loss, there is a failure to provide for other emotions such as hostility and guilt and the needs they create. The greater these feelings are, the greater is their tendency to create new demands, for the hostility must somehow be discharged and the guilt must be released or displaced. The bereaved person is therefore vulnerable in bereavement unless the prescribed social role adequately meets these needs.

In other cultures, mourning customs and expectations provide opportunities to meet emotional needs. Ambivalence towards relatives in the Apache culture, which is induced by their social structure, finds socially sanctioned displacement in Apache mourning rites and customs (Opler, 1936). The obligation of the bereaved to avenge the death of the deceased provides sanctioned opportunities for the ridding of guilt feelings and hostility among the Murngin (Warner, 1937). Volkart (1976) further notes that there are numerous examples in the anthropological literature of the bereaved being required to inflict pain and disfigurement upon their bodies, which fastens their attention upon themselves and consequently hastens their emancipation from the deceased.

Mourners in American culture are seriously vulnerable to psychological problems:

> If the bereavement problems of a given culture are adequately perceived, functionally adequate social roles for the bereaved may be devised that can blunt such vulnerability to breakdown as may appear. But to the extent that social and cultural conditions [as in American culture] encourage interpersonal relationships in which overidentification, overdependence, sense of loss, hostility, guilt, and ambivalence are bred in profusion and to the extent that the social role of the bereaved person does not take account of these feelings and the needs they inspire bereaved persons may often be unintended victims of their sociocultural system. In our case, the sense of loss may be handled satisfactorily by the role that encourages expression of loss and grief; but the role does not, and cannot, adequately provide for replacement when this need is strong, and the added burdens of accumulated and unrelieved guilt, hostility, and ambivalence, when they are strong, can only increase vulnerability to psychic break down. (Volkart, 1976, p. 255)

In the "Family Problems" section of Chapter 12 there is a more thorough discussion of the effects of American culture on the grief experience.

DETERMINANTS OF BEREAVEMENT OUTCOME

Recent findings have indicated that early intervention is successful in reducing the damaging effects of bereavement for high-risk widows and widowers, although such intervention may not benefit those in low-risk or unselected groups (Parkes, 1980; Parkes & Weiss, 1983). This means that, in order to intervene effectively, it is necessary to know which mourners are at risk. Through a series of investigations with widows and some widowers, Parkes and Weiss (1983) identified what appear to be those variables most predictive of bereavement outcome. From these they derived the three major determinants of pathological grief syndromes: bereavements that were sudden, unexpected, and untimely, leading to unanticipated grief; those associated with ambivalence towards the deceased with reactions of intense anger and/or self-reproach, resulting in conflicted grief; and those related to an abnormally dependent relationship with the deceased, generating reactions of intense yearning that became chronic grief.

In analyzing the factors that were associated with unresolved grief Parkes and Weiss identified a list of precursors. The eight variables appearing during the first 2 months after death that, combined, gave the most satisfactory prediction of bereavement outcome at 13 months (and that appeared to predict the trajectory for the future outcome) are listed in order of significance as follows:

• *Coders' prediction of outcome.* This was an educated guess made by the coders of the Harvard Bereavement Study, from which the data for these investigations came (Glick et al., 1974).

• *Respondent's level of yearning* (3 to 4 weeks after bereavement). Intense yearning, much greater than that typically seen, appeared to have been associated with undue dependence on the deceased. Interestingly, this further provides evidence that it is not solely those who avoid or repress grief who are most likely to become disturbed a year later.

• *Respondent's attitude toward own death* (3 to 4 weeks after bereavement). This involved the expression, at the first interview, of the wish for one's own death. It is unclear as to why this variable had such predictive value. It arose under a variety of circumstances and did not appear associated with any particular antecedent or outcome variable. It seemed to be equally expressive of several different syndromes of pathological grief.

• *Duration of terminal illness.* This was closely associated with the pathological syndrome of unanticipated grief.

• *Social class.* Social class may represent a constellation of variables. For instance, low social class may indicate an environment in which there are special stresses and/or a lack of resources. Whatever social class represents, it is interesting to note that it affected the outcome of bereavement without changing the actual course of grief: respondents of lower socio-economic status grieved in much the same way as those of higher status, although the outcome appeared to be poorer. Surprisingly, poor financial status and low income did not correlate with outcome, leaving this variable requiring more analysis.

• *Years of marriage.* The importance of a long marriage can be evaluated only in light of other evidence. While brief marriages appear to be easier to give up than longer marriages are, a long marriage cannot be assumed to be a major cause of pathological bereavement, as witnessed by the studies of older widows and widowers who appear less vulnerable to the effects of conjugal bereavement than younger ones.

• *Respondent's level of anger* and *Respondent's level of self-reproach* (3 to 4 weeks after bereavement). Both anger and self-reproach may reflect ambivalent marriages. Since such marriages appear to result in more problematic grief, it is not surprising that these variables are associated with poorer outcome.

Several other variables appeared to be clinically important, but were not statistically significant in this study because of its design. When the design deficiencies were controlled for, it was clear that bereavement symptoms are worse for young widows and widowers than for older ones, and for widowers than widows. Other possible impediments to recovery observed during the study were a tendency to doubt one's own capacities, a lack of hope for the future, and a deathbed statement from the deceased amounting to prohibition of recovery.

PSYCHIATRIC PROBLEMS DUE TO BEREAVEMENT

Bereavement has been significantly associated with psychiatric admission (Parkes, 1965) and with first entry into psychiatric care (Stein & Susser, 1969). In 1964 Parkes found that within a 6-month period following the death of their husbands a group of London widows under 65 had tripled their psychiatric consultation rates and had received prescriptions for sedation at seven times the amount prior to the death of their husbands. Parkes and Brown (1972) found that the bereaved in their study obtained professional help more frequently and had more social difficulties in comparison to the control group. Stroebe and Stroebe (1983) noted that there is near unanimous agreement in the literature that bereavement can be a cause of mental illness. While depression is the most common disorder, other disorders such as neurotic disorders, phobias, obsessions, hypochondriasis, and conversions have been described as well (Raphael, 1983).

MORBIDITY AND MORTALITY DUE TO BEREAVEMENT

Some degree of physiological disturbance is a common component of the normal grief process. Nevertheless, it often escalates into a health risk for the bereaved. In some instances, the mourner even dies from grief-related illnesses. The following sections describe the nature and extent of the risks that bereavement poses to physical health. Despite its being discussed in this chapter, physiological symptomatology does not signify unresolved grief in and of itself; it is mentioned here to illustrate that normal physiological disturbances accompanying grief can themselves become pathological to the mourner.

Morbidity

There have been a number of investigations of the physical sequelae of a loss through death (Clayton, 1979; Glick et al., 1974; Lindemann, 1944; Maddison, 1969; Maddison & Viola, 1968; Maddison & Walker, 1967; Parkes, 1964, 1970, 1972; Parkes & Brown, 1972; Rees & Lutkins, 1967; Young, Benjamin, & Wallis, 1963; Parkes, Note 2). All of these concluded that the death of a loved one carries with it a definite physical risk for the griever much greater than that of the normal population.

Maddison (1969) summarized several studies and noted that in studying the health status of widows in Boston and Sydney 13 months after bereavement there was deterioration in 21% of Boston subjects and 32% of Sydney subjects. When matched to a control group these figures became more significant, as only 7% of the control group in Boston and 2% in Sydney reported a comparable deterioration in health. Glick et al. (1974) discovered that within 8 weeks after the death of their husbands 40% of the widows they studied had consulted their physicians because of headaches, dizziness, sleeplessness, and loss of appetite. Parkes (Note 2) reported that this same population spent considerably more time in bed than did the control group and had three times as many hospitalizations in the year following bereavement.

When comparing bereaved widows and widowers to a non-bereaved control group 13 months after the loss of their spouses, Parkes and Brown (1972) reported that bereaved subjects exceeded the control group in physical symptoms, especially in autonomic symptoms. They found that widows reported 50% more autonomic symptoms than women in the control group and widowers displayed four times as many symptoms as married men in the control group. Twelve bereaved individuals were admitted to the hospital during the year after their loss, while only four members of the comparison group had hospital admissions, and these were for conditions less serious than the bereaved group. The emotional distress of the bereaved sample was greater than the control group. Insomnia and changes in appetite and weight were also more frequent. Of the bereaved group, 28% reported an increase in smoking, 28% reported an increase in alcohol consumption, and 26% had either begun taking tranquilizers or increased their use. There had been virtually no increase in drug use in the control sample, with the exception of an unexplained increase in smoking among 20% of the married men. Other studies have suggested that bereavement is a precipitant for ulcerative colitis (Lindemann, 1944), neoplastic diseases (Klerman & Izen, 1977), thyrotoxicosis (Lidz, 1949), and asthma (McDermott & Cobb, 1939), as well as for psychosomatic disorders in general (Breslin, Note 3).

A series of more recent investigations provides additional data illustrating the physical assault experienced by the griever. These studies have been more narrow in focus and have revealed that specific physiological processes are altered as a direct consequence of the stress of bereavement. Acute grief was found to be associated with relatively higher 17-hydroxycorticosteroid excretion rates in parents of leukemic children after the death (Hofer, Wolff, Friedman, & Mason, 1972). Grief also has been shown to affect the pituitary-adrenal axis and to lead to hypersecretion of cortisol, causing suppression of the immune response and resulting in increased susceptibility to infectious diseases and malignancies (Fredrick, 1976-77, 1982-83). Depressed lymphocyte function has been demonstrated in bereaved individuals (Bartrop, Lazarus, Luckherst, Kiloh, & Penny, 1977), and recent evidence has documented that suppression of mitogen-induced lymphocyte stimulation in widowers is a direct consequence of the loss (Schleifer, Keller, Camerino, Thorton, & Stein, 1983). The effects of this last study were found to be visible during the first month after bereavement, in contrast to previous findings in which they were seen only after 6 weeks (Bartrop et al., 1977). Additionally, they were found to persist longer than responses to other physically stressful conditions.

Mortality

The combined evidence of mortality statistics suggests that there is a strong mortality risk to the bereaved. Kraus and Lilienfield (1959) found an increase in death rates of 40% for widowers in the first 6 months subsequent to the loss. In 1963, Young, Benjamin, and Wallis found almost the same 40% increase in the mortality rate of British widowers for 6 months following the death, after which it declined to expected levels. Subsequent analysis of these deaths revealed that three-quarters of the increased death rate was attributable to heart disease (Parkes, Benjamin, & Fitzgerald, 1969). Studies by Cox and Ford (1964) and Rees and Lutkins (1967) also found a significant increase in mortality for the bereaved as compared to control populations.

Stroebe et al. (1981-82) originally found that the evidence traditionally used to sustain the assumption of a "loss effect" (a predisposition to mortality due to bereavement) was insufficient, but that numerous indirect sources of evidence seemed to support it. They urged continued research on the issue, with particular attention to psychosocial processes that might cause the bereaved to either take an active self-destructive role or cease adequate health care. In a later extensive review Stroebe and Stroebe (1983) found that, compared with marriage, widowhood was associated with higher mortality for both sexes, with the excess risk being greater for men and the younger widowed. (This supports the findings of

Jacobs and Ostfeld, who reviewed the literature in 1977.) Synthesizing the evidence from longitudinal studies, Stroebe and Stroebe found that for widowers there appeared to be a peak in the mortality risk during the first 6 months after the death, while for widows the period of highest risk appeared to be during the second year of bereavement.

Taken together, all these studies of morbidity and mortality corroborate clinical observations that bereavement is a state of great risk physically, as well as emotionally and socially. For this reason, the importance of adequate resolution of grief work cannot be stressed too much.

CHAPTER 5

Therapeutic Interventions with Grievers

Expressing the feelings of loss, anger, and sadness that come with death of a loved one is a necessary part of the resolution of grief. But by itself it is not enough.

> *Case Example:* Cheryl had been in therapy three times over the past 8 years before coming to her present therapist. During these ventures into the psychotherapeutic process she had addressed the death of her father 7 years before . . . or at least she thought she had. Through a variety of techniques, including Gestalt exercises and identification and expression of feelings through different eclectic methods, she "dealt" with her father's death. However, at the time she came to her present therapist, it was clear that she still struggled with a number of unresolved issues around his death. She had symptoms of an agitated depression and continued to act out, which kept her from developing satisfying relationships. When informed by her therapist that she needed to work on the death of her father, Cheryl was incredulous since she had already spent a significant amount of time working on that issue.

This paradoxical situation stems from an incomplete understanding of the importance of the cognitive and intrapsychic aspects of grief work. Many such grievers are left wondering why they have failed to resolve their loss despite having expressed their emotions: "But I cried for my father," "I saw a therapist and we talked about my child's death. . . ," "I let myself feel the pain." The feeling that they have done what they were supposed to, but somehow have been betrayed by themselves by still being stuck in grief, can be profound. Even more often, they have a sense that some particular loss really has been resolved, and then, to their surprise, they are told that there is more work to be completed. They have indeed worked on resolving the loss—the problem is that they simply have not finished with it.

Lindemann (1944) outlined the three tasks of grief—emancipation from the bondage of the deceased, readjustment to the environment in which the deceased is missing, and formation of new relationships—that must necessarily be completed for the successful resolution of the process. However, relatively little has been written about the cognitive and intrapsychic processes that accompany the affective procedures of expression of feeling and catharsis in grief. Most caregivers focus on these affective procedures. While these are critical and crucial for successful resolution of the grief process, a number of cognitive and intrapsychic processes *must* take place as well.

COGNITIVE AND INTRAPSYCHIC PROCESSES OF GRIEF

What are the cognitive and intrapsychic processes of grief? They can be divided into three main categories: decathexis; development of a new relationship with the deceased; and formation of a new identity. They should be addressed in this order. Although they will be discussed individually here, they are not mutually exclusive; in fact, they are quite interdependent.

Decathexis

The early psychoanalytic theorists gave the clearest explanation of decathexis. Freud (1913) said, "Mourning has a quite precise psychical task to perform: its function is to detach the survivors' memories and hopes from the dead" (p. 65). To reach this end, the process of decathexis must occur. Anna Freud (1960) summarized the processes by which this inner adaptation is achieved as follows:

> The process of mourning *(Trauerarbeit)* taken in its analytic sense means to us the individual's effort to accept a fact in the external world (the loss of the cathected object) and to effect corresponding changes in the inner world (withdrawal of libido from the lost object). (p. 58)

Too often therapists and caregivers focus solely on the reactions to the external world (i.e., emotional responses to the separation from the loved one) and not enough on the changes in the inner world (i.e., decathexis, development of a new relationship with the deceased, and formation of a new identity).

When someone experiences a significant loss, she wants to deny that it has occurred. However, repeated frustration of the desire to unite with and obtain gratification from the lost loved one finally convinces the griever that the loss has indeed occurred. In order to avoid the overwhelming feelings that accompany recognition of this separation, the griever creates within her mind a representation or mental image of the deceased. In this way, the griever attempts to hold on to the deceased. This process is called introjection. It is from this introjected image of the deceased that the mourner must withdraw her emotional energy (Fenichel, 1945). All the feelings, thoughts, memories, and expectations that bound the mourner to the deceased are gradually worked through by being revived, reviewed, felt, and loosened. Freud (1957) described the process and how the mourner becomes compelled to relinquish previous investment in order to survive and maintain pleasures in continuing to live:

> Reality-testing has shown that the loved object no longer exists, and it proceeds to demand that all libido shall be withdrawn from its attachments to the object. . . .
> Each single one of the memories and situations of expectancy which demonstrate the libido's attachment to the lost object is met by the verdict of reality that the object no longer exists; and the ego, confronted as it were with the question whether it shall share this fate, is persuaded by the sum of the narcissistic satisfactions it derives from being alive to sever its attachment to the object that has been abolished. . . .
> . . . mourning impels the ego to give up the object by declaring the object to be dead and offering the ego the inducement of continuing to live. (pp. 244, 255, and 257)

Thus, decathexis is a crucial intrapsychic procedure that must be accomplished in order for the bereaved to successfully resolve the loss and have the unattached emotional energy to invest in subsequent relationships. The operations of decathexis can be summarized as follows (Siggins, 1966):

> The process of mourning, then involves the following steps: under the influence of the reality that the object no longer exists, the ego gives up the libidinal ties to the object. This is a slow piecemeal process in order that the ego will not be overwhelmed by a flood of feeling. The mourner pursues this task by introjecting the relationship with the lost object, and then loosening each tie to the now internalized object. For a normal person it is apparently easier to loosen ties with an introjected than with an external object (Fenichel, 1945, p. 394), presumably because in this case our inner world is more tractable than the world around us. Thus introjection acts as a buffer by helping to preserve the relationship with the object while the gradual process of relinquishing is going on. The ties of relationship are represented by hundreds of sep-

arate memories, and the dissolution of the tie to each one of these takes time (*ibid.*, p. 393). In this process, of course, the relationship to the lost person is not abandoned, but the libidinal ties are so modified that a new relationship can be established. (p. 17)

Development of a New Relationship With the Deceased

The death of the loved one separates the mourner from the deceased. However, it does not constitute the end of their relationship. As the mourner's life is reorganized in the absence of the deceased, a new relationship is structured, one based largely on recollection, memory, and past experience (Irion, 1966).

The griever must decide what the new relationship with the lost loved one will be like. First, the deceased must be remembered in context as someone who lived *and* died (Irion, 1966). A clear, realistic image of the deceased needs to be developed, reconciling all the differing aspects of the deceased's personality and all the experiences the griever had with that person. It is also necessary for the griever to consciously decide which parts of the old life and relationship should be retained and which must be relinquished. This includes finding ways to healthily remember the deceased as life continues, without impeding decathexis and reinvestment in others. Some possibilities are rituals, anniversary celebrations, prayers, commemorations, memorializations, and healthy identification. (See "Rituals" in this chapter for more on this topic.)

Formation of a New Identity

The griever must necessarily come to the realization that the major loss of the loved one has changed her personally. Part of an individual dies when one with whom she has been emotionally involved dies. The interactional part of the self created by the unique and special relationship between them now exists only in memory. For example, the death of a mother destroys the part of the interactional self that was a mother's daughter, although the role probably continues internally for the daughter (Weigert & Hastings, Note 4). However, she can also augment her self: she can adopt new roles, skills, behaviors, relationships. A perspective is needed on both what has been lost and gained as a consequence of the death. That which has been changed (either positively or negatively) must be recognized and grieved for; that which continues must be affirmed; that which is new must be accommodated. It is important to define and integrate the new and old selves, and to explore the new life options available. There should be an awareness that a transition is taking place as the new identity shifts from "we" to "I." New assumptions about the world, a world without the deceased, must be developed. These will also bring about changes in the griever's identity.

Identification with the deceased first occurs as a way of perpetuating the mental image of the loved one to prevent the pain of the loss from being felt. By temporarily preserving the loved object, it allows the griever to work at the process of decathexis without becoming overwhelmed. Later it helps to partially conserve the lost loved one while it adds to the ego, thereby contributing to the enrichment of the personality (Furman, 1974). Just as the ego is constructed in childhood by the process of incorporation of and identification with others, the griever's identity may be changed through her identification with the deceased. For example, the griever may change her personality and sense of self by taking on the deceased's values, acting on his concerns, adopting his mannerisms, or feeling as he would have felt. However, when incorporation and identification become ways to avoid experiencing the loss and relinquishing the loved one, rather than aids to decathexis, the process has become pathological and it must be vigorously confronted.

This description of the formation of a new identity assumes that the mourner had appropriately differentiated herself from the deceased prior to the death. If this is not the case, the mourner will be unable to let the deceased go, since it would mean losing a primary part of herself.

INTERVENTIONS FOR GRIEF

To help the griever reach these goals of grief work, we can intervene in many ways. In the next section, some useful strategies will be suggested, followed by a discussion of the therapeutic use of private rituals with the bereaved and some descriptions of forms of psychotherapy for unresolved grief.

Intervention Strategies

What the griever needs most is acceptance and nonjudgmental listening, which will facilitate the expression of emotions and the necessary review of the relationship with the lost loved one. He will then require assistance in integrating the past with the new present that exists.

In his excellent book, *Understanding Grief,* Jackson (1957) states that the goal of the caregiver is to assist the griever in releasing emotional ties to the deceased despite the discomfort and sorrow it causes, and in subsequently replacing the type of interaction lost. The individual must be persuaded to therapeutically yield to the process of grief, and this involves accepting the pain of looking realistically at the loss. The griever is encouraged to participate actively in the work of mourning instead of trying to escape or deny it, and to realize that the grieving period can be delayed but not postponed indefinitely, for it will be carried on, directly or indirectly.

There are a number of specific strategies that can assist grievers in meeting the goals of grief work. These strategies have been grouped into seven broad phases. They roughly correspond to the process of grief from initial shock to reintegration into normal life.

Make Contact and Assess

At first we must try to make some sort of connection with the griever. In the early aftermath of bereavement grievers are dazed and often in shock, with little energy or motivation to help themselves. Our main tasks at this time are to establish a relationship and simply be present. We also need to conduct an assessment of the bereaved individual in her grief in order to plan appropriate interventions.

Reach out to the bereaved. Do not say "Call me if you need me." The bereaved frequently do not have the energy to initiate contact and often feel overwhelmed. We need to reach out in practical and concrete ways. While the professional therapist may be slightly more limited here, and may need to remain somewhat more nondirective for ethical and professional reasons, most of us can be very specific in the types of help we offer the newly bereaved. For example, instead of merely saying that we are concerned, we can make specific offers of assistance: "Why don't you let me get you a cup of coffee?" "How about if I accompany you to choose the casket?" "Suppose I arrange for a babysitter so you can attend the Widow-to-Widow meeting?" We must figure out what it is the bereaved person needs and what we can offer, then offer it as specifically as possible. The griever may well politely refuse our assistance, but this should not keep us from offering assistance again at another point. Such a refusal should not be discouraging or be taken personally—it is simply a statement of the griever's emotional, physical, and social state, in which she is temporarily unable to respond to or appreciate attempts at care and consolation. The griever may require a number of offers of help and will benefit in the long run from the continued efforts of concerned individuals who do not give up on her because of a few rejections. This is a true test of the empathic caregiver.

Be present physically, as well as emotionally, to render the griever security and support. This is especially important during the initial period of shock and disorganization, in which consistent physical presence and physical contact (hugging, handholding, touching) not only convey to the griever that she is not alone, but help reorient her to the world that has gone out of focus and control with the loss of the loved one. Such physical support will become critical again at the time when the true implications and reality of the loss sink in, weeks and months after the death. Most social support has dwindled by then, as people assume the bereaved are well over their grief. For many grievers this period of time is actually the most difficult, as the pain of loss is felt most acutely when the griever is forced to resume life without the loved one.

We need to recognize that feelings about the deceased's death per se are only part of the experience for the newly bereaved. Demands such as making funeral arrangements, notifying relatives, and dealing with the responses of others all engender further emotional reactions. Besides encouraging expression of feelings by the bereaved, immediate treatment should also be aimed at minimizing the tendency of the bereaved to become overwhelmed and unable to function.

Especially during the early period of shock and disorganization, it may be helpful for someone to take charge of some of the routine functions and responsibilities of the bereaved, such as providing meals or doing errands. During this time it may also be therapeutic to render the security of some direction, as the bereaved may be unable to provide their own. We may do things such as remind the bereaved to eat; make sure they get adequate rest; suggest priorities; help them with funeral decisions; or gently confront unrealistic or precipitous plans.

Intervention at this time should be geared toward helping the family focus on problems one at a time, addressing solvable problems to which practical solutions can be found, before progressing to more complicated issues at the feeling level (Berlinsky & Biller, 1982). This is not to deemphasize or negate the critical importance of facilitating expression of feeling as soon as possible. However, if the bereaved become so engulfed in the immediate demands for decisions and action that they become convinced of their inability to cope with the situation or abrogate all responsibility, an unhealthy passive tone is set for the rest of their grief experience.

Make sure you give the person "permission" to grieve. Because grief is often such a foreign experience, and since it inherently contains many traditionally unacceptable thoughts and feelings, the griever will often consciously or unconsciously seek permission from others to grieve. If permission is denied (implicitly or explicitly), the griever may censor her expressions in an effort to be socially acceptable. Consequently, we must demonstrate verbally, and through our nonjudgmental attitudes and behaviors, that the expression of grief is not only appropriate, but essential for therapeutic resolution of the loss. Lazare (1979) describes the "critical moment" in the interaction with the griever when the griever's voice cracks, her facial muscles quiver, her eyes water, and she turns toward the caregiver to see if he can tolerate and support the crying and the entire process of mourning. If the caregiver can communicate compassionate support through verbal and nonverbal expressions, the griever will receive the message that it is acceptable and will express her grief. However, the entire therapeutic process will cease if the caregiver gives indications that he is uncomfortable (e.g., leans away, changes the subject, appears anxious, or urges the griever not to cry).

Do not allow the griever to remain isolated. Social support is critical throughout the entire grief process. It enables the bereaved person to tolerate the pain of loss and provides the acceptance and assistance necessary for completion of grief work and reintegration back into the social community. Research repeatedly confirms that one of the most significant factors contributing to the failure to appropriately resolve grief is the absence and/or inappropriateness of social support and interaction. Nothing is more therapeutic in the process of grief than the presence of an accepting and nonjudgmental caring other. Especially early after the death, the griever may require the presence of concerned caregivers to feel grounded in the midst of the chaos. At the time of such intense emotional reactions, it is particularly helpful to have the accompaniment of others to lend security, order, and a sense of reality to the griever. Therefore, we must work to connect the griever with appropriate social supports if these are lacking in her social system.

Group psychotherapy or self-help groups may be particularly therapeutic in this regard. Research has indicated that there are a number of curative features inherent in group treatment that are absent in traditional individual psychotherapy (Yalom, 1975). Group members develop a sense of connection with others who have similar problems; they have the opportunity to help others; they can obtain hope from seeing others who have overcome their problems; they can model their behavior on members who are successfully coping; and they can get unconditional acceptance and a feeling of belonging (Spiegel & Yalom, 1978). Both psychotherapy groups and self-help (or mutual support) groups benefit from the "helper-therapy principle" (Reissman, 1965), in which the member experiences an enhanced sense of interpersonal confidence, self-worth, and purpose and meaning through being of help to others. This allows the members to break out of the passive victim role. In contrast to psychotherapy groups, self-help groups have the additional advantages of providing concrete guidance for an indefinite period of time; recruiting their members from those who share a specific and often stigmatized attribute (e.g., specific loss); encouraging public confession of the stigma through specific or ritualized discussion (e.g., discussing the deceased), often an important criterion for membership; and being in a position to effect real changes in the outside lives of its members, with many moving in the direction of public and political involvement and thereby enhancing their self-esteem and assertiveness (Spiegel & Yalom, 1978). Clinical evidence, increasingly backed by research reports, documents the particularly therapeutic results of self-help group intervention in bereavement (Raphael, 1983), especially when helping members have received training in their roles and when the group is supported by professionals with considerable experience with the bereaved (Parkes, 1980).

Maintain a family systems perspective in dealing with the griever. Recognize that not only is the bereaved individual dealing with the loss of a special relationship and of parts of herself, but also with the irretrievable loss of her family as she has known it. It should be remembered that a series of social factors makes Americans more vulnerable to death in the family (Volkart, 1976) and that, as a system and as separate individuals, the family itself will profoundly influence the grief experience of its members. (See "Family Problems" in Chapter 12 for more on this topic.)

Conduct an assessment of the mourner's grief. Prior to planning any intervention for the mourner we must have an accurate assessment of where she is in her grief and of the significant factors that influence it. Intervention without appropriate understanding of the dynamics of a given bereavement situation may not only be inappropriate, but possibly do more harm than good.

The following therapeutic assessment of the bereaved taken from Raphael (1983) not only yields information, but also facilitates the expression of emotions and promotes the mourning process.

• *Can you tell me a little about the death? What happened? What happened that day?* This gives the griever permission to talk about the death. It provides information on the nature and circumstances of the death; how the bereaved heard of it; whether it was expected or unexpected, timely or untimely; what effect it had on the bereaved; whether the griever's presence or absence at the time of the death may have been a source of guilt; whether it occurred at a time when there were special conflicts or stresses in the relationship. The griever's capacity to talk about the death and her pattern of emotional responses to it will become obvious. Defenses of denial and avoidance may become clear. It also will become apparent from the discussion whether the bereaved had the opportunity to see the body and say private good-byes.

• *Can you tell me about him, about your relationship from the beginning?* This allows the caregiver to get the history of the relationship from the start, determining the expectations and disillusionments that went into it, as well as determining the images

and interactions it involved. It clarifies the quality of the relationship with the deceased, the level of ambivalence and dependence
it involved. There also is an opportunity to assess the degree to
which the bereaved still is denying the loss. The degree to which
the griever can talk of the person in real terms, recalling him
truthfully rather than in an idealized fashion, will become apparent. The emotions associated with mourning may be assessed to
determine risk factors from the relationship and indicate the appropriateness of the griever's progress and also the quality of
mourning at this point after the loss.

   • *What has been happening since the death? How have things
been with you and your family and friends?* This permits exploration
of the patterns of family and social response and the support that
is perceived to be available. It yields information about the experience of the bereaved, her feelings about the absence of the lost
loved one and the finality of death. It also provides for assessment
of other crises or stresses that may have occurred or blocks to the
resolution of grief.

   • *Have you been through any other bad times like this recently
or when you were young?* This area of inquiry allows for more
specific assessment of concurrent crises and stresses and also of
earlier losses.

   Several other issues must be addressed in this assessment.
   • *Evaluation of the presence of illogical or magical thinking.* This
     mode of thinking is not unusual in adults under stress. For
     example, one woman was convinced for years that in trans-
     porting her aunt to the emergency room following a major
     heart attack, it was her hitting the potholes in the road that
     ultimately proved fatal to her loved one.
   • *Detection of increased feelings of guilt and responsibility.* Such
     feelings may stem from illogical thoughts.
   • *Description of what the loss means to the mourner by the mour-
     ner.* This gives the mourner an opportunity to point out her
     most salient concerns.
   • *Analysis of all the psychological, social, and physiological fac-
     tors influencing the individual's grief response.* Special attention
     should be given to the socio-cultural norms that influence the
     overt expression of grief.
   • *Collection of a complete history of prior losses.* This includes
     not only normal losses, but those events not normally per-
     ceived as losses, such as psychosocial losses or socially denied
     losses like abortion.

   Any assessment will need to be continuously updated, as recent
research suggests there are previously unexpected fluctuations in

the experience and needs of the bereaved (Alexy, 1982; Hardt, 1978-79; Rando, 1983). An initial assessment without subsequent revisions is inadequate.

Another reason for conducting a thorough and ongoing assessment is that recent evidence seems to show that, in regard to unresolved grief, some forms of intervention that are appropriate for one type of bereavement are useless or even harmful in others (Parkes & Weiss, 1983). For example, the most effective treatment following the loss of ambivalent relationships resulting in conflicted grief is using interventions that facilitate normal grief. The aim is to promote the overt expression of all the feelings of grief. In contrast, with the chronic grief often found with the loss of relationships of dependency, such attempts at promoting expression of grief would only make the situation worse. In such cases it is better to insist on forward movement and increased autonomy for the griever, and to encourage her to play a more active role in developing goals and making decisions. As a further contrast, those bereaved from unanticipated losses require repeated opportunities to talk through the implications of their loss and to react emotionally. They must make sense out of the loss and bring order to their lives to diminish the feeling of being overwhelmed with stress and insecurity.

Assess to determine which tasks of grief are incomplete. Regardless of the schema of tasks used, it is important that grievers make progress in achieving those tasks. The focus of treatment should be on helping grievers with any task they seem unable to meet (Worden, 1982). First they must accept the reality of the loss. If they do not, treatment must focus on the fact that the person is dead and that the mourner will have to let her go. They also must experience the pain of grief, not just accept the loss. Treatment then is aimed at making it safe to feel positive and negative emotions so grievers can work through them. Part of this task is the redefinition of the griever's relationship with the deceased. Grievers must then adjust to the environment in which the deceased is missing. Here problem-solving is a large part of the treatment. Mourners are taught to overcome their helplessness by trying out new skills, developing new roles, and returning to living. The final task is the withdrawal of emotional energy and the reinvestment of it in other relationships. Mourners learn to stop grieving, decathect from the deceased, say a final good-bye, and cultivate new relationships.

Make sure that the griever has appropriate medical evaluation and treatment when symptoms warrant. Since grief has a large impact upon the mourner's physical health, the mourner must receive appropriate medical evaluation, treatment, and follow-up when necessary. To ignore the somatic aspects of grief in favor of the psychosocial ones is to incompletely address the needs of the griever. Just as previously there was danger from overreliance on medical intervention in grief (e.g., too liberal prescription of tranquilizers), there is now danger in failing to recognize when medical treatment is necessary to prevent mortality or morbidity, or to manage physical symptoms of psychological distress that interfere with the grief process (e.g., vegetative signs of clinical depression such as not sleeping or eating).

Maintain a Therapeutic and Realistic Perspective

In order to be most helpful to the bereaved, we must be realistic about the extent to which we can relieve their suffering. We must be aware that we will often feel helpless when they are in pain, without allowing this to interfere with our interventions. The temptation must be avoided to say or do things that, while they may be intended to be comforting, will not ultimately help the bereaved to resolve their grief.

Remember that you cannot take away the pain from the bereaved. Despite our most fervent attempts and our best efforts, we cannot rectify the situation that is agonizing the bereaved: we cannot bring back the deceased loved one. This does not mean we have nothing to offer; it merely means that we must be realistic about what we can accomplish. A caregiver can only make the experience relatively better than it would be if she were not there, by listening to the griever and facilitating appropriate grief. Grief is painful and the pain of loss cannot be taken away, no matter what a concerned and committed caregiver may do. To expect otherwise is to set yourself up to fail!

Do not let your own sense of helplessness keep you from reaching out to the griever. Especially during the initial response to grief, the griever may appear unapproachable, inconsolable, or out of control. These reactions should not keep us from approaching the griever, just being with him, or attempting appropriate interventions. To be effective we must realistically accept our inability to take away the pain of loss as a natural part of interaction with the bereaved.

Expect to have to tolerate volatile reactions from the bereaved. We must learn to tolerate the intense angry protest that is directed towards us by the bereaved. Especially in the early stages of bereavement, hostile emotions are often directed towards others. Additionally, we must be prepared to deal with the fact that the griever finds us ineffective, since all he wants is the return of the lost loved one and we cannot provide it. The pushing away that may result must be understood in this context. We must realize that the griever is in pain and desperately misses the deceased,

although reasonable limits can be placed on expression of anger
by the bereaved.

In some cases the bereaved may be hesitant to respond to us
even though they may desire to do so. They may put on a brave
front and/or assert that there are others who need our help more.
Often this is done to test the extent of our concern and our willingness to share their distress It may also reflect their fear of the
pain that discussion will produce. There are three questions in the
minds of grievers as they contemplate their caregivers: (1) Can I
trust you? (2) Do you know what you're talking about? and (3) Do
you care about me? (Healy, Note 5). As caregivers we must be
prepared to tolerate, as well as address, all three questions, and
not be insulted if our good intentions are not recognized by the
bereaved at this time.

*Recognize the critical therapeutic value of "the gift of pres-
ence."* Although we cannot do anything to take away the griever's
pain of loss, we can be helpful to him by being present to share it.
Caregivers are traditionally trained to "do" something to assist
others. In this instance what is needed is to just be, not do. This
is actually a more difficult task, for when we are able to "do"
something, we can combat our own feelings of helplessness. When
someone is wracked with sobs, with a heart breaking with acute
grief, it takes immense courage and determination to just be there
with him and avoid trying to take away the pain by saying that
things will be fine or that he shouldn't feel so upset. Trying to
rescue the griever from his grief is harmful and countertherapeutic. The compassionate acceptance of the griever's feelings and
experience, signaled by our willingness to remain present, is what
will eventually help him, since it encourages the necessary review
and processing of the loss experience.

*Make sure you view the loss from the griever's unique per-
spective.* Goals of intervention must be appropriate to this person,
this loss, and this relationship (Raphael, 1980). The loss cannot be
viewed from our own perspective if we are to be effective. Our
assumptions must be thoroughly checked before proceeding, for
what we believe to be problems may not be for particular grievers.
This means we must help grievers to define and decide for themselves what is most problematic for them, to prioritize their concerns, and to deal with those concerns as therapeutically as they
are able. Most importantly, we must suspend personal judgment
about the meaning of any loss to the griever. For example, a client
once became very upset about the possibility that her mother
would be hospitalized for some routine tests. While this situation
appeared trivial in contrast to others in which loved ones were
dying, it was disturbing to this very dependent woman because it
made her aware of the probability that her mother would one day

die before her. It is clear that the seriousness of any loss must be evaluated in the context of the individual's perspective and cannot be compared to other losses for other people.

Let your genuine concern and caring show. Do not be afraid to be emotionally moved by the sadness of the griever, if in fact this is what prompted it. If this reaction is a direct response to the present situation, and does not solely reflect personal issues, the griever often perceives it as confirmation of his loss, acceptance and empathy on the part of the caregiver, and normalization of his feelings. It often is very therapeutic for the bereaved to know that caregivers can care enough about them to be emotionally touched by their situations. If you personally knew the deceased, appropriate comments sharing your reaction to the loss are often especially meaningful and helpful to the bereaved.

Do not let your own needs determine the experience for the griever. For example, do not close down a conversation about the deceased because it hurts you to see the griever cry. Always ask yourself if the interventions you are considering are for your own benefit or for the bereaved's.

Do not try to explain the loss in religious or philosophical terms too early. To say "It's God's will" or "Everything happens for a reason" will not be helpful when grievers need to ventilate their anguish and feelings. Later on such explanations may assist grievers in finding some meaning and/or perspective in their loss.

Do not tell the griever to feel better because there are other loved ones who are still alive. This robs him of his legitimate sadness. People cannot be replaced. No matter how many other loved ones are surviving and what other resources the bereaved may have, they cannot diminish the loss. This is one of the comments that most often raises the ire of the bereaved. It is frequently employed by well-meaning but insensitive consolers in an attempt to diminish the pain of the bereaved.

Do not try to unrealistically "pretty up" the situation. Legitimize the situation as the difficult one that it is. Do not try to paint an unrealistic picture of it, for this will only infuriate the griever and create distance between the two of you. It is more therapeutic to tell it as it is: "It is very painful right now," "You are right, it does not make any sense!" Do not act as if something could happen to lessen the pain, as if the griever could run away and escape from it. This does not preclude hope that it will get better, for hope is critical in sustaining the griever through the pain. It is the unrealistic, falsely cheerful responses that must be avoided.

Do not forget to plant the seeds of hope. While recognizing the pain and difficulty of grief, do not fail to give the griever hope: hope that someday the pain will decrease, hope that someday there will be a reunion with the deceased, hope that life will have some meaning again at some point. These are not unrealistic hopes offered in a way that denies or invalidates the current intense experience of grief or the permanent changes that will result from it. Rather, they are realistic aspirations that can offer the bereaved needed support and comfort. For a majority of grievers, the reassurance that someday they *will* be in less pain is critical in allowing them to carry on. This is one reason why self-help support groups are so therapeutic, as they illustrate that people can get past the anguish and the agony and that life can have some meaning again. Even though the newly bereaved cannot feel this at the time, seeing that there is hope for it is often helpful enough.

Do not encourage responses antithetical to appropriate grief. For instance, do not tell the griever not to cry, censor his anger or guilt, or to take a tranquilizer merely to avoid some distress. While such responses may momentarily stop the pain, it is only deferred until later, when it may have to be dealt with by the griever alone. Everything should be aimed at reaching the goals of grief work and promoting the resolution of the loss.

Maintain an appropriate distance from the griever. We must be close enough to share in the griever's suffering, but not so close that we succumb to his despair or encourage inappropriate dependence.

Do not fail to hold out the expectation that the griever will successfully complete the tasks of mourning and that the pain will subside. While the griever needs to feel his present pain is legitimate, he also needs to believe that he can successfully address the tasks of mourning. We must convey to him that, as long as he continues to deal with his grief, he can look forward to overcoming the pain and carrying on with his life. The self-assurance and confidence this gives him will support him through the many doubts that arise in the course of grief.

We must not only be compassionate, sensitive, and empathic, but also insist that the griever continue to make forward progress through the grief process. Excessive commiseration, or tolerance of inappropriate dependency or chronic grief, will not help the griever. Previous expectations of rapid recovery from grief were inappropriate, but it is equally inappropriate to fail to encourage the griever to once again participate in life when he is ready.

Encourage Verbalization of Feelings and Recollection of the Deceased

In order to successfully complete grief work, the griever needs repeated opportunities to be heard nonjudgmentally, to express the pain of the separation, to accept the finality of the loss, to articulate and process the many different feelings about the loss and its consequences, and to engage in the recollection and review procedures that facilitate healthy decathexis. These opportunities can be promoted through a series of specific techniques.

Help the bereaved to recognize, actualize, and accept the loss. This means assisting the griever in coming to an intellectual acceptance of the fact that, despite all wishes to the contrary, the loss has actually occurred, the loved one is indeed dead, and she will not return (at least in this life). Understandably there is frequently a need to deny this, especially early in the bereavement. However, continued review of the relationship and discussion of the loss, the events that surrounded it, its meaning and implications, and the frustrating inability to gratify needs with the deceased will help the griever to come to accept the loss. Repeated reality testing will confirm the absence of the loved one and the finality of the separation. Grievers who fail to achieve an intellectual acceptance of the loss will be unable to deal with it emotionally. This is similar to the uncertainty over the loss mentioned by Lazare (1979), in which grief could not occur until the loss was finally confirmed and acknowledged by the griever. If the loss is not made real to the griever, he doesn't have to grapple with its implications or his feelings about it.

Listen nonjudgmentally and with permissiveness and acceptance. The griever must be able to ventilate emotions without fear of rejection. This is critical because many of the emotions of grief are unacceptable and guilt-provoking to the mourner. It is important for the griever to give words to grief and sorrow, for, as Shakespeare wrote, when a passion can expend itself in words it is less apt to result in deeds: "Give sorrow words; the grief that does not speak whispers the o'er-fraught heart and bids it break" (Shakespeare, *Macbeth*, Act IV, Scene 3). Unless the mourner feels accepted, this very necessary therapeutic process will be thwarted.

Assist the griever in identifying, accepting, and expressing all the various feelings of grief. This is one of our most important tasks, for failure to express grief prevents its resolution. There first may be a need to work through some societal, cultural, ethnic, religious, or idiosyncratic resistances to accepting certain feelings of grief as tolerable or normal. Unless grievers can be made more comfortable with these feelings, they will be incapable of working them through. Feelings then must be identified and expressed in order to achieve appropriate decathexis. In the early phases of grief the bereaved will feel painful yearning and angry protest. They may need help in recognizing some of the causes of their distress, such as unfulfilled needs. Often simply naming the feeling or experience the griever is undergoing helps. For example, identifying emotions by saying "It seems like you're aching for your husband" or "Sounds like you're feeling frustrated by your inability to change this situation" allows the griever to understand and perceive her-

self as more in control of the experience. It can clarify and help
normalize unacceptable, unrecognized, or unexpected thoughts
and feelings, and make them more manageable.

The mourner will need to differentiate clearly among the feelings of grief: sorrow, anger, depression, relief. This will permit
each feeling to be fully experienced. Specific sources for the feelings
should be identified. For example, anger may result from the sense
of desertion the griever feels; helplessness may be a result of the
inability to reverse the loss; and anxiety may develop over concerns
of being alone. In order to be able to focus more fully on the content
at hand, the griever must also learn the difference between old
business situations, reactivation of previous conflicts, present conflicts, and existential dilemmas (Clark, 1982). This will lessen
emotional confusion.

Intellectualized treatment of emotion will do little good, for
grievers must "own" their feelings. They must internally process
them, not just express them behaviorally: a griever may cry, but
not experience or come to terms with the separation pain. If this
is not done, those feelings will resurface later in more destructive
ways. An unpleasant but effective analogy is that grief is like gar-
bage—if it isn't put out, it begins to smell!

**If the griever appears to be resisting the grief process, explore
the griever's defenses to discover the reasons behind it.** Many people are afraid to express the emotions of grief, fearing they will
lose control or break down. There may be excessive dependency,
anger, or guilt that is interfering with the normal grief process.
We can explore these feelings directly and query the absence of
expectable feelings with statements such as "People often seem
worried about things that didn't go right at a time like this—an
argument or misunderstanding or something they meant to do and
didn't before the person died. Have there been any concerns like
this for you?" (Raphael, 1980, p. 163). Of course, feelings cannot
be demanded from the bereaved. Their resistances have to be
worked through before they can progress any further in resolving
the loss.

Frequently there is resistance to dealing with anger and guilt.
It sometimes helps to tell the mourner that, while it is not unusual
for people to be afraid of dealing with anger for fear of finding that
there was nothing positive about the relationship with the deceased, it is only if the anger is worked through that the griever
will be able to see the positive aspects of the relationship. Other
individuals may not want to relinquish anger or other intense emotions because they feel it is the only thing that binds them to the
deceased. In this case, they need to be told that by relinquishing
the inappropriate emotion, they will be able to remember the deceased more clearly and feel closer to her. In grieving they will be

able to formulate a relationship with the deceased that will bring her closer than perpetuating unresolved grief ever could.

Anger often requires legitimization by the caregiver:

> *Case Example:* Ed lost his father suddenly, without a chance to say good-bye to the man to whom he was so devoted. When he arrived at the hospital, his father's body had been removed minutes before. In therapy, Ed spoke of how his Irish Catholic family wanted to focus on all the good memories they had of the father. Crying was viewed as inappropriate, since they believed it indicated a lack of faith, and anger was unheard of. Family members were supposed to assuage their grief and dismiss their feelings by focusing on the good times.
>
> One day in therapy it was strikingly clear that Ed was absolutely furious over the death of his father and the lack of opportunity for closure. When he was given the interpretation he was angry, he found it impossible to accept, pointing out the "inappropriate" and "unnecessary" nature of this emotion. Ed was then asked how he would feel if his car were to be stolen while he was in the session. He immediately responded that he would want to kill the thief and that it would confirm to him the degenerative nature of our society. He went on for several minutes in a heated tirade. When he calmed down, Ed was asked how he felt about his father being "stolen" from him. At that moment he could finally recognize that while he could allow himself to be angry over the loss of his car, he had not permitted himself the same luxury over the loss of his father. The analogy assisted Ed in realizing the appropriateness of his angry response to the death of his father and his being "robbed" of the farewell that he would have desired.

Because grievers have so much trouble facing anger, this emotion may need to be relabeled before they can deal with it. Lazare (1979) suggests the use of words such as "irritate" or "annoy." Worden (1982) uses the word "miss" by asking "What do you miss about him?" and allowing the person to respond in positive ways, then asking "What don't you miss about him?" and eliciting the more negative feelings. This balances the positive and negative feelings and teaches the griever that both kinds of emotions can exist together.

Another emotion that may pose thorny problems for the griever is guilt. As noted previously, there is always some guilt after someone dies. This guilt comes from the lack of perfection and ambivalence inherent in all human relationships, and from the unrealistic expectations and standards that mourners often have (e.g., "I should have been able to protect her from death" or "I never should have felt any anger towards her during our relationship"). Guilt that is out of proportion to the event is termed *illegitimate guilt*. It requires that grievers discuss their guilty feelings, and the acts, omissions, thoughts, or feelings that generated the guilt, with nonjudgmental others. They must rationally examine the events to determine if, given the amount of information available at the time, they did in fact act in the best way possible. Mourners also have to be reminded that they are human and that humans make mistakes and have ambivalent relationships. They must be helped to see the positives that existed in the relationship and be cautioned against emphasizing the negative. They also will need to forgive themselves, find constructive ways to expiate their guilt, and change the unrealistic standards or irrational beliefs that contribute to their guilt. However, these interventions must not be made too soon. Premature reassurance will deny grievers the necessary opportunity to ventilate their guilt feelings.

Legitimate guilt occurs when there is a direct cause-effect relationship between what the griever did or failed to do and serious harm resulting to the deceased. In this situation, where guilt is appropriate, it must be acknowledged and plans must be made for restitution and expiation. This guilt can become destructive if it is used as self-punishment. When legitimate guilt warrants punishment, the griever should do something constructive about it, such as doing something altruistic for others as a way of atoning. Guilt that cannot be expiated must be accommodated; the individual must learn to live with it and not continue to punish himself. If this cannot be accomplished, the stage is set for unresolved grief.

> *Case Example:* Georgia was an alcoholic whose drinking resulted in the death of her son in an automobile accident. Her remorse and guilt were boundless as she continually tortured herself about the accident and death of her child. In therapy she came to realize that this was just another way of feeling sorry for herself (as her drinking had been), and she subsequently turned her energies over to working in an alcohol rehabilitation program, where she did her part to ensure that no such tragedy would ever happen again.

Allow the bereaved to cry and cry, talk and talk, review and review without the interruption of your sanity. This is a necessary part of the process, especially in the early stages of grief. Do not close it down in any way, shape, or form; in fact, try to facilitate it. It enables the bereaved to complete the requisite grief work. Each story told, each memory relived, each feeling expressed represents a tie to the deceased that the griever must process by remembering, feeling the emotions generated by it, and then letting it go. Encourage such expression without analyzing or interpreting it. Limits can be imposed later, if therapeutically necessary.

Do not be amazed if the griever talks about many of the same things repeatedly. Grievers need to review again and again their attachments and relationships to the deceased and the circumstances of the death. It is not only the dramatic memories, the ones that bring tears, that need to be reviewed—they all do. This repetition is part of the critical process of decathexis. It is only by repeatedly seeing that their needs, feelings, hopes, desires, and expectations are being frustrated that the bereaved start to accept the finality of the death and appropriately detach from the loved one. They may need to go over situations obsessively in an attempt to understand how they occurred, put them into perspective, and find some meaning and sense in them. In essence, the griever is trying to get some mastery and control in an uncontrollable situation. It is very similar to the need of the person who almost has an accident on the way to work and then must inform everyone of what happened. The process is vividly seen at the wake, where the griever may repeat his story to each person that files through. Each time the story is told, he gets more of a handle on it and a little more control of it.

Do not be afraid to mention the dead person to the griever. To avoid doing this will only isolate the griever further in his own grief, possibly fostering denial or other unhealthy reactions. Try to incorporate the name of the deceased in conversations with the bereaved in order to personalize the situation and to make it more real for them. This will confront their natural urge to deny and distance, but fear of prompting an emotional response should not inhibit mentioning the deceased. These responses are precisely what must be addressed if grief is to be adequately resolved. In many cases bereaved individuals actually are gratified to hear the name of the deceased spoken aloud. It is a way of having the deceased remembered and kept "alive" in a healthy way. It shows them that they are not alone in remembering and caring that the loved one existed.

Encourage the griever to realistically review and talk about the deceased and their mutual relationship. Have the griever repeatedly review the entire relationship, back to its earliest origins and the hopes and fantasies that formed it. Have him discuss its ups and downs, its course and development, its crises and joys— all aspects of it through the years. As these events are gently unfolded, associated feelings can be examined, such as anxiety, ambivalence, and guilt. Only by repeatedly reviewing this unique relationship will the griever be able to identify the feelings that must be processed and slowly begin to decathect from the deceased.

Initially most bereaved individuals idealize the deceased. Over time they usually become more realistic and see her as having both positive and negative traits. To reach this point, repeated discussion of the negative as well as the positive aspects of the deceased and the griever's relationship to her is necessary. Raphael (1980) suggests how to gently open areas of discussion that may be less than positive: "You've told me a lot about the happy times you've shared; could you tell me a little bit about the times that were not so happy?" (p. 157). It will be important for the griever to develop a realistic composite image of the deceased that adequately represents the *real* person and the *real* good-bad relationship (Raphael, 1983). This is especially necessary for legitimizing ambivalent or negative feelings about the deceased that necessarily must be worked through.

Help the Griever Identify and Resolve
Secondary Losses and Unfinished Business

It is not enough for the griever to mourn the death of the loved one; she also must mourn the secondary losses that occur as a result of the death. Too often these secondary losses, especially if they are symbolic ones such as loss of status or loss of a dream, or if they are losses of part of the self, fail to be identified and grieved for. Such losses, and any unfinished business that may remain between the bereaved and the deceased, interfere with the successful completion of grief work and impede healthy readjustment to life without the deceased. When these are present, they must be uncovered and adequately addressed.

Help the griever to identify current and potential secondary losses (physical and symbolic) resulting from the death. These losses will require their own grief responses. Nevertheless, they are often overlooked and not identified as legitimate losses per se. Simply because they are secondary does not mean they are insignificant; frequently they are harder to resolve than the initial loss. Examples of such secondary losses are loss of that part of the self that was in a role relationship with the deceased (e.g., that part of the self which was a father's daughter); loss of the family as it was; loss of a sexual partner; loss of time with children because of the necessity of working; loss of social life as it had previously been experienced; or loss of the home to pay for medical expenses.

Help the griever to identify any unfinished business with the deceased and look for appropriate ways to facilitate closure. At times this may require a referral to a psychotherapist, but it often may be resolved by allowing the griever to say aloud in the presence of a caring witness the things that were unsaid to the deceased. Fancy techniques are not needed to assist the griever in finishing the unfinished business, as frequently in-depth discussion of what the griever would have wanted to say·or do can help. In fact, the griever should be asked what he feels he must do in order to achieve a sense of completion. (See "Rituals" in this chapter for more on this topic.)

Assist the griever in recognizing that not only must she grieve for the deceased individual, but also for the dreams, fantasies, and expectations that she had for and with the deceased. Similar to secondary losses, these need to be identified and grieved for individually, for they are also important losses. Unfortunately, they often are not recognized as losses because their existence was not tangible. However, the lack of ability to fulfill these is a loss in the truest sense, since it is the loss of something that was highly valued.

Support the Griever in Coping
With the Grief Process
The griever frequently has unrealistic expectations about herself and the grief process. To help the griever cope with and productively yield to the grief experience, we must correct these misconceptions, and give her support in coping with the pain and permission to care for herself.

Design interventions that capitalize upon the griever's positive coping skills and compensate for deficient ones. All individuals do not cope alike and all grievers will not grieve alike. Rather than being directive at this point, which might engender more feelings of helplessness in the griever, it is best to assess the strengths and weaknesses of the griever and work with them. When the griever is doing healthy things, such as talking about the deceased, we should encourage it; when she is choosing unhealthy ones, such as drinking too much, we should suggest alternative behaviors or sources of help.

It is not our task to remake the griever into a psychologically different person. We only need to understand the griever's personality so we can maximize the chances of reaching that person. It may take time to learn about the griever, but it can make our interventions much more effective. For instance, a husband might find it less threatening to discuss his reactions to the death of his spouse in the context of a discussion of the family's responses, rather than in an individual session focused on his own personal feelings.

Provide the griever with normative data about the grief process. Help her recognize that grief normally involves reactions that would be pathological in other circumstances, or that may be contrary to the way she usually is, e.g., she may not want to be involved with others despite her usual sociable personality. This will alleviate normal fears about going crazy and help the griever understand the issues she needs to work out. It is necessary to normalize the person's grief because unrealistic expectations or negative feelings about essentially normal reactions cause the majority of problems with grief. However, this must be done in a way that does not minimize or trivialize the griever's experience. Educate the mourner about grief. For example, inform her that it does not mean she is bad because she wishes someone else died instead of her loved one; let her know she is normal in feeling overwhelmed. Fulton's (1967) two guidelines for helping bereaved children are also applicable here: prevent distorted grief responses and facilitate normal grief processes.

Make sure the griever understands that her grief reactions will be unique. Explain to the griever not only what people in general undergo in grief, but also that each individual's grief is unique. For example, although two sisters each lose their brother, they will grieve differently according to their specific relationship to their brother and other variables that influence their idiosyncratic grief responses. This is important because grievers may compare themselves to others without recognizing the significant similarities and differences, and berate themselves for their feelings.

Communicate your realistic understanding of the pain and the griever's natural wish to avoid it. This will be helpful to those who may be inhibiting some of their grief, as well as those undergoing the normal grief process, as long as it does not seem to imply that the griever does not have to address her pain. It normalizes the pain and expresses empathy, understanding, support, and respect:

> The elements that are intrinsic to this work involve the following: a general recognition of the bereaved's inner pain which is obviously difficult for him to bear and express; a general recognition that this and his other fears are common amongst bereaved people and thus understood by the counselor; a recognition that his defenses serve some psychological purpose and therefore will not be torn down harshly or without due consideration of their function; a recognition that he is reluctant, probably for a variety of reasons, to relinquish the person who has died, and that, *together*, the bereaved and the counselor may be able to explore and understand the reasons and feelings involved in this; and a recognition that he, like many other bereaved people, dreads and wishes to avoid the pain of loss and other intense emotions that occur naturally at this time, especially anger, sadness, and guilt. Such understandings may be made explicit in interpretation, or they may be more gradually worked toward with the bereaved. (Raphael, 1983, p. 376)

Help the griever to recognize that she must yield to the painful process of grief. There is no way to go over, around, or under grief—we must go through it. Grievers must be helped to understand that grief cannot be delayed indefinitely, for it will erupt in some way, directly or indirectly. (See Chapter 4 for more on unresolved grief.) Whether or not their loss was fair is of no consequence; whether or not they deserve what is happening does not matter. The inescapable fact is that they have sustained a major loss requiring a painful period of readjustment that demands excruciatingly hard work and causes more pain and trouble if not attended to. Help them put it in the context that, although the pain is distressing, the experience and release of it is a healing part of the process.

   Make it clear to the griever that the process of grief will affect all areas of her life. For example, she may find that her concentration or memory may not be as sharp as it usually is and that she may need to temporarily compensate for this by keeping notes or making a list. Or she may find herself experiencing feelings that are out of the ordinary for her. Predicting the widespread effects of grief is not done to frighten grievers, but to prepare them for the unexpected intensity and extensiveness of the experience. In this way, too, the grief will not precipitate other problems. For example, with this knowledge, a couple may be able to see the increased tension in their marriage as a symptom of their mutual grief, and not of another loss about to befall.

   Assist the griever with appropriate time and course expectations. Our society has placed inappropriate expectations on the bereaved, and these, unfortunately, have been internalized by grievers. They frequently exacerbate their problems by being unrealistic about the amount of time the process of grief will require and how linearly it will proceed. (See "Expectations for Grief" in this chapter for more on this topic.) We need to provide more realistic information. They need to know that grief is a choppy, "two steps forward, one step back" experience that will continue for much longer than they had anticipated and will expose them to feelings they never knew they could have. Initially they should be encouraged to adopt a "one day at a time" perspective to help them avoid being overwhelmed. Anniversary and holiday upsurges in grief should be explained and predicted, and it should be suggested that significant life events such as getting married or having children may trigger new feelings of grief. Normative time spans for grief should be provided only within the context of general responses; grievers should not see them as self-fulfilling prophecies.

   Encourage the griever to be patient and not to expect too much of herself. See that the griever does not impose any "shoulds" on herself about the grief process. Hopefully this will be helped by the provision of appropriate normative data and the placing of this particular loss into a realistic context that reflects the important variables influencing the griever's response.

   Encourage the griever to give herself a respite from the grief. She should enjoy other people and other aspects of life. Help her to clearly understand that this is not a betrayal of the loved one, and stress the importance of caring for the self, despite the emphasis on the deceased and frequently on other survivors. This may have to be repeated often, since it is not uncommon for grievers to care for everyone else but themselves while grieving.

Help the griever find a variety of ways to replenish herself following the severe depletion resulting from major loss. Such things as adequate rest and nutrition are essential, as grief work requires enormous energy. The griever also needs social support in order to face the painful process of grief, decathect from the loved one, and subsequently reinvest in others. Physical activity or sports provide physical outlets for feelings. Intellectually, religion or philosophy, literature, art, and the media can aid the griever in finding meaning in the loss or simply escaping reality for a while. The griever also needs sources of emotional nurturance to recover from the pain of loss and decathexis. The continuous strain of grief on the griever, in which she is continually giving out and giving up, makes it essential for her to replenish herself in a number of ways.

Suggest some form of physical activity to release pent-up feelings. Many of the feelings of grief are difficult to articulate or, if they can be verbalized, have become somatized. Research has indicated that physical activity can work to reduce tension and anxiety, externalize aggression, and relieve depression, all components of the grief reaction. Such activity also helps prevent further somatic and psychiatric problems due to the grief process.

Help the griever maintain good physical health. Optimum physical health is necessary if she is to endure the arduous grief process and avoid psychosomatic complications. Make sure she gets sufficient exercise and rest, and is free from drugs. A balanced diet is also important, and special attention should be given to calcium, vitamin D, and phosphorus, all of which are depleted by the stress of grief.

Do not support flight by the bereaved. Some grievers will attempt to cope by moving, taking a vacation, or making significant changes. If this occurs too early, they will find they are stripped of their roots and the security of familiar surroundings. In the future, changes may be very helpful to the griever who is attempting to relinquish some of the past and integrate new roles into her life and personality. However, changes that happen too soon will result in more loss for someone who is already overwhelmed by many losses.

To prevent unnecessary changes we should look for ways to minimize secondary losses to the bereaved. For example, the family that can be spared having to move out of their home after the death of a father will have less trauma to deal with than if they are forced to leave too close to the death. If possible, we should also discourage grievers from making important decisions and major changes during the first year of bereavement. While such actions may appear viable and productive to the bereaved, they may only contribute to further disorganization or stress.

Help the bereaved to deal with practical problems that develop as a consequence of the death. Not only do emotional matters require attention, but practical ones as well. Worries about finances, a lack of education that precludes a better job, and other practical, day-to-day concerns are significant stressors to any bereaved individual. This does not mean that we must become involved in all of these practical matters, but that it is important to recognize their significance to grievers and to at least refer them to appropriate resources. No matter how effective the clinical interventions are, if the griever cannot afford food or transportation to the caregiver, they will be useless.

Help the Griever to Accommodate
to the Loss

These interventions are suggested for when the griever is well into his grief work. They will be inappropriate if used early in the process. As the grieving individual progresses through the process of grief, we can be especially helpful to him by assisting him in understanding the changes that grief brings to the self and in helping him in developing healthy ways to maintain a relationship with the deceased loved one.

Assist the bereaved in getting and maintaining the proper perspective on what resolution of grief will mean. People never forget, but the pain can diminish. Grievers need to know that they can survive, but will not be the same. Freud (1961) himself noted how, although grief subsides, it is never forgotten:

> Although we know that after such a loss the acute state of mourning will subside, we also know we shall remain inconsolable and will never find a substitute. No matter what may fill the gap, even if it be filled completely, it nevertheless remains something else. (Letter 239, p. 386)

This does not mean avoiding decathexis; it only points out that there will always be reminders of a significant loss. The goal is to help the griever recognize this fact and continue living, without inappropriate clinging to memories of the deceased.

Help the griever recognize that a major loss always changes us to some extent. He will never be exactly the same. Sometimes this is upsetting for the griever and those who know him, but it is a normal consequence of a major loss. Just as we must expect the griever to be a different person after the loss, so must the griever anticipate and be made aware of the transformations in himself.

Help the bereaved to discover his new identity and the psychological and social roles that he must assume or relinquish as a consequence of the death. Where once there was a "we", now there is an "I." This is a highly significant and painful transition to make. Ask the griever what experiences, roles, expectations, values, opportunities, and fantasies he has had to give up, and what new ones have had to be assumed. Also have him think of how identification with the deceased has added to or changed his previous identity. The griever must try to be specific and operationalize these changes so they can be more readily "owned" and understood in the context of normal reorganization after a major loss. He must appropriately identify and grieve for these changes, both losses and gains. Help him also identify what has remained consistent despite the trauma of the loss. This will provide a much needed sense of security and continuity.

As the individual develops a new identity there will be a corresponding need for new friends to validate this identity. This does not dismiss the need for the support and continuity provided by old friends, but new relationships with people who share important elements of the new identity can prevent feelings of alienation and isolation. For example, a newly widowed woman may be interested in associating with other widows because they have coped with similar problems and may understand what it is like to feel like a "fifth wheel" in social situations.

Assess with the griever which roles and skills must be assumed and work to help him accomplish this. This not only insures adequate replacement of necessary functions, but also gives the griever a sense of control and assists in the development of a new identity in the world without the deceased. For example, the widow may have to be taught how to handle the time management problems of being a single parent, and the widower may benefit from some cooking classes.

Help the griever to understand that a healthy new relationship with the deceased must be formed. Although death has separated the mourner from the deceased, it has not ended the relationship. It simply means that the relationship has changed from one based on the deceased's presence to one relating to memories of the past. This transition occurs during the grief process as the mourner reorganizes and restructures his life without the presence of the deceased. It is important for the griever to achieve the proper balance and perspective on this new relationship. While it is distinctly unhealthy for the griever to attempt to bring back the loved one by clinging to memories, neurotically perpetuating the relationship through illusion, neither is it healthy to extinguish all memories of the deceased, wiping out part of his own past life. The deceased needs to be remembered as one who was once alive but is now dead (Irion, 1966).

Ask the griever in what appropriate ways he will keep the deceased's memory alive and continue to relate to her. It is important for the griever to find new ways to relate to the loved one. Ask him to consider how he has identified with the deceased, confronting self-destructive ways and supporting therapeutic ones. Together discuss what parts of the previous life will be retained (special times, routines, mementos) and how reminiscences can be kept life-promoting rather than death-denying. Anniversary celebrations, prayers, commemorative donations, and mention during grace over dinner are all examples of ways to relate to the deceased while maintaining the proper perspective on the new relationship. Indeed, "learning how to cherish the irreplaceable memory of the missing member in your family is a healing part of grief" (Hogan, 1983, p. 6).

Do not allow the griever to equate the length and amount of his suffering with some kind of testimony to his love for the deceased. This will only promote unresolved grief. The griever must understand that healthy grief does not mean abandoning the loved one, but rather maintaining a relationship based on loving memory. This will eventually liberate the griever to have other relationships, which should not be seen as betrayals of the deceased. Neither should suffering be seen as a bond to the deceased or as proof of the value of the relationship.

Assist the griever in reestablishing a system of belief or meaning. A major loss often precipitates a quest for meaning, not only for the loss itself but also for the griever's life. Since the continuity of life has been disrupted, a new set of assumptions about the world must be developed to accommodate the death and the situation of being without the deceased. For example, the person who previously assumed that the good will be protected by God probably will have to reexamine this idea when his young child is senselessly killed. Once he considers the possibility that his belief is untrue, he is free to change his construct system and adopt a new view of the world.

When trying to understand why the loss occurred, the bereaved will need guidance in answering the questions that can be answered and accepting the fact that some cannot. They will have to arrive at a point where they realize that they may not ever understand why the loss happened, but that there may be a reason that cannot be ascertained. This is particularly important for those who have had an untimely loss, such as the death of a child.

Since everyone needs a reason to live, we also must help the

bereaved identify those beliefs and actions that will provide a renewed sense of purpose in their lives. At first mourners may feel
there is no reason to go on, and they will have to be reassured that
in time meaning will be restored. To those for whom death has
provoked a crisis of faith in previously held beliefs, new or renewed
religious and philosophical ideals may supply reason and order.
Activities not formerly significant can become meaningful, such as
campaigning for stiffer drunk-driving legislation after the death of
a loved one in an accident caused by a drunk driver.

Work With the Griever to Reinvest in a New Life

At this point, well along into the grief process, interventions
are directed toward appropriately supporting the griever's reinvestment in a new life.

*At the appropriate time, encourage the griever to find reward-
ing new things to do and people to invest in* (Lindemann's third
task). If the griever has appropriately decathected from the deceased there will be energy to reinvest in other people, things, and
causes—anyone or anything that gratifies the needs of the griever.
This is difficult, but necessary, after any major loss; however, it
may be particularly problematic for those who had been involved
with caring for a loved one with a long-term chronic illness prior
to death. In this case much of their time had been focused around
the care of the dying loved one and now this time may weigh all
too heavily on their hands (although some may be relieved).

Grievers may require some direction in getting back into cir-
culation. People may avoid them because of the anxiety-provoking
nature of the loss. Parents who lose children or individuals whose
loved ones die through socially unacceptable means (e.g., suicide
or murder) often find themselves without any social support. We
must help these grievers find the support they need to adapt to the
loss and to form new relationships with others. It may come
through family, friends, or self-help or other organized helping
groups. If they are encouraged to choose new tasks to accomplish
and new causes to invest in, they may also find supportive people
in social, educational, religious, or political groups.

*Do not push the bereaved into new relationships before they
are ready.* Grievers are often reluctant to disclose their feelings to
others because they fear being forced into uncomfortable social
situations too early. Many feel it is an insult to the memory of their
loved one or that it is an unbearable burden at the present time.
The decision to encourage a griever to enter into new relationships
depends on the individual and her specific loss and progress
through the grief process.

*Help the griever identify the gain that has derived from the
loss.* In every loss there is a gain. This is not to dismiss the intensity

of the bereavement experience, nor to minimize its tragedy. However, whenever a loss takes place there is a gain that accrues. For example, although a husband may lose his wife, the situation may force him to spend more time with his children. In this case, a "gain" that has occurred is that the husband may now be more closely involved with his children than he was previously. This does not mean that he is glad that the loss occurred or that he would have wished for his wife's death. The point is that at times it is helpful for grievers to recognize gains and to capitalize on them in their recovery process. It may help them cope with the painfulness of the loss by putting it in the perspective of the gains and losses that continually ebb and flow through life, or giving it some positive meaning.

Obviously all of these suggestions only hold true within certain limits. Grief that is absent, distorted, or too prolonged or intense will require more in-depth treatment. Referrals to mental health professionals should be made for grievers as needed. There will also be times when we will need to be more directive and assertive with particular grievers. For, although the bereaved require non-judgmental acceptance and support, there will be occasions, after a period of time, when they could benefit from a gentle, loving, and well-timed nudge in the direction of meeting the goals of appropriate grief work.

Rituals*

Rituals are a part of every social group. They are found in a surprising variety of forms and are practiced in some manner by all societies. Rituals can provide powerful therapeutic experiences that symbolize transition, healing, and continuity (van der Hart, 1983). Consequently, they can address and catalyze many aspects of the grief process. Like funerals, they can initiate the process of grief. However, they are not magic. Their power comes from the faith that the individual has in their ability to provide meaning.

> *Case Example:* Al's teenage brother committed suicide by shooting himself in the head with a shotgun in a field near their house. Now that Al can finally admit to the feelings of anger and betrayal that have complicated his grief, and has worked them through to a large extent, he is able to return to the spot of his brother's demise and plant a tree to mark his brother's life and to offer something living in place of death.

---

*Adapted from "Creating Therapeutic Rituals in the Psychotherapy of the Bereaved" by T. A. Rando, *Psychotherapy: Theory, Research and Practice*, in press–a. Reprinted by permission.

As discussed here, a ritual is a specific behavior or activity that gives symbolic expression to certain feelings and thoughts of the actor or actors individually or as a group. It may be habitually repeated or a one-time ocurrence. Rituals can be particularly helpful in assisting an individual or family to successfully resolve grief, both prior to and after the death (ideally building successfully on the therapeutic foundation supplied by the funeral as described in Chapter 7). These rituals need to be tailored to help the bereaved individual or family accept the reality of the loss, express and work through the feelings attendant to that loss, and accomplish the tasks of grief work.

For the individual, rituals provide a structured way to recall the lost loved one and to make some statement about the mourner's feelings. They encourage the necessary formulation of a new relationship with the deceased by acknowledging the physical loss while allowing the memory to continue. In terms of the social group, rituals can work to solidify family relationships and assist in the realignment of family roles. Like funeral rituals, therapeutic rituals can increase group cohesion following the death of a significant other in several ways: they give the group a commonly experienced symbolic behavior; they provide a way to cope with the separation; they make a statement of communal support; and they provide meaning to counteract the loss of it experienced after the death.

Rituals have many specific therapeutic properties.

• *The power of acting-out.* Acting-out enables the griever to constructively do something to overcome the feelings of emptiness and powerlessness that often accompany bereavement. It gives the individual a sense of control. Acting-out cuts through intellectualization and other resistances to mourning to directly reach the emotions; the physical reality of ritual behavior touches upon the griever's unconscious feelings far more effectively than any words can. It allows the griever to externally express his inner feelings, and may help him in expiating feelings of guilt.

• *The legitimization of emotional and physical ventilation.* Rituals give the mourner permission to outwardly express his feelings, providing acceptable outlets and symbols to focus upon.

• *The delimitation of grief.* Grief can seem overwhelming when it is experienced as a diffuse, global reaction. Ritual can channel feelings of grief into a circumscribed activity having a distinct beginning and ending with a clear purpose, making the feelings more manageable.

Case Example: The Morrison family plants a special tree in memory of their deceased toddler, Andrew, on his birthday. This provides them with an activity through which they can

demonstrate their love for the child and illustrate to themselves and others that they have not forgotten him. Consequently, the Morrisons find it less painful and not a betrayal
of Andrew if they do not feel constant pain throughout the
anniversary date. They find it easier to give themselves permission to experience whatever joy is available to them on
this day without as much guilt.

A ritual designed to express but also delimit grief, such as this one,
can be especially therapeutic during holidays and other anniversary times.

 • *The opportunity for the bereaved to "hang on" to the deceased
without doing so inappropriately or interfering with grief work.* Participation in ritual behaviors may give the griever a chance to
interact intensely with the memory of the deceased for a limited
period of time without crossing over into pathological dimensions.
Ritual legitimizes such emotional exchanges.

 • *The provision of assistance in mourning and in confronting
unresolved grief.* Rituals allow the griever to state consciously and
unconsciously, implicitly and explicitly, that a loss has occurred.
Through them the mourner can channel his feelings of grief or
finish unfinished business. They aid in the process of decathexis.

 • *The learning gained through doing and experiencing.* Participation in ritual behavior "teaches" the mourner that the deceased
is gone. It provides the experience necessary to validate the loss
and prepares him to readjust to the environment in which the
deceased is missing.

 • *The provision of structure for ambivalent or nebulous affect and
cognition.* Ritual provides a focus that is especially helpful in managing the confusing disorganization and loss of control commonly
experienced in grief.

 • *The provision of experiences that may allow for the participation
of other group members.* Collective rituals promote the social interaction that is a requisite for successful grief resolution and reintegration into the social group.

 • *The structuring of "celebrations" of anniversaries and holidays.*
Participation in ritual activities commemorating a special date
may provide an unusually effective way of tapping into or confronting a grievers' anniversary reactions, which are not always
easily recognized or owned by grievers.

Certain variables must be assessed and taken into account in
designing a therapeutic ritual: the psychological, social, physical,
cultural, and religious/philosophical characteristics of the griever;
the nature and extent of his psychosocial support; the specific characteristics of the loss; and the griever's present phase in the grief
process and the issues and possible conflicts attendant to it. A ritual

may be created to assist grievers in the normal process of their grief work.

Case Example: Michaela, a 17-year-old girl, was killed in an automobile accident. Her family was told they needed to commemorate her at Christmas, a day that they were dreading. They decided to burn a candle throughout the holiday to symbolize that she was still an important part of their lives, although in a radically different fashion. At dinner her empty chair was occupied by a senior citizen who otherwise would not have had a holiday feast.

It may also be a tool to help those whose grief has been unresolvable.

Case Example: Rita was accompanied by her therapist as she visited the grave of her daughter who died 19 years ago. She laid a bouquet of flowers on the grave, spoke of what she had lost in the intervening years, and talked of when she would reunite with her child. She then divided the bouquet in half, taking one half home with her and leaving the remaining flowers on the grave. She had told herself symbolically that while she had lost the physical presence of her daughter forever, her relationship continued based on loving memory. She had been fearful that if she acknowledged the death and grieved her loss, she would lose her daughter permanently. However, the ritual enabled her to acknowledge the death, grieve her loss, and still keep her daughter's memory.

Once the impediments to successful grief resolution are known, an appropriate ritual can be designed to overcome them. For instance, in the case described at the beginning of this section, Al needed something to symbolize that he could forgive his brother for committing suicide. Consequently, he chose planting the tree in his brother's place of death to illustrate that even though his brother had died, Al had a living attachment to him as represented by the tree. Ritual doesn't have to be dramatic, but it should be tailored to the needs of the griever if it is to be meaningful and helpful. There must be an appropriate amount of emotional distancing for the ritual to be effective. Rituals that are too overwhelming (under-distanced) or do not have enough emotional meaning or content to the griever (over-distanced) will be nontherapeutic (Scheff, 1977).

It is important to recognize that rituals can be as effective in dealing with the terminally ill as they are with the bereaved following the death. The same therapeutic properties exist since grief work is being addressed by both populations.

Case Example: Sam was the patriarch of a large Italian family. As he was succumbing to a long-term illness, both Sam and his family had difficulties with his relinquishing his control and authority over the family. However, when Sam had come to the point where he had worked this issue through in his mind, he called his family together and gave his ring to his eldest son to wear to signify the investiture of authority. Through this ritual behavior, he communicated to his family that he was "letting go of the family reins," but that he did not want to be forgotten. All the family now knew that the eldest son had authority that had been legitimized by Sam. They would also remember Sam whenever they saw the ring.

Therapies for Unresolved Grief

Psychotherapy must often be used when normal grief turns to unresolved grief. Much of the grief work will necessarily be done outside of the therapy session. The following section provides brief descriptions of some of the forms of grief therapy that are presently available.

Focal Psychotherapy

Raphael (1983) provides a model of focal psychotherapy that involves assessment of the particular form of pathological bereavement response and specific treatment to manage it and address the etiological processes involved. The goal is to convert the pathological bereavement response into one in which the individual is able to grieve more appropriately.

Therapy may be carried out either during the crisis following the loss or at a later point in time. Raphael believes that the optimal time for preventive intervention is probably between the first 2 to 8 weeks, perhaps even up to 3 months, after the death. In the first several weeks many people are so preoccupied by the necessary practical tasks and family matters that they are not ready to talk and work through the various aspects of their loss. Since after about 6 to 8 weeks some of the urgency of the crisis settles and old defenses return, it is important to intervene before the griever is less open to influence and has developed maladaptive grief responses. This is consistent with crisis theory, which states that a little help rationally directed and purposefully focused at a strategic time will be more effective than more extensive help given when the person is less emotionally accessible.

Focal psychotherapy as applied to three categories of pathological bereavement will be discussed here. Although many of the strategies described in the preceding "Intervention Strategies" section are used in this therapy, only those specific to particular categories will be mentioned.

Inhibited, suppressed, or absent grief. The therapist must explore the reasons why the bereaved cannot accept the death. Among the possibilities are dependence on the deceased, fear of the emotions of grief, and guilt about the death. The therapist's principle task will be to identify the griever's defenses, which will be revealed through repeated review of the griever's relationship with the deceased. Mourning itself will be facilitated by this process. An absence of appropriate affect may be due to the mourner's fear of releasing emotions. The therapist must communicate recognition of the bereaved's inner pain, the purpose of her defenses, and her reluctance to experience grief. (See "Support the Griever in Coping With the Grief Process" in this chapter for more on this topic.)

Distorted grief. In this grief there will be some suppression or inhibition of grief along with powerful distortions. These distortions usually fall into two patterns: extreme anger and extreme guilt. Angry distortion is often found following the loss of a dependent relationship or where there is a sudden or unexpected death for which someone is blamed. Particular emphasis in the treatment will be on assisting the bereaved in working through the problems created by the loss of a very dependent relationship or one that symbolized something special and irreplaceable for the griever. The pattern of distorted extreme guilt is usually found when the relationship between the bereaved and the deceased had been one of intense ambivalence, possibly even filled with conscious or unconscious wishes for the death or departure of the deceased. The guilt may be personally borne or projected onto others. The special aim of treatment is to explore the origins of ambivalence in the relationship, its links to earlier repetition compulsions, and the bereaved's parent-child relationships. Early in treatment, the therapist must refrain from reassuring the griever that she did her best or all she could for the deceased. In most cases the griever is well aware on some level of the extent of her anger. She will only receive reassurance when this anger or "death wish" is brought into the open and faced with a therapist who can assist her in coming to terms with it. If the guilt is legitimate, the therapist will need to help the griever accept it and learn to live with it. This group of bereaved individuals may relish the pain of their guilt and use it to pacify the deceased. If the guilt becomes unmanageable, they may sink into a psychiatric depression; if there are fantasies of reunion with the deceased, suicidal preoccupations may have to be assessed.

Chronic grief. This form of bereavement is similar to acute grief but it has been prolonged. It is often seen following the deaths of individuals with whom the bereaved were in dependent and irreplaceable relationships, those that were unexpected, and those of children. It usually indicates that an extraordinary and possibly pathological emotional investment had been maintained in the deceased. Many individuals experiencing this type of grief are not motivated to relinquish it, for it assists them in keeping the deceased "alive." Specific treatment goals are to explore why the relationship has such a special meaning and cannot be relinquished. It will be critical to explore the roles and identity that the griever had in terms of the deceased, since decathexis may only result following the adoption of new roles and identity. It must be noted that chronic grief can develop as a method of controlling and punishing others, eliciting their care, and receiving secondary gain. Therapists may want to establish a set of concrete tasks for the chronic griever to complete, e.g., sorting through the deceased's effects or decreasing visits to the cemetery. The griever needs to develop other sources of gratification and to create an alternate role for herself. However, such grievers are notoriously difficult to treat and frequently retain their symptoms unremittingly. Parkes and Weiss (1983) caution against using traditional treatment modes that stimulate or extend grief expression with chronic grievers. (See "Make Contact and Assess" in this chapter for more on this topic.)

Re-grief Therapy

Volkan has written extensively on re-grief therapy (Volkan, 1971, 1975; Volkan & Showalter, 1968), which is designed to

> help the patient bring into consciousness sometime after the death his memories of the one he has lost and the experiences he had with her, in order to test them against reality, to accept with affect—especially appropriate anger—what has happened, and to free himself from excessive bondage to the dead. (Volkan, 1975, p. 234)

The criterion for utilization of this treatment is intellectual acknowledgment of the loss accompanied by emotional denial 6 months or more after the death. The griever has a chronic hope that the deceased will return and consequently is fixated in the initial reaction to death. Many of these grievers have not fully participated in funeral rituals and never saw nor believed the final interment to have taken place. There is usually great ambivalence towards the deceased.

In the beginning of therapy rational distinctions are made between what actually belongs to the griever and what belongs to the deceased. The individual is helped to form boundaries demarcating herself from the deceased through the taking of a detailed history of the deceased and the lost relationship. Sometimes a photo of the deceased is brought in to clarify the differentiation. The griever is helped to understand why she could not permit the deceased to "die." The circumstances of the death are carefully examined. Next, the therapist focuses on the griever's "linking objects," which are highly symbolized objects representing the deceased and providing contact with him. The therapist asks the griever to bring these to the session and they are used to stimulate memories and make the griever aware of the magical ties with the deceased. The concepts that are symbolized by the linking objects are identified and interpreted to loosen the griever's contact with the deceased. Further review of the circumstances of the death is conducted and emotional release is encouraged. Dreams and fantasies are analyzed, and the griever is encouraged to take responsibility for her feelings of anger, ambivalence, and guilt. Re-griefing is a short-term therapy and the griever is usually seen four times a week to promote intensity.

Behavioral Therapies

Behavioral approaches are best suited for chronic pathological bereavement that contains strong phobic avoidance components. A number of researchers have suggested that a modified flooding technique of confrontation with pain-evoking stimuli breaks down denial and evokes the affects of grief (Gauthier & Marshall, 1977; Gauthier & Pye, 1979; Ramsay, 1977, 1979; Ramsay & Happée, 1977), which can then be desensitized and extinguished.

Several studies offered guided mourning (Lieberman, 1978; Mawson, Marks, Ramm, & Stern, 1981), a treatment in which individuals with unresolved grief were exposed both in imagination and in real life to avoided or painful memories, ideas, or situations related to the loss of the deceased. They were encouraged to repeatedly describe such thoughts, feelings, or ideas until the distress that had initially prompted the phobic avoidance response was diminished. Individuals were encouraged to say good-bye to lost loved ones by writing notes or visiting the cemetery. There was an intense reliving of painful memories and feelings associated with the bereavement. Individuals were also given instructions to write about the deceased, think about that person, force themselves to face the grief, and look at a photo of the deceased each day. When compared to a controlled group that had been encouraged to avoid thinking about the death or the deceased, those who had received guided mourning intervention evidenced modest improvement as compared to the controlled subjects. This was most evident for phobic avoidance and least evident on measures of depression, suggesting less of an association between mood disturbance and avoidance of bereavement cues than previously assumed.

A behavioral approach also has been used to treat grief among the elderly (Averill & Wisocki, 1981). In such an approach, the intrapsychic aspects of grief are not the focus of therapy, but rather the symptoms of grief. The goals and procedures are established according to the individual's reactions and their affect on her func-

tioning. Five broad categories of behavior are considered grief reactions for which goals are set:

- Physiological complaints, with goals such as reducing symptoms or increasing physical activity
- Subjective (private) events, with goals such as changing self-
  concepts or maladaptive thought patterns
- Overt behavior, with goals such as reducing use of alcohol
  or drugs or eliminating compulsions
- Interpersonal relationships, with goals such as reducing isolation and improving the quality of social interaction
- Environmental support, with goals such as changing physical
  or social structures to support or facilitate therapeutic gains

Many techniques are available to the behavioral therapist in
treating various symptoms of grief: relaxation, systematic desen-
sitization, covert conditioning, cognitive rehearsal, role-playing,
contingency contracting, and various kinds of skill training, to
mention a few.

> In many instances, the application of these techniques to the
> symptoms of grief is a relatively straightforward extension of
> ordinary clinical practice. For example, relaxation procedures
> may be used to help the bereaved overcome general feelings of
> anxiety and, on a more specific level, to alleviate such symptoms
> as insomnia. The thought-stopping procedure described by Cau-
> tela and Wisocki (1977) can also be used to reduce the stress
> associated with bereavement. This procedure consists of targeting
> a stress-inducing perseverative thought pattern in training the
> client to interrupt the pattern with distracting stimuli.
>   The experienced clinician can easily extend the list of tech-
> niques to include his or her preferred modes of treatment. How-
> ever, a caveat should be noted. Because of their complex origins,
> the symptoms of grief may not yield to treatment as readily as
> other forms of distress. Indeed, it is not always easy to decide
> which symptoms of grief should be treated, and at which point
> in time. Consider again the technique of thought-stopping. This
> procedure should be used only for thoughts that are troublesome
> to the client because they are impeding recovery (e.g., negative
> self-references which add to the person's feelings of guilt, anxiety,
> or depression). The client should not be encouraged to shut out
> all thoughts of the deceased, even if those thoughts are sometimes
> quite painful. (Averill & Wisocki, 1981, p. 145)

A treatment method for those suffering from unresolved grief
has been developed that uses present-time guided imagery (Melges
& DeMaso, 1980). The process begins with preparation for making
the decision to re-grieve and clarification of the procedures. This
is followed by guided imagery for reliving, revising, and revisiting

scenes of the loss. The individual is asked to relive a sequence of the loss by viewing it in her mind's eye as if it were happening now. She is then told to revise that scene in order to remove the barriers or binds that inhibit grieving. Finally she is instructed to revisit the revised scene in the present tense as if it were taking place here and now in order to acknowledge the finality of the loss and experience the full range of grief that was previously prohibited. In many cases the individual is encouraged to engage in

> "dialogues with the deceased" in order to acknowledge the finality of the loss, differentiate himself from the deceased, express tears and rage, deal with ambivalence and misdirected anger, tease apart interlocking grief reactions, emancipate himself from unspoken binds, reveal secrets and deal with unfinished business, express love and forgiveness, and get permission from the "presence" of the deceased to look for new relationships and options, especially those that seem to flow naturally from what the deceased would have wanted for the bereaved. (Melges & DeMaso, 1980, pp. 56-57)

Following this the therapist works with the griever to build new hopes and plans of action following completion of the intense work of grieving. The authors note that the patient's decision to re-grieve is often therapeutic in and of itself. Results have been found to be good, sometimes dramatic, after 6 to 10 sessions. They note that in most instances it has been integrated with other forms of therapy. They feel that one of its greatest advantages is

> that the present-time guided imagery, or components of it, can quickly get at the core issues needing resolution. It serves to highlight the obstacles and binds which are often only dimly perceived when the patient talks about the loss in the past tense. (p. 59)

EXPECTATIONS FOR GRIEF

As mentioned before, there are many false expectations in our society about the nature of the grief process. To help the bereaved, we must be able to give them a more realistic view of how grief will change over time and how long it will take for them to recover from a loss.

Time as a Treatment Variable

Frequently time is viewed as a healing factor in the process of grief. It is not uncommon to hear "Time heals all," "It just takes time," or "Time will ease the pain." But time can be helpful in the grief process *only* if the griever is dealing with the loss, not if he is denying, inhibiting, delaying, or otherwise not working through the loss. It is like the healing of a wound. If the wound is cleaned and properly dressed, with time and treatment it will heal; however, if the wound is not appropriately cleaned and tended to, time will not be helpful. It will only mark the progress of festering infection. In grief, time is therapeutic in that it can allow the griever to put things in perspective, adapt to change, and process the feelings and attend to the tasks of grief work. The passage of time plus these experiences reduces the pain. But for the person who seeks to avoid his grief, time is distinctly malignant; it only increases the pressure and strengthens the resistance to healthy mourning, providing fertile ground for the development of other pathology. For the griever who has not attended to his grief, the pain is as acute and fresh 10 years later as it was the day after. During those 10 years, other symptomatology has probably developed as well. In contrast, the griever who has successfully completed his grief work will still feel a sense of loss, but time will have helped the healing and the pain will be more in memory than experienced at that moment. In sum, the passage of time can help resolve grief, but only if it is accompanied by the active undertaking of grief work.

The Course of Grief

In general, people assume that they should be over grief in only a fraction of the time it actually takes. The intensity of grief in fact fluctuates over time, and this must be identified, predicted, and legitimized for the griever.

One example of how grief progresses is the "6-month phenomenon," in which the griever has been coping for some time immediately after the death and then experiences a resurgence of grief months later. It is often disheartening and discouraging to the griever, who may imagine she is losing control or going out of her mind. Actually, however, she is merely coming out of the daze that she has been in through the early months following the loss. Now that everyday life has commenced, she is confronted with the painful reality of the loss in striking, unexpected ways. For example, the widow may only truly comprehend her aloneness when she struggles to put up the storm windows by herself the first autumn after her husband has died. When the griever has to go Christmas shopping alone, or when the daily routine settles in enough to emphasize the loneliness, there is a more complete understanding of the ramifications of the loss, and acute symptoms recur. Grievers are not usually prepared for the impact of these experiences and mistakenly believe that they are back where they started from in terms of working through the grief. This intermittently acute awareness of loss is not uncommon for several years after the death. Thus, grievers need to be told that bereavement does not follow a decreasing linear pattern. It has many ups and downs, twists and turns.

It may be difficult to determine where a person is in grief at any given time. Hardt (1978-79) found that there was a series of stages that the bereaved pass through prior to being able to accept the death of a loved one, and that in several of those stages the mourner appears to have a greater acceptance of the death than in fact has been internalized. The research of Rando (1983) suggests that bereavement symptoms may initially subside over a period of time, then increase again long after the death. And even the person who is acutely grieving may not show it 24 hours a day, as the grief must sometimes be put aside for the demands of living.

The Duration of Grief

The duration of grief is variable and will depend upon the factors influencing the grief response. The research that has been conducted on the duration of grief is scant and inconclusive. It also is artificially biased since the follow-up period is usually only 18 months, which precludes knowledge of what happens after this time period. This prohibits making valid, generalized statements about the length of normal grief. A rule of thumb is that as long as a grieving behavior is not dysfunctional (physically or psychosocially), harmful, or representative of more severe pathology, it can be viewed as not abnormal and seen as part of the process of grief. This allows for a wide variety of reactions and fluctuating symptom intensities. Although it was once thought that the symptoms of grief lasted only 6 months, it is now known that some symptoms may take up to 3 years to be resolved. Most of the more intense reactions of grief subside within 6 to 12 months. However, the saying "Once bereaved, always bereaved" still remains true. There are some parts of the loss that will continue to be with the griever until he dies. It should be remembered that *no* evaluation can be made about grief and its duration without taking into account all of the psychological, social, and physiological factors that influence a specific grief response.

Anniversary reactions are to be expected. These are brief upsurges in grief that occur during certain times of the year (e.g., during anniversaries of important events, holidays, birthdays) or in the presence of certain stimuli (e.g., a special song, photograph, location) and are normal within limits. All of us have an unconscious time clock within us that keeps track of anniversary dates whether or not we consciously recognize it. It is very common for someone who is experiencing an inexplicable increase in symptoms to later realize that it is the anniversary of a significant event. It can be predicted for grievers that they may feel more vulnerable at anniversary times and that this is quite normal. Continued vulnerability to these intermittent pangs of grief is not incompatible with recovery, as long as the defense against the vulnerability does not take too much effort, reduce grievers' capacity for gratification, or interfere with their functioning (Parkes & Weiss, 1983).

It can also be predicted that certain experiences later in life may temporarily resurrect intense grief resulting from earlier losses. These new experiences may make aspects of the lost relationship important that were insignificant at the time of the bereavement (Siggins, 1966). The man who attains the same age as his father when his father died; the woman whose husband is not there to walk her daughter down the aisle at the daughter's wedding; the young adult who misses the presence of his sibling at his college graduation; the young woman who recognizes she is now an adult and laments the fact that she never got the chance to know her parents as adults since they died when she was so young; the woman who grieves for the loss of her mother when she becomes a mother—all these individuals are experiencing normal grief reactions occasioned by certain specific changes and experiences that poignantly illustrate to them the loss they have sustained. Within appropriate limits these, like anniversary reactions, are normal and expectable.

What indicates the ending of grief? Freud (1957) summed up his criteria for the successful resolution of the grief process rather succinctly. He felt that the work of mourning was completed when decathexis was accomplished and the ego became free and uninhibited again. Others feel that grief is ended when the individual completes the final mourning phase of reorganization (Bowlby, 1980; Parkes, 1972). Both Lindemann (1944) and Parkes and Weiss (1983) assert that their three tasks of grief work must be effectively carried out prior to being able to call the grief process complete. (See "Descriptions of the Grief Process" in Chapter 2 for more on this topic.) These are quite abstract concepts and difficult to operationalize.

Some behavioral criteria suggested by Lazare (1979) indicate the resumption of life with successful resolution of grief. As with other aspects of grief, these will be evidenced in a waxing and waning fashion.

- The depressive symptomatology of bereavement disappears.
- The individual's time sense goes back to normal—he can let time go on now.
- There is a different kind of sadness, a change from a bitter sadness to a sweet one.
- The individual displays more equanimity when discussing the loss.

- The individual starts to be able to enjoy holidays again.
- The "searching" for the lost loved one ceases.
- The individual relates better to others.
- There is a healthier relationship with the deceased.

Ten general areas of assessment reported by Parkes and Weiss (1983) appeared to capture all the various facets of recovery for the bereaved individuals they studied:

- Level of functioning comparable or better than prebereavement level
- Movement towards solution of outstanding problems
- Acceptance of the loss, including an absence of distortion (belief in the permanency of the death and a realistic image of the deceased), comfort in talking and thinking about the deceased, and a socially acceptable, rational explanation for the death
- Ability to socialize as effectively as before the death
- Positive and realistic attitude towards the future
- Health back to prebereavement levels
- General level of anxiety or depression appropriate
- General level of guilt or anger appropriate
- General level of self-esteem appropriate
- Ability to cope with future loss

Most of the bereaved eventually come to terms with their grief and carry on with their lives, but total resolution of grief may never occur:

> In our earlier formulations we had thought that a widow "recovers" at the end of the four to six weeks of her bereavement crisis on condition that she manages to accomplish her "grief work" adequately. We believed that thereafter she would be psychologically competent to carry on with the tasks of ordinary living, subject only to the practical readjustments demanded by her new social roles. We now realize that most widows continue the psychological work of mourning for their dead husbands for the rest of their lives. During the turmoil and struggles of the first one to three years most widows gradually learn how to circumscribe and segregate this mourning within their mental economy and how to continue living despite its burden. After this time they are no longer actively mourning, but their loss remains a part of them and now and again they are caught up in a resurgence of feelings of grief. This happens with decreasing frequency as time goes on, but never ceases entirely. (Caplan, 1974, p. viii)

CHAPTER 6

Different Bereavement Situations

In this chapter four specific bereavement situations will be examined to highlight the diverse issues that arise under different loss circumstances: the death of a child, the death of a spouse, death by suicide, and the grief of children. As all losses are not the same, neither are all grief reactions.

GRIEF AFTER THE DEATH OF A CHILD*

In the thanatological literature there has been relatively less writing devoted to the topic of parental loss of a child as compared to other losses. This has occurred despite the fact that there are unique psychological and sociological issues that make parental bereavement particularly difficult to resolve. These issues must be recognized in clinical treatment work with bereaved parents.

Factors Causing Difficulty in Parental Grief

There are a number of factors that make the experience of loss of a child particularly difficult: social expectations for parents, the unexpectedness of a child's dying before a parent, negative social reactions, loss of support from spouses, and the need for caring for the surviving children.

---

*Adapted from "Bereaved Parents: Particular Difficulties, Unique Factors, and Treatment Issues by T. A. Rando, *Social Work*, in press–b. Reprinted by permission.

The Parental Role

A primary factor contributing to the intensity of parental bereavement is the role of a parent. Studies have found that the grief of parents is particularly severe when compared with other bereaved individuals (Clayton et al., 1968; Schwab et al., 1975; Sanders, 1979-80). Psychologically, the process of mourning for one's child involves not only dealing with the loss of the child, but with the loss of parts of oneself, since parental attachment consists both of love for the child and self-love (Furman, 1976). The unique dynamics of the parent-child relationship intensifies the losses to self usually sustained by any individual subsequent to the death of a loved one. There is an assault on the self and sense of immortality:

> With the death of a child in the family the blow is felt narcissistically and as a threat to the sense of our immortality. . . . The bereavement for the child is intimately connected with, and related to, the libidinal investments. The child serves as a tie with the traditional past, but also, and perhaps more importantly, with the future and with our sense of immortality. (Schwartz, 1977, p. 196)

There is also the unique closeness of the relationship and the failure to sustain the basic function of parenthood:

> Physiologically, psychologically, and socially, the relationship that exists between parents and their children may well be the most intense that life can generate. Obviously, then, vulnerability to loss through death is most acute when one's child dies. . . .
>
> Not only is the death of a child inappropriate in the context of living, but its tragic and untimely nature is a basic threat to the function of parenthood—to preserve some dimension of the self, the family, and the social group. (Jackson, 1977, p. 187)

There are numerous other losses resulting from this initial loss:

> Parents who lose a child are multiply victimized. We are victimized by the realistic loss of the child we love, we are victimized by the loss of the dreams and hopes we had invested in that child, and we are victimized by the loss of our own self-esteem. Not unlike the survivors of the concentration camps, we cannot comprehend why we did not die instead. (Kliman, 1977, p. 191)

For this reason parents experience themselves as "victims of an overwhelming assault on their parental identities as protectors and providers" (Wallace, 1967, p. 515) and actually feel "mutilated" and "disabled" (Stephens, 1974). Survivor guilt runs rampant.

Much of the adult identity centers around providing and doing for children, a basic function of the adult. The parent who has been in the roles of provider, problem-solver, protector, and adviser, and who has been accustomed to being self-sufficient and in control, must now confront the interruption of these roles and the severing of the relationship with the child. The death of a child robs the adult of the ability to carry out his functional roles, leaving the parent with an overwhelming sense of failure and loss of power and ability. It assaults the sense of self to have these basic roles shattered and have parental omnipotence over the child rendered useless and ineffective. Survival guilt may develop not only because of existence after the death of the child, but because of the feeling that the child has been "let down" by the failure to carry out the basic duties of parenthood. In no other role are there so many inherently assumed and socially assigned responsibilities. In no other relationship is the individual expected to be so loving and good, so totally concerned and selfless—unrealistic expectations that cannot be fulfilled. This is a major reason why the resolution of parental grief is such a difficult task and why it places additional demands on the bereaved parent as compared to other bereaved individuals in different roles.

The Unnaturalness of a Child's
Predeceasing a Parent

Given that a basic function of the parent is to preserve the family and protect the child, there is an implicit expectation that the parent will die before the child. The orderliness of the universe seems to be undermined when this expectation is unmet.

> Bereaved parents come in all ages. It does not appear to make a
> difference whether one's child is three, thirteen, or thirty if he
> dies. The emotion in each of us is the same. How could it be that
> a parent outlives a child? (Schiff, 1977, p. 4)

The unnaturalness is not determined by the age of the child, but by the fact that the child dies "out of turn" with the parent. The strangeness of the event becomes a major stumbling block for the bereaved parent who cannot comprehend why it happened and can take no solace in the idea that the loss was inevitable.

Survival guilt appears to be fostered by the uncommon nature of the loss of a child. The guilt is fueled, and the needed coping mechanisms lacking, because this is an age where infant and child mortality are at the lowest rates ever, leaving parents now unprepared to deal with the loss of their children in comparison to the centuries past.

There has been much discussion in the literature of the child's age as a determinant in parental grief. Although researchers may argue about it, the clinical evidence suggests that the question is academic and meaningless to bereaved parents. No matter what the age of their child, they have lost their hopes, dreams, and expectations for that child, and have lost parts of themselves and their future. Often this is forgotten when the child who dies is an adult. The parents are usually pushed aside in favor of the spouse and the children of the deceased adult. However, no matter what the age of the deceased, the parents have still lost their "baby." Even if the deceased is a grandparent in his own role, he is still a child to the parents and the loss is just as unnatural.

The age of the child does define some specific issues that will need to be addressed in the parents' grief. For example, if a child dies during the tumultuous stage of adolescence, and has been actively involved in normal adolescent rebellion and conflict with his parents, his death may be relatively more difficult for the parents to resolve because of the normal ambivalence that may have existed in the relationship.

Another factor contributing to the unnaturalness of the child's death is that, especially with children and adolescents, death is often sudden and dramatic, the result of accident. Such deaths are more likely to produce traumatic effects and poorer bereavement outcomes (Parkes, 1975; Parkes & Weiss, 1983). They are often more likely to involve violence, mutilation, and destruction, leaving the survivors with a greater sense of helplessness and threat. This type of death prompts enormous efforts by the parents to find meaning in the death, determine who is to blame, and regain a sense of control. (See "Psychological Factors" in Chapter 3 for more on sudden, unanticipated death.) Deaths in these circumstances have been associated with increased mortality in the bereaved (Rees & Lutkins, 1967).

A final issue, one that may be uncomfortable for some parents to admit, is that in losing their child, they lose someone who could care for them later in life. This may be particularly important to elderly parents who may have been receiving emotional, physical, or financial assistance from the adult child who died.

Social Reactions to the Death of a Child

Society has a uniquely strange and callous response to the bereaved parent. Although all bereaved people are somewhat socially stigmatized, parents whose children have died appear to report more of this than other mourners. They often experience abandonment, helplessness, and frustration when they frequently are avoided by other parents or are the subject of others' anger when they do not return to normal quickly enough. These other parents are made anxious by the bereaved parents, who remind them that this unnatural event could happen to them and their own children. As a result, bereaved parents are often left without many of the social and emotional supports desirable for coping with the grief process. Fortunately, self-help groups such as The Compassionate Friends or groups devoted to specific types of loss such as Mothers Against Drunk Drivers (MADD) have arisen to help meet some of the psychosocial needs of bereaved parents and to fill in the gaps left by other members of society. This further supports the common feeling that only other bereaved parents can offer solace and understanding.

Loss of Support of Spouse

One of the most difficult aspects of parental bereavement is that the death of the child strikes both partners in the marital dyad simultaneously and confronts them with the same overwhelming loss. Consequently each partner's most therapeutic resource is taken away, as the person to whom each would normally turn for support is also deeply involved in his or her own grief. The closeness that characterizes the marital relationship also makes partners particularly vulnerable to the feelings of blame and anger that grievers often displace onto those nearest to them.

Partners can greatly disappoint each other if they assume that they both will experience the same grief simply because they have suffered the death of the same child. Each of them will have had a unique relationship with the child, influenced by their social roles and the sex of the child. Different things will constitute losses to each parent. For the mother who was at home with the child on a daily basis, there may be acute awareness of the physical absence of the child, the inability to touch, hear, or see him. Duties such as cleaning the child's room may remind her of the lost child. The father working outside the home may miss having the chance to play sports or games with the child and feel the pain more keenly on the weekends.

Each spouse will also respond idiosyncratically according to such variables as personality differences, coping abilities, previous loss history, and other psychosocial factors. One of the major variables contributing to differences in grief experience is sex-role socialization. The male has been conditioned to exert emotional control. He prides himself on the role of the provider, protector, and problem-solver. However, with the death of his child he fails in each of these roles. Conversely, women have traditionally been socialized to express emotions other than anger. The situation is ripe for conflict if one spouse interprets the other's grief response as indicating a lack of love for the deceased child. There must be a wide latitude for differences in grief expression.

Couples may also lack synchronicity in their grief experiences, with one spouse being up emotionally while the other is down. This may occur in four grief work areas: expressing feelings; working and doing daily activities (one may find comfort in work, while the other is overwhelmed by it); relating to things that trigger memories of the deceased (one may desire all photographs to be removed from the house, while the other will cling to them); and searching for the meaning of what has happened (one may find solace in religion, while the other relinquishes her former faith) (Montgomery, 1980). Couples may have widely divergent styles of grief expression or avoidance and these may fluctuate over time, bringing the spouses closer together or separating them further from one another. Any of these differences may cause spouses to erroneously conclude that their mate has rejected them, especially when the mate is depressed and withdrawn. Although partners may have pulled together to meet crises in the past, they will have to recognize that they will seldom be in the same place at the same time in their grief process and that this does not mean that they do not still love one another. They will also need to recognize that the grief experience will change each of them and that consequently they cannot expect their mate to be exactly the same person as before. This will create a change in the marital relationship that also must be accommodated.

One of the primary areas in which a partner's response to grief can dramatically alter the couple's relationship is in the sexual realm. A classic and quite frequent problem is the inhibition of sexual response and intimacy in bereaved parents. This may be the result of the fear of having and losing other children, or may be a symptom of the grief or depression experienced by one or both of the partners. While the intimacy of sexual contact may be comforting to one spouse, it may be precisely what the other cannot endure at that moment in her grief. If the barriers to feelings are let down in order to experience the closeness of sexual intimacy, then the spouse may also be vulnerable to having to experience other less positive feelings, such as the pain, loss, and grief against which she has attempted to shield herself. Since sexual intimacy and orgasm can put individuals in touch with their feelings at a deep level, individuals may seek to avoid it for fear of tapping into painful emotions. Unless each member of the couple understands the difference between themselves and their differing grief styles, and can appreciate the fact that the sexual relationship, as well as other aspects of the relationship, can be intensely affected by grief, there will be further problems. It is not unusual for the sexual relationship to be compromised by disinterest, depression, avoidance, or other grief-related responses for up to as long as 2 years after the death.

Other marital difficulties arise when normal patterns of relating are disrupted. For example, communication dysfunction often develops. One partner may ask the other unanswerable questions, such as why the death occurred, or may avoid communicating with the spouse for fear that it will precipitate a mutual downward spiral. Irrational demands may be made, as when one spouse expects the other to take away the pain. Day-to-day problems may not be confronted because of preoccupation with the loss of the child, or because one spouse seeks to protect the other. Unfortunately, such problems tend to accumulate until there is an explosion. This may result in greater misunderstandings and feelings of helplessness.

A sensitive issue that spouses must confront is that their physical presence and their mannerisms can remind one another of the deceased child. Part of the couple has been lost irretrievably, both in terms of the past they have shared and the future of which they had dreamt. To be constantly reminded of this by the sight of each other is a very painful experience.

All of these secondary losses place additional burdens of grief, loss, and adaptation on couples already overwrought with responsibilities and demands. These problems contribute to the higher divorce rates in bereaved couples sometimes cited in research.

Parenting of Remaining Children

Parents who have other children must continue to function in the very parenting role that they are trying to grieve for and relinquish. This places them in an enormously psychologically difficult situation. Frequently it becomes difficult to deal with the other children because they also serve as a painful reminder of the child who died. If the bereaved parents have trouble caring for the surviving children due to preoccupation with the deceased child and/or problems secondary to the grief process, there is more frustration. In addition, the normal displacement of hostility onto others in close proximity may be expressed as anger with the surviving children, making parents feel even more guilty.

Surviving children are themselves in very vulnerable positions. There is too frequently the expectation that the other children will take the place of the deceased. This is unhealthy both for the children and their parents. Severe problems have been documented with regard to "replacement" children (Cain & Cain, 1964; Poznanski, 1972). While there is always some role realignment and reassignment in a family subsequent to the death of a family member, parents may inappropriately place expectations on children that repress the children's own identities in an attempt to keep the deceased child alive. This is usually caused by one or both parents' inability to work through their grief over the loss of the child. Often they had intense narcissistic investment in the child who died. In cases where a new child is born, that child enters a world of mourning with apathetic and withdrawn parents who focus on the past and literally worship the image of the dead. In the classic Cain and Cain (1964) study of replacement children, parents had not been interested in having another child until their child died. For many, the home was turned into a shrine, daily schedules were dictated by visits to the grave, and photographs of the deceased filled the house. Frequently these parents imposed the identity of the dead child upon the substitute child and unconsciously identified the two. The deceased child was idealized and the new child could never hope to compete. Such replacement children have been found to have psychopathologies ranging from moderate neuroses to psychoses.

Other problems can occur between bereaved parents and remaining children. Resentment that the others continue to exist or distress because it appears that the children have adjusted too quickly or have grieved insufficiently are not uncommon. Parents may become concerned that their relationships with the remaining children are less intense than the one they shared with the deceased and may fear that they have lost the ability to love their children. Usually this is temporary and can be worked through as the bereaved parent continues the mourning process and starts to reinvest again. At times it may reflect the desire not to invest in the remaining children because of the fear of losing them too.

It is crucial for parents to have an understanding of the different grief responses of children (see "The Grief of Children" in this chapter for more on this topic) so they do not erroneously interpret the children's reactions and can better communicate with the children about death and loss. It is also important that parents recognize when remaining children have unrealistic expectations of themselves. They may try to take away their parents' pain, to be perfect, or to replace the deceased sibling.

Unique Parental Grief Reactions

Parents whose children have died undergo all the normal reactions of grief, but are particularly susceptible to guilt or problems due to their relationship with the deceased. Their symptoms are usually more severe and long-lasting, and they are more compelled to find a justification for the death.

Parental Guilt

Guilt appears to be the most pervasive response to the death of a child. According to Miles and Demi (in press), such guilt feelings arise from parents' sense of personal responsibility for the child's well-being and helplessness to have prevented the child's suffering and death. They have suggested six sources of this guilt:

• *Death causation guilt.* This guilt is related to the belief that the parent either contributed to the child's death or failed to protect the child from death. Examples of this would be a parent's feeling guilty for giving permission for some activity that resulted in the death (e.g., to go swimming); not being more vigilant about some aspect of the child's health (e.g., not taking the child to the doctor sooner); and being responsible for allowing the child to have the vehicle that caused the death (e.g., buying the bicycle involved in the accident).

• *Illness-related guilt.* Here guilt is related to the parental role during the child's illness or at the time of death. The parents feel they did not live up to their own expectations in fulfilling that role either by their actions or thoughts and feelings. Situations parents have reported as initiating this guilt include not taking the child home to die; leaving the child's bedside to meet personal needs for rest; not being with the child at the time of death; and wanting the child to live despite the pain or to die because of it.

• *Parental-role guilt.* With this guilt there is a belief that the parent failed to live up to personal or societal expectations in the overall parental role. It is related to the societal image of the parent as all knowing, all loving, always available, and superhuman. For example, parents reported feeling guilty for not spending more time with the child who had died, not expressing their love to the child more often, not providing enough structure and/or discipline, or not attending events related to the child's activities.

• *Moral guilt.* Moral guilt comes from the belief that the child's death is punishment or retribution for the parent's violation of a moral, ethical, or religious standard. It is more likely to be experienced by parents with strict consciences or with religious/philosophical backgrounds that emphasize guilt and punishment. Concerns that the death of their child was retribution for such things as an abortion, an extramarital affair, or poor church attendance are not uncommon.

• *Survival guilt.* This is guilt from violating the standard that a child should outlive her parents. Such emotion is implied in phrases like "I am here and she's gone; she had so much to live for" and "It doesn't seem right that I am still alive and enjoying life and she is buried in a casket across town."

• *Grief guilt.* Grief guilt is related to the behavioral and emotional reactions of grief at the time of or following the child's death. Parents may feel guilty for overreacting or for being too stoic. They may feel guilty for the way they treated other family members during acute grief. Recovery guilt is not uncommon, as parents may feel they are unfaithful to the deceased child if they ever again enjoy themselves.

To cope with this guilt, several strategies can be used. These are taken from Miles and Demi and suggestions made earlier in this book. First, parents should confront and admit to feelings of guilt and then examine the reality of the situation and their actual intent at the time. They may then come to see their actions in a more positive light. A mother who felt guilty for planning the party that resulted in her child's death found that when she carefully examined her motives for planning the celebration she realized that she had been a good mother and had simply tried to fulfill her child's wishes.

When this cannot work, parents may need assistance and permission to forgive themselves, or constructive ways to atone for their guilt, if they realize that in fact their acts did cause serious harm to the child. This is termed "legitimate" guilt. Writing a letter of self-forgiveness in a journal or writing a letter to the child who died speaking of regrets and need for forgiveness can help. Discussing the events with a nonjudgmental other and finding socially constructive ways to work out the guilt can also serve this purpose. Parents must learn to live with guilt that cannot be worked through.

Many parents will require assistance in identifying and changing irrational beliefs and expectations that may be producing guilt. Guilt usually results when we perceive ourselves as falling short of our self-image or violating our beliefs. Some common and irrational beliefs and expectations that fuel parental bereavement guilt include "I must be perfect in everything I do," "My child's needs should always come before my own," and "I must always feel love for my child." Once the irrational belief has been identified the bereaved parent can be helped to change it into something more realistic and therefore less guilt producing.

Another method for reducing guilt is to focus on the positives in the relationship and experiences with the child who died. Although legitimate guilt must be admitted to, parents should be instructed to focus on the positive things they did, felt, and thought about the child during her lifetime, during the illness, or at death. This focus can be consciously sought whenever the parent concentrates on guilty thoughts or minimizes the positives that did exist in the relationship.

Guilt may also be mitigated through altruistic efforts to help others or contribute to society in some way. By turning the tragedy of the child's death into a social movement to help others, parents may find some meaning in the situation and reduce their feelings of guilt at the same time.

Normalizing the ambivalence and guilt in human relationships can be exceptionally helpful in ameliorating some of the effects of personal guilt. Parents may need assurance that previous ambivalence about the child did not cause the death. Identifying unrealistic social expectations that fuel parental guilt and fail to recognize normal human ambivalence can also be very therapeutic. Spiritual beliefs may assist the parents in accepting their lack of perfection, and also allow them to attribute some meaning to the death and to hope for a reunion after death.

Self-punishment or self-defeating thoughts or behaviors must be confronted. The support of a nonjudgmental significant other will go a long way in assisting bereaved parents to put their guilt in perspective.

The Parent's Relationship to the Child

Parents may have trouble resolving their grief when their attachments to the child are less than ideal. They may have feelings of ambivalence or anger towards the child that are quite normal, given the burdens of child rearing and of coping with loss, but develop guilt because of social expectations. Even though no one can be a perfect parent at all times, there is no social support for normal parental ambivalence. Additionally, a parent may also have overidentified with the lost child, especially if the child occupied the same place in the family as the parent did, was the same sex as the parent, took on roles similar to the parent's childhood roles, fit in with the parent's neurotic problems, or symbolized something extraordinary for the parent (Raphael, 1983). Because the relationship with a child may be as ambivalent or conflicted as any relationship with an adult, parental grief must be evaluated in light of each parent's unique history with the child.

The Severity of Parental Bereavement

Because of the factors cited earlier, parents' grief responses tend to be more intense than those of other mourners. This increases the likelihood that they will feel they are going crazy or are out of control. The social isolation they are subjected to may exacerbate their perception of losing touch with reality. Parents may find themselves searching the obituaries to find other young children in order to assure themselves that others share their fate. Or they may have a particularly bad time on the day of the week or at the time of the day the child died, having an unconscious feeling that if they can stop those times from occurring, they will be able to stop the death from having happened. (This is similar to an anniversary reaction, and it resurrects acute feelings of grief.)

It is often unrecognized that parents must "grow up with the loss," in a grieving process spanning the years. The times at which their child would have graduated, gotten married, or had children are often marked by upsurges in grief. Since parents are rarely prepared for these occurrences, and frequently are not aware of their source, they may feel they are acting abnormally or have not adequately addressed their grief. For this reason, parents need to have this phenomenon explained to them in advance.

There is also some evidence that parental bereavement may not necessarily decrease linearly over time. In a study by Rando (1983), 78% of the bereavement variables measured decreased in intensity during the second year of mourning and then increased in intensity in the third year. Denial appeared to rise each year, while guilt declined steadily. There was a steady increase in atypical grief responses over each of the 3 years following the death and a steady decrease of the percentage of parents experiencing high adjustment. Interestingly, there appeared to be little change in anger or hostility over time. This analysis indicates that time does not necessarily provide full relief from symptoms, and that there are significant fluctuations in the bereavement experience.

The Search for Meaning

The search for the causes and meaning of the death is especially important to parents who have lost a child. It is seen as an essential component of the parental grief process (Craig, 1977; Miles & Crandall, 1983). Especially because of the role of the parent and the unnaturalness of the child's predeceasing the parent, bereaved parents are often left with overwhelming questions. Some of the questions can be answered. How the death took place can be answered medically or seen as a direct consequence of a given action. Bereaved parents need to answer questions of causes as much as possible, so they can deal with their guilt and sense of failure. However, the reason it happened, the understanding of how it fits into the scheme of life, is more difficult to come up with. Why children must suffer and die is a question that few can answer satisfactorily unless responding on the basis of some faith or belief. Reasons that cannot be understood have to be assimilated as that— something that cannot be comprehended, but must be accepted. Accepting the fact that there is a reason, although unknown, is the therapeutic step that frequently helps bereaved parents cope with the unfathomable.

It would be a mistake to assume that all parents remain bitter and resentful after the death of their child. Despite the everlasting grief with which they must contend, many parents have reported growth responses following the death of their child. The most commonly reported ones in a small, circumscribed study by Miles and Crandall (1983) were having a stronger faith, being more compassionate and caring towards others, and living life more fully because of an increased awareness of its preciousness and fragility. Negative outcomes were reported, but were less frequent: being unable to resolve the loss, having a negative and meaningless view of life, and feeling that life had stopped. Although this study is not very generalizable, it does suggest that even in situations of the

most devastating grief mourners can find some meaning in loss
and can channel their pain and rage into endeavors that contribute
to their personal recovery and assist society.

Miscarriage, Stillbirth, Neonatal Death, and Sudden Infant Death Syndrome

There are unique issues that arise in the loss of a fetus, a stillbirth, or the death of an infant. Frequently these losses fail to be
socially legitimized or supported because it is not understood that
the relationship to a child begins long before birth. From the moment of conception, whether the child is desired or not, there are
positive and negative feelings attached to the image of the child.
They multiply and intensify during the period of gestation. Mothers
seem to be more able to form a bond with the child quickly because
they carry the child and feel it develop within them. However,
many fathers begin to cathect to the image of their child from the
time the news of the pregnancy is delivered. As the fetus develops
within the woman, and body changes occur and movements can
be felt, the father may participate more actively in his bonding
with the unborn child.

The fantasized baby may represent to the parent-to-be a number of either positive things, such as a way to share love with
another or to perpetuate the family line, or negative things, such
as a way to resolve an intrapsychic conflict or to gain a weapon in
a relationship. Whatever the baby may represent, it is the object
of the feelings, thoughts, and fantasies of his parents. Therefore,
even prior to the birth, there is definitely some relationship that
exists in the hearts and minds of parents with regard to the unborn
child. If the baby dies, there still is a relationship and a host of
hopes and feelings that must be grieved for.

Miscarriage (spontaneous abortion)

Up to 25% of all pregnancies end in miscarriages, and others
are terminated because of such conditions as diabetes, eclampsia,
or twinning (Shaw, 1983). Despite this, little clinical attention has
been paid to the grief reactions that result. A miscarriage is even
less defined as a loss than is a stillbirth, or neonatal or sudden
infant death. The fetus, according to many social and legal definitions, was never an actual human being. But most parents-to-be
are invested in the blood and tissue that would have become their
child. Maternal grief has been found to be the same for miscarriage
as for a stillborn child or the death of a neonate (Peppers & Knapp,
1980; Stack, 1980). An example of grief following miscarriage is
offered by Raphael (1983). A 24-year-old woman, Sandra, describes
her grief in her own words:

They said it was nothing . . . just a miscarriage. I was only a few weeks overdue. I had seen those pictures, and I know it was only tiny, but it was *my baby*, and it counted as a real baby.

I wanted to see it, but really all there was was blood. They say I couldn't see anything in that. When I got home I cried and cried and they couldn't understand. Jim tried to comfort me. He kept on saying it would be alright because we could have another baby right away. But that was another baby—it wasn't the same at all. It was *this* baby I was crying for, and there'd never be another one just the same as it. . . . Some days I would think of how it would have been—a little boy or a little girl.

Anyway, my tears went. I was a bit sad again now and then. Each month I used to think, *now* the baby would have been this big; *now* I would have been feeling the movements; *now* it would have been due. I felt a failure until I became pregnant again and then it faded. Really, I got over it alright when you look back. But it wasn't "nothing." For me I really did lose a baby—not just a miscarriage. (pp. 236-237)

Several important issues are highlighted by this case example:
- Although the embryo hadn't developed, it was still a baby in the mind of the mother.
- There was a need to validate the life that was lost and to perceive the loss, i.e., to see what there was of the baby.
- There was a genuine grief reaction consequent to the miscarriage, especially since the child was desired.
- The grief was triggered by thoughts of how the baby *would* have been, or *could* have been.
- The mother felt like a failure because of her inability to deliver a live, healthy child and because of the failure of anticipated body changes to occur.

Normal grief symptoms can be expected after a miscarriage. Typically, guilt is a common feeling, even more so than anger or frustration. Seibel and Graves (1980) found that 25% of the women in their study felt they were responsible for the miscarriage. This parallels clinical observations that often couples attribute the miscarriage to something they have done. In such cases factual information about the probable cause of the abortion should be supplied, emphasizing the reality that pregnancies are not that easily terminated (Shaw, 1983). Previous feelings of ambivalence about the pregnancy also escalate guilt feelings, and other grief reactions such as sadness, anger, and resentment may be present. They all will require processing. The couple needs to share their fantasies, thoughts, and feelings about the unborn child in order to effectively complete the mourning process. Otherwise, unresolved loss can lead to pathological grief.

A point must be made here about abortions. Whether they are

elective or therapeutic abortions, there is still the loss of a child involved. Additionally, social and psychological factors contributing to the decision to have an abortion may complicate the grief experience: the psychological and physical health of the mother, poor social support and environment, ambivalent feelings about the pregnancy, guilt. After an elective abortion society usually gives a covert message to the woman that she should be pleased and relieved rather than sad, failing to recognize that the two diverse emotions may coexist (Raphael, 1983). Distress and sadness may initially be denied by the woman, since she feels that they are incompatible with the decision she has made. She needs to understand that even though the decision to have an abortion is made and acted upon, it in no way dismisses her ambivalence about the choice. Both sets of feelings will need to be processed in the grief period. Even among those who uphold the right of the woman to make such a decision there may be a feeling that they have "killed" their child. This, plus society's lack of recognition that abortion is traumatic, may contribute to lower self-esteem and depression for the woman consequent to the abortion. Failure to resolve the loss of a child in this way may lead to behavioral acting out of the conflicts, perhaps in repeated abortions and unplanned pregnancies. The theme of guilt is common, and some women develop a self-destructive lifestyle that may be a form of self-punishment.

Stillbirth
With stillbirths other issues arise. The mother has been able to keep the child for a longer period of time, so there has been more opportunity for intensified bonding. Some women have gone through the whole pregnancy only to have the child die right before its completion. In addition, the woman may have had to continue carrying the damaged or dead child until the natural onset of labor.

It is often difficult for the woman to return home after hospitalization, for she has nothing to show for all those months of "work," for all the changes her body went through. There may be anxiety about seeing the room that had been prepared for the baby, confusion about what to do with baby shower gifts, and a dread of making the necessary explanations to others. Those outside of the family often do not comprehend the loss and assume there will be no grief, for while the baby had been very much a part of the lives of the mother and family, it had not even existed for others. This isolates the parents and family from support.

It is critical for siblings to be involved in mourning, for they too had hopes and feelings about the child's coming to join their family. Young children will need sensitive and factual information about the loss, for they may erroneously assume responsibility for the death as a consequence of previous jealous and angry feelings towards the new child. They may experience profound guilt. All children will require support in completing their grief work because it will be exceptionally difficult for them to separate from a sibling they have never seen. (See "The Grief of Children" in this chapter for more on dealing with children's grief and Chapter 12 for more on the loss of a family member.)

Parents' feelings can be expected to span all possible grief reactions. As with miscarriage, a stillborn baby raises the issue of the parents' defectiveness in producing a baby that cannot survive. Especially with the woman, there is a feeling that she is damaged and has failed to prove her womanhood by her inability to conceive and deliver a healthy baby. Fathers, too, can feel guilt over having impregnated their wives and contributed to the emotional turmoil the couple currently experiences. It is not uncommon for couples to believe that sexual activity during pregnancy caused the stillbirth. As with parents of older children who die, questions about the couple's competency as parents and feelings of guilt, inadequacy, and defectiveness arise. Fantasies about certain thoughts or feelings causing the death add to the normal parental guilt. There additionally can be problems in the marital relationship, or with the entire family. Future parenting may be affected. There may be a profound disturbance of mothering a subsequent child (Lewis & Page, 1978); overprotection of remaining or subsequent children (Rickarby, Single, & Raphael, Note 6); or opposition to having other children and choosing to become permanently sterilized (Wolff, Nielson, & Schiller, 1970).

Fathers are often ignored during mourning, even more than they may be following the death of an older child. Many fathers dismiss or underestimate their own grief, and receive little social support because of it. This may be especially true because the focus of people's concern may be the physical health of the mother. The father may also have to make decisions about his wife's care and burial of the child, which adds even more stress.

Mourning may be made more difficult for the mother by her physical condition. It reminds her that she has given birth, but there is no child and only empty arms. She feels that part of herself has died with the baby (Wilson & Soule, 1981). Additionally, there are hormonal and physical changes that contribute to her emotional responses and make her grief more intense.

Because the mother's physical condition may keep her from immediately participating in the funeral, it makes sense to attempt to postpone it so she can be involved and gain the therapeutic benefits possible. (See Chapter 7 for more on funerary rituals.) In addition, especially when the child was dead at or shortly after birth, parents require some validation and confirmation of the child's existence. Mothers trying to orient themselves following a stillbirth or the death of a child in the first 24 hours of life were found to be most vulnerable about their needs to see or touch the child, reach out to others for emotional support, and test their own feelings against the perceptions of others (Davidson, 1977). Without this, they were found to resort to bizarre behavior in an attempt to avoid the chronic disorientation that arose. In the study, one woman was found to weigh vegetables to find one that had the identical weight and height of the child she had given birth to but had never been allowed to hold. Until the loss could be made real to her by holding such an object, she continued to search for what she had lost.

In treating individuals who are mourning a stillbirth, the therapeutic task is to counteract the unreality of the child's existence that impedes mourning. Lewis and Page (1978) suggest that parents be encouraged to look at or hold their dead baby; help lay out their dead baby; take an active part in the certification of the stillbirth; and name the child and provide it with a memorable funeral. Burial in a common and nameless grave should be avoided; there should be a ritual to mark the loss and a personalized place for the remains. Siblings should be included in this funeral ritual. In helping bereaved parents, Lewis and Page ask direct questions about the stillbirth and help the parents create memories designed to make the baby more real in their minds so they can mourn her. With other bereavements there is much to remember and memories can be shared and cried over; but with stillbirth there is little to talk about and few to discuss, cry, and share it with. The parents are isolated and often find themselves avoiding contact with others because of unconscious feelings of shame and guilt. This deprives them of the opportunity to talk about the loss, which would aid their mourning.

Perhaps one of the most important points that must be made to the parents who have experienced a stillbirth is that they have just as much right to grieve as any other parent. No matter how brief their baby's life, they did have a child, a child who died. Unfortunately, stillbirth is seen by society as less tragic than the loss of a child. It is considered an "unfortunate occurrence," but one that can be rectified through a replacement child, something rarely felt when an older child dies. As a result, parents whose infants have died before birth are often not considered to be parents. This, coupled with the lack of memories of the child, makes it more difficult for parents to define themselves as parents and to feel their grief is justified. They need to remember and review their thoughts and feelings about the child from the very beginning of the pregnancy to make it seem real.

Neonatal Death

A neonatal death shares many of the same characteristics of bereavement as stillbirth. However, in this case the parents have a limited opportunity to know and experience the real, live child. They have something besides fantasy to relate to. Unfortunately, their experiences with the child may be painful, as the child may be critically ill and attached to strange machinery, and they may have to make treatment decisions that later cause them regret. But despite this, parents need to be made aware of the child's condition as soon as possible and allowed to see, hold, and interact with the baby and be involved in its care. Separation from the child should be minimized, although treatment in neonatal nurseries may require it. When this is true, visiting hours should be unlimited and as much contact as possible should be provided for parents to view and experience their child.

As in the case of a stillbirth, the importance of viewing and holding the infant after death also cannot be overemphasized. In far too many hospitals the practice has been to whisk the infant away from the mother and to provide no explanation of what occurred or what would happen to the remains. This practice often stems from the concern that allowing parents to see the dead child is detrimental to their later adjustment. In reality, the reverse is true. While viewing the baby may be upsetting, it is critical for parents to have this experience. They should not be sedated when this occurs, for holding and spending time with the dead baby helps bring the reality of the loss into focus, even if it is painful. Fantasies are often far worse than reality and the inability to conceptualize the lost child will make grief resolution much more difficult. Interestingly, one investigator observed that parents would examine their dead baby in close detail, finding familial resemblances and engaging in the same processes of identification observed to follow live births. This enabled the parents to be able to both incorporate the baby as a tangible loved object that was a part of themselves and separate from it as well (Montgomery, Note 7). Even in situations where the baby is deformed it is important that parents view the child. It is not uncommon for parents to find some beauty in even the most deformed child and it provides them with the necessary experience to make the event real.

Fathers are often expected to make decisions about the disposition of the remains of the child. Frequently they are advised to make these decisions without consulting the mother in an attempt to spare her any more trauma. This forces the husband to suppress his own grief and robs him of the chance to share with his wife the experiences of making decisions about the child's funeral and grieving together. Additionally, the women are usually very resentful at being prohibited from making decisions for their child's burial. When funeral services are held prior to their release from the hospital, they can become quite hostile towards their spouse and interpret his actions as a statement of lack of love for the child.

The mourning process will involve the parents' repeatedly going over the details of the pregnancy, the birth, and the child's short life. Their sense of helplessness at watching their child, their anger at hospital personnel, and all of the other feelings that the experience creates will have to be worked through so they can relinquish the lost baby. The cause of death will be very important to these parents, and information should be related honestly, factually, and as completely as possible to them.

Research findings suggest that grief and mourning after neonatal loss may be intense, but are by no means indicative of pathology. When pathological outcomes do occur, they appear to arise from highly ambivalent attachment to the child, failure to come to terms with the reality of the death, suppression of grief, failure of social support, and the reawakening of the grievers' unresolved feelings of helplessness, inadequacy, and irrational guilt (Raphael, 1983).

Sudden Infant Death Syndrome

Sudden infant death syndrome (SIDS) is the leading cause of the deaths of infants between 1 week and 1 year of age in the United States, accounting for 8,000 to 10,000 deaths annually (May & Breme, 1982-83). This particular type of loss often involves a major crisis for the bereaved family and any number of symptoms of unresolved grief, including family disruption, general symptomatology and distress, psychosomatic reactions, depression and other psychiatric illnesses, changes in interpersonal relationships, both within the family and outside of it, and parenting problems with subsequent children. There are five unique features of a SIDS loss that complicate the grief and actually "victimize" the parents and family members left behind (Markusen, Owen, Fulton, & Bendiksen, 1977-78):

- *Suddenness.* There was absolutely no opportunity to prepare for the loss.
- *Absence of a definite cause.* This prevents a complete definition of the situation by family and caregivers and consequently increases the likelihood of intense guilt, since parents are given no rationale to feel blameless and others can create doubts through criticism of parental care or insinuations about their actions.
- *Problematic grief reactions.* The intense and critical mother-infant bond is abruptly severed. This, plus the possibility that such a loss is the first experience with death that many

young married couples encounter, creates an extremely intense and harsh grief experience for the mother. There are similar problems with the father-infant bond for many men. Although culturally they may be less involved at this point in time than mothers are, they still suffer from this particularly difficult grief.

- *Sibling bereavement.* Siblings suddenly must struggle with guilt over the ambivalent feelings they had had about their new sibling. Additionally, they are forced to cope with the disruption that their parents' own grief creates for the family.
- *Legal system involvement.* Because the death is sudden and of no known cause, families are forced to deal with police, medical examiners, and hospital personnel who must protect the interests of the child and the state by investigating such deaths. However, there is often an insinuation that the death was caused by some act of commission or omission on the part of the families, which places an additional burden of guilt and pain on them.

An additional complication is that the infant dies at a time when the family is still oriented to taking care of the infant. The abrupt absence of the baby and the futility of the parenting role that has been negated increases the overwhelming nature of the loss. Guilt, such a difficult issue for all parents who lose children, is often perpetuated by all five of the factors cited. For this reason, it is absolutely critical to provide parents with appropriate information about what is known and not known about SIDS so they do not internalize more guilt.

The grief after a SIDS death is very intense for all family members. The mother often feels that her child has been torn from her. Searching for the baby and preoccupation with his image are strong components of this grief. Anger, frustration, and irritability with others are common. The entire family is disrupted, not only because of individual grief responses, but because the intense grief of the mother often renders her unable to provide any of the other nuturant functions in the family. Children are bewildered, communication is disrupted. "The loss of the baby seems to cut at the heart of the family life" (Raphael, 1983, p. 260).

The SIDS Family Adjustment Scale identifies the critical tasks for adjustment following SIDS death (May & Breme, 1982-83). The family is rated on a 5-point continuum ranging from a maladaptive response indicative of poor adjustment to a highly adaptive response associated with good adjustment. The areas rated are:

- *Communication of feelings within the family.* The more open communication is permissible, the better the possibilities for successful readjustment.

- *Lifestyle resumption.* The degree of resumption of usual individual and family activities measures individual and family adjustment.
- *Use and perception of community and family support.* Families who can utilize outside support seem to have better bereavement outcomes.
- *SIDS information.* Provision of factual information about SIDS to the family immediately after the death can help to prevent subsequent emotional problems.
- *Preventability.* If the cause of death is believed to have been preventable, the grief process will probably be prolonged; if the death is considered to have been unpreventable, it may be shorter, but intense.
- *Subsequent children.* If the decision to have subsequent children is not made through thorough and rational discussion, the "replacement syndrome" may be in operation.
- *Religion.* It appears that families having a deep religious orientation and spiritual values achieve a better emotional adjustment to the death than families without similar religious convictions.
- *Family morbidity.* The number of physical symptoms observed in family members may reveal blocked or incomplete emotional expression of grief.
- *Infant centrality.* Preoccupation with the deceased infant may indicate failure to appropriately decathect and unresolved grief.
- *Family emotional health.* Extreme emotional dysfunction and lability are concomitants of ongoing grieving and indicate a failure of resolution at the time of assessment.
- *Functional role of infant in the family.* The assigned role of the infant in the family (e.g , marriage stabilizer, family heir) may give an indication of the functioning and needs of the family system
- *Family solidarity.* The perceived closeness of family members following the SIDS death indicates the possibilities for successful grief resolution and identifies the need for emotional support that exists at the time. In families that were well-adjusted before the death, increased closeness will enhance the resolution of grief.

Families should be regarded as mourners of a sudden, unanticipated death, and treated with strategies appropriate to resolution of this type of grief. (See "Psychological Factors" in Chapter 3 for more on the effects of sudden death and "Intervention Strategies" in Chapter 5 for treatment strategies.) They will need confirmation of the death through the funeral and mourning rituals, and repeated opportunities to talk about the loss. Social support is critical in order to validate the child's existence and to provide comfort to the family.

The Question of Having Another Child

For many couples who have lost a child, the question of whether or not to have another will inevitably arise. If the couple does not have an older child that they have successfully raised, they may question their ability to produce a normal, healthy child or to protect and care for one. The following points must be kept in mind when helping a couple decide whether or not, or when, to have another child.

- The couple must have achieved some resolution of the loss of the deceased child. They must have successfully reviewed their fantasized and real relationship with the child, and relinquished their hold on her. They should not feel that they need to have another child to resolve their grief.
- The couple should conceive the child because they want to have a child, not to prove that they can produce a healthy baby or resolve their lingering guilt.
- The couple must consider all the pros and cons for having another child at this time.
- Any pregnancy that stems from a desire to avoid dealing with the grief of the first child's death will create serious psychological problems from the beginning.
- Any pregnancy that is meant to alleviate the stress between marital partners or among family members subsequent to the death of the first child is equally doomed to failure.
- Before having a child, the couple should show by their actions that they clearly understand that the new child will involve a new pregnancy, need a new name, and will be a unique person with her own needs and wants. The new child should not be seen as a surrogate for the deceased child.
- When a new child arrives, the parents will understandably be concerned about her welfare, but they must recognize the dangers in being overprotective in an attempt to avoid what happened to the deceased child.

Parents should be told that research indicates that, for couples who have lost a child to SIDS, there may be some difficulty in the woman's becoming pregnant and carrying the child full term (Mandell & Wolfe, 1975; Markusen et al., 1977-78). When the new baby does arrive, family members should be prepared to experience a combination of both joy and pain. If at this time or during the pregnancy there appears to be a need for family members to talk or there is evidence of undue conflict or symptoms suggestive of unresolved grief, help should be offered or an appropriate referral should be made.

Treatment Recommendations for Parental Grief

So far the focus has been on the factors that make parental bereavement such a unique stress. This knowledge is necessary so techniques are not misapplied, expectations are appropriate, and opportunities to intervene are not missed. But there are also some specific interventions for grief resolution besides those normally used that are particularly effective for working with bereaved parents. The following interventions are meant to help mourners clarify their expectations for grief, adjust their parental and marital roles, and develop coping skills.

Clarifying Expectations for Grief

• Tell parents that research data suggest parental bereavement may not automatically decrease with time (Rando, 1983). Help them develop appropriate expectations for the course of their grief.

• Help parents to see that the age of the child is inconsequential to their being bereaved, but that it will determine some of the issues that arise during the bereavement. Especially try to legitimize grief for parents who grieve for a miscarriage, stillbirth, or neonatal or SIDS death. Too often there is a social negation of this type of loss.

• Make it clear to parents that not only do they have to grieve for the loss of their child, but also for the loss of their hopes, dreams, and expectations for that child. They must grieve for what they have lost individually, as a couple, and as a family.

• Make sure parents understand that just because they have lost the same child does not mean they experience the same loss or will grieve the same way.

• Assist parents in developing the proper perspective on what resolution of their grief will mean. They will never forget the death, the emptiness will remain, but the pain can diminish and they can learn to live with the tragedy. However, they will not remain unchanged. They will survive, but they will not be the same as before the loss.

• Predict for parents upsurges of grief at specific points in time, e.g., when the child would have graduated or gotten married, when it is September and all of the rest of the children are returning to school.

Adjusting the Parental Role

• Challenge some of the unrealistic expectations parents may harbor about themselves as parents, such as the idea that they could have protected their child from everything. Help them to work through their guilt and find ways to forgive themselves for failing to live up to societal expectations for perfect parenting. Then identify with them ways to make the tragedy meaningful and channel their intense feelings.

• Show parents that their relationship with the child was unique, and not just determined by their role as parents. The personal attributes of the child and parents, as well as their specific roles in the family, make each loss idiosyncratic.

• Provide parents with information about family reorganization after the death of a family member. (See Chapter 12 for more on this topic.) Work with them to make sure they do not abandon the remaining children or place them in unhealthy or replacement roles. Give the parents information about how to communicate with the surviving children and help those children with their grief. (See "The Grief of Children" in this chapter for more on this topic.)

• Assist parents in disengaging themselves from the parental role with the deceased child while maintaining this role with the surviving children.

Adjusting the Marital Relationship

• Assist men in dealing with the socially conditioned responses that block grief resolution. Give men permission to grieve and help them learn how to cry; encourage discussion with other fathers; support the idea that the father cannot "fix" everything despite his roles as protector and problem-solver. Too often the father attempts to protect his family from the effects of grief, both his and their own. It must be made clear that this is unrealistic and unhealthy. Help men to see that changes in their spouse's responses are not related to them or the family, but are reactions to the grief. Suggest physical activity as a method of release of anger, frustration, and other responses to the grief. As society becomes more androgenous, these traditional issues for men can be expected to be increasingly seen in women as well.

• Help women to express their feelings of anger, which have traditionally been suppressed. Also give them a perspective on the socially conditioned male response to grief so they can understand it and not interpret it as a lack of love for them, the deceased child, or other family members.

• Make it clear to the couple that they cannot overestimate the effects of grief on their relationship. Help them with the normal tendency to place blame on each other and, if this cannot be worked through, refer them for appropriate therapy. Encourage communication and understanding of problems due to the grief process. Help them cope with unmet expectations when they grieve in different ways and have different interests. They must recognize that recovery will proceed for each of them in different areas at different times. However, they also need to remember that despite such differences, and the volatile feelings resulting from the loss, they still love each other. They must treat each other as very fragile people who will require patience and understanding in order to survive and recover from the loss together.

• Help couples recognize that grief probably will have an impact on their sexual relationship for a while, and that this is unrelated to their feelings of love for one another.

• Explain to the couple that grief will change both of them and consequently will result in a different relationship in the marriage. This does not have to be a negative change, but there must be a recognition that some changes will occur as a result of the major loss. They will not be the same people after the loss as before.

Teaching Coping Skills

• Parents must be advised to take life one step at a time. The loss of the child may be so overwhelming that they feel they will not be able to continue to survive, so they must break down the future into small discrete steps of an hour or a day, and focus only on each step.

• Help parents create appropriate rituals for the therapeutic expression of grief.

• Work with parents to reestablish a sense of meaning in their lives. Help them to answer those questions that can be answered and to accept the fact that some will never be answered or understood. They need to learn to live with what is unknown and to believe that there may be reasons for the death that we cannot be aware of.

• Assist parents in expressing their needs to others. Many people want to be supportive, but are at a loss for what to do. Bereaved parents, even though they are grieving, may have to be the ones to take the first step to reach out to others.

• Have the parents write a journal to complete the necessary process of review. The possibility of forgetting even the smallest detail of the child's life is a great fear for them. Consequently, a journal will allow them to record all the details of the child's life from the moment of awareness of pregnancy through the day of death. Pictures, remembrances of friends and relatives, thoughts and feelings that occur to them can all be included. The negative as well as the positive acts of the child should be included in order to remember her as she really was. The parents can be encouraged to pour out their feelings to the child and tell her of their anger, guilt, love for her, and longing for her. Finishing unfinished business can be facilitated by writing down such things as what they wish they had said or not said, done or not done; what they wished the child would have done or not done; what they are regretful, angry, or resentful about; what they remember fondly; and what they still owe the child, and what the child still owes them, to finish the relationship.

• Encourage parents to give themselves permission to take a break from their grief to enjoy their other children and other aspects of their lives. Help them to see this is not a betrayal of the deceased child.

• Enourage parents to adopt coping strategies that are active and externally directed, as these have been found to be most useful to parental adjustment. In her study Videka-Sherman (1982) found that altruism and investment in a new role or meaningful activity both preceded reduction in depression of bereaved parents. The least adaptive coping mechanisms were found to be escape by not thinking about the death or using drugs or alcohol, and persistent preoccupation with the deceased child.

• Point out to others that the older parents of the adult child who dies may be in a uniquely vulnerable situation, as most of the support will be given to the child's spouse or children, and not to the parents. In some cases they may fear losing their grandchildren after their own child has died. When a grandchild dies, grandparents also may be in a difficult position, as they see their own child suffering with the loss and there is nothing they can do.

• Refer the parents to the nearest chapter of The Compassionate Friends, a self-help group for bereaved parents.* Through mutual sharing, support, modeling, learning that they are not "going crazy," and helping others, parents are supported in their grief. This is especially important for bereaved parents, as they often have trouble gaining needed emotional and social support for the expression and resolution of their grief. (See "Psychological Factors" in Chapter 3 for more on the benefits of the self-help process to the bereaved.)

GRIEF AFTER THE DEATH OF A SPOUSE

There appears to be relatively more social understanding of the sequelae of the loss of a spouse than any other loss. It is not as uncommon an event as the death of a child is. Much of our knowledge about bereavement comes from investigations of conjugal loss. Indeed, the majority of women in our country can expect to be widowed in their lifetime.

In the last several decades in the United States the number of

---

*For information on the location of The Compassionate Friends chapters write to The Compassionate Friends, P.O. Box 1347, Oak Brook, Illinois 60521.

widows relative to widowers has increased until now there is a 4½ or 5:1 ratio (Berardo, Note 8). The three factors accounting for this are that mortality among women is lower than among men and therefore larger numbers of women survive to advanced years; wives are typically younger than their husbands and consequently have a greater probability of outliving their mates; and, among the widowed, remarriage rates are considerably lower for women than men (Berardo, 1968).

Up until recently the empirical research that was available on sex differences in bereavement appeared to be mixed in results. However, an extensive review of the bereavement literature that controlled for many confounding variables has just been reported (Stroebe & Stroebe, 1983) and concludes that, if there is a sex difference in conjugal bereavement reactions, it is the men who suffer more both physically and psychologically. They also found evidence of a sex difference in the period of the highest risk after the death. Widowers appeared most vulnerable shortly after bereavement, while widows reached the peak of their risk during the second or third year of bereavement.

In the Harvard Bereavement Study, Glick et al. (1974) examined the contrasts in the experiences of widows and widowers, providing some insight into the differences in experiences of the two sexes. They noted that men and women reacted similarly to the immediate loss of the loved one. However, men responded differently than women to the traumatic disruption of their lives. Men tended to define their experience as a "dismemberment," while women tended to emphasize a sense of "abandonment." Widowers were more likely than widows to be uncomfortable with the direct emotional expression of grief and seemed to require more rational justification for their thoughts and feelings. The widower appeared to make more rapid social recovery than the widow, but it was suggested that emotional reaction seemed to center around realism and control. This is evident in the findings that, compared to women, men were more unable or unwilling to display grief; stopped displaying any emotional signs of grief sooner after the death; were initially higher in guilt, which then decreased; and were more realistic and quicker to accept the death. After the death men required more assistance in coping with the practical problems resulting from the death, such as obtaining help with the housework and children, while women appeared to require more assistance in coping with their emotional responses.

Other studies have been done, most of them focusing on widows. The status of widowhood has long been known to entail a variety of social problems. This makes it hard to determine which problems are due to the loss and which are due to other problems. Some of the problems are associated with aging, since a majority of the widows are older. Serious economic problems frequently result in the widow and her family having to exist in below-average economic circumstances. For example, in one study approximately 70% of the men who died left their families without a will, and on the average family income decreased 44% (Healy, Note 5). Widows often have trouble getting well-paying jobs because of their long absence from the labor market, discrimination towards older women, and disproportionate employment in low-paying jobs. Then there are the many problems that come with single parenthood. Finally, widows have higher death rates, a greater incidence of mental disorders, and higher suicide rates than their married counterparts (Berardo, 1968). These social problems magnify the stresses and secondary losses experienced by the widow.

The traditional social attitudes towards American widows have posed some particularly difficult stresses for them to overcome subsequent to their loss. Lopata (1970) notes that the American and European cultures, with their emphasis on mate selection based on love and the exclusivity and privacy of marriage, plus the nuclearization of the family, have thrust the widow into a unique situation. As the importance of marriage increases in these societies, there is a corresponding decrease in the importance of other relationships. The couple bears most of the burden of emotional, social, and economic support alone. When the spouse dies, there is no strong kinship system or set of traditions to which the widow can turn and know she can receive support. She is additionally handicapped in her quest to build a new life by the fact that she frequently had been discouraged from developing the needed competencies to socially and financially manage a career, family, and home. As a result, she often finds herself less competent in social and economic matters than she needs to be following the death of her husband.

Widows also are victims of stigmatization. They tend to be socially ostracized, as they make others feel uncomfortable and are very threatening to other women whose husbands are still alive. It is not uncommon for best friends to drift apart after one of them becomes widowed, as the friend who is still married will be less inclined to include her friend in social events. Therefore the social life of widows tends to diminish, while it may expand for widowers. Widowers are perceived as less of a threat, and they have more women available to choose from for remarriage because women tend to live longer.

There are a number of reasons why the woman experiences more change than the man following the death of a spouse. In her study Lopata (1973b) found that these changes were dependent on the extent of the woman's involvement with her husband and the strength of the bonds they had, in addition to the number of varied sets of relationships the woman had with him. First, the woman loses a partner with whom she has shared the process of defining the world. Frequently this results in the widow's trying to imagine what the husband would do in certain circumstances if he were alive, which becomes increasingly difficult over time. Then, the widow has to reformulate her identity, which is exceedingly difficult, especially if she has lived her life doing things "for him." In such a case the widow has lost the object of her work, as well as the partner in her life. As the widow develops a new identity, she may have to seek new friends to support it, ones who understand what she is experiencing. Her task of redefinition is made harder by the fact that there is little general tolerance for her grief and there are few role models to follow (Vachon, 1976). Finally, she has lost a social link between herself and society. In a culture that has traditionally only reinforced a woman's identity as part of a couple, the widow may now be lost. She is forced to deal with feelings of incompetence, incompleteness, and isolation, as well as with the other normal components of grief.

An additional problem is that women have historically been socialized to be passive and therefore tend to lack the tools for the development of new social roles and friendships. These factors have made loneliness one of the greatest problems of the widowed. There may be many forms of loneliness, as suggested by Lopata (1973a):

- Loneliness as a desire to carry on interaction with the particular person who is no longer available
- Loneliness arising when a husband dies and the widow feels that she is no longer an object of love, thus losing a major source of her identity
- Loneliness due to the absence of anyone to care for or to be the recipient of love
- Loneliness for a companion relationship of the depth provided by the deceased, for the sharing of experiences with another human being
- Loneliness for the presence of another human being in the home
- Loneliness as unhappiness over the absence of another person to share the workload or carry out tasks that the widow cannot or does not wish to do
- Loneliness as a longing for the previous lifestyle or some set of activities formerly carried out with the deceased
- Loneliness as alienation due to a drop in status and/or disengagement from a prior lifestyle and set of relations as a result of the husband's death
- Loneliness as a result of rifts in social relations with long-time friends
- Loneliness as the consequence of an inability to make new friends

- Loneliness as a combination of any of the previously mentioned forms

Techniques to deal with these forms of loneliness fall into the categories of keeping busy, developing new roles and relations, and focusing on one's social role. In Lopata's study, despite the loneliness, most widows preferred living alone to moving into the homes of their married children. The women said they wanted their independence. Glick et al. (1974) had a similar finding. While many widows expressed a need to have someone take over their lives, few actually relinquished their autonomy.

Interestingly, widowhood appears to be less disorganizing to the identity of the lower-class woman, since she has not devoted as much of her time and resources to constructing a world-view around the presence of (and with the help of) the man she married. Although the woman of a higher class has a closer relationship with her husband, she tends to become more disorganized when widowed, even though she possesses more resources to assist her in rebuilding her life.

Despite the many social problems of widowhood, it has been found that most widows eventually seem to adjust to their change in status, with some even deriving a good deal of pleasure from their new lives. Indeed, Lopata (1972) found that compared to when their husbands were living many widows were more independent, competent, active, and free.

The circumstances of widowhood will probably change over time as society becomes more androgenous. But at that point, as now, it will still be imperative to understand what roles and functions a particular spouse performed for the partner. It is the only way to accurately assess the symbolic losses resulting from the death of that spouse and to appreciate and understand the needs and experiences of the survivor.

In addition to the usual therapeutic interventions to facilitate appropriate grief, these specific recommendations are made for working with bereaved spouses.

- Help the griever identify those functions or roles previously assumed by the spouse that will have to be adopted by the griever or assumed by someone else in order to continue with as similar a lifestyle as possible. For example, sometimes men may need more help with domestic tasks, whereas women may require more assistance with financial planning.
- Especially with elderly widows and widowers, be aware of any consequent loss of social connection that may have been provided by the deceased. Also, when it has been necessary for the elderly couple to rely on each other to assure the adequate survival of each individually, it must be determined whether the survivor

can manage independently. If not, supportive help or, if necessary, relocation must be suggested.

• Assist the survivor in maintaining appropriate relationships with and role expectations for children. Children, especially when living at home, may have unrealistic and unhealthy expectations placed upon them by an overburdened or emotionally depleted single parent. Introduce the parent to those agencies and organizations that support single parents, such as Parents Without Partners or They Help Each Other Spiritually (THEOS).

• Provide the surviving parent with appropriate information about family dynamics (see Chapter 12) and grief in children (see "Children's Grief" in this chapter) to maximize the chances for healthy resolution of grief in individual family members and the family as a whole.

• Work towards appropriate redefinition of identity as a goal of the grief process. Whereas once there was "we," now there is "I." Help the mourner grieve these changes and make necessary adjustments. Assist the griever in learning skills needed to accomplish new role tasks, e.g., encourage the widow to take an auto repair course. Foster the development of new relationships with people who can validate and support the griever's new identity.

• Recognize that there are differences in the periods of vulnerability for widows and widowers (Stroebe & Stroebe, 1983). Widowers appear more vulnerable shortly after the bereavement, in contrast to widows, who seem this way 2 or 3 years later. Predict these periods to the bereaved to ensure appropriate expectations, without developing a self-fulfilling prophecy. Design treatment interventions to take this into account for individual mourners.

• Be aware of other sex differences between widows and widowers with regard to perception of loss, expression of grief, social versus emotional recovery from bereavement, and differing focus of needs.

• Assess the different educational, occupational, and social skills of middle-aged and older widows. Gear specific interventions and education to their needs, without failing to appreciate that the loss of their stereotypical traditional role, which you are now seeking to broaden, will constitute a major secondary loss in itself.

• As needed, refer survivors to one of the many self-help widow/widower support groups, such as Widow-to-Widow or They Help Each Other Spiritually (THEOS). Many churches and synagogues now sponsor such types of groups.

GRIEF AFTER SUICIDE

Suicide poses difficult problems in grief resolution for the surviving loved ones. Indeed, the survivors have been termed "victims" themselves. Kastenbaum (1977) notes how, although the deceased from suicide is neither more nor less dead than one who dies after a long debilitating illness, the phenomenon of suicide itself has a special set of meanings for us. Our culture perceives suicide as sinful, criminal, or a weakness or madness. In contrast, some other cultures have viewed it as "The Great Death" and there exist cultural traditions that support it as a rational alternative. Individual meanings of suicide to the suicide perpetrator may include suicide as reunion; rest and refuge; retribution; penalty for failure; or an unintentioned mistake. All of these cultural and individual meanings will affect how people respond to the suicide death of a loved one.

Schuyler (1973) discusses the additional burdens placed on suicide survivors over and above the normal trials of the grief process. The social stigma due to society's attitudes towards suicide frequently results in a lack of social and emotional support for the survivors. For example, Rudestam and Imbroll (1983) investigated the reactions of people to four different newspaper accounts of the death of a 10-year-old girl. The child was described as having died from either a bone marrow disease, an automobile accident, a barbituate overdose, or hanging. The results indicated that when the child's death was reported as being due to suicide (barbituate overdose or hanging), compared to when the child's death was from illness or accident, the child was perceived as being more emotionally disturbed and as coming from a more disturbed home environment. The child's parents were blamed more for the death and subjects were more interested in asking questions about the death when it was from suicide than when it was from accident or natural causes. This kind of lack of support jeopardizes survivors' successful resolution of the grief process. Survivors also are forced to deal with the shame for the actions of the deceased, a shame they have difficulty differentiating themselves from. And in cases of suicide, survivors usually are subjected to investigations by police, coroners, and insurance agents. These unpleasant experiences serve to strengthen negative grief responses and heighten the already existing anger at the deceased, who now is at rest but has left the survivors behind to pick up the pieces. This anger is difficult to cope with, as the deliberateness of the act fuels feelings of rejection and abandonment. Being consciously deserted by a loved one attacks the survivors' sense of worth, self-esteem, and meaning. The suddenness of the loss also precludes a period of anticipatory grief to allow feelings and unfinished business to be worked through. This further burdens the griever and leaves him suffering from the effects of the unanticipated bereavement reaction (Parkes & Weiss, 1983).

Since the death was intentioned, there is often a tendency for the survivors to blame themselves for failure to prevent the suicide. This results in one of the most marked features of grief following suicide—guilt. Guilt is exacerbated by the fact that there exists no external cause to blame it on; the death was not inevitable, caused by a disease, or brought about by an unforeseen accident. If there happens to be a sense of relief that a loved one's sufferings may now be over, the griever may subject himself to even more self-recrimination.

It is not uncommon for suicide survivors to go on to develop a fear of their own self-destructive impulses. Questions about the inheritability of suicidal tendencies frequently arise. The need to know why the death occurred, a normal search in bereavements, is especially pertinent here.

Clearly, the dynamics of a loved one's choosing to die and leave close ones behind sets up the grievers for intense feelings towards the deceased (anger and guilt) and, when combined with the normal social reaction to a suicide, intense feelings towards themselves (guilt and shame). When treating suicide survivors, it is necessary to be especially aware of the increase in these feelings, the intensity of which sets them apart from the normal bereavement reactions.

If suicide is consciously and freely chosen as an alternative to debilitating illness, there may be mediating variables that attenuate some of the survivors' grief. The suicide may be planned, and therefore expected, with time for experiencing anticipatory grief and finishing unfinished business. In such cases there is a sense of control and an answer to why the death occurred.

As an addition to the normal course of therapeutic intervention, some recommendations will now be made for working with suicide survivors.

• The guilt of the suicide survivor is especially intense. As with any griever, legitimate guilt must be constructively addressed, not dismissed; however, in suicide the survivor frequently assumes more unrealistic guilt. Normalize this for the survivor and pay special attention to dealing with it therapeutically. Help the survivor see that regardless of what he did or didn't do, he is neither responsible for nor in control of the choices of another. Watch for behaviors indicating self-punishment, self-sabotage, or unhealthy attempts at expiation and atonement.

• In the search for understanding and an effort to put the suicide in a logical chronology, the survivor may look back in time and see hints or clues about the impending suicide that make sense now in light of the death, but were then imperceptible or unrecognized. Work with the survivor to keep him from assuming undue guilt over not having acted on these clues or not having successfully prevented the suicide if they were perceived. Challenge him about whether it is realistic to have expected himself to have picked up on those clues at that time with the information that was then available.

• The anger of the suicide survivor towards the deceased, God, or the world is often more torturous and vehement because of the deliberateness of the rejection by the deceased. This must be vigorously addressed, with an emphasis on appropriate externalization of the anger. The internalization of such emotion, coupled with intense guilt, can lead to unhealthy acting-out. This must be monitored.

• The sense of rejection wrought by suicide is particularly profound. Help the survivor to identify this and the feelings about himself that arise from it. Feelings of unworthiness, as if there is something wrong or "bad" about the survivor, may develop as the survivor struggles to understand why he has been so viciously rejected. Beware of the ripple effect of these types of negative thoughts. Like secondary losses, they must be identified and worked through.

• Help the survivor identify and deal with the unfinished business that remains. Like the survivors of any sudden death, suicide survivors must cope with the sequelae of being unprepared and of lacking the opportunity to say good-bye. Such sudden deaths tend to leave the survivors with relatively more of a sense of unreality about the loss and heightened intensity of feeling.

• Suicide often leaves the survivor stigmatized. Social isolation may result because of the fact that it is a "socially unspeakable loss" (Lazare, 1979). Obituaries may be omitted, and insurance payments are often invalidated. Find ways to help the survivor to connect with others. Predict the possibility of negative social reaction, but make it clear that this stems from problems in those doing the reacting. People may wonder why the survivor's love was not enough to stop the victim from killing herself. Work with the survivor in not accepting responsibility for the actions of the deceased and not "buying into" shame or guilt.

• Encourage the survivor to hold funeral rites for the deceased. Previously such rites were often refused to those who committed suicide. However, they are critically important to the survivors of suicide, as to the survivors of any death. Help them to see that their discomfort with the mode of death need not and should not interfere with their being able to reap the psychological benefits of these funerary rituals. The postdeath activities following suicide should be kept as much as possible like those following a normal death. Work with the survivor to ensure that the unique guilt, shame, and stigma of a suicide do not deprive him of this.

- Normalize for the survivor the sense of relief that frequently comes when suicide ends a life that was filled with pain. If the relationship had placed onerous burdens and worries on the survivor, this emotional response will be quite natural. Help the survivor to see that relief always follows the end of an unhappy situation, and that it should not create more guilt. Point out that it is possible to feel relieved that something is over and yet still grieve for it. Relief at the time of death does not mean that the survivor did not love the deceased.

- Do not be surprised if the survivor evidences a fear of "contagion"—a fear that he will lose control and kill himself as did the deceased. Explain that suicide is not hereditary and is based on choice.

- The survivor will attempt to come to some understanding as to why the deceased chose the option of dying. Allow the survivor to play out different scenarios about the deceased's frame of mind, choice of method, reasoning, and decision-making process. It is a way of trying to make sense of what has happened and of working it through.

- Help the survivor undergo the necessary medical, legal, and insurance investigations that may be demanded by the mode of death. Predict the probable discomfort of these and assure the survivor that you will be available during the process, since it may generate more anger, guilt, betrayal, rejection, and other emotions of grief.

- Work with the survivor to see the deceased clearly in both her positive and negative aspects. The voluntary choosing of death, and at times the violent nature of the death, may prevent the survivor from remembering the deceased realistically. The survivor needs to have a realistic composite image of the deceased in order to recover, but this usually cannot be achieved until many of the emotions have been worked through.

- Help the survivor to see that although he may disagree with the action of the deceased in ending her life, it was her choice. Work with him to appreciate the fact that frequently it was the last and only option that was perceived by the loved one at that time. Whether or not he accepts the fact that the deceased had a right to end her life, the survivor must recognize that it was the deceased's choice, not his. Predict for him that he may accept this intellectually long before he can accept it emotionally.

- Refer the survivor to a self-help group of suicide survivors. Such groups are uniquely helpful in addressing the issues of the grief of survivors. Two such resources are Safe Place, run by the international suicide prevention group called The Samaritans, and Ray of Hope. Check with local suicide prevention centers for other available resources.

THE GRIEF OF CHILDREN

The fact that children do not continuously evidence grief in overtly visible ways erroneously leads some to believe that they do not understand the loss or recognize its implications, or else that they are not grieved by it. Nevertheless, children do mourn, even when it is not clearly evident:

> It may be, as seemed to be the case for many of the children we saw, that the grief and mourning were often intermittent. The child may initially respond as if nothing of importance has happened. At another time he may show periods of intense upset and indicate that he is missing the dead parent. At other times he may carry on happily playing as if nothing has happened. At such times the child's denial is high and his ego is not preoccupied with mourning. But this does not indicate he does not or cannot mourn. His quiet periods may also be times of lingering in memory and fantasy with the dead parent, and as such constitute part of the ebb and flow of mourning. Such rests from grief, such bouts of "shutting out" what has happened also occur in adult bereavement. There is nothing to suggest they indicate a pathological response in adult or child unless they become the predominant pattern, diminishing all reality testing. (Raphael, 1983, pp. 94-95)

Most of what is true for adults in grief also holds true in age-appropriate ways for children. Like adults, children display a variety of reactions to the death of a loved one. They go through the same types of grief as long and intensely as their adult counterparts, and have many of the same needs as adult grievers. Many of the same symptoms and issues arise, caused by many of the same variables.

There has been immense controversy over the age at which a child can legitimately be said to mourn in a process similar to an adult's. Many of the theoretical arguments about the child's capacity to mourn center around the requirements necessary for mourning. According to different theorists, variables such as complete identity formation, maintenance of object constancy, and cognitive understanding of the concepts of irreversibility, permanence, universality, and inevitability are prerequisites. Part of the problem in resolving this controversy may stem from the comparison of the child's grief to the adult model of mourning. It may well be that there needs to be a separate children's model of mourning that takes into account the child's social, developmental, and emotional context. Just because a child's response differs from an adult's does not mean that the same processes are not occurring. In fact, they very well may be, but they may appear in more child-like, immature ways. Intellectual debate may rage ad infinitum about the child's ability to classically mourn; but what is undeniable and incontrovertible is that children, even young infants, will have dramatic and long-lasting reactions to the separation from a loved one. They experience intensely painful responses that adults must understand, legitimize, and help them through.

Issues in Child Mourning

Some people feel it is wiser to protect the child from death and loss and to find ways in which to cushion its impact. Yet all the available evidence suggests that not to assist the bereaved child in actively confronting the death is to predispose him to significant pathology and life-long problems.

> Why is it important that a child master his emotional response to the loss of a loved one? First of all, not to assist a child in perceiving and understanding his responses to the most important event of his life would be to participate in denying him something of his basic birthright as a human being. In addition, psychoanalytic studies have shown that when a person is unable to complete a mourning task in childhood he either has to surrender his emotions in order that they do not suddenly overwhelm him, or else he may be haunted constantly throughout his life with a sadness for which he can never find an appropriate explanation. (Furman, 1970, p. 76)

For this reason not only must children be provided adequate intellectual explanation of the death, but they must be assisted in coping and mastering the tasks of mourning. These tasks are the same as for the adult griever. However, the unique conditions of childhood bring up some special issues that must be addressed. There are three needs of children that deserve special attention according to Furman (1970) because they are so easily overlooked. First, the small child's ability to remember a loved one in her absence may be inadequate. He may require assistance up until puberty. Pictures of the deceased, particularly those taken with the child, help the child to recall that person so that the feelings associated with her remain available for resolution. Remembrance of dates of important birthdays and anniversaries should be respected and observed by those with a surviving child in order to keep alive the memory of the deceased. Those who care for the child can remind him of the love, concern, pride, and joy that had characterized the relationship between the deceased and the child. They can share and reinforce the memories of the deceased and offer possessions as keepsakes and cherished mementos.

Second, children must grow up with the loss. Important events in the child's life will remind him of the lost loved one he misses. The "firsts" will be times when the continuing significance of the deceased's death is remembered.

Third, there is a special need of young children to have both a male and female figure to whom to respond. Consequently, a consistent surrogate for the deceased parent will be helpful to allow the child to experience and work out some of the feelings he would have had with that parent, and allow him to find out what adults of that sex are like. This does not mean that a single parent should rush into a hasty remarriage, but merely illustrates the importance of giving young children the opportunity to identify and interact with adults of both sexes. Older children often select their own parent substitutes from teachers or family friends.

There are a number of factors that can inhibit the mourning process of the child:

- The surviving parent's inability to mourn
- The surviving parent's inability to tolerate the pain of the child and to allow the child to mourn (denying his feelings and their expression)
- Fear about the vulnerability of the surviving parent and the security of the self
- The lack of the security of a caring environment
- The lack of a caring adult who can stimulate and support the mourning process
- Confusion about the death and his part in it
- Ambivalence towards the deceased parent
- Unchallenged magical thinking
- An inability to put thoughts, feelings, and memories into words
- Issues of adolescence that exacerbate normal conflicts in mourning
- Cognitive inability to accept the finality and irreversibility of the death
- Lack of opportunities to share longing, feelings, and also memories
- Instability of family life after the loss
- Reassignment of an inappropriate role and responsibilities

Mourning may take an intermittent course depending on these factors. Many children do not resolve their loss but mark time until more favorable circumstances arise and they can acknowledge the pain of loss and grief and mourn for the dead parent, e.g., when the family becomes stable and secure again, or when they form some stable relationship with a surrogate who can make them feel secure enough to express their feelings (Raphael, 1983).

It also is not uncommon for a child who has lost a loved one earlier in life to experience a reaction of grief later on and to require more working through of the loss at that time. As children grow they require new information about the death; their cognitive capacity increases, and they become intellectually, emotionally, and verbally mature enough to ask questions about the death. In effect, they will need to fill in the pieces of the story that they may have been unable to comprehend when younger. Sometimes it is only at later points in time that people recognize they are lacking information that would be important to them regarding the death of a loved one. For example, one woman recognized 45 years after the death of an infant sibling that she did not know where that sibling had been born. All of this does not constitute a pathological chronicity of grief, but illustrates that "working through" is a process that continues over time. Indeed, for both adults and children, "mourning is never really over, for new life-situations may appear at any time which evoke for the mourner aspects of the lost relationship insignificant at the time of bereavement" (Siggins, 1966, p. 18).

Bereavement at Different Ages

Raphael (1983) has synthesized the existing descriptions of childhood responses to bereavement (usually bereavement of a parent, although not always), looking at the relationships, concepts of death, and bereavement experience and responses of the child across several age groups. A summary of her findings provides a framework for understanding the bereavement of children.

The very young infant in the first months of life often cries and shows distress because of the withdrawal of vital supplies when the mother dies. Good surrogate mothering often soothes this reaction quickly.

For the infant from 4 or 5 months to 2½ years of age, bereavement may be expressed by nonspecific ongoing distress in reaction to the absence of the mother. This is probably the earliest manifestation of grief. Although this child probably lacks any true internal image of the mother, part of him responds to the absence of the mother as a specific person. There is no evidence of any internal grief work or feelings of grief, only undifferentiated precursors of emotions such as the "primary affects of unpleasure" (Engel, 1962). The deaths of other significant individuals may be experienced by the infant through reaction to the mother's grief.

The older infant, from 6 months to 2 years of age, shows the initial beginnings of grief and mourning. This child experiences separation from the mother in a way vividly described by Bowlby (1980). At first there is shock, rapidly followed by protest at the separation. This protest is designed to bring the mother back and "punish" her to prevent future repetitions. Prolonged absence and frustration of his wishes teaches the child that his protest is to no avail and despair arises. Recollection, yearning, longing, and pain ensue. These feelings may be followed by a period of withdrawal or distracting activity, as the child's immature ego cannot tolerate pining and longing for prolonged periods. Eventually the child gives up looking for the mother, no longer expecting or hoping for her return. Despair and sadness become evident, and there is a lack of interest in usually pleasurable objects and activities. This typical separation response will persist if the separation is unabated. The child will become detached from everyone if a constant and caring person does not take over. In studies where the mother returns after a separation, the child's responses reveal an image and memory of her. First denial and then eventual acceptance of and reunion with the mother occur as the child explores her and reestablishes her presence. Some of the responses displayed by bereaved children of this age are exaggerated separation responses: clinging, screaming, refusal to separate from other attachment figures, distress, and sleeping and eating disturbances. Regression may be prominent. If the reaction is to the loss of someone other than the mother, such as a father or sibling, it is difficult to tell if it is truly a reaction to the loss itself or a mirroring of and identification with maternal grief. When relationships with people other than the principle caring person are lost, two factors govern the level of response of the child: the quality and intensity of the relationship, and its significance for the mother. In the responses of the child of this age is the kernel of difficulty that all individuals face with loss:

> It is at this age that the infant is first unconsolable for his "own and only mother" whom he has lost. No other person can replace her, can take away the anguish of his screams, at least initially. So that no matter how much comfort and consolation is offered, it is not what he wants. He wants simply her. . . . The cry of the infant's anguish awakens every fiber of our response to hold and comfort him. It reawakens the pain of our own inner experiences of separation and fear. Yet our comforting does not ease the pain, at least initially, for he wants only her. Yet it is only with our comforting that the pain will eventually ease and he will be supported to accept his loss, to relinquish the bond. This same pattern applies to bereavement throughout the life cycle, but never so poignantly as at this early stage. (Raphael, 1983, p. 82)

From the age of 2½ on, the processes and responses of grieving children differ little from their elders, although the children may lack the capacity to put their thoughts, feelings, and memories into words (Bowlby, 1980; Raphael, Field, & Kvelde, 1980). For children from 2 to 5, grief responses are quite variable (Raphael, 1983). Because their grief is frequently only intermittently evident, parents commonly perceive these children as being relatively unaffected. However, this lack of outward evidence does not mean mourning is not occurring. Initially, many do not appear to understand the news of death fully and ask seemingly inappropriate questions immediately afterwards. In ensuing weeks younger children often show a degree of bewilderment and may exhibit some regressive behavior, such as being clinging and demanding. They are likely to repeatedly inquire about the whereabouts of the dead parent and demand to know why she has not returned and what she is doing. There is obvious yearning for the parent's return and angry protest when it does not occur. In addition to regression, these children may seek and cling to transitional objects, such as soft toys and blankets, and their aggressive behavior may increase. There is often anger with the deceased for desertion and for the resulting chaos in family life. This anger may be directed towards the surviving parent, or the parent may engender such anger by withdrawing and being unable to provide comfort. The children suffer multiple bereavements as they not only lose the parent who died, but also lose (at least temporarily) the security of the relationship they had with the surviving parent. This loss will be worse if they are sent away to an unfamiliar environment as protection from adults' grief and from funeral activities. Anxiety is often an unrecognized result of this experience, as the children are deprived of the secure and predictable world of the family as it is plunged into grief. Their sense of security may be totally disrupted and they may have concerns for their own survival. Preoccupation with the deceased, longing, and sadness are common. Children of this age will be likely to review and remember their relationship with the lost person. Evidence suggests that mourning and decathexis may take them a long time, if they even feel secure enough to let it occur (Furman, 1974; Raphael, 1983). There is a tendency to overidealize the deceased. This can cause problems later if the child compares the survivors to an idealized loved one. Finally, at this age it is unfortunately true that family members and other adults may find it intolerable to acknowledge the child's painful mourning. They may deny the child's feelings and inhibit their expression. Such inhibition of mourning may occur at any age, but it is a greater problem for the child since he lacks the security and resources to address the grief in the absence of support from others.

For the child from 5 to 8 there is more of a cognitive understanding of death and its implications, although not to an adult level. Children of this age are particularly vulnerable, since they understand much about death, but have little coping capacity (Polumbo, Note 9). Denial is often the prime defense in the face of loss. At this age children are particularly likely to behave as if nothing had happened. They need to hide their feelings out of concern about being babyish; they have a great fear of loss of control, exposure, and infantile dependence on adults; and they may have internalized parental demands for containing emotions or identified with parents' own restriction of feelings (Furman, 1974). These children may indeed cry and express deep feelings, but do so only in private. Even adults close to them may not be aware of this. Thus, while their inner life is affected, it is not reflected in their overt behavior. They may be perceived as uncaring, unloving, or unaffected, and may not receive the support and comfort they desperately need. This is particularly unfortunate because, given the developmental tendency to shut out feelings, such children may not deal with their grief unless given permission and support to do so. To cope, these children may develop a strong fantasy life in an attempt to keep the relationship with the deceased alive. Again, survivors may compare poorly with this fantasized, idealized person. It is important to provide these children with more constructive ways to address their grief:

> Given the opportunity to talk about their feelings, children in the middle-childhood age range will eventually, in a trusting relationship, feel safe enough to broach their distress and sadness. However, this opportunity is often not available to them in the family because of the family's denial of their grief at this age. Within our study children in this age group showed that they yearned strongly for the dead parent but were hesitant to show this. Boys, especially in this group, had particular difficulty in expressing their sadness and longing, frequently exhibiting aggressive responses and play. (Raphael, 1983, p. 101)

Other responses at this time may be guilt due to fear that hostile wishes may have caused the death; concern about being different than peers since one parent is gone; fear about the vulnerability of the surviving parent; and a compulsion to become self-reliant and helpful (e.g., the 8-year-old girl who becomes "a little mother" to her younger siblings) in an attempt to inhibit grief, overcompensate for yearning, and act out their own needs for care.

For the child from 8 to 12, sudden death will usually elicit shock, denial, and possibly great anxiety and distress. The child appears frightened by what has happened. When death has been anticipated there appears to be less need for the extreme denial that often comes into play following a sudden death. However, some denial is likely to occur. Although the child of this age is not as dependent on the parent as before, the independence that has been attained is still fragile and parental loss can precipitate the reawakening of feelings of childishness and helplessness. Although the child experiences yearning and longing for the deceased, he believes that these "childish" feelings must be controlled and may be quite unable to share them with anyone. Consequently, the child may put on a facade of independence and coping. Anger may be more easy to manifest, since it is a more powerful feeling. General irritability may be a symptom of this anger, but is often not recognized as such by either the child or those around him. In fact, it is often inappropriately labeled as difficult behavior and the child loses support or receives punishment. The child of this age is still unable to accept the finality of his personal loss, although the finality and irreversibility of the death in general is recognized. This, coupled with the fact that the yearning is often repressed, puts this child at risk of failing to resolve the loss. The child may hold on to the relationship in a fantasized idealized way that can create further problems with the surviving parent. The negative affects that once were attributed to the deceased parent may be projected onto the survivor. This child needs to share his longing and initiate the process of mourning. However, the grief and mourning of many children in this age group goes unrecognized. This especially happens when they do not act out their bereavement but take it quietly and become withdrawn, marking time until they can acknowledge the pain of the loss and appropriately grieve. At times grieving can begin when the family becomes stable and secure again, or when a relationship is established with a surrogate who can make the child feel secure enough to express his yearning and sadness over the death. Teachers in particular may provide such relationships. Some children may choose to retreat into some symbolic behavior linked with the deceased parent, identifying with the parent's behavior or style. They may also try to act "grown-up" in an attempt to master the pain of their loss and deny their helplessness. They, too, may compulsively care for others, or may actually become controlling or bossy. In this age group, more than any other, there is a tendency towards fearfulness, phobic behaviors, and some hypochondriasis. Research indicates that most children bereaved at this age lack opportunities to share their grief and are frequently conflicted about their inhibition of their grief.

After a significant loss, adolescents may feel helpless and frightened. They may want to retreat to childhood, where there was a sense of protection from death and its consequences, but be compelled to act more adult by social expectations. This conflict is painful when the adolescent is expected to comfort family members while feeling childlike and frightened himself. In addition, the strong yearning for the deceased parent may seem as if it is drawing the adolescent back into childhood, with its symbiosis and powerlessness. This is hard to accept for the normally rebellious adolescent; consequently, the yearning is often repressed, making him more susceptible to pathological mourning. Anger is more easily expressed, and can give the adolescent a sense of power to counteract his helplessness. However, it can also fuel depression or be used to inappropriately punish self or others for the death.

Denial may also be used as a defense, for the adolescent greatly fears losing control of his already strong emotions and is especially threatened by the idea of mortality. Like adults, adolescents can now conceive of the future effects of the death, such as the absence of the father who would have walked the bride down the aisle. Many adult responses to the death will be seen, but they will be complicated by typical adolescent problems: resistance to communicating with adults; overconcern about the acceptability of their responses to others; alienation from adults and sometimes peers; lack of knowledge of the social expectations; and other developmental issues that may compromise the task of mourning, such as problems with separation and dependency, identity, heightened emotionality, and sexual conflicts. At times the ongoing tasks of adolescence will preclude mourning from being successfully completed. It may be delayed, possibly until secure relationships are present to facilitate it, or occur intermittently. One of the issues that makes this mourning particularly difficult is that the adolescent may be experiencing guilt as a result of the normal rebelliousness and separation that had been occurring prior to the death. This can prompt conflicted mourning behaviors. When adolescents' grief and mourning cannot proceed directly, grief may be evidenced through exaggerated pseudoadult behaviors; identification with the dead person; withdrawal and depression; sexual acting-out; and care-eliciting behaviors designed not only to secure care, but to release tension, self-punish, and sometimes replace the deceased (Raphael, 1983).

Variables Influencing the Child's Grief

As with the adult, the child's emotional responses to the death of a loved one will be influenced by a number of psychosocial variables. (See the factors discussed in Chapter 3 and consider them in age-appropriate ways.) Bowlby (1980) places the major variables in three classes:

> (a) The causes and circumstances of the loss, with especial reference to where and what the child is told and what opportunities are later given him to inquire about what has happened;
> (b) The family relationships after the loss, with special reference to whether he remains with his surviving parent and, if so, how the patterns of relationship are changed as a result of the loss;
> (c) The patterns of relationship within the family prior to the loss, with special reference to the patterns obtaining between the parents themselves and between each of them and the bereaved child. (p. 311)

As in adult grief, the secondary losses resulting from the death of a parent also must be assessed in order to determine the impact of the parent's death upon the child. For example, the remaining parent's emotional capability to provide for the care and security of the child will strongly influence that child's grief and experience after the death. Due to the lack of maturity and self-sufficiency, the bereaved child is vulnerable not only to her own emotional responses to such a major loss, but also the consequences of the remaining parent's grief and the interruption of normal care and interaction patterns necessary for growth and security (Kastenbaum, 1977). This places the bereaved child in a precarious position of double jeopardy. The role reorganizations that occur in the family as a consequence of the death, and the new role assignments and responsibilities that result from them, also will obviously influence the child's bereavement. The subsequent changes in family rules for expression of feelings, patterns of gratification, and types of support, and the family's acceptance of the mourning tasks will have a profound influence on the child's experience. Families in which children have a particularly difficult time include those in which death is taboo; those in which someone must be to blame; those in which emotional relationships are cool and detached; those in which things must go on as before; those for whom the loss means chaos; and, to a lesser extent, those who must do the "right" thing (Raphael, 1983). (See Chapter 12 for more on this topic.) In addition the responses of the social group (peers and schoolmates) will be as critical to a child in resolving her grief as they are to an adult.

The death of a sibling can cause its own unique difficulties for the child. Because of the commonalities between siblings and the shared experiences and events they undergo, it is not uncommon for the death of a sibling to be particularly traumatic to a child. More than other losses, this type of death profoundly illustrates to the child that she can die too. One factor that may complicate responding to sibling death is the intense guilt that results from previous hostile wishes and feelings of ambivalence in the relationship. There may be strong anger with the parents for being unable to protect the sibling and prevent the death from happening, for, if it happened to the sibling and they failed to protect that child, they could fail to protect the surviving child as well. (See "Siblings' Responses" in Chapter 13 for more on this topic.) Often siblings have a changed role in the family after the death; for example, they may move from second to oldest child. This transition may be a difficult one, and may require sensitive handling by caring adults. It may be even more problematic for the sibling who becomes an only child following the death of a brother or sister. As documented in the literature, if there is inappropriate assignment of roles and responsibilities. as well as identity, it may be particularly harmful to the surviving children (Cain & Cain,

1964). Sibling bereavement can be made more difficult by parental overprotection after the loss of a child, comparison with the deceased child, or parental inability to attend to the surviving family members' needs due to involvement in their own grief. Reaching the age at which a sibling died can be particularly frightening. Children need an adequate explanation of cause of death in order to be able to confront this anxiety. Siblings may also have trouble dealing with the deceased child's effects. For some, inheriting these may be comforting; for others, disturbing. Each child will feel differently, and sensitivity should be used in deciding what should be done with the deceased child's belongings and room.

Effects of Childhood Bereavement

What happens to people who experience bereavement early in life? There have been numerous studies documenting the general symptomatology of bereavement during childhood. From these studies it is clear that children's symptoms are quite similar to those manifested by adults, usually disturbances of sleep, appetite, or habit patterns. However, there may also be effects leading to psychosomatic disorders, depression, and adjustment disorders, neuroses, and conduct disorders.

There also have been studies investigating the correlation between early childhood loss and later adult behavior. In their extensive overview of the available research on parental death and psychological development, Berlinsky and Biller (1982) concluded that almost all relatively sound methodological studies demonstrated differences between children who had lost a parent and those who had not. These differences were evidenced both shortly after the death and many years later.

In the studies younger children appear to be more adversely affected by the parent's death than older children. It was unclear whether this was a result of the inability of younger children to understand death, the greater need for parental involvement, the lack of the benefits of a two-parent home, or a combination of these factors. The sex of the child appeared to make little difference in the overall effect of parental bereavement. When compared to children from other family backgrounds, the bereaved children were more submissive, dependent, and introverted, and less aggressive. The specific correlates of parental death include: emotional disturbance, specifically suicidal behaviors; general maladjustment and, to a lesser degree, psychosis; juvenile delinquency and criminal activity; and frequent deficiencies as well as occasional superior performances in cognitive, academic, and creative areas. Paternal bereavement has been studied relatively more than maternal bereavement. Sequelae of this loss include emotional disturbance, delinquent and criminal behavior, and sex-role assumption that is typically feminine (e.g., submissiveness, dependency, low aggression, ability to delay gratification, and externally oriented locus of control). It should be noted that the sex-role behavior of both male and female children is affected by the death of the father and results in less traditionally masculine behavior. Paternal bereavement can be either an asset or liability to achievement in the cognitive, academic and creative areas, although it is more often a problem. The death of the mother has been studied less and has been linked only to emotional disturbance. In contrasting children who had lost a parent with children whose parents were divorced (a significant loss itself), the bereaved child was again apt to be more submissive, dependent, introverted, anxious, and less aggressive. He also was less likely than the child whose parents had divorced to have cognitive, academic, impulse-control, and later marital problems. Sex-role adoption was more feminine in both male and female children. Taylor (1983-84) found that those who sustained early losses were more easily reminded of the theme of death than those who had not, and they tended to structure death in a more cognitively remote fashion. Other studies of childhood bereavement sequelae in later life have indicated that there may be general symptomatology and ill health; psychosomatic problems; psychiatric disorders; relationship problems; sensitivity to loss; and anniversary and "age-correspondence" phenomena (Raphael, 1983).

Since childhood bereavement may result in a number of emotional, cognitive, behavioral, social, and physical problems, the resolution of grief is important. However, it is invalid to conclude that childhood bereavement invariably leads to dysfunction. Raphael (1983) has critically reviewed a number of childhood bereavement studies in terms of childhood sequelae and effects during later life. While discussing the many possible consequences of bereavement for young children, she astutely observes that "despite all these possibilities, no clear-cut findings have really emerged, for the vast majority of studies have been retrospective, and the variables are many and complex" (p. 126). Berlinsky and Biller (1982) note that it is not the simple fact of the occurrence of the death, but rather "the variables associated with the loss of the parent as well as characteristics specific to the child, that will predict the child's subsequent adjustment and development" (p. 127). A more appropriate conclusion to make is that reached by Bendiksen and Fulton (1975), who found that "childhood bereavement is a serious personal crisis that can have serious consequences for later adult life, but that there is also a 'normalizing' effect that is particularly evident when data are compared with a similar age cohort that have experienced divorce during the same childhood period" (p. 57). Even though death precipitates a severe reaction, it is not completely unlike other traumatic events and its effects may lessen over time.

Therapeutic Interventions

As noted previously, what differences there are between grief in adults and grief in children are usually the result of limitations in children's cognitive grasp of death (see "Reactions to Death Across the Life Cycle" in Chapter 9), developmental experiences, and the manner in which information about death has been conveyed to them. Many children's problems with death and grief arise from the dishonest ways in which adults often interact with children about the topic of death. Children are not automatically afraid of death. Ironically, fear is instilled in them by the adults who try to protect them.

Children are often told myths or fairy tales about death instead of the truth. Grollman (1974) gives some examples and their unexpected detrimental effects.

> *Example 1*
> "Mother has gone on a long trip."
> *Child's Reaction*
> - Anger and resentment ("Why didn't she take me?" "Why did she leave?")
> - Abandonment and guilt ("I must have done something bad to make her leave me.")
> - Illusion that Mother will return
> - Wonder at why everyone else is sad and crying
>
> *Example 2*
> "God took Daddy when he was so young because your father was so good that He wanted your father for Himself."
> *Child's Reaction*
> - Resentment and anger against God ("*I* needed him.")
> - Fear of being good ("I might be taken.")
>
> *Example 3*
> "Grandma died because she was so sick."
> *Child's Reaction*
> - Associates all sickness with death
>
> *Example 4*
> "Your aunt died. Now she's sleeping forever."
> *Child's Reaction*
> - Associates sleep with death and becomes afraid to go to sleep

Information that is not truthful and realistic will be harmful to children, despite any intent to protect or help them. Children need honest explanations, given at age-appropriate levels of understanding, that will enable them to grapple with the terrible but unavoidable experience of loss. Several important things should be remembered when telling a child of the death of a loved one:

• The child should be told immediately in order to prevent his hearing it from someone else. Use a normal tone of voice, avoiding hushed, unnatural whispers that may convey an undesirable message of death being unreal or spooky.

• The child should be told by someone close to him, preferably in familiar surroundings that afford him some security.

• The child should be given as honest an explanation as possible within limits of understanding. Very young children are not able to understand irreversibility and permanence, but, for example, they can understand something like the analogy of death to a broken toy (something the child can definitely comprehend). In both cases, that which is lost does not function anymore, and although we would like to fix it, it cannot work again.

• Convey to the child that he is loved and will continue to be taken care of even though a very sad thing has happened and the adults are very upset. It is frightening for the child to see adults upset, but this must not be hidden since it is a natural reaction. Children need to know that it is permissible and normal to express grief. Of course its expression should be somewhat tempered in order not to overwhelm them. Jackson (1965) points out that sadness is quite different from despair and that reasonable expression is different from complete collapse. He advocates that children be spared extreme expressions of adult breakdown, which might overtax them emotionally. However, children can contend with much stronger reactions than adults believe and, in general, it is better to err in the direction of sharing the feeling than concealing it from the children. The most important thing is that the child receive an explanation of the adults' feelings as normal responses to grief. This must be accompanied by an attempt to make the child feel secure even though there is a great deal of change occurring. Other family changes should be kept to a minimum, although of course there will be reorganization following a death.

• Predict for the child that he may feel sad and even have strange or different feelings for a while. Let him know that this is natural and that he should talk about those feelings. Convey that such feelings will not last forever.

• Include the child in funerals and other rituals of mourning. Children often are sheltered from the grief expressions of adults, yet they have a *right* and a *need* to be included. They should be allowed to share their grief with those that they love. Silence about the death and isolation from significant others at this time deprive children of the opportunity to deal with their emotions. In addition, if children are not included, they start to feel insecure and abandoned as they see adults reacting to and sharing in an experience that they cannot share. They are shut out at the time they most need to be included. This does not serve to protect children but only to harm them. Coupled with this is the fact that the fantasies of children are often much worse than the reality. Lacking explanation for the responses of parents, and being withdrawn from a secure environment, children will engage in magical thinking and fantasy that will do nothing but cause problems later.

Children should be given the opportunity to decide whether or not to attend the funeral. If they decide not to go, that decision should be respected. They should be told that they may visit the grave or the church when they want to, with the accompaniment of an adult if they desire. If they decide to go, the details should be explained in advance so that they will have some idea of what to expect.

Frequently, adults project their own fears and concerns onto children and assume that the funeral will be devastating to them. It definitely need not be. In and of themselves the funeral rituals offer nothing for the child to fear. Of course the funeral will be sad, but it is always sad to lose a loved one. Since parents try to prepare their children for dealing with life in the real world, they must also try to prepare their children for the losses and deaths that they inevitably will confront. It is best if parents allow their children to face the sadness of grief while they are present to help the children cope with it. The alternative is to try to hide the children from the real world, perhaps causing them to confront its grief at a time when the parents are no longer there to support them—at their parents' deaths.

It is important to watch out for children's causal connection of their personal wishes or actions to the death of their loved one, called *magical thinking*. This may also be observed on the adult level, but is especially prevalent in children due to their immature cognitive development. For example, a child may feel responsible and guilty for her father's death because she had engaged in a fight with him or had said "Drop dead!" For this reason, it is important to develop an understanding of what children think and feel about their loss; they may have significant misconceptions. Since these can interfere with appropriate grief resolution, they must be corrected as soon as possible. This requires explaining to the child the difference between expression of a thought or feeling and causation of an actual physical event. The child will also benefit from the reassurance that it is normal at times to feel angry or upset with the people we love, and that it has nothing to do with the death of a loved one.

A child's grief should not be evaluated solely in comparison with an adult's (although there are more similarities than differences). Sometimes children will not react at all to the news that a loved one has died. It may seem that they are insensitive to the death or that they do not understand, but this conclusion may be quite incorrect. Children engage in denial just as adults do, and these behaviors may be more primitive manifestations of adult denial processes. Also, children tend to act out their feelings more than adults. Play is the natural means of communication for children, offering them safe modalities for self-expression. It enables them to experiment with different identities and rehearse difficult or anxiety-provoking events. Because they often lack the capacity to put feelings and memories into words, children must act out their grief through their behaviors, their art work, and their play. This is the symbolic language that adults must attempt to understand. Relying exclusively on verbal expressions will miss a major source of information about the children. When children talk about the death in a way that is contradictory to external behavior, the discrepancy must be accounted for in order to understand what is really going on. Adults should check whether they are subtly sending out messages of how they want the children to react. Children are very sensitive to the cues of adults and, if they feel their expressions of grief will upset or in some way further disturb someone they are already concerned about, they will cloak and inhibit these responses. Similarly, if the emotions of grief conflict with a child's age-appropriate or idiosyncratic concerns, there may be further inhibition of grief expression. For example, the adolescent who wants an adult image may be reluctant to express the very normal (and adult) feelings of helplessness.

The most therapeutic posture to take with children is that loss engenders intense feelings that must be dealt with. They need to be aware that adults are willing to discuss the death and the children's feelings when the children are ready. Adults must be cognizant of the needs of children to express feelings not only about grief, but also about the changes in the family following the death. They must attend to the children's behavior, for frequently that behavior conveys more about the children than their words. However, their behavior must be interpreted carefully, as it will not necessarily correspond with their inner feelings. Sensitive inquiry will help in determining exactly how they feel. Sometimes children just need the catalyst of an adult's interest to talk, especially to discuss feelings they have been reluctant to express or that have been surprisingly intense. Most children will need adults' "permission" to grieve.

It is necessary for adults to discuss death with children in order to demystify it. Ideally, prior to the loss of any loved one, children will have had some conversations with an adult about death and its natural part in the course of life. Parents can utilize the numerous "teachable moments" that occur in everyday life to instruct their children about death and grief. For instance, the death of a pet or a famous person can provide a natural opportunity for parents to discuss death and its ramifications with their children. One of the most striking findings from LaGrand's (1981) extensive investigation of the loss reactions of college students was that the students wished that there had been more preparation for the loss through open and honest family communication about death, sharing of grief with parents, and greater exposure to death earlier in life. This is a prime indication of the need for death education in the schools and at home.

Treatment Recommendations for the Grief of Children

In general, the treatment interventions used to assist the bereaved adult are equally as effective in assisting the bereaved child when age-appropriate considerations are taken into account. Grieving children are not unlike adults. The same principles will apply, the same types of psychological, physiological, and social variables will influence grief reactions, and many of the same symptoms and outcomes can be expected. Here are some critical considerations when dealing with bereaved children.

• Keep in mind the developmental capacities of the child and his age-related concerns at the time of death. Both of these will profoundly influence the grief experience. For example, the normal problems of adolescence serve to intensify the conflicts of grief for older children.

• Openly discuss and truthfully disclose facts when dealing with children about death in general or about a specific loss. Gear communication and interventions to the child's cognitive level.

• Make sure you give the child permission to mourn. Try also to make the bereaved child feel secure enough to let the process occur. Do not deny his feelings or disallow his mourning, even if it is painful to you.

• Model appropriate grieving behavior. Do not be afraid to let the child see you cry or express feelings related to the grief.

• Recognize the importance of a surrogate adult for very young children in order to provide them with an appropriate sex-role model and to work out psychological issues that would require the relationship of an adult of that sex.

• Recognize that the grief of children may be evidenced only intermittently. A lack of observable grieving behavior does not indicate that mourning is failing to occur. Children's inner feelings may not be conveyed by their external behavior.

• Understand that much of the child's grief will be expressed through play, acting-out behaviors, or artistic creation. Attempt to understand the symbolic messages that are conveyed through these mediums.

• Look for magical thinking involved in the child's explanations of the death and correct it to avoid guilt and inappropriate grief reactions.

• Recognize that not only does the death have a profound impact on the child, but also the surviving parent's reactions and the changes in the family. The secondary losses that accrue from the loss of the parent are particularly disruptive for a child, who is vulnerable due to a lack of personal resources and who may be unable to understand the relation of the losses to the death.

• Make the child feel secure. Assist him in identifying and expressing his feelings. Try not to make too many changes in order to minimize the transitions to which the child must adapt. Consistency is critical for children whose worlds have been shaken by the death of a parent.

• Recognize that children "grow up with the loss" and often will require additional information or working through of the original grief at later points in life. This is a normal process and not a pathological symptom.

• Work to make sure that the roles that are reassigned after the death of a family member are appropriate for everyone involved, especially the children. Educate the adults about the harm done by assigning inappropriate role responsibilities to a child. To expect a child to be "the man around the house" or "the little mother" is unfair to the child, detrimental to the child's future development, and often limiting to the mourning process.

• Take for granted that children suffer from separations from people to whom they have been connected. Regardless of whether or not you can believe that children mourn in a process similar to adults, recognize that there are intense separation reactions that are quite painful and need to be addressed and supported by adults.

• Recognize the normalcy of idealization of the deceased parent and work to gently prevent this from causing problems with relationships with survivors.

• Recognize that children are not born afraid of death and that their fears are instilled in them by adults. "Protecting" a child from death and loss is unrealistic and only serves to predispose the child to future problems.

• Help the very young child remember the deceased and integrate these memories appropriately into his life. Provide mementos and stimulate recollections.

• Recognize that if children lack opportunities to express feelings and raise questions about the death or to explore fantasies and concerns about their future care, they will be unable to complete mourning and feel secure. The more openly issues are dealt with, the better will be the child's chances of working through the loss and making a successful adaptation.

• The child who experiences a sudden death may need extra support in coping with the unanticipated grief response that results from untimely and unexpected deaths. The child will need to get some sense of security again, something even adults have trouble with when such deaths occur.

CHAPTER 7

Funerals and
Funerary Rituals*

Virtually all societies and cultures have been found to have some form of funerary rituals. Such practices appear to have developed quite early in man's history. Anthropological reports substantiate that the Neanderthals buried their dead with ceremony in Iraq some 60,000 or more years ago (Pine, 1969). Early civilizations are also known to have had intricate ritual systems for care of the dead. The link between funerary rituals and society is a strong one. From the time of the ancient Egyptians, Greeks, and Romans to present-day Americans there have evolved specific funerary practices that reflect each society's philosophical and religious beliefs and values. These practices have in turn served as symbols to influence and shape those beliefs and values (Irion, 1966; Mandelbaum, 1959). In this sense, funerary rituals bolster the solidarity of the social group. It is important to recognize the connectedness of these rituals to the society as a whole, for while funerary rituals are created by the psychosocial tasks demanded by death, they are regulated by social factors such as the extent and type of social organization and the demography within it (Pine, 1972).

> Certain things must be done after a death, whether it occurs in a very simple or in a highly complex society. The corpse must be disposed of; those who are bereaved—who are personally shocked and socially disoriented—must be helped to reorient themselves; the whole group must have a known way of readjustment after the loss of one of its members. These things "must" be done in the sense that they *are* done. When people find that they have no set pattern for dealing with death—as may occur in newly coa-

*The author gratefully acknowledges the helpful comments of Vanderlyn R. Pine, PhD, on an earlier version of this chapter.

lesced groups—or when they discover that the former pattern is
no longer a feasible one, they tend quickly to establish some clear
plan for coping with the occasion of death. (Mandelbaum, 1959,
p. 189)

Despite the variety of ways funeral rites are observed through-
out the world, a striking number of similar ties suggest that these
rituals meet critical universal needs that exist at the time of death
(Pine, 1969). These similarities include the following:
  • Social support is provided to grievers through the gathering
    of relatives and friends. There is an extension of sympathy
    and empathy, recognition of the loss, and communication of
    care and support aimed at bringing comfort and support to
    the bereaved.
  • Some sort of ritual and ceremony is involved. Often, but not
    exclusively, the ceremony may be religious in nature, utilized
    to explain the reason for and meaning of death.
  • Visual confrontation of the dead body is common. This may
    occur at the place of death, the home of the deceased, the
    funeral home, or a neighborhood meeting place. The body
    may be prepared in different ways but is generally put on
    display.
  • There usually is a procession. This can be viewed as a "family
    parade" that enables individuals to display their grief pub-
    licly. It frequently concludes the funeral, ending at the place
    of final disposition.
  • Some kind of sanitary disposition of the body is carried out.
    This includes burial, entombment, or cremation. In instances
    of donation of the body to science, embalming, or some form
    of sanitization of the body, occurs.
  • Funerals generally require material expenditure. This
    enables the bereaved to communicate their loss to society
    and support this sentiment with tangible, measurable
    means.

Such similarities confirm the necessity for some form of funerary ritual to address the psychological needs of the immediate
survivors and surrounding social group. The requirement is seen
by Blauner (1966) as a social mandate: "Since mortality tends to
disrupt the ongoing life of social groups and relationships, all societies must develop some forms of containing its impact" (p. 378).
Funerals serve as severance rites to separate the deceased from the
living; rites of passage for mourners to psychologically, socially,
and spiritually assist them through bereavement; and means of
providing societal continuity and affirmation, expression of beliefs
and values, and group solidarity. The way in which cultures develop funerary customs is outlined by Pine (1969):

Death gives rise to immediate personal emotional responses which seem to trigger certain culturally oriented responses and reactions which evolve into specific patterns of bereavement. Every culture has deeply entrenched traditional customs for handling death, and as grief ensues, societally based reactions become more pronounced in the form of funeral practices. These customary practices aim at providing meaningful structures upon which bereaved people may lean, hopefully giving them some sense of consolation and easing the transition caused by the termination of personal interaction. (p. 62)

CRITICISMS OF CONTEMPORARY FUNERARY RITUALS

In recent years some people have become dissatisfied with traditional funerary rituals. Complaints range from general griping about funerals—they are too impersonal, traumatic, morbid, anxiety-provoking, artificial, or expensive—to the well-articulated criticisms of Jessica Mitford's (1963) scathing attack on exploitation in the funeral industry in *The American Way of Death*. From the investigation of the funeral industry by the Federal Trade Commission in the 1970s to the establishment of memorial societies as an alternative to the high cost of funerals, charges and criticisms have been leveled against the funeral director, who has been a major scapegoat of death since ancient times (Pine, 1969). However, these charges have been made without an understanding of the necessity and usefulness of funerary rituals and the many alterations in funerary customs due to social changes.

The social changes that have fostered contemporary American funerary practices are those that have modified the American way of life since the Industrial Revolution: urbanization, increasing technology, secularization of society, and social reorganization. First, they have altered the way American families relate to society. As Americans have developed fewer social ties, become more alienated from each other, been more mobile, and had less stability in their roles than before, the family has become more nuclearized. This has resulted in strong emotional attachments to fewer people, and overidentification and overdependence among family members, which make the individual in American culture a victim of "high vulnerability in bereavement" (Volkart, 1957). Consequently, "he experiences grief less frequently, but more intensely, since his emotional involvements are not diffused over an entire community, but are usually concentrated on one or a few people" (Blauner, 1966, p. 389). (See "Family Problems" in Chapter 12 for more on this topic.) This, plus the legislative guidelines for embalming and other undertaking functions, have resulted in decreased participation by the American family in the funeral. It is now almost exclusively under the direction of the professional funeral director. It is a uniquely American custom for the family to participate so minimally, other than by attendance, in funerary rituals. (Pine, 1975).

Advances in medical science, changes in mortality rates, and the segregation of the ill and elderly, together with the previously mentioned social transitions, have made death seem remote in America. It is no longer a part of everyday existence. In earlier times, children and adults were repeatedly exposed to experiences that familiarized them with death. The deaths of everyone in the extended family, from infants to elders, were as witnessed as the births. Nature also was observed in its continual cycle of life and death. For people in preindustrialized America there was a sense of unity, of an integrated process that took one from birth to death and related both events. That sense is now lacking in contemporary society, and it partially accounts for a widespread American tendency to deny death and the need for funerary rituals.

Another result of advances in medical science is an increase in the length of illness before death. This provides more opportunities for anticipatory grief. If too much decathexis occurs prior to the death, the survivors may feel they have already said good-bye and do not require a funeral service. However, this also robs them of other benefits of the funeral, such as confirming and enhancing their social and community relationships (Fulton & Fulton, 1971).

The last major change influencing contemporary funerary practices is the deritualization of American society. In the past, society was less mobile. People were more religious, and life centered around a large and extended family that shared a unified view of life, fostering feelings of belonging and predictability. Emphasis was on the individual, not on his productive or technological capabilities. At that time ritual celebration of significant events was a public display connoting security, control, and predictability. It expressed the beliefs of the social group and symbolized its values. Participants could communicate through symbolic activity. Ritual provided cultural prescriptions for formal patterns of behavior to guide and sustain the individual during confusing and chaotic periods of transition. It provided meaning at a time of inconsistency. Today, because of the changes in American life, there is a decrease in formal ritual behavior. People are left without support and direction during times of change and flux.

> American culture has, in certain respects, and for some Americans, become deritualized. Persons bereaved by a death sometimes find that they have no clear prescription as to what to do next. In such cases, each has to work out a solution for himself.

After the typical period of shock and disorganization, these mourners can receive little help toward personal reorganization. When
individual solutions to such recurrent and poignant problems are
repeatedly made, they may tend to coalesce and to become institutionalized. Hence it may be that the people who have reacted
strongly against the older rituals—because they were rituals—
may institute some new version of the old ritual forms. (Mandelbaum, 1959, p. 214)

Thus, death is more removed from our society; we try to deny
it, but we are more vulnerable to it. We have altered our funerary
rituals to reflect these facts and have turned the final rites surrounding death over to professionals. As a reaction to these developments
some observers and consumers have criticized funerals. However,
while some of their points are valid, this does not mean that contemporary funerals are harmful or useless. As yet there are no
suitable alternatives for the funeral in providing a way of coping
with the highly emotional and upsetting experience of death
(Keith, 1976; Pine, 1976b). Moreover, doing away with funerals
may result in a culture "with even more juvenile death-denying
ways, haunted by unresolved guilt, pent up anger and half-finished
relationships" (Cassem, 1976, p. 20). There is striking evidence that
the increasing deritualization in American society is having an
effect upon our behavior in the face of death. Lacking the traditional ceremonies that help to control the expression of anger and
hostility and lessen guilt or anxiety (all normal emotions following
loss), we turn to less therapeutic outlets for expressing our emotions, such as psychosomatic illness or aggressive and hostile acts
against society (Fulton, 1976b). There is strong ethnographic evidence that there is an increased risk of anger and aggression as
Americans move away from traditional funeral services, since these
emotions tend to be more frequently expressed and are much more
intense if ritual specialists (e.g., funeral directors, clergy) are absent (Rosenblatt, Jackson, & Walsh, 1972). Consequently, grievers
should be encouraged to effectively utilize rituals in therapeutic
ways, while minimizing the undesirable effects that are pointed
out by critics.

While basically funerals are no different than other rituals,
funeral directors are the only ritual specialists who are criticized
while performing the precise functions they are supposed to perform. For instance, there is a belief that funeral directors over-
charge for their services in the celebration of the ritual as compared
to other rituals:

It is of interest here to mention that statistics suggest that people
are prepared to pay for a wedding, on the average, twice what
they pay for an average funeral, and this without benefit of "wed-

ding insurance." We know of only one published statement con-
demning the uneconomical behavior of parents at this festive
occasion and know of no charges publically made of exploitation
by the dress-making industry, catering industry or Brewers Association of America in connection with the wedding. (Fulton,
1976b, p. 171)

This hostility appears to be less related to the funeral director
as an individual than it is to his role with regard to the anxiety-
provoking topic of death.

Further, the public may feel hostile toward the funeral director
because of the role he plays. The guilt generated by desire on the
part of the bereaved to rid themselves quickly of the body and by
the death itself, the possible confusion and anxiety in the selection
of the "right" casket, and the attitude toward the funeral director
as the constant reminder and associate of death prompt the public
to lash out at him. (Fulton, 1976b, p. 171)

FUNCTIONS OF FUNERALS

The funeral consists of five parts, as outlined by Raether and
Slater (1977):

- *The removal of the body.* This symbolizes the separation of
  the dead from the living. It was a more integral part of the
  funeral process in the past, when the body was removed
  directly from the family home. Currently most deaths occur
  in institutions, and this action is not usually witnessed by
  the family.
- *The visitation period.* This is when the community comes to
  the mourners and expresses its empathy, sympathy, and support for them.
- *The funeral rite.* During this time a ritual is invoked to meet
  the needs of the mourners. For 75% of the people this will
  have a religious orientation. Others will have an alternate
  form of humanist or secular funeral service. A third form is
  available, the memorial service, which is a funeral without
  the body present.
- *The procession.* This conveys a symbolic message about both
  the deceased and the mourners. In terms of the deceased, it
  acknowledges the finality of what has occurred through the
  movement of the deceased from the place of death and/or
  the final service to the place of final disposition. In terms of
  the mourners, the procession away from the place of final
  disposition without the deceased illustrates the movement
  back into the mainstream of society. "Psychologically, the
  procession adds to the impact of the movement which occurs
  as a person moves from the place of death to taking those

firm steps of resolution and living a life without the presence of the deceased" (p. 241).

- *The committal.* This is the conclusive phase of the process and it entails the act of committing the body to its place of final disposition. It may be an interment, in which the body is buried in the dedicated ground of a cemetery or memorial park; entombment, in which the body is entombed in an above-ground mausoleum; or cremation.

The overriding function of a funeral is to serve as a rite of passage. Transitions into different states of being are celebrated throughout life in all cultures. Major changes such as birth, puberty, marriage, and death all have rituals to help individuals and society adapt to the changed state and cope with the disequilibrium that occurs during transition. Van Gennep (1960) first conceptualized the "rite de passage" and outlined its three phases: the separation from a former state, the transition into a new state, and the incorporation into that new state. (Note how these parallel Lindemann's [1944] three tasks of grief work: emancipation from the bondage of the deceased; readjustment to the environment in which the deceased is missing; and formation of new relationships.) These occur during the funeral for both the mourners and the deceased. For the mourners it involves separation from the deceased loved one, transition into the state of being without the loved one, and reincorporation into the social group in their changed state. The deceased is symbolically removed from the surviving social group, put through a transition during the funeral in which she moves from the living social group to the state of death, and then is acknowledged to be dead by being left in the land of the dead through interment, entombment, or cremation. During the interim transitional period it is made clear through behaviors that mourners are beginning to have a diminishing relationship with the deceased.

One of the most important functions of a funeral is to validate the life of the deceased. This assures people that they will be remembered at the time of their passing and is a testimony to the fact that a life has been lived. A lack of recognition for the ending of a life is depersonalizing and invalidating. It is tantamount to dismissing the importance of the person who had died. Thus, it is not unusual to see survivors go to great lengths to assure themselves that they have fittingly marked the end of the life of their loved one. Society has its last opportunity to relate to the deceased publically, to bestow rank or classification (Kastenbaum, 1977). The specifics of the ritual, the number of mourners, the impact the death has on society all reflect the value placed upon the deceased individual. Kastenbaum (1977) mentions the relationship between the splendor of final arrangements and the status of the deceased and points out that such arrangements can serve as a validator of the worth or distinction of the individual. In this regard Pine and Phillips (1970) assert that monetary expenditures have taken on added importance as a means for the bereaved to express to themselves and others their sentiments for the deceased.

> Our view is that *because* people increasingly lack both the ceremonial and social mechanisms and arrangements that once existed to help them cope with death, monetary expenditures have taken on added importance as a means for allowing the bereaved to express (both to themselves and others) their sentiments for the deceased. For with so few modes of expression remaining to the bereaved, funeral expenditures serve as evidence of their concern for both the dead and the conventional standards of decency in their community of residence. (p. 416)

Funerals have been established to meet specific needs of the mourners and society. Although they do address disposition of the body of the loved one, they are primarily for the living, not the deceased. "A funeral rite is a social rite *par excellence*. Its ostensible object is the dead person, but it benefits not the dead but the living" (Firth, 1964, p. 63).

How Funerals Benefit the Mourner

The mourner derives psychological, social, and spiritual benefits from well-designed funerary rituals. (The following discussion is based on the analyses of Cassem, 1976; Fulton, 1976a; Irion, 1966, 1976; and Pine, 1976a, 1976b.)

Psychological Benefits
Funerals confirm and reinforce the reality of the death. The natural urge to deny the death is confronted by the ceremony of leave-taking. Viewing the body is often quite helpful, as it challenges the normal desire to deny the loss while promoting acceptance of the death. Participating in the funeral ritual—standing at a wake and repeatedly looking at the deceased in the casket, attending a funeral service, accepting the condolences of others, witnessing the casket at the grave—graphically illustrates to the bereaved that the death has indeed occurred. Even if it cannot be emotionally accepted at that time, the memories of these experiences will later help to confirm to the bereaved the reality of the loss of the loved one.

Viewing the body has been criticized in recent years, as some mourners have wished to avoid the painful reactions that seeing the body can engender. However, it is precisely the impact of the finality of the loss that viewing seeks to promote. Clearly the body of the deceased is the best symbol of the individual and therefore the most effective one to focus upon in attempting to perceive the deceased in a new relationship, as someone who is no longer alive and will only exist in memory.

The custom of viewing the body not only promotes realization of the loss, especially after sudden or accidental death, but also, through proper preparation and restoration of the body, assists in recall of the individual prior to any disfigurement from pain, accident, or violence. This preparation is not designed to make the deceased look alive, but to provide an acceptable image for recollection of the deceased. The presence of the body provides an immediate and proper climate for mourning and is a natural symbol to stimulate discussion and expression of emotion about the deceased.

Funerals assist in the acknowledgment and expression of feelings of loss. Focusing directly on the loss in a socially legitimized situation where catharsis and ventilation are supported, stimulates the emotional responses of the mourner to the loss. Aided by the presence and acceptance of concerned others, the mourner confronts the pain of the separation that must be dealt with and accommodated. The presence of the body during the funeral is a meaningful symbol that the griever can focus upon to activate those emotions and memories that need to be expressed.

> We must be able to show emotions and affective behavior; not to do so is, in a sense, a denial of death. As we strive to express our bereavement, to give vent to our grief, to share our mourning, we can opt for the rituals and ceremonies of the funeral as a means of coping with the reality of loss in a satisfactory fashion. Thus, the funeral serves as an important community and personal event during the period of acute grief because it provides a setting for emotional catharsis with *social support*. (Pine, 1976a, p. 113)

Funerals offer the survivors a vehicle for expressing their feelings. This allows the mourners a public and socially legitimized opportunity to display certain feelings about the lost loved one and act out emotions and behaviors necessary for resolving grief (e.g., demonstrate love, expiate guilt, finish unfinished business).

Funerals stimulate the recollection of the deceased, a necessary aspect of decathexis. Mourners can begin to review their relationship with the deceased, which will be necessary to effectively complete grief work. Each story told, each incident remembered, each emotion shared with others assists in the process of decathexis.

Funerals assist mourners in beginning to accommodate to the changed relationship between themselves and the deceased loved one. In the process of grief the mourner must develop a new relationship with the lost loved one based on recollection, memory, and past experience, in contrast to the relationship of presence and interaction that formerly existed (Irion, 1966). To do this the griever must remember the deceased in a clear and realistic manner, as someone who has lived *and died*. Funerals help to accomplish this by promoting review of the relationship and processing of the accompanying feelings. By supporting remembrance of the deceased and confirming and underlining the reality of the loss, the ritual facilitates remembering the deceased in a context of finality. This is not the end of the relationship, although it certainly signals separation. Instead, the relationship between the griever and the deceased must move from one of presence to one of memory.

> Building on this foundation [Freud's 1917 discussion of decathexis] Lindemann's research has pointed to the necessity of "learning to live with memories of the deceased." [Lindemann, 1942] This is a matter of delicate balance. It would not be healthful for the mourner to try to recall the deceased from the dead by his memories, trying neurotically to perpetuate the relationship through illusion. Neither would it be healthful to seek to extinguish all memory of the deceased because of the painfulness of such recall. The deceased must be remembered in a context of finality as one who has lived and died. The rememberances help to maintain a relationship which is not radically ended but radically changed. In time the mourner becomes able to think of his relationship to the deceased, in both its positive and negative aspects, without pain. The funeral is of important help here because it can reinforce both the remembering process and the fact that the one who is remembered has died. (Irion, 1966, p. 103)

Funerals allow for input from the community that serves as a living memorial to the deceased and helps mourners form an integrated image of the deceased. Tributes paid to the deceased emphasize the worth of that person and establish that she is worthy of the pain currently sustained by the mourners. This not only legitimizes the discomfort for the mourners, but puts it in a meaningful perspective that often allows it to be better tolerated. Many people are bolstered by the comments, feelings, and thoughts they receive from others about their deceased loved one. Comments from community members also may help the mourners establish a well-rounded, realistic composite memory of the deceased to maintain.

Funerals in and of themselves contain the specific properties of rituals employed in therapy. The power of acting-out in rituals enables the individual to actively "do" something. It cuts through intellectualization, providing an objective focus in the present for the expression of feelings and reaching emotions on unconscious levels more effectively than mere verbalization. It allows emotions to be integrated and channeled more easily, assisting in the more efficient expiation of guilt. (See "Rituals" in Chapter 5 for more on these properties.)

Social Benefits

Funerals allow the community to provide social support to the mourners. Through the funeral, the community shows that it recognizes that the mourners now have a new relationship with the deceased, and that it wants to help them maintain this new relationship through memory, commemoration, and ritual. There is a manifestation of shared loss. These rituals strengthen the relations among the living as well. The consolation of those who care gives acceptance to the mourners' feelings and affirms that the mourners are not alone in grief. The mourners' path back into the social group is smoothed by the support gained from others through their presence, thoughtful gestures, and expressions of feelings of sadness and loss. Indeed, if the funeral is conducted in the absence of others, it will not serve to meet the needs of the bereaved individuals (Pine, 1975).

Funerals provide meaningful, structured activities to counter the loss of predictability and order frequently accompanying the death of a loved one. They prescribe a defined social role and provide things to do at a time when self-directed actions and purposeful behavior are not easily attainable. This is especially true given the recent sociological changes that have decreased the mourning period in American society and taken away the markings that previously identified the bereaved as individuals requiring special consideration (e.g., the black arm band, mourning clothes, formal 1-year mourning period). This has left Americans without prescribed roles and norms and often with unrealistic expectations about how to act after the death of a loved one. There are no guidelines on how to be a mourner, and few models to emulate. Therefore, the funeral can be therapeutic in providing this structure to the bereaved at a time when direction is so sorely lacking and so much needed.

Funerals begin the process of reintegrating the bereaved back into the community. The bereaved person is reincorporated into the community with a new identity, one that reflects the fact that the relationship with the deceased loved one has radically changed. There is still a relationship, but it is based on memory and identification. Additionally, the mourner probably has had to assume new roles and responsibilities as a consequence of the loss. This necessitates a change in identity (e.g., a "wife" is now a "widow"), which is validated by the community through the funeral. This process of reintegration was more clearly visible when society maintained more formal periods of mourning, with distinctive mourning garments and standardized roles of behavior indicating who was bereaved. At that time it was easier to perceive when the transitional period of social mourning had ended. Following this the community would welcome the griever back from the more isolated experience of mourning (the incorporation into the new state that is van Gennep's third phase of the rite de passage). Complications arise in today's society when this transitional period is abbreviated and routines are expected to be reestablished immediately. This makes the funeral exceptionally important, since it contains a condensation of experiences that formerly were more prolonged and constituted the important transitional phase. Today the mourner does not have adequate time to make the transition to life without the deceased prior to being incorporated back into the community. This indicates why many bereaved individuals have such a struggle with this part of the process. If they had a longer period of time to adapt, many could more adequately address the change in their relationship with the deceased and accommodate themselves to their new identity prior to being readmitted into the social group.

Spiritual Benefits
Funerals with a religious orientation give mourners a context of meaning as they attempt to fit the death of their loved one, and ultimately of themselves, into their religious/philosophical framework. According to Irion (1966), religious services provide the mourners with many benefits. They offer mourners meaning that transcends the death of the loved one, bearing witness to the hope for new life beyond death. Suffering can be comprehended and accepted with the help of religious resources, keeping it from becoming overwhelming. Mourners can confront the meaning of their own life and death, come to terms with it, and rededicate themselves to worthy purposes. The nature of humans as a unity of body and spirit can be understood more fully, both intellectually and emotionally. Finally, the services themselves provide the chance to praise God and offer thanks for life, and to pronounce a benediction on the deceased and the life she lived.

How Funerals Benefit the Social Group
Funerals have designated social purposes. "Rites performed for the dead generally have important effects for the living. A funeral ceremony is personal in its focus and is societal in its consequences" (Mandelbaum, 1959, p. 189). The social group benefits from the therapeutic effects of funerary rituals as it struggles to adjust to the loss of one of its members and to cope with the reactions that ensue.

> [Death] . . . threatens the very cohesion and solidarity of the group . . . [and the funeral] counteracts the centrifugal forces of fear, dismay, demoralization, and provides the most powerful means of reintegration of the group's shaken solidarity and of reestablishment. (Malinowski, 1948, p. 53)

Funerals help the group to adjust to the loss of one of its members. The recollection of the deceased and the catharsis of feelings stimulated by his death have therapeutic benefits for the community as well as the intimate survivors of the deceased. Like the close mourners, the community will need to deal with its grief, adapt to the changed circumstances resulting from the death of the member, and redefine itself without the existence of the deceased. The funeral ritual offers the first display of this new community. In 1963 the funeral of President Kennedy was helpful in allowing the nation to reorient itself without the presence of its leader.

Funerals affirm the social order by offering testimony that despite the death that has occurred, the community lives on. This was essentially the message that American politicians wanted to send the world when President Kennedy's funeral was broadcast. Despite the intense emotional response to the loss of a national leader, the succession of government proceeded at an orderly pace and the government continued to function. Such a message of continuity is also comforting in the face of the pain and longing experienced as a result of separation from a loved one. There is some sense of reassurance (although at times this can be maddening for the bereaved) that although a major loss has been sustained, life will continue, an important recognition when one's world is out of focus. The funeral not only assists the mourners most directly involved, but also signals to the group as a whole that readjustment and adaptation is occurring, and that although the group has been changed because of the death, it still exists. It confirms that the group is relatively indestructible in the face of personal death.

Funerals bind the social group together through present experience and collective memory. Members of the social group share a common loss. In addition, the members are often reunited at funerals after long absences. The collective memory of the group helps to define it and solidify its cohesiveness. Individual members often reestablish a focus on memories from the past that made them what they are in the present. Not infrequently relatives will recall shared experiences from the past and benefit from this additional definition of themselves, even though many years have passed and there may be little contact with one another now. For all groups weddings, wakes, and funerals bring the family together, strengthen it, and provide a sense of identity to its members.

Funerals demonstrate to members of society that they themselves will someday die, and serve as vehicles of anticipatory grief prompted by the rehearsal of their own mortality. The community receives crucial cumulative experiences of anticipatory grief through participation in the funeral rituals of its members. Community members benefit from the funeral rituals of others by receiving confirmation of the reality of their own future demise. A number of theorists are concerned about the decreasing community involvement in funerals, for this robs the community of the benefits of the rituals (while leaving the bereaved without critical social support). It especially deprives individuals of the chance to rehearse their eventual roles as primary survivors (Keith, 1976). Participation in funerals also illustrates to both the bereaved and community members that grief can be resolved, as former grievers provide excellent proof that grief can be overcome and adjustments can be made.

Funerals are a way in which the community conveys its values and beliefs regarding the meaning of life and death. Since funerals are shaped by social values and meanings, the celebration of these rites is an occasion to symbolically and concretely demonstrate the values and beliefs of the society.

Funerals are means by which the community may maintain symbolic connection with the dead and reap therapeutic opportunities to complete unfinished mourning. According to Warner (1959), the unending repetition of funerals in a community offers the members of that community appropriate opportunities for ritual connection with the dead. The funeral involves many more people than the immediate survivors, for the funeral is a public ceremony that puts each participant in connection with her own feelings towards death and the dead she has known. This is supported by Cassem (1976) when he discusses the therapeutic value of funeral rituals in providing mourners with "an occasion to cry, a chance to continue the unfinished business of grieving which all of us have" (p. 19).

Funerals provide for the final disposition of the body or the remains of the deceased. This is necessary for hygienic reasons, as well as for the symbolic transition of the deceased into the world of the dead. It also signifies the parting from the mourners, who are now effectively separated from the deceased. At times this is required for fulfilling certain religious prescriptions.

ALTERNATIVES TO TRADITIONAL FUNERALS

In addition to the traditional wake and burial services, cremation or memorial services can be chosen as alternate means of disposing of the body and honoring the deceased. Funeral preplanning allows the dying person to choose the mode of disposition she feels most comfortable with, assures her control of the situation, and takes some of the burden of decision-making off the shoulders of the family.

Cremation

Cremation is one of the available modes of body disposition. When it occurs immediately after death, with no ritual of any kind, it is called simple disposition. Cremation also may be employed in conjunction with the memorial service. The funeral director cremates the body and at a later date a public memorial service is held. Still another option exists in which all of the rituals of a wake and funeral are held, but the family accompanies the body to the crematory and deposits it there instead of at the cemetery.

In ancient times there were religious prohibitions against cremation. Some of these centered on the interpretation that it was pagan, since it had been widely used in Graeco-Roman culture and the Romans had burnt the bodies of Christian martyrs in an attempt to deny Christian resurrection. This position continued through most of Western history until the late 1800s, when the modern cremation movement developed in Italy as a reaction to the Catholic Church's monopoly on burial arrangements and as a rebellious act against the Church's authority. To counteract this the Church enacted laws forbidding cremation, stating its objection was not based on theological reasons, but was a matter of Church discipline. However, since the 1960s priests have been authorized to participate in cremation when requested and the Catholic Church now permits this mode of body disposition, although it tends to prefer interment. Its usage has increased in recent years due to the rising costs of land burial, the shortage of land for cemeteries in urban centers, concerns over public health, and the greater number of people preferring it for esthetic reasons.

There are several available modes of disposition of the deceased's remains following cremation. They may be placed in a small metallic or stone container, a process called *inurnment*. The urn may be buried or placed in a type of mausoleum known as a *columbarium*. A third option is strewing or scattering the remains. This process is subject to legal prohibition in some places and legal requirements must be investigated in advance. It also requires pulverization of the remains into ashes (sometimes bone fragments are left after cremation). Most survivors choose to scatter the ashes in places of sentimental attachment or in specially designated areas in cemeteries. A focused memorial is often important because there is no particular site the survivors can turn to as a final resting place. Consequently, memorial plaques, trees, or inscriptions in Books of Remembrance are frequently employed. Finally, some survivors may choose to personally retain the remains themselves.

There are psychological advantages and disadvantages to cremation (Irion, 1974). If this mode of body disposition is not chosen to circumvent the pain of the mourning process by getting the deceased out of sight quickly, it can have helpful psychological benefits. Cremation can facilitate mourning by effectively symbolizing the finality of the relationship that one has had with the deceased and suggesting that life must go on without her presence. The dissolution of the body in cremation makes it quite clear that the relationship does not continue as previously experienced. Since the body has been the medium of the relationship in the past, reducing it to ashes and bone fragments is a very graphic way of signaling a major shift in the relationship. Seeing the cremation process as a quick and clean incineration of the body that precludes the slow process of decomposition in earth may make the survivors feel better. Some feel comforted that the body is reduced to its natural elements and then mixed with elements of the earth. For them, it symbolizes oneness with nature.

Irion feels that cremation should never be done when it is seen as a way to escape the grief process as rapidly as possible. It also should not be done when survivors have strong reservations against being cremated themselves. Mourners should never arrange the cremation of another if they themselves are unwilling to be cremated (although it does not have to be their preferred mode of body disposition). Those who plan to be cremated should permit the closest survivors to alter that plan if the survivors have deep personal reservations about it. Still another problem may result from cremation when there has been a strong negative relationship between the deceased and the mourners. It may become a symbol of hostility, an acting-out of negative feelings towards the deceased. Consequently, it is important to look at both the psychological advantages and disadvantages, as well as the symbolic meanings cremation may have for those involved, before making a final decision:

> Simply put, the following are the conditions that should be met before the decision to cremate is made:
>
> One should be sufficiently secure to be willing to follow practices that may not have total acceptance in the community, to innovate.
>
> One should be convinced of the necessity for facing the reality of death and loss and be alert to tempting easy ways of avoidance and escape.
>
> One should not feel the need of a tangible focus for remembering the deceased.
>
> One should be willing to be cremated himself, although it is not essential that he actually plan to do so.
>
> One should freely acknowledge that the relationship with the deceased has ended as it has been known, and that life must go on without the presence of the deceased. (Irion, 1974, p. 252)

Memorial Services

A memorial service is a service that is held after the body has been buried or cremated. It differs in this respect from the funeral service, which is conducted in the presence of the body. Usually a memorial service is held 3 or 4 days after the death, but it should be scheduled for whatever time best meets the needs of the survivors. Programs are varied and can be arranged according to the desires of the survivors. Music, prayer, reflection, and sharing of remembrances and feelings about the deceased with the others present may be included. Morgan (1975) sees several advantages in such a memorial service. It focuses on the life as opposed to the death of the deceased, fostering *rehabilitation*, bringing the image of the deceased into focus and recalling what she did for the good years of her life so the survivors have a strong, happy image to carry with them. This is especially important after a long-term illness or a decline in the individual's capabilities. *Identification*, a sense of identity with the deceased, also is fostered as survivors recognize that they have shared her life and that they are now custodians of the values by which she lived. In a sense, their lives can be a memorial to the deceased; they have the ability to immortalize her. Like funerals, memorial services also reestablish relationships between mourners and the community, assist mourners in adjusting to new identities and relationships, and relieve guilt by reaffirming the values and identity of the deceased as they continue in the lives of family and friends.

In practice, the features of memoral services are sometimes incorporated into funeral services. If significant events that the deceased shared with the community are recalled, and the individuals are allowed to express the meaning of their relationship to the deceased, the funeral will have achieved the same goals as a memorial service. Indeed, Raether and Slater (1974) have observed that all funerals are memorial services, but not all memorial services are funerals.

Memorial societies have been developed by individuals who have banded together to obtain dignity, simplicity, and economy in funeral arrangements through preplanning. They charge modest fees and provide information and counsel. Although simple arrangements and low rates can generally be arranged by anyone, membership in a memorial society assures that decisions and plans have been made beforehand and expenses are reduced by membership in the organization.*

---

*For information about the nearest memorial society, contact the Continental Association of Funeral and Memorial Societies, 1828 L Street N.W., Washington, D.C. 20036.

Funeral Preplanning

The caregiver is in a unique position to assist dying patients in preplanning their funerals. There are compelling reasons why all individuals should consider preplanning (Morgan, 1975):

> 1. You know what you want, how to get it and what it will cost. You don't have to choose a casket or negotiate for a funeral.
> 2. Your family understands what is being done. Simplicity will reflect dignity rather than lack of respect.
> 3. By accepting in advance the reality of death, and by discussing it frankly, you and your family are better able to meet it when it comes. (p. 38)

In addition, proponents of the funeral offer reasons why it should be prearranged (Raether & Slater, 1974). Prearrangement allows individuals, especially those who are alone, to have the assurance that the funeral and burial will fit their personal beliefs, standards, and lifestyle. It also helps survivors by providing approximate funeral and burial cost guidelines. Finally, it allows those who have moved numerous times or maintained several residences to make certain that they will be buried at the location of their choice. In essence, preplanning of funerary or memorial rituals allows people the ability to exert some control over their final connection with society.

It is important for planners to recognize that basically funerals are for the living, not the dead. They must review the possible effects of their plans on the survivors. Discussion of funeral and burial preferences with potential survivors is suggested to insure that decisions will not be made that could be difficult or upsetting for them to carry out. Failure to do this in a coherent, interactive manner will probably cause problems later for some of them.

THE VALUE OF FUNERALS

Despite recent criticism, funerals fulfill critical psychological and social needs following a death. A rite of passage is necessary after the death of a loved one, for the passing of that person must be recognized, his survivors must be supported as they start a new life without him, and they must be reintegrated into the community, which itself must reaffirm its continuity after the loss of a member. By design, funerals catalyze acute grief responses, prescribe structured behaviors in a time of flux, and encourage recognition of the loss and development of new relationships with both the deceased and the community.

It is not coincidental that these rituals take place so soon after death. Early problems with the grief process are often the worst ones, predisposing mourners to even further difficulties. Some psychologists and sociologists argue that at times these rituals occur too early, when the bereaved may be unable to appropriately benefit from them due to their being in a state of shock or disorganization. However, this does not contradict the necessity for the rituals to occur early after the loss; rather, it points out the need for continued ritual throughout the mourning process. For example, the Roman Catholic anniversary mass and the Jewish "unveiling" take place a year after the death, thereby providing additional ritualistic activities that continue to offer the therapeutic advantages of the funeral.

Whatever rituals are adopted, the important issue is that they be personally meaningful to the bereaved. This does not preclude formal religious rituals, if they hold some meaning for those involved. When the bereaved have no organized religious or philosophical system of belief, humanist services suited to their personal needs can be developed. Rituals that are not personally meaningful to the bereaved have no therapeutic value, whereas those that are meaningful are perceived as positive parts of the grief process.

It is the instances in which rituals have not properly addressed grievers' needs that have given funerals a negative image for some. These, when combined with the practices of a relatively few unscrupulous funeral directors have contributed to the overindictment of funerals. But in reality, there are far more instances of research findings confirming the value of funerals than the critics of the funeral industry would have us believe (Binger, Ablin, Feuerstein, Kushner, Zoger, & Mikkelsen, 1969; Fulton, 1976a; Glick et al., 1974; Pine, 1976a). Mourners with pathological grief often indicate that their experience with the funeral did not go well and that their participation in it was insufficient, suggesting the critical psychological importance of the ritual and the benefits of full participation in it (Volkan, 1975). In a large scale study of widows and widowers (Fulton, 1976a), subjects who participated in what would be termed a "traditional" funeral (i.e., who viewed the body and who involved their friends and relatives in the ceremony) reported fewer adjustment problems, more positive recall of the deceased, and closer ties and warmer relationships with their relatives than did subjects who had less than the traditional funeral. The funeral seemed to bring surviving members closer together. A greater sense of urgency with respect to being kind and considerate of other survivors was reported. Those who did not view the body or had arranged for immediate disposition of the remains (excluding the normal Jewish custom of not viewing the body) reported the greatest hostility following the death; the greatest increase in consumption of alcohol, tranquilizers, and sedatives; the greatest increase in tension and anxiety; the lowest positive recall of the deceased; and greater problems in adjustment to the death, particularly among male respondents.

While there may be some global accusations against the funeral industry, funeral directors do seem to be serving the living well in their position of caring for the dead. Although funeral directors in general are derided by some, it is not unusual for people to comment positively on individual funeral directors whom they know and with whom they have had contact (Fulton, 1976b; Pine, 1976a).

Wakes, funerals, memorial services, and other mourning rituals have a great potential to facilitate resolution of grief. If the purposes of these rituals are distorted, resolution of grief is made more difficult. Thus, it is important to separate errors in interpretation of rituals from the usefulness of their design. Such rituals are unparalleled in providing a good beginning for the healthy grieving process.

SUGGESTIONS FOR PLANNING FUNERALS AND FUNERARY RITUALS

Funerary rituals can be a potent means of promoting effective grief resolution when properly planned with survivors. Here are some suggestions to follow when planning in addition to those already discussed in Chapter 5.

Confronting the Death

• Ask the bereaved how they want the deceased to be remembered, especially when interviewing to collect information for the obituary notice. This is a critically important psychological opportunity, since it prompts recollection of the deceased, promotes recognition of the fact that the relationship has been changed, and assists in the process of decathexis.

• Give the bereaved adequate private time to be with, touch, caress, and hold the body. This may occur prior to public viewing or before the body is taken to the funeral home. Do not rush the survivors, as time with the deceased may be very critical in helping them to finish unfinished business, accommodate to the changed relationship they must have with the deceased, and accept the reality of the loss.

• Encourage questions from the bereaved and answer them as fully as possible. At times upsetting information may have to be given to the bereaved, but gentle honesty should be the rule. For example, to try to hide the fact that the individual was decapitated may predispose the bereaved to more problems later when the autopsy report is finally received. What is imagined is often worse than reality. You cannot protect the bereaved from reality, but you can present it in the most compassionate way.

• Address the unique issues involved in special cases of death. For example, in cases of stillbirths and neonatal death, encourage the family to have a funeral ritual in which the mother participates. Do not acquiesce to the practices of some newspapers that refuse to print obituary notices for such deaths.

In cases of suicide, be firm in suggesting that the ritual be held despite discomfort with the possible reactions of the community. Point out the important issues (see "Grief After Suicide" in Chapter 6 for more on this topic) and help the survivors to see that it is necessary to mark the death and to respond in ways that will be helpful to their own bereavement.

In cases of disfigurement or deterioration of the body, prepare the body to make it as presentable as possible to the family. In those situations where it is inadvisable to display the body publically, the family should be encouraged to view some portion of the body that would confirm for them the death of their loved one. They need to see some identifying aspect of the body, such as a hand with a birthmark, that will help them to recognize the body as the remains of their loved one.

In those cases where a body is not available (e.g., when lost at sea or buried in a cave-in), a memorial service should be suggested. You may even want to tape the service, since the unreality of the death may be difficult for the survivors to later combat and a tape of the service may help.

• Especially in untimely and sudden death cases, consider saving a lock of hair (get permission first) or taking a photograph of the deceased. Such items are especially meaningful and can be delivered to the bereaved later on to help confirm the reality of the loss.

Planning the Funeral

Incorporating Grievers' Needs

• Listen to the specific needs of the survivors. Help them articulate those needs so they can be included in the funeral in some form.

• Assist the bereaved in making the funeral as adaptive and meaningful as possible. It should reflect their emotions and their image of the deceased. Feeling that the ritual would be approved of by the deceased and that they have appropriately honored her according to their ethnic or cultural standards can be meaningful to them.

• Be aware of the family's values, norms, expectations, and religious/philosophical preferences. This is important in order to provide a funeral that will be meaningful to the family and congruent with their psychosocial history.

• Encourage the family to perform those specific personal behaviors that are important to them in terms of saying good-bye and finishing unfinished business. For example, allow a child to put a favorite toy into the casket of his brother.

• Because some mourners may resent your preparing the body, you should ask them if they wish to participate in this. For example, the mothers of children who have died may want to dress their child for the last time and resent your taking over this function. Be aware of this possible need.

• Explain in advance to the bereaved, in as much detail as possible, exactly what will happen during the funeral rituals. This will allow them to be more prepared for the experience.

• If the funeral does not contain some elements of a memorial service, encourage the creation of a memorialization of the life of the deceased for incorporation into whatever funerary rituals are chosen. Encouraging discussion about the deceased and the sharing of feelings is therapeutic.

• Do not force grievers to participate or express feelings. Encourage them to act as they wish, as long as it does not prevent grief resolution. If the griever opts for denial and withdrawal, it should be permitted, but the consequences of such actions should be gently pointed out.

• Recognize that the bereaved's sense of ceremony may be different than yours. While you should try to dissuade them from carrying out plans that are psychologically unhealthy, they otherwise should be allowed to honor the deceased in whatever way they see fit.

Making Decisions

• Since bereaved individuals may not be aware of the possible options for funeral services, explain the various options open to them.

• Do not force bereaved individuals into any choices that appear to contradict their stated needs. In fact, if their own choices do contradict their needs, gently point this out.

• Respect the choices made by the bereaved. Remember, this is their funeral, not yours.

• Convey to the bereaved that the amount of money they spend is not necessarily a meaningful indication of their love of the deceased.

• Recognize that within a given family there will be different needs among individual family members. At times it will be difficult to design rituals that will accommodate all of them. These differing needs should be discussed openly, since ignoring them in order to promote a false unity will only create problems later on.

• Make sure that the mode of disposition is one that the mourners can live with. This is especially critical in cases involving cremation, where unresolved issues may make such a choice a conflicted one that causes later problems for the survivors.

• Be sensitive to the fact that some decisions may be regretted later. For example, double check if spouses truly want the deceased's wedding ring buried with her, asking if perhaps they would want to save this as a memento. Of course this must be done in a gentle, undemanding way. Sensitively pointing out the consequences of certain courses of action will allow the bereaved to become aware of possibilities they had not considered.

• Determine if the decisions the survivors are making reflect their own needs or the advice of others. It is acceptable for them to take others' advice if it meets their needs, but try to ascertain whether or not they recognize all their options and are in fact taking care of their own needs.

• Understand that although you must call upon the bereaved to make a number of decisions, the process of grief renders such decision making enormously difficult. Explain matters as simply and clearly as possible, for the bereaved person is most probably confused and overwhelmed. Repeat the explanation as often as necessary for comprehension.

Including Others

• Encourage the participation of family members and of the community (if not disputed by the family). Allow them to participate as much as is possible, and/or desirable.

• Be sure to assess the needs and wants of the quiet ones in the family. Do not forget those individuals who may still be hospitalized, such as the mother of the stillborn baby or the other victim of an auto accident. Work to incorporate these individuals into the funerary ritual and possibly arrange for a delay of the services until they can attend.

• Involve the clergy in funerary rituals. Work with them to see that the mourners' needs are met.

• Help the bereaved to include children in the funerary rituals and try to keep them from being omitted or pushed aside. Future pathology and problems in the family can be prevented when the children are included in the funeral.

• It is important to involve other family members besides the immediate family. Recognize that they often get overlooked, even though their grief may be quite intense. This is especially true when parents have lost an adult child. In most cases, the attention is directed towards that child's spouse and children, and the parents of the deceased are left unattended. Recognize this phenomenon and work to include or at least to validate the experience of these other mourners.

• Recognize the importance of the survivors who may not be next of kin. Frequently they have sustained relationships with the deceased that may even be closer than the family, yet often they are forgotten in funerary rituals. Your recognition of their importance and their relationship to the deceased will go far to help them in their grief and validate their participation.

Preparing for After the Funeral

• Suggest that the bereaved appropriately reach out for support from friends or family if needed.

• When directing many of the activities following the death, make sure that the bereaved take care of their own physical and emotional needs (e.g., suggest adequate rest and eating, discourage overreliance on tranquilizers). They will need their strength if they are to continue to address their grief.

• Normalize the intense reactions of acute bereavement so they are not interpreted as abnormal and responded to inappropriately.

• If and when appropriate, help the bereaved with matters of estate and financial concerns to whatever extent possible. When proper, advise them to contact professionals. You may have to be an advocate for them or direct them to the benefits that are due them.

• It may be important for you to gently predict that it may be difficult for the family to go home following the funeral activities. After the excitement and chaos of the several days of rituals following the death it may seem very lonely. This experience should be normalized for survivors.

Fulfilling the Funeral Director's Role

• Understand the customs and socioeconomic, religious/philosophical, and cultural values, norms, and mores in the community from which your clients come. Otherwise you will not be able to adequately address their needs.

• Recognize that you are part of a community and attempt to integrate into that community. You can symbolize the continuity of the life-death cycle. The very same limousines that carry the families of the deceased to the cemetery are also those that carry families to weddings.

• Do not become a "surrogate sufferer" (Nichols, 1983). In order to overcome your feelings of helplessness in the face of intense grief responses, do not try to suffer in the place of the sufferers or reduce their pain. In the long run this makes them feel more helpless, passive, and out of control. Work to help the grievers help themselves.

• Realize that you may be one of the few people who will have the opportunity to deal with the whole family and the support system together. While you should recognize individual differences, the family and support system themselves form a system, and should be responded to as such.

• You must show respect at all times for the deceased and for her survivors. While you may have buried numbers of mothers before, it is a first-time occurrence for the mother's survivors and sensitivity about this must be maintained at all times.

• Recognize that the mourners may be hostile towards you because of some negative publicity that has been received by the funeral industry. They may resent that you are making your living off the death of their loved one. This is a professional issue that you must deal with in a manner that will not interfere with your effective servicing of the bereaved. If this is not possible, you should seek professional advice.

CHAPTER 8

Death and
the Dying Patient

Becoming aware of having a terminal illness means facing the fact that life, as it has been known, is now limited. The terminally ill patient must reorient his life, values, goals, and beliefs to accommodate this sudden realization. Although from late childhood almost everyone is cognitively aware that death is universal and that each of us must someday die, the news of terminal illness alters a patient's perspective radically. Previously the fact of personal death could be denied. It was an event in the future that could easily be repressed and sublimated. But after death is known to be imminent, the patient is compelled to take a good hard look at death and its personal meaning. It cannot be avoided any longer.

INITIAL AWARENESS OF
IMPENDING DEATH

A patient may become aware that he is dying in many ways other than receiving a direct diagnosis from a physician. He may learn in any one or more of the following ways (Kalish, 1970):
- A direct statement from the physician.
- Overheard comments made by the physician to others.
- Direct statements from other health care personnel, particularly nurses.
- Overheard comments made by other health care personnel.
- Direct statements by others involved, such as a family member, a social worker, a clergyman or the family lawyer.
- Overheard comments by others involved.
- Changes in the behavior of others, e.g., visits of the physician dropping off, staff interactions becoming more abrupt, the sudden visit of a loved one from a long distance away.

- Changes in medical care procedures, e.g., different medication is administered, pain-killers are more readily dispensed, surgery is cancelled.
- Changes in physical placement. The patient may be moved to another room, sent home, or put in an extended care facility. The physical location will have great significance in terms of the progress of the illness.
- Self-diagnosis. Through reading, listening to the fatal symptoms of others, assessing the reactions of other individuals, a reasonable self-diagnosis can often be made.
- The signals from within the body.
- Altered responses to personal futurity, e.g., discussion of the future suddenly is responded to with reluctance or else is aggressively avoided.

Because patients can ascertain information that is not directly presented to them, an *open awareness context*, in which there is shared knowledge and communication about the illness among patient, family, and caregivers, is very important to establish (Glaser & Strauss, 1965). It is the only context in which it can be determined exactly what the patient is aware of, and, by implication, exactly what needs to be responded to by caregivers. (See "Avoidance of Withdrawal From the Patient" in Chapter 11 for more on awareness contexts.)

Despite how it is learned, the knowledge of impending death precipitates a crisis for the patient. Pattison has analyzed the knowledge of death in terms of the five aspects of crisis defined by Parad and Caplan (1960):

- This stressful event poses a problem that by definition is insolvable in the immediate future. In this sense dying is the most stressful crisis because it is a crisis to which we bow but do not solve.
- The problem taxes one's psychological resources since it is beyond one's traditional problem-solving methods. One is faced with a new experience with no prior experience to draw from, for although one has lived amidst death, that is far different from one's own death.
- The situation is perceived as a threat or danger to the life goals of the person. Dying interrupts a person in the midst of life; and even in old age it abruptly confronts one with the goals one set in life.
- The crisis period is characterized by a tension that mounts to a peak, then falls. As one faces the crisis of death knowledge, there is mobilization of either integrative or disintegrative mechanisms. The peak of anxiety usually occurs considerably before death.

- The crisis situation awakens unresolved key problems from both the near and distant past. Problems of dependency, passivity, narcissism, identity, and more may be activated during the dying process. Hence one is faced not only with the immediate dying process but also with the unresolved feelings from one's own lifetime and its inevitable conflicts. (Pattison, 1978, pp. 145-146)

In confronting the crisis the patient faces limit, loss, and change (Davidson, 1966). He feels (and is) limited and trapped by the illness. He feels loss as he recognizes that he must lose all that he has ever known and loved. And he faces many changes: changes in his body, changes in his assumption of futurity, changes in his independence, changes in his abilities and capacities, changes in relationships with others. All of these attack the ego's attempts to maintain homeostasis, and seriously destabilize the person. The patient will struggle to attain a new equilibrium using psychological defenses and coping mechanisms. However, psychological defense is difficult for terminally ill patients for these three reasons (Verwoerdt, 1966):

- The illness itself and its physical sequelae deplete the individual of energy required to maintain appropriate coping mechanisms.
- The individual has had no previous experience with death to assist in the adaptation to it.
- Healthy adaptation requires the expectation of pleasurable results in the future. This is absent in the patient facing a terminal illness.

For these reasons, the crisis of the knowledge of death is an overwhelming one to face.

There are various ways in which patients may react to the news of terminal illness. They may accept or deny the news, vacillate between accepting or denying, or do both simultaneously. They may overtly express knowledge that they are dying, but emotionally be unable to accept it. Conversely, they may accept it, but be unable to verbalize it. Whatever the response, it is undertaken to protect the shocked ego and meet the emotional needs of the patient at that moment.

TASKS OF THE DYING PATIENT

Anyone who is forced to cope with serious illness or injury must meet some basic adaptive tasks. Moos and Tsu (1977) have identified seven sets of tasks that are generally encountered with any serious illness, not just terminal ones. The relative importance of each type of task will vary widely depending on the nature of the illness, the personality of the individual, and the environmental circumstances.

The first set of tasks is straightforward. It involves dealing with discomfort, incapacitation, and other symptoms of the illness or injury itself.

The second set is the management of the stresses of special treatment procedures and the institutional setting itself. Radiation, chemotherapy, surgery, prosthetic devices—all represent therapeutic measures that demand adaptation both to them and their side effects. Additionally, there are new and highly specialized technical environments for treatment. The intensive care unit, the radiation treatment room, or the waiting room of the oncology clinic are all foreign environments that place additional demands on patients and their families. The separation of patients and family and the unfamiliar nature of treatment create problems and additional secondary losses for them.

The tasks in the third set consist of developing and maintaining adequate relationships with caregivers. The patient and family must consider how to cope interpersonally with the health care system. They may feel insecure about expressing their honest concerns, feelings, or needs, and be uncertain how to get specific information or what procedures to follow.

> Consider the questions patients may ask themselves: Can I express my anger at the doctor for not coming to see me? How can I ask for additional medication for pain when I need it? How can I deal with the disagreements among different physicians regarding how I should be treated? How can I handle the condescension and pity I sense in the nurses who care for me? How can I tell the physical therapist not to give up on me even though my progress is disappointingly slow? How can I engage my doctor in a meaningful discussion of how I wish to be treated if I am incapacitated and near death? These are problems which plague patients and their families. The frequent turnover and change in personnel, particularly those staff who come into more direct contact with the patient, makes this an unusually complicated set of tasks. (Moos & Tsu, 1977, pp. 9-10)

The fourth category of tasks concerns preserving a reasonable emotional balance by managing upsetting feelings aroused by the illness, such as anxiety, anger, alienation, inadequacy, or guilt. It will be critical for the patient to maintain some hope, even when it is sharply limited by the realities of the illness.

Preserving a satisfactory self-image and maintaining a sense of competence and mastery is the fifth set of tasks. Changes must be incorporated into a new and revised self-image, to which personal values and lifestyles may have to be accommodated. Losses must be grieved, and goals and expectations must be readjusted. The patient must define the limits of independence and find a personally and socially satisfactory balance between accepting help and taking an active and responsible part in his life.

The sixth set of tasks includes preserving relationships with family and friends. The patient will need continued contact with loved ones, despite the isolation or alienation sometimes caused by hospitalization, the illness, or the reluctance of others to stay in contact with the sick or dying. Communication must be kept open to meet this need.

The final set of tasks involves preparing for an uncertain future in which significant losses are threatened. This means dealing with anxiety over the uncertainty, as well as grieving for current and potential losses.

In addition to the seven types of tasks just discussed, there are others unique to the terminally ill patient. Most, if not all, of these tasks only serve to remind the patient even more acutely that time on earth is limited. It is important that those close to the terminally ill patient recognize this and assist in any possible manner with the execution of these seven tasks. These tasks are outlined by Kalish (1970).

The patient must arrange a variety of affairs. Each one signals impending death; each one brings the patient one step closer to it. These include getting the will in order; paying back debts; checking on insurance policies; leaving messages for friends, neighbors, and co-workers; making funeral and burial arrangements; and providing for the welfare of those left behind. Often pain and discomfort, fear, anxiety, confusion, or disability hinder the patient from taking a direct role in these arrangements. If denial has caused the patient to reject the notion of immediate death, such arrangements may not be made at all. Although this task may be uncomfortable, it gives the patient a sense of control and allows her to take care of survivors. (See "Assistance With the Practical Considerations of Dying" in Chapter 11 for more on this topic.)

The patient must undertake the task of coping with loss, both of loved ones and the self. Dying persons are often deeply concerned with what effect their death will have upon their survivors in ways other than legal and financial. They will frequently consider their survivors' grief, their needs, their vulnerability, and their coming need to establish replacement relationships. There is a potential for bringing patients and their loved ones closer together if the feelings can be openly and honestly discussed. Ignoring these feelings through mutual pretense precludes this, and the deceit wears emotionally on all those involved and robs them of meaningful interaction.

Similarly, the dying patient must accommodate the self to its own loss. The patient is going to lose the entire known world and all of the people in it. Coping with this impending loss is one of the most difficult tasks for the dying person, whose fears are a combination of the reaction to the loss of self and empathy with the sorrow of the loved ones.

The patient must see to future medical care needs. Often this task can be left to others, but many times the patient derives a sense of satisfaction in exercising some control in such matters. With analgesics, the kind, dosage, frequency, and types of effects tolerated can be decided by the patient. The choice of kind of medical treatment and the point at which it can be discontinued may be left up to the patient; so can the location of death, whether in the hospital, nursing home, hospice, or the patient's own home.

The patient must plan the future. Whatever remaining time, energy, and financial resources there are must be allocated by the patient. For example, the patient may want to plan disbursement of personal possessions and make arrangements to see long-lost friends. She may desire to spend her dwindling resources on a last vacation or set up a trust fund for survivors. In any case, the patient should continue to plan for and enjoy living as long as possible.

The patient must anticipate future pain and discomfort and face possible loss of various forms of sensory, motor, or cognitive abilities. All of these prospects are extremely anxiety-provoking to the patient. However, changes in appearance and loss of performance and function must be realistically anticipated, grieved, and planned for. It often turns out that the realities of the situation are less frightening than the anticipation of them. Nevertheless, the patient should make arrangements for a time when she may no longer be capable of carrying out her own wishes and plans. For instance, she may assign power of attorney, enroll in a hospice home-care program, or make a "Living Will" to ensure that heroic resuscitation measures will not be initiated when they would not contribute to the further quality of life.

The patient must cope effectively with the loss of self and identity and with the death encounter. The patient will be forced to relinquish control in vital areas of her life and face the coming destruction of the body and its suggestion of loss of self and identity. Consequently the patient must consider being a nonperson, a forgotten person, someone who continues only in memories, pictures, and the temporary results of work and human relationships. There is also the fear of a rite of passage from which no one has returned with descriptions of the new role. The possibility of permanent extinction must be acknowledged.

Coping with the death encounter inevitably brings up concerns of immortality. Many are comforted through their religion at this time. Others, while religious, find no such comfort. The research on the role of religion has produced mixed results. Living memories may be hoped for in one's children, or artistic or industrial contributions. It is at this time that patients who do not feel fulfilled, or do not believe they have contributed to society, will sink into what Erikson (1950) has termed "the state of despair."

The patient must decide whether to attempt to slow down or speed up the dying process. The patient's will to live influences the dying process. If it is relinquished, the patient stops fighting or complying with treatment and may succumb to the illness earlier than medically anticipated. If it is strong, the patient may experience additional remissions.

The patient must deal with numerous psychosocial problems. In this and following chapters, the patient's struggle with the problems of dying will be examined.

THE PATIENT'S STRUGGLE FOR CONTROL

It is what the patient wants. And the physician . . . the nurses, the relatives. It is what janitors want as they mop the floor and hospital administrators as they pick up the telephone. Should psychiatrists or social scientists appear on the scene, then we just have a wider assortment of people seeking the same goal if by different means.

Everyone affected by the dying situation wants to stay in control. This is not the only desire of people in this situation, but it is a need that must be attended to if other goals are to be met. (Kastenbaum, 1978, p. 227)

One of the major themes of the chapters devoted to the dying patient will be the theme of provision of control. Practically all clinical interventions suggested are attempts to put more cognitive, emotional, social, or behavioral control back into the hands of the dying individual from whom it is so incontrovertibly slipping away. The control issue surfaces in all phases of the illness, for from the moment of diagnosis to the moment of death the patient struggles to cope with many different kinds of losses. Since the patient is incapable of avoiding these losses, a feeling of loss of control is inevitable.

As a society we are poorly equipped to handle this phenomenon. We value our sense of control too highly, and stress possession of the tools to achieve it—independence, effectiveness, power. They defend us against the painful experience of helplessness. The desire for control is natural and understandable, but control is continually threatened with dissolution by illness and by the ultimate situation over which we are powerless and ineffective—death. It is not surprising, then, that the terminally ill patient uses direct and indirect methods to secure, maintain, and assert as much control as is possible.

Unfortunately, the patient's control is not only challenged by the intrinsic aspects of the illness and its treatment, but also by the health care and family systems within which the patient exists. As illustrated in the quote opening this section, everyone involved in the dying situation wants, indeed needs, control. Conflicts arise when one person's attempts at gaining control take it away from another. The family's need to get medical information may interfere with the patient's need to talk about his feelings at the same time. A physician's need for authority, manifested by an order forbidding a nurse to discuss the diagnosis with the patient, keeps the nurse from meeting her need to be responsive to those who are in her care.

Although all participants in the dying experience struggle with control issues, no one does so more than the dying patient. Others can assume control in different areas to compensate for their losses, but the dying patient is seldom afforded this luxury as his capabilities dwindle. One of the most critically important services a caregiver can perform is to maximize the patient's opportunities for control and minimize situations destructive to it.

SUFFERING

It is important to differentiate between the experience of pain and that of suffering. Pain alone does not equal suffering. For instance, a woman may experience pain in childbirth, but not necessarily suffering. Bodies do not suffer, a person suffers, and this usually occurs when the intactness of the person is threatened or lost (Cassell, Note 10). For suffering to take place, a loss or disruption of the sense of wholeness must occur. Physical pain is unnecessary. For example, the mother watching the distress of a child may suffer, but she does not necessarily experience physical pain. For the dying patient, this issue is a critical one. The illness taking the patient's life may bring with it physical pain, but suffering does not automatically proceed from it. Whether or not it does is dependent upon what meaning is given to the pain. "Thus pain is not the issue per se, but our response to pain that makes it either *sufferable* or *suffering*" (Pattison, 1978, p. 150).

Medical intervention can ease physical pain, as well as some nontraditional methods. (See "Pain Management" in Chapter 11 for more on this topic.) However, the mere diminution of pain will not and cannot eradicate suffering. Suffering must be attended to by awareness, understanding, and comfort. It is psychological in nature and must be ministered to through the therapeutic intervention of a concerned and present other. Indeed, relief from pain is less closely related to drugs than to the individual's attitudes and feelings about pain:

> The patient who fears pain is more likely expressing a fear of suffering. And what is suffering? It is pain that has no meaning, no location, no explanation. Clinical studies of pain in the dying bear this out: pain relief is not closely related to the dosage of pain-killing drugs, but rather relief is closely tied to the person's attitude toward pain.
>
> The fear is not just a physical fear, but a fear of the unknown and unmanageable. Senseless pain is perhaps intolerable. On the other hand, pain may be accepted and dealt with if that pain does not mean punishment, or being ignored, or not being cared for. People will not suffer long, but they will endure pain. (Pattison, 1978, p. 150)

Caregivers can do much to alleviate the suffering of dying patients. Minimizing the losses that disrupt the individual's sense of wholeness—isolation, rejection, loss of control—will reduce the individual's suffering, despite the presence of physical pain (Cassell, Note 10). Additionally, working with the patient to put the experience into a religious, philosophical, or personally meaningful perspective can make it understandable or lend it a transcendental frame of reference that will give it some meaning and allow it to be better tolerated.

TYPES OF DEATH

There are four types of death that each dying individual actually undergoes (Sudnow, 1967) *social death, psychological death, biological death,* and *physiological death.*

Social death represents the symbolic death of the patient in the world the patient has known. Socially, this world begins to shrink. This occurs naturally when the illness forces a change in lifestyle or the individual is hospitalized and removed from the familiar environments of work, home, and neighborhood. The number of social contacts the patient has diminish accordingly. Withdrawal and separation from others result from the patient's increasing preoccupation with the illness and grieving for the losses to come. Usually by the end of the illness contacts are limited to only those who are closest to the patient.

In some cases, however, social death occurs much earlier than necessary. In these situations, dying individuals may be deserted and placed in nursing homes by families who already consider them "dead." They may be the victims of too much and too effective anticipatory grief on the part of their loved ones, resulting in premature detachment. They also may be isolated at the end of the hospital floor so as not to provoke anxiety in the hospital staff, who are all too often still made uncomfortable by a dying patient. Studies have been done illustrating that the needs of the terminally ill tend to be met much less efficiently than do those of the acutely ill. One classic study noted how nurses took longer to respond to the call lights of terminally ill patients than to those of the acutely ill. All of this reflects the discomfort that the dying provoke in those around them. Although such anxiety is understandable, it needs to be managed in ways that are therapeutic and not deleterious to the patient. Social death is a natural part of the dying process, but care must be exercised to ensure that it results from the natural sequence of the patient's dying trajectory and not from the defensiveness of those around the patient.

Psychological death refers to the death of aspects of the dying individual's personality. The dying process will cause this to occur. Terminal illness will demand some degree of regression and dependency just by the fact that the individual is no longer capable of the same degree of autonomous functioning as previously. Grief over the losses (symbolic and physical) resulting from the illness will affect the personality. The disease process itself often fosters personality changes biochemically, as do medication and pain. Coinciding with this, patients will experience changes in their relationships with others, all too often leading to isolation and invalidation. As the end draws closer dying individuals also begin to decathect from the world and most people they know, withdrawing into themselves. In essence, the individual, as others know that person, dies.

Biological death refers to death in which the organism, as a human entity, no longer exists. There may be artificial supports that keep certain organs functioning, but the human traits of consciousness and awareness in a self-sustaining mind-body organism are gone.

Physiological death occurs when there is a cessation of the operation of all vital organs.

Ideally these four types of death succeed one another in this order, facilitating each other. Therapeutic intervention would attempt to structure the environment so that these first two types of death do not occur too far in advance of the latter two. When biological death precedes physiological death by too great an interval, crucial questions of bioethical concern arise in such legal and moral issues as euthanasia, transplantation, and "pulling the plug."

Obviously, the goal should be to try to promote circumstances in which all four types of death can occur as coincidentally as possible. This can be achieved by minimizing premature detachment from the patient, socially and psychologically. Continued interaction with family, friends, and caregivers is critical in affirming the social and psychological existence of the patient. The patient and his family can be helped to expect, adjust to, and deal with the psychological changes resulting from the disease process and its accompanying losses. The patient needs to be supportively accompanied throughout the illness and permitted to die in a natural manner at the time of biological death.

THE LIVING-DYING INTERVAL

A useful conceptualization of the process of dying has been offered by Pattison (1977, 1978). Although each of us has the potential to die at any moment, we usually operate under the assumption that we have a certain lifespan in which to plan our lives. The diagnosis of terminal illness abruptly confronts us with a crisis, the crisis of knowledge of death. Our expectations for the future are drastically altered. The period of time between the crisis of knowledge of death and the point of death is called the *living-dying interval*. Due to recent advances in medicine, this living-dying interval has been lengthened for most illnesses, and in fact often encompasses a number of years. While in the past knowledge of impending death would be rapidly followed by death itself, there now are often chronic conditions with which the patient and his family must cope. Living with a chronic terminal illness brings a number of problems:
- Remissions and relapses
- Lengthened periods of anticipatory grief
- Increased financial, social, physical, and emotional pressures
- Long-term family disruption
- Progressive decline of the patient and emotional responses of the family to this
- Longer periods of uncertainty
- Intensive treatment regimens and their side effects
- Dilemmas about decision-making and treatment choices

They are the price we pay now that serious illnesses no longer are inevitable and immediate death sentences. Some believe that this price is too high, especially when it involves prolonging the patient's physical and emotional pain. But the reality is that illnesses are becoming more chronic in nature and placing new demands on caregivers who work with the terminally ill.

The living-dying interval is divided by Pattison into three clinical phases, each with independent tasks:

The period of living-dying can be conveniently divided into three clinical phases: (1) the acute crisis phase, (2) the chronic living-dying phase, and (3) the terminal phase. We can respond to the acute phase in terms of crisis intervention, so that it does not result in a chaotic disintegration of the person's life during the rest of the living-dying interval. Thus, our first task is to deal appropriately with the crisis of knowledge of death, so that the dying person can move into an appropriate trajectory that integrates his dying into his lifestyle and life circumstance. The second task is to respond to the adaptive issues of the chronic living-dying phase. Finally, the third task is to assist the patient to move ineluctably into the terminal phase when it becomes appropriate. (Pattison, 1978, p. 141)

The Acute Crisis Phase

When a patient receives a terminal diagnosis, he is immediately thrown into the acute crisis phase of the living-dying interval. Annihilation anxiety arises. He may experience an *ego chill*, the shudder that stems from the sudden awareness that nonexistence is entirely possible (Leveton, 1965). The usual reaction is one of acute crisis anxiety. This escalates until it reaches a peak, after which the patient calls upon whatever psychological mechanisms are available to reduce the anxiety. Continued functioning under such stress cannot occur for very long. If ineffective psychological mechanisms are utilized to cope with the anxiety, the patient will fall into a disintegrative dying style. In this regard it is helpful to look at the knowledge of death as a crisis event. (See "Initial Awareness of Impending Death" earlier in this chapter for more on this topic.)

People react to the crisis of the knowledge of their impending death in different ways. For some, there will be anxiety, panic, and an intense sense of helplessness, abandonment, and vulnerability. For others, these may be absent and in their stead there may be a feeling of immobilization and possibly depersonalization. Feelings of inadequacy, confusion, and bewilderment are not uncommon, for no answers are available. Indeed, for dying patients and their families, the time of diagnosis is most often cited as the most difficult and stressful period within the entire experience. The need to deny, the confusion and the shock, the high anxiety, the lack of time to assimilate—all make it difficult to decide how to proceed and to mobilize effective coping mechanisms. The fact that individuals react intensely, with what in other situations would appear to be pathological responses, needs to be put into perspective:

> We should not be surprised to see many pathological defenses in this acute stage, and we should perhaps not react too vigorously to them. For if we focus on the reduction of anxiety through a focusing on reality issues and appropriate emotional support, it is likely that the dying person will move toward appropriate emotional responses to his living-dying. (Pattison, 1978, p. 146)

The *trajectory* is the path of the individual's dying experience. There are four different types of trajectories or death expectations that can be set up by the crisis of knowledge of death. These are based on the certainty of the death and the time at which it is anticipated (Glaser & Strauss, 1955, 1968). Certain trajectories are easier to cope with than uncertain ones, since ambiguity is always difficult to contend with and generates anxiety. In fact, one of the reasons that the acute crisis phase of dying is usually the time of peak anxiety is because it is the time when the uncertainty of events is highest.

The first type of trajectory is certain death at a known time. In this case the time frame for resolving issues is quite clear, so there may be rapid movement from the acute crisis phase to the chronic living-dying phase. In very acute illnesses or after serious accidents the death may occur so swiftly that there is no time for anything but the acute phase and the death itself.

The second type is certain death at an unknown time. This is the typical trajectory for chronic fatal illness. Because the length of the living-dying interval is uncertain, there is additional stress on the patient and family. Treatment should focus on those things that are certain in the patient's life:

> Here there is certainty of death, but the living-dying interval may stretch out over several years. It is clear that here we have prolonged emotional stress for the dying person and for the family. They live with dying. To follow the principle of certainty, the lesson here seems to be the importance of *focusing on what is certain.* Since the exact time of death cannot be reasonably predicted, it is important here to shift the focus to predictable daily issues of life. Thus the dying person and the family can turn to specific issues and deal with life on a predictable day-to-day basis. Whereas in the acute trajectories one is faced with the imminent expectation of death, in this chronic trajectory it is important to shift the focus from death per se to the issues of living while dying. (Pattison, 1978, p. 143).

Third is the trajectory of uncertain death, but a known time when certainty will be established. In this case, the dying trajectory is suspended until there is further information, as when a patient waits for the results of a biopsy or an organ transplant. Intense emotions are aroused for those involved, as the anxiety generated in the acute crisis phase cannot be responded to until the question of the certainty of the death can be resolved.

The final type of trajectory is uncertain death and an unknown time when the question will be resolved. These trajectories are associated with the overall uncertainty and anxiety of serious chronic illnesses such as multiple sclerosis and genetic diseases. It is ambiguous as to when the question of the certainty of death will be resolved. For some, this breeds a high degree of anxiety that leads to dysfunctional defenses and a hypochondriacal fixation on the physical state. Others, especially younger patients, are helped to successfully adapt to the illness by new advances in medical management of uncertain illnesses such as of hemophilia and cardiac conditions (Pattison, 1978).

The different dying trajectories will affect the types of emotional responses and coping mechanisms patients and their families will display, as well as the interventions that will occur during the clinical process. Caregivers should be aware that their attitudes and behaviors are strongly influenced by their perception of the patient's dying trajectory. For example, they may find it easier to interact with the patient while he is awaiting the results of the organ transplant than after it is clear that the organ is being rejected and he will most probably die. It can also be a problem when the patient does not follow the expected trajectory and lives longer than expected. This can be quite unsettling to family members and to caregivers, who must alter their expectations. When there is much ambiguity, or there are numerous remissions and relapses, people may experience increased anxiety when expectancies fail to materialize. This occurs even if the changes are favorable, as when the patient survives an operation that he was not expected to survive. Despite this, trajectories are useful, for they contain expectations about certainty of death and time remaining that can give everyone involved guidelines for responding and interacting.

The Chronic Living-Dying Phase

In this phase the individual, his family, and caregivers struggle to cope with the illness and its problems, and the psychosocial responses to the illness and the impending death.

Dying as a Gradual Process

For most patients all losses will not occur at once and it will be a gradual process that will lead them to their deaths. This must be recognized by caregivers and families so that they relate to patients appropriately according to the stage of illness. To immediately treat patients as if they were in the final days of life, when in fact they may have many more months or even years to exist, is forcing them into an inappropriate role that denies their living while they are dying. (See Chapter 12 for more on this topic.)

During the chronic living-dying interval, it is important that reasonable expectations for continued normal living be maintained by the patient and family. Frequently patients unnecessarily restrict their lives or are avoided by significant others because of a misunderstanding of their symptoms. It is not uncommon for family members to express a fear of contamination from the patient and for the patient to experience rejection, isolation, and possibly abandonment as a consequence of family members' fears. For example, cancer patients have been known to be forced to eat off paper plates to prevent what others perceived as contamination of dishes. Patients also must learn to cope with the fact that support may be offered at one moment and rejection the next as people are inconsistent in their ability to relate to them. Feelings of alienation may develop, fueling their fears of abandonment, unacceptability, and isolation. In analyzing cancer patients' feelings of alienation, one researcher found "people who have cancer speak of themselves as the new lepers: of being rejected, overprotected, and misunderstood, all at the same time and by the very people they look to for support" (Severo, 1977).

Caregivers need to provide specific information to both patient and family as to realistic expectations about the disease process. For example, the patient needs to know that during the times she is symptom free she can feel comfortable in resuming a designated amount of her previous functioning. Family members may need to be calmed about fears of touching or being intimate with the patient. The main idea is to provide the patient and family with as much realistic information as possible to enable them to enjoy to some extent whatever aspects of living still remain open to them.

Dying patients must be recognized as being fully human during the course of their living-dying interval. Few of them will become bedridden immediately. They will still want to work, play, relate to others, and be involved in social activities. Here is where the attitudes of families and caregivers are especially important. Dying patients will still want to be related to as they were previously. They will still want honest communication and interaction. Indeed, departure from traditional patterns of relating to loved ones will be unsettling and will only indicate to them that they are already perceived as socially dead. For this reason, caregivers and loved ones are advised to avoid treating dying individuals only as patients. This does not mean that they are not treated sensitively, but that their status as dying individuals will not take away the opportunity for honest relationships with others during the time they have remaining. The phrase "living-dying interval" is important to take literally: the patient is still living, although on a dying trajectory.

Treatment Modalities

In an effort to either treat the illness or keep the patient free of pain because there is no hope of cure (known as palliation), surgery, radiation, and chemotherapy are the most frequently used modalities.

Surgery. While surgery is the most effective form of treatment for many types of cancers, and is a necessary part of treating many chronic illnesses, patients often approach it with apprehension, misconceptions, and fears of mutilation. Patients' responses to surgery depend on many variables:

- Fear of anesthesia and loss of consciousness
- Misconceptions from others who have had surgery
- Fear of pain
- Amount of preparatory information about the surgery and its sequelae
- Extent of the surgery
- Meaning of the affected body part or organ to the patient, e.g., the loss of a breast is anxiety-provoking to a woman because of its importance to her sexual identity and sense of self
- Visibility of the damage and the extent to which it interferes with the body's function
- Degree of dependence it causes the patient and any secondary losses as a result of it, e.g., having to relinquish a job.
- Amount of postoperative support provided by caregivers and family
- The psychological dynamics of the patient that affect the adaptation process, e.g., if notions of guilt and punishment have been aroused by the surgery, the response may be complicated
- The losses caused by hospital admission, e.g., increased dependency, decreased self-worth, interruption of normal lifestyle

The home environment and family relationships will determine the quality of postoperative care (Dyk & Sutherland, 1956). It should not automatically be assumed that release from the hospital will be welcomed by the patient or the family. Consequently, caregivers will need to assess the patient's home situation and try to smooth the transition from hospital to home.

Radiation. Of all the various treatment forms, radiation therapy is the most misunderstood and feared one (Rotman, Rogow, DeLeon, & Heskel, 1977). There are a number of reasons for this:

- The treatment is received from a large machine in a room with no other human being present.
- The treatment is invisible.
- There are concerns that the treatment itself will cause cancer.
- The side effects (e.g., hair loss, sterility, nausea and vomiting) are frightening and uncomfortable.
- There are patient and family concerns about loss of sexual function and sterility.

Because of these problems, caregivers are well advised to assess the patient's knowledge and concerns about both the disease and radiation treatment in general before providing more specific information. The well-prepared patient and family will be better able to cope with the treatment and its side effects. What the radiation machinery does and how it works should be explained to the patient and family. A brief tour of the treatment area will help assuage many of the fears associated with both the equipment and the procedure. Patients are often frightened by the size of the machinery and the fact that they will be required to lie absolutely still for a period of time alone. Side effects should be explained in advance so patients have time to adapt and to take compensatory action if necessary (e.g., purchasing a wig for hair loss or investigating sperm banks if permanent sterility is a potential outcome). Information on medication to control side effects and appropriate nutrition to increase tolerance for therapy will be important as well. Patients may need continual information about the radiation process since, with recent public interest in radiation and nuclear issues, there may be some confusion as to how radiation can be beneficial. They also will need to understand the place of radiation in the overall treatment regimen. To be told that after surgery they must endure radiation, and then possibly chemotherapy, may be quite overwhelming and cause patients to wonder why previous treatment modalities were prescribed in the first place. The particular impact of each treatment modality must be explained in advance, as well as how these different treatments will interact with each other.

Chemotherapy. This form of therapy raises a number of questions for the patient about its effectiveness, its side effects, and its interference with normal life. Additionally, there is the threat that the side effects can be not just unpleasant and discouraging, but even life-threatening. In this case, the cure can truly be worse than the disease. Family members often feel a great sense of outrage when complications from the side effects cause the death of their loved one, rather than the disease itself.

Living with chronic illness and adjusting to the many side effects of chemotherapy can be debilitating for the patient and his family. (See "Treatment" in Chapter 13 for more on this with regard to the dying child.) Side effects include loss of hair, nausea and vomiting, weakness and fatigue, any number of neurological and physical changes, and sterility. Adapting to changes in personality and mood, physical appearance, and functioning that occur because of the chemotherapy is an arduous task for the patient and family. The inconsistency of some of the symptoms (e.g., sometimes hair loss will occur and at other times it will not) and the varied schedules of the treatment regimen may make life for the patient and family seem like a roller coaster ride. However, even when the patient is feeling well and the side effects are minimal, the knowledge that another treatment day is imminent often creeps into awareness and causes an emotional reaction. Planning for clinic visits, allowing time for side effects to pass if they are transitory, supporting the patient during and after the chemotherapy procedures—all these demands are placed upon the patient's family. Such demands require that the resources of the family be directed towards the seriously ill member. This often causes family members to resent the sick person, which in turn creates ambivalence because they still care about the one whom they resent. (See "Emotional Responses of the Family" in Chapter 12 for more on this topic.)

As with other treatment approaches, it is recommended that patients and their families be given as much information as they can accommodate initially. In this way they can be more prepared for the side effects and plan for them. In addition, the patient and family will have more realistic expectations of the process and will be able to anticipate when they will need support from others. During this time, good relationships with caregivers will be essential, for the experience is very trying for everyone involved.

Remissions and Relapses

Remissions and relapses are a normal part of chronic illnesses today. Psychologically these are very difficult transitions for the patient, the family, and caregivers. Following an extended remission, the news of a relapse is a stunning blow. The patient and family may feel angry that they were not spared this after going through so much in treatment and following physicians' orders carefully. This anger may be directed at caregivers or displaced onto others. Many patients are frustrated at again having to cope with potential death after it has already been dealt with and successfully beaten. They are forced to confront all of the emotional issues that they may have been able to avoid during the remission. If the initial treatment was difficult, patients may be understandably reluctant to undergo it a second time. Some may opt not to undergo the treatment, and may choose to live a shorter life, but one without the side effects of a particular treatment approach. This can be an especially painful time for patients and families as the activities to which they may have returned during remission must again be relinquished. Their new hopes may be dashed and they are often forced to confront even more intimately the knowledge that the disease is ultimately uncontrollable. When remissions and relapses occur in frequent cycles, family members may detach from the dying patient because it is too painful to continually reinvest and then decathect from him. The Lazarus syndrome, when the individual is expected to die and then experiences a reprieve or gets better, is a major psychological problem for families and caregivers. (See "Anticipatory Grief" in Chapter 2 for more on this topic.)

Because of the painful issues involved in remissions and relapses, caregivers must be especially sensitive to the emotional reactions of patients and families. Caregivers themselves are not immune to the same reactions of disappointment, anger, fear, and frustration as the patients and the families. When a relapse does occur, an explanation should be given as to why it happened, what treatments will be tried and why, and what the possibility for a subsequent remission is. Disappointment in the negative turn of events and disillusionment with traditional medicine can make patients and families especially vulnerable to unproven remedies such as special diets, plant extracts, and vaccines (Schmale, 1976). While some of today's unproven remedies may be tomorrow's cures, serious consideration should be given when patients and families decide to depart from traditional medical practice. Caregivers can be helpful in this regard by openly and honestly discussing the possibility of alternative treatments while, eliciting the patient's feelings and level of knowledge about them, and communicating their knowledge about or willingness to investigate such alternative methods (U.S. Department of Health and Human Serivces, Note 11).

Sexuality

Diagnosis of a terminal illness does not necessarily diminish interest in sexual contact with others. In fact, it often heightens the need for physical as well as emotional closeness, for continued affirmation of desirability and attractiveness. However, for many, emotional responses to the illness and the side effects of the illness or its treatment interfere with sexual satisfaction. The woman who fears resumption of sexual relations with her husband because she feels he will be disgusted by her mastectomy, the man who feels less manly because he is no longer as physically active, the increased marital tension that can develop as each spouse copes with the impending loss of the other, the absence of privacy resulting from hospitalization—all of these are examples of impediments that can interfere with satisfying sexual contact. In addition, unrealistic expectations may further complicate sexual adjustment following diagnosis of a terminal illness. Often people feel as if they should not make advances towards the patient with an illness, assuming that there is something wrong with them because they have such desires. They fail to understand the integral part of sexuality in patients' lives, even when there is a terminal illness.

Caregivers must recognize the importance of sexual contact to those who are ill. Only recently has there been more of a recognition of the need for a double bed for patients in the hospital so that they may reexperience closeness and sexual contact with their loved one. However, many caregivers have a difficult time accepting sexuality as a normal component of behavior and often are disgusted by masturbatory activity or other forms of autoeroticism by patients. They need to see that terminal illness does not preclude sexuality.

Wasow (1978) argues for the inclusion of a course on sexuality in medical schools to help the physician overcome avoidance of the sexual concerns of patients. She believes that caregivers have an obligation to bring up questions about sexuality in their conversations with patients. In the Sadoughi, Leshner, and Fine (1971) study on chronically ill and disabled individuals, over 50% of the patients would have liked to have discussed their sexual concerns with a hospital staff member of the same sex if one had been available. Patients often need encouragement to discuss these matters and sometimes even require medical permission to experiment with new or modified patterns of sexual behavior necessary because of the illness. It is the responsibility of caregivers to respond to these needs. Patients are more likely to express their sexual concerns if their physician routinely discusses sexuality and appears to be comfortable in doing so (Beeson & McDermott, 1975). Wasow notes that to give adequate attention to the sexual problems of seriously ill patients, physicians will need to consider sexuality as an important part of emotional health, recognize that they themselves are plagued by anxieties and myths about human sexuality, and work to overcome the prevalent denial and/or ignorance of the sexuality of the terminally ill patients.

The importance of access to sexual stimulation cannot be underestimated. Leviton (1973) argues persuasively for the significance of sexual contact as a deterrent to premature death and to suicide among the aged. He sees it as an antidote to despair, hopelessness, and depression. Studies on the deleterious effects that deprivation has on humans and animals illustrate that touching and sexual contact prolong life and improve health. Consequently, Leviton advocates that affectional-sexual relationships be encouraged through appropriate social and physical planning of the environment in nursing homes and hospitals. He feels that the status of sexual functioning should be considered part of any medical work-up, and that, when appropriate and desirable, sexual therapy should be part of the total therapeutic approach. With regard to terminally ill patients this may mean identifying alternative sexual behaviors, providing education to alleviate fear of injury, and giving emotional support to help patients cope with threats to their sexuality. Woods (1975) suggests allowing patients predictable times during which they can enjoy solitude or be alone with their partner, and discusses how these are ways of conveying a respect for sexuality and sexual behavior as a natural aspect of living.

Caregivers do not have to be experts in human sexuality to help patients and their families. They merely have to view human sexuality as an integral component of the human personality that should be considered during terminal illness. With patients who are dying, who may feel inordinate amounts of alienation as a consequence of rejection by others, the importance of continued validation as worthwhile and desirable human beings cannot be overstressed.

There are some indications that female patients are more successful at getting their affectional needs met than males (Leiber, Plumb, Gerstenzang, & Holland, 1976), and that more male patients and their spouses report sexual difficulties than do female patients and their spouses (Wasow, 1978). It may be that females have a greater ability to express their desires, fears, and worries than males.

Specific sexual needs may change with time. Although the dying patient's desire for sexual intimacy may decrease over time, the desire for nonsexual physical closeness increases (Leiber, et al., 1976). Demonstrations of affection—holding hands, embracing, and kissing—appear to be needed more than sexual stimulation and release. All types of intimate physical contact should be permitted to the terminally ill patient. From the time of birth to the time of death there is a need for intimate touching and closeness.

Financial Issues

As terminal illness becomes more chronic, issues come up that previously were nonexistent. Two of these are the employability and insurability of the terminally ill. Problems in these areas create considerable psychological and financial stress for patients and their families, and constitute legitimate areas of intervention for caregivers.

The economic toll of chronic illness is devastating. In a 1976 national study on cancer, the direct medical costs were estimated at over $6,000,000,000, and the total costs, including losses due to mortality and morbidity, were put at over $30,000,000,000 (Scotto & Chiazze, 1977). Another study of 115 families of advanced cancer patients found that the total course of the illness (including hospital, physician, and burial expenses) ranged from less than $5,000 to more than $50,000, with an average cost of $21,718 per family (The National Cancer Foundation, 1973). Since survival times have lengthened considerably since these studies were done, it can be assumed that the costs are now even higher.

Expenses for the family include medical costs and nonmedical, out-of-pocket costs. The latter are hidden expenses that accompany terminal illness: transportation; prosthetic devices; new clothes for an altered body; childcare; telephone calls; food purchased at the hospital or eaten out; gifts for the patient; lodging for the family if the patient is hospitalized out of town. These out-of-pocket expenses often must be paid immediately, are not tax deductable, and are not anticipated by the family. In a study by Lansky, Cairns, Clark, Lowman, Miller, and Trueworthy (1979), the out-of-pocket expenses for families with terminally ill children were analyzed. When combined with the loss of wages on the part of parents staying with the sick child, the median loss of income was 26%.

Often the patient's financial position will dictate the kind of medical care she can obtain and affect the quality of the patient's remaining time with her family. Financial concerns may prevent family members from being able to be with the patient, for they may have to remain at work to keep the family financially solvent. The "price" exacted is more than money—loved ones cannot be present at the time they are most needed. In addition, the patient may lose self-esteem and feel guilty because she must rely on others for financial support and is unable to contribute to the family's finances.

Caregivers need to be more comfortable addressing financial issues with patients. Research has confirmed that the dying patient is quite concerned with the circumstances and grief of those left behind and would welcome assistance with financial concerns (Kalish & Reynolds, 1976; Koenig, 1968). Anything that helps the dying patient financially will relieve some of the overall stress of the illness. (See "Assistance With the Practical Considerations of Dying" in Chapter 11 for more on this topic.)

Employability. Resumption of the work role, at least to some extent, is a critical goal for many patients. Work is more than what we do; it helps us define who we are and supports our self-identity, self-esteem, independence, productivity, and self-sufficiency. It is a meaningful connection with life, and it has important social and interpersonal advantages as well. Because of this, it is highly therapeutic for most terminally ill patients to resume some measure of their previous work. However, work may be denied them not only because of the physical or emotional sequelae of the illness and its treatment, but also because of fear, ignorance, or discrimination on the part of employers.

Estimates of the percentage of patients subjected to job discrimination have run as high as 90% (Dietz, 1978). In a 1976 study by the American Cancer Society, it was found that 22% of their sample of the "most employable" recovered cancer patients reported at least one job rejection because of their previous illness. Subtle, work-related problems were found to exist as well: hostility from co-workers; changes in work location designed to force them to resign; lack of raises; denial of promotions or opportunities for advanced training; reduction in health benefits; and ineligibility for newly available group life insurance. Counts, Rodov, and Wilson (Note 12) reported an employment discrimination incidence of 23% among adult cancer survivors. Of the employers who refused to hire cancer survivors, 61% cited their fear of increases in insurance premiums as their justification. Other fears mentioned by employers included decreased productivity, excessive sick leave, increased absenteeism, long-term disability payments, and the possibility of the employee's sudden death. Disproving these fears, Stone (1975) studied 1,417 employees at the American Telephone and Telegraph Company and discovered that for cancer survivors employee absenteeism, turnover, and job performance were within normal limits, and there were no increased insurance costs.

In a study examining consequences for recovered pediatric cancer patients over 18, 40% of the 60 survivors had experienced some form of employment discrimination. Many of them reported they had been unprepared for such discrimination and poignantly discussed how they were made to feel worthless or at immediate risk. Most of the survivors and their families were unaware of their rights and of the remedies available to them. As a result, the research investigators said that one of the key aspects of social rehabilitation for patients is for caregivers to provide them with information on how to be effective advocates for themselves in regard to these issues (Koocher, O'Malley, & Foster, 1981). The rights of cancer patients in certain work situations are protected by federal statute in the Rehabilitation Act of 1973. However, cancer patients are not being made aware that they may be eligible for vocational rehabilitation services. The Vocational Rehabilitation Act of 1973 has not had a substantial impact on the rehabilitation of cancer patients, as special programs for them are being conducted in only five states. In addition, some medical criteria used in the evaluation of cancer patients' eligibility for vocational rehabilitation services appear to be unreasonable (Mayo Clinic Rehabilitation Program, 1977).

Less than a third of the respondents in a study of recovered cancer patients in blue collar occupations thought that their physicians were aware of work-related problems (Feldman, 1976). This implies that caregivers may need to take the initiative and ask about conditions at work. They can also interpret medical information to help patients understand and cope with the disease and plan for returning to work or searching for a different job; discuss with them whether or not to report the nature of their illness when returning to or seeking new employment; and assist them in understanding and dealing with co-workers and communicating about their illness.

Insurance. Individuals with a history of cancer often have trouble getting new or additional insurance. Concern over losing health insurance benefits appears to be one of the major barriers to changing jobs (American Cancer Society, 1976). The waiting lists for eligibility for some insurance companies may extend up to 10 years after treatment. In the study of recovered pediatric cancer patients by Koocher et al. (1981), few patients were able to obtain individual health insurance policies, and when they did, most policies contained clauses excluding a wide range of coverage related to cancer. Most patients were covered by some form of group policy through an employer. While almost 64% had life insurance coverage of some sort at the time of the investigation, most of them had been denied a policy at least once, were required to pay a higher than normal premium, or were made to observe a waiting period of some sort. It was also found that discrimination or rejection associated with employment and insurance often led to increased anxiety about the disease and lowered self-esteem in the recovered patients. In contrast to this, it was concluded in the Mayo Clinic Rehabilitation Program Study (1977) that insurance-related problems experienced by cancer patients following treatment were not necessarily discriminatory and that insurance coverage was available for most patients following treatment. However, it was found that patients were subject to waiting periods and unreasonable underwriting actions for individual coverage, cancellation of insurance, and refusal of applications.

The Terminal Phase

The onset of the terminal phase of living-dying is not precise and is roughly thought to begin when the dying person starts to withdraw into herself and respond to those internal body signals that tell her she must now conserve her energies (Pattison, 1978). There appears to be a psychic as well as physical turning away from the outside world into the self. (See "Acceptance, Withdrawal and Detachment, and Hope" in Chapter 11 for more on this topic.)

THE CONCEPT OF APPROPRIATE DEATH

Appropriate death (Weisman, 1972a; Weisman & Hackett, 1961) is a useful concept when dealing with terminally ill patients. Basically an appropriate death is one with which the individual is relatively at ease or which might have been chosen, "a way of living as long as possible" (Weisman, 1972a, p. 41). With regard to a terminal illness, the following criteria have been identified for an appropriate death:

- *Conflict is reduced.* The internal conflicts of the patient, such as fear of loss of control, have been addressed and worked through as much as possible.
- *Compatibility with the "ego ideal" is achieved.* This means "I am going to die as the person I think I am." The patient's

basic sense of identity is maintained even in the approach of death.

- *Continuity with important relationships is preserved or restored.* Unfinished business is attended to and the patient has the support of important others until death.
- *Consummation of a critical wish/concern is brought about.* Critical last acts or last wishes are brought to fruition, such as the patient's living long enough to see the birth of a grand-child.

Additionally, the patient should be as pain-free as possible. Suffering and emotional and social impoverishment should be kept to a minimum. Within the limits of disability the patient should be operating at the optimum level of functioning.

An appropriate death will be different for each person, and a death can be appropriate even if the person does not willingly accept dying. (See "Acceptance, Withdrawal and Detachment, and Hope" in Chapter 11 for more on this topic.) The caregiver's goal should be to facilitate as appropriate a death as possible for each individual. To gain insight into this concept, complete Exercise V, which follows.

EXERCISE V

*An Appropriate Death and
Finishing Unfinished Business*

Decide what would constitute an appropriate death for you (excluding a terminal illness). What are the important criteria or variables that would make this death appropriate for you? What things would be important for you to do or have?

Decide what would constitute an appropriate death for you if you were dying from a terminal illness. What are the important criteria or variables that would make this terminal illness death appropriate for you? What things would be important for you to do or have?

Do the criteria or variables that would make your death appropriate have any implications for the manner in which you are, or should be, conducting your life now? (Do you need to make more time in your life for the people who are really important to you in order to have as little unfinished business as possible at the time of your death? Should you be pursuing a task you always wanted to accomplish?) If so, what are they?

How much unfinished business would you have in your life if you died right now? What would it be? Who would it be with?

What, if anything, prevents you from doing these things now that would finish your unfinished business? Why, if it is true, do you fail to live as if you could possibly die at any moment?

Ideally people should live so that if they died tomorrow they would have a minimum of unfinished business left. What could you do to help yourself in this regard?

How can you help your patients identify what they would need to achieve an appropriate death for themselves and to finish their unfinished business?

CHAPTER 9

The Dying Patient's Reactions

The grief of the person with a terminal illness is similar to the anticipatory grief of family members. However, the dying patient grieves not only for future losses but for losses in the past and present as well. From the past, grief from previous losses and re-membered acts committed or omitted tend to emerge. In the pres-ent, the dying person must relinquish many of the capabilities and attributes that define his identity. He may be treated differently now that he is terminally ill. His former roles may be reassigned to others. He also may experience the gradual decathexis of loved ones, some of whom may start to invest in others. Unfinished busi-ness may further complicate the entire process. And in addition to all this, he grieves in anticipation of future losses as well. Here are some of the possible losses:

- Loss of control
- Loss of independence
- Loss of productivity
- Loss of security
- Loss of various types of psychological, physical, and cognitive abilities
- Loss of predictability and consistency
- Loss of experiences
- Loss of future existence
- Loss of pleasure
- Loss of ability to complete plans and projects
- Loss of dreams and hopes for the future
- Loss of significant others
- Loss of familiar environment and possessions
- Loss of aspects of the self and identity
- Loss of meaning

The terminally ill patient often struggles with ambivalence over the fact that it is he, not other loved ones, who is going to die. Feelings of anger and jealousy, along with the sense of being cheated, contribute to this ambivalence. As a result, there may be more denial of potential losses as the dying patient tries to cope with negative feelings that are often quite unacceptable to himself. Ambivalence may also be present for the bereaved after a death, but the unique situation of terminally ill grievers tends to make them more vulnerable to it. They are also vulnerable because of it, since they do not want to alienate others with their negative feelings and end up left alone.

Dying individuals struggle with many of the same feelings as mourners after a death. The same processes of grief must occur. There will necessarily be a need to identify losses, ventilate and express feelings, review, and finish unfinished business. They too will require "permission" to grieve from their loved ones and care-givers. There will not be a period of reestablishment for these patients as there is for postdeath mourners, but for many there is a state of realization or resolution that can be reached. (See "Acceptance, Withdrawal and Detachment, and Hope" in Chapter 11 for more on this topic.) Emotional reactions may be similar, but the dying patient will experience them much more intensely. Finally, postdeath mourners may not experience the intense loss of self-esteem that accompanies terminal illness. Human beings have common aspirations (Bibring, 1953): they want to be worthy, that is, loved and appreciated; good, not aggressive or hateful; and strong, not dependent and helpless. Failure to fulfill these aspirations frequently leads to depression and other psychological problems. Since terminal illness prevents people from meeting these desires, it is not surprising that a myriad of emotional reactions occur throughout the dying process.

VARIABLES INFLUENCING THE RESPONSES OF THE DYING PATIENT

Four classes of variables influence an individual's response to terminal illness. The first is *personal characteristics*. This includes some of the same factors that influence an individual's grief response:

- Personality
- Sex
- Age
- Coping style and abilities
- Religion/philosophy of life
- Social, cultural, and ethnic background
- Previous experience with loss and death

- Maturity
- Intelligence
- Mental health
- Fulfillment in life
- Perceived timeliness of impending death
- Lifestyle

There are some additional personal characteristics that influence a patient's response to terminal illness:
- Specific fears about dying and death. These will be discussed later in this chapter.
- Expectations about the illness and death, taken from previous experiences and other sources of information (reading, watching television, talking to others). These may be negative, as when a terminally ill patient has been seen to have been abandoned, or positive, as when the well-managed, pain-controlled death of a person surrounded by supportive friends has been witnessed.
- Degree of presence or absence of the will to live. It has been well documented that psychological factors play a critical role in the development and progress of disease.
- Remaining unfinished business. This can serve as a motivator for longer survival, as with the patient who fights to witness his son's childhood, or a discouraging factor, as with the patient who gives up because she has little hope of healing the rift between herself and her sister.

The second class of variables is *characteristics of interpersonal relationships*, and they apply to relationships with caregivers as well as family and friends:
- Quality and quantity of the patient's relationships
- Degree of support and security provided by the patient's relationships
- Degree of openness and honesty of communication with significant others
- Social milieu of the patient

The third class of variables is *socio-economic and environmental factors:*
- Financial resources and their expected stability
- Economic status
- Degree of access to quality medical treatment
- Occupation and employment status
- Education
- Social class
- Physical environment

The final class of variables is *characteristics specific to the illness of the patient:*

- Type of illness. This will determine such things as the length of the dying trajectory, the type of problems to be encountered, type of social reaction, the patient's expectations, and the treatment regimen to be endured. It will dictate the circumstances of the death and influence the quality of life preceding it.
- Personal meaning of the specific illness and its location to the patient. For some patients, cancer is such a frightening concept that they would gladly opt for a terminal renal disease and would be able to handle it much better than "the big C." If the site of the cancer is in the reproductive system it is likely to be responded to differently than, say, cancer of the liver, since the reproductive system affects the person's self-image more.
- Expected death trajectory. The expected course of the illness will influence how the patient plans the rest of her life, what expectations about the illness experience develop, and how much time is available to finish unfinished business. Trajectories that are not met, even in the situation where the patient survives longer than expected, can be unsettling for patients, families, and caregivers.
- Physical milieu of the patient (e.g., home, hospice, institution).
- Presence and amount of pain.
- Effects of mental and physical deterioration.
- Effects of drugs and medications used.
- Effects of treatment regimen.
- Rate of loss of control.
- Number and rate of secondary losses.
- Proximity to death.
- Rate of progression towards death.

Certain patterns of these variables seem to predict how well patients will cope with illness and how long they will live. In 1975 Weisman and Worden published the results of their study analyzing the psychosocial considerations influencing the quality and duration of survival in cancer deaths:

> *Longer survivals* are associated with patients who have good relationships with others, and manage to preserve a reasonable degree of intimacy with family and friends until the very last. They ask for and receive much medical and emotional support. As a rule, they accept the reality of serious illness, but still do not believe that death is inevitable. Hence, at times they may deny the gravity of illness or seem to repudiate the fact of becoming

more feeble. They are seldom deeply depressed but may voice resentment about various aspects of their treatment and illness. Whatever anger is displayed, it should be noted, does not alienate others but commands their attention. They may be afraid of dying alone and untended, so they refuse to let others pull away without taking care of their needs.

Shorter survivals occur in patients who report poor social relationships, starting with early separations from their family of origin, and continuing throughout life. Sometimes they have had diagnosed psychiatric disorders but almost as often talk about repeated mutually destructive relationships with people through the years. At times, they have considered suicide. Now, when treatment fails, depression deepens, and they become highly pessimistic about their progress They want to die—a finding that often reflects more conflict than acceptance. (p. 71)

Subsequent research has tended to confirm their conclusions. Holden (1978) found support for the idea that life expectancy is influenced by psychosocial variables. She discovered that patients who lived longer tended to express more anger towards their disease and their doctors. Conversely, those whose illnesses resulted in a shorter life span were more apt to utilize denial and repression, tended to be more despairing, and had few supportive relationships. Derogatis, Abeloff, and Melisaratos (1979), in their investigation of women dying of breast cancer, found that the characteristics of those who survived the longest were that they were more demanding of physicians and less satisfied with treatment. However, they also found that such patients were rated as less well-adjusted, more hostile, and more demanding. From his many years as a practicing oncologist, Krant (Note 13) has developed the following description of poor copers: they suppress information; they act passively and tend to submit; they behave stoically and are fatalistic; they communicate little with family and staff; they inappropriately act-out; and they project blame on others. He has found lessened emotional distress during illness to be associated with strong interpersonal support, openness with physician and family, a general confident outlook, and few physical symptoms.

Synthesizing the research, it appears that patients who are assertive about their needs and wants, who can appropriately express and direct their anger, who maintain some optimism, and who have the open communication with family and physician that accompanies strong, supportive relationships are the ones who will cope better and live longer in their illness. Depression, despair, denial, and poor communication with a minimal or absent system of interpersonal support are associated with less effective coping and shorter survival times.

The issue for caregivers will not only be how to maximize those factors associated with better coping and longer survival in patients, but also how to cope with the assertiveness, anger, and frank communication that is so healthy. Traditionally passive, depressed patients are not threatening, while vocal, demanding ones may be. Those who really believe that dying patients should be expressive, not only because it is healthy for their survival, but because it means they are functioning, alive persons with human dignity, will go the extra mile to support, accept, and deal with more vocal and demanding patients.

EMOTIONAL REACTIONS AND FEARS OF THE DYING PATIENT

Anxiety

Anxiety is apprehension in the absence of a specific danger. It differs from fear in that it is nondirected. In fear, the threat is recognizable; in anxiety it is difficult to specify what is causing the feeling. Some degree of existential or annihilation anxiety will be common for anyone contemplating his own death. It is a natural reaction that is expected to be present during some, if not all, of an individual's terminal illness. Since it is fairly certain that terminal illness will generate some anxiety, any and all manners of intervention should be tried that will alleviate this uncomfortable emotional response. This will be a continuing responsibility throughout the changing course of the illness.

The major way in which a dying person can be helped to manage anxiety is by being assisted in breaking down the anxiety into its component parts. The person is helped to delineate his specific fears and concerns and each one is addressed and problem-solved individually. It is easier to cope with specific fears than to try to grapple with more global, undifferentiated (and thus more terrifying) anxiety.

Pattison (1977) has described a number of fears of the experience of dying. He notes that although the ultimate problem of death cannot be conquered, the terminally ill person can be helped to cope with the various parts of the process. By focusing on these specific fears, the crisis can be made more manageable. Patients can cope more efficiently, enhancing the self-esteem, dignity, and integrity that are so easily compromised when death is confronted.

Although most people are afraid of and anxious about their deaths, the same issues will not be equally important to each person. Each individual will have his own unique combination of specific fears about death. What is of the utmost concern to one person may be negligible to another. Each person will respond idiosyncratically, depending upon personality, previous experience, coping mechanisms, support, and other factors.

The therapeutic goals are to ascertain which specific fears concern the patient (almost like conducting a differential diagnosis), to assist the patient in confronting his pertinent fears, and to isolate each issue (since they cannot all be dealt with simultaneously). Problem-solving can begin on each fear, leading to a reduction in the patient's anxiety.

There are many possible specific fears (many of these are adapted from Pattison, 1969, 1977, 1978).

The fear of the unknown. This is usually manifested most strongly in the acute crisis phase. The fear is a strong and basic one in all human beings. That which is unfamiliar or which cannot be anticipated frightens us at all levels. From the child afraid of the dark to the adult confronting death, we all cling to the security of the familiar. Like the rest of us, the terminally ill patient is afraid of death. This fear is exacerbated by the fact that the patient will have to confront this anxiety-provoking situation in the immediate future.

For the dying individual it is important to separate that which can be answered about the unknown from that which cannot be answered. Some of the possible questions are as follows (Diggory & Rothman, 1961):

What life experiences will I not be able to have?
What is my fate in the hereafter?
What will happen to my body after death?
What will happen to my survivors?
How will my family and friends respond to my dying?
What will happen to my life plans and projects?
What changes will occur in my body?
What will be my emotional reactions?

Some of these questions are answerable immediately, while others require time in order to be answered, and still others will not be answerable during this lifetime. Those questions that can be answered, should be answered. It is helpful for the patient to distinguish between questions about the reality of life, for which answers can be legitimately given, and those related to philosophical, religious, and speculative concerns, for which only opinions, but not answers, can be offered. A patient may also make plans that will ensure that his preferences will be respected with regard to some questions, such as "What will happen to my body after death?" To answer that question, the patient can make his own burial arrangements. Doing these things will eliminate some of the unknown quantity with which the patient must contend. Anything that can do this will be therapeutic for the one facing this fear.

The fear of loneliness. When people are afraid or in uncertain situations, the presence of others can be reassuring or comforting. We all derive some amount of security from others. In sickness this security is not always available, since people tend to be isolated when they are ill or in pain. Unfortunately, as family, friends, or caregivers, we often try to avoid witnessing others' sickness or discomfort and consequently the social world of the seriously ill person diminishes.

If it is anxiety-provoking to see others ill, it is especially difficult to see them when they are dying. For this reason the dying person becomes increasingly isolated from social contacts. Not only are the dying frequently removed from a familiar environment and hospitalized, but too often friends and relatives will remove themselves because they want to avoid acknowledging the fact that they too will die some day. This leaves people alone and without support at the very time when they most need it: during the crisis of their own dying. As in any other crisis the individual benefits from the support and nurturance of others during this period. Deprivation of social contact, as illustrated in experiments in sensory deprivation, can foster ego-disintegration. This fear of loneliness appears to be most paramount when individuals initially face the prospect of death and dread that they will be deserted in dying. Consequently in the acute crisis phase caregivers and family should be present on a frequent basis and determine who will be with the patient at certain times. In the chronic phase the task is to engage the patient's interest in everyday relationships and tasks so dying does not become the sole focus of the person's life. In the terminal phase it is important to assure the patient of the continuing interest and availability of people to the extent that they are desired. The idea is to indicate to the dying person that he need not feel loneliness, although at times he may be alone. It is quite ironic that this should be one of the most widespread fears of dying individuals, since it is one that can most easily be eliminated by the supportive presence of loving others.

The fear of loss of family and friends. The dying individual mourns the loss of family and friends just as they will mourn him after he dies. In order to face the permanent separation entailed in death, he must work through this grief, wrapping up any unfinished business he has with those who will be left behind. This means clarifying and accepting the ambiguous and conflicting emotions between himself and his loved ones in an effort to achieve some acceptable resolution and to reaffirm the meaning and value of the relationships. This process of working through grief is very similar to that seen in the bereaved. After this occurs the dying patient may then be able to appropriately separate from loved ones as death approaches.

The fear of loss of self-control. The patient who is progressively debilitated from a deteriorating disease worries about adequacy and dependence. These are very important issues in our culture, which rewards and prizes self-reliance and independence. The terminally ill patient experiences this loss of self-control over an extended period of time with no recourse but to become more dependent as the illness progresses. It is often a humiliating and anxiety-provoking experience. The most therapeutic interventions will encourage and allow the patient to retain whatever control is possible (e.g., making decisions about daily tasks, arranging the funeral) in order to enhance his sense of control and self-esteem. In this situation, anything that can render some measure of control can help ease the frustration, helplessness, and sense of guilt arising from dependency.

> *Case Example:* A 42-year-old mother of three teenagers chose to die at home. In order to support the maintenance of control and self-image, the caregiver worked with the family and patient to situate the hospital bed in the dining room, right next to the table where all the family gathered. In this way the patient was able to participate in family activities and discussions. She had input in all family decisions. Her purse was kept next to her bed and she could continue to dole out the allowances for her children. She still supervised activities in the household and was available to the family. All of these things helped the patient to maintain control of her motherly duties, which constituted the major role in her life and a main factor in her self-image.

The fear of loss of body parts and disability. Because our bodies are so very much a part of our self-image, the loss of body parts, disfiguration, or bodily deterioration results not only in a loss of function, but a loss of self. This blow to our self-integrity brings shame, inadequacy, and guilt feelings, which are accompanied by feelings of being unloved and unwanted. It is especially problematic in our culture, where there is such an overemphasis on attractiveness, beauty, and youthful appearance. We need to assist dying individuals in grieving the loss of body parts and body-image, along with helping them cope with subsequent disability without a loss of integrity or self-esteem. We must continue to show respect for them in their deteriorating conditions and not disclose any aversion that their unsightliness may engender, although we can concur with their realistic perception of it as unattractive if we are in a position where we have to comment upon it. To pretend that disfiguration is pretty would only indicate untruthfulness to patients, who desperately need to believe their caregivers are honest with them. However, although we may, for example, agree that a particular ulcer is unappealing, we can still make it clear to patients that they do not repulse us and that they will not be rejected by us and should not reject themselves because of their physical degeneration. Convey to them that they are still valued as people, despite their deteriorating condition.

We can also provide opportunities for the dying to exercise as much physical management over their own bodies as possible. This will enhance self-control, reduce possibilities for shame and guilt, and minimize the amount of loss to which patients must surrender. Such things as encouraging patients to feed, bathe, groom, and exercise themselves whenever possible will facilitate these goals. When a patient is unable to do such things himself, we should assist him in accomplishing these behaviors. Even if it means putting a hand over a patient's to direct the brushing of his teeth, it is better than not having the patient involved at all and taking over the total job ourselves. As patients become progressively weaker, they need to be provided with whatever supports are available (e.g., walker, bedside commode, three-pronged cane) to help them maintain whatever degree of physical activity is available to them. Their environment needs to be planned to conserve their energy, for instance, moving the bed to the window so they don't have to walk across the room to see outside, or bringing necessary items to them.

The fear of suffering and pain. The fear of dying in screaming torment is a common one. People can usually endure pain better if it makes sense to them and they know that after the pain there will be some relief. For the dying patients these comforts are absent. There is no expectation of a pleasurable future after the pain, as there is for the patient with postoperative pain. There seems to be little reason for it to continue in the face of the fact that the person must die anyway. In light of this, it is important to develop the most efficacious program of pain management possible and to involve the patient in that program. (See "Pain Management" in Chapter 11 for more on this topic.)

Knowing that the pain does not constitute punishment, that it will not result in being left alone or ignored, and that it will be explained and managed as rigorously as possible all add to the patient's ability to tolerate the pain. (See "Suffering" in Chapter 8 for more on this topic.) In 1956 Lemon observed that cancer pain is often most unbearable because hope, understanding, and personal interest are withheld, consciously or unconsciously, by caregivers. The effective caregiver recognizes that "staying" is an important element of pain management. It requires staying with the patient not so much through physical presence (although this is critical), but by remaining open and available to the patient despite the pain and anxiety involved in attending to the terminally ill (Benoliel & Crowley, 1974). If the patient has the comfort of human presence and is not isolated in his pain, the tolerance of it may be much higher.

The fear of loss of identity. The losses of human contact, family and friends, body structure and function, and self-control and consciousness all threaten the patient's identity. These things normally affirm us to ourselves, defining who and what we are. At the point of dying, the issue will not be that we die, but how we die.

Confronted with the threat of death and dissolution, the dying individual is faced with the tasks of attempting to retain self-respect, integrity, and dignity in the process of dying. There are three major mechanisms for this. The first is contact with those who have been and are part of the person's life. Continued contact with the familiar reaffirms to dying individuals that they are still the same people they have always been. Being treated as a living person (who also happens to be dying) rather than as one who is already dead is helpful also. It is critical for health care personnel to continue to think of the person and not the "disease." A second mechanism is maintenance of the continuity of the individual through family, friends, work and bequeathed possessions. Assisting people to live as much as possible until they die will strengthen this recognition of continuity after death. A third mechanism for some people is a desire for union with loved ones who have died previously, as well as those who will die subsequently. There is a belief that there will be an inevitable reunion with significant others. This reunion with parents and progeny allows the person to place himself within a continuum of human relationships, in which death is merely one point in the more universal span of existence.

The fear of sorrow. As patients contemplate the losses they will undergo as part of the dying process, there is a fear that they will be unable to tolerate the attending sorrow. Sources of sorrow must be identified and worked through individually, rather than all at once, and it must be made clear that grief is acceptable and necessary. On the other hand, intervention should also focus on enabling the dying patient to experience the joys and pleasures that remain possible, especially since all losses do not occur simultaneously. Premature sorrow and detachment should be avoided, as the dying person could be kept from available satisfactions by concentrating solely on the anticipatory grief work. There needs to be a melding of the two: anticipatory grief and enjoyment of remaining satisfactions and accomplishments.

The fear of regression. As the dying person grows closer to death the fear of regression becomes more salient. Previously it had been a concern about final behavior related to the fear of loss of control, such as a fear of acting foolishly or childishly. But nearer to death, as there is a lessening of physical capacity and a clouding of consciousness, the sense of regression, of losing concrete and hard reality until there are no boundaries of self or others and no sense of time and space, may be frightening to the dying individual.

Therapeutic intervention will assist the individual in comfortably shifting away from reality to turn inward, allowing the withdrawal and surrender that accompanies the turning away from life and signals psychic death. At this time active engagement is no longer appropriate, as it would communicate to the patient that this natural regression is fearful or undesirable. Such intervention requires being very attuned to the psychic changes in the patient and responding to his cues. There will be signs of turning inward: the patient may show no interest in others, stop watching television and reading the newspaper, or lie down facing the wall instead of the door. At this point the amount of stimuli reaching the patient can be reduced. He can be assisted in determining which people he still wants to see. His surroundings can be kept from being intrusive; for example, the television and newspaper may still be present, but they will not be extended to him if he expresses no interest in them. More quiet time should be spent with the patient by both caregivers and family. They need to be careful about withdrawing too soon, for the patient may still need them, not to actively do anything, but just to be present. (See "Acceptance, Withdrawal and Detachment, and Hope" in Chapter 11 for more on this topic.) Occasionally in the final hours extensive regression occurs in which the patient relives childhood memories vividly.

The fears of mutilation, decomposition, and premature burial. These fears are not specific to the dying process but are included here since they may arise as issues for a dying patient. They are focused on what happens to the body after death (e.g., fear that the body will be eaten by worms after burial) and on the horrible fear that the individual could be misperceived as dead and buried while still alive, as has occurred in some famous horror stories. A person may sustain one or several of these related fears. These can be addressed by having patients choose their own preferred mode of body disposition and providing appropriate information about it, as well as telling them about the medical precautions always taken prior to pronunciation of death.

This passage seems to summarize the process of coping with fears of dying:

> Given our interest, support, and guidance, the dying person may turn to use his available capacities to deal with the several distinct part-processes of dying. He can face death as unknown with the realization that he cannot know, and instead consider the process of dying that he can know and deal with. He can learn to endure the inevitable degrees of separation that begin to occur if he is not actually deprived of human contact. He can face the loss of relatives, friends, and activities and actively mourn their loss and become reconciled to it if this grief is defined and accepted. He

can tolerate the loss of self-control if it is not perceived by himself and others as a shameful experience, and if he can gain control of himself to the degree that he is able. He can retain dignity and self-respect in the face of the completion of his life cycle, gradually relinquishing the unattainable and respect himself for what he has been. Then one can place one's life in a perspective of both reunion and continuity with one's personal history and human tradition. If this is accomplished, then one can move toward an acceptable regression where the self gradually returns to a state of non-self. (Pattison, 1969, p. 13)

Patients' fears can best be understood when we are aware of our own anxieties about death. Doing Exercise VI at the end of this chapter can help uncover our feelings and explore ways of coping with them.

Depression

Depression is another emotion experienced by the dying patient, as a natural reaction to the perception of imminent loss. It is both a symptom of and tool for the patient's preparation for the loss of all she knows and for coming to grips with the reality of demise. This type of depression should be treated differently than a reactive depression for a loss that has already befallen. For example, in the situation of a woman who has undergone a mastectomy, reassurance, encouragement, and attempts to cheer her up, as well as support for her grief work, are often therapeutic. However, in a preparatory or anticipatory depression, there will be times when it is necessary to focus on the imminent losses. These need to be contemplated and worked through to whatever extent is possible. This will be assisted if the patient is allowed and encouraged to express her sorrow as any griever would and to face her fears of dying with the continued caring presence of others. Most of the time depression is clearly evidenced by characteristic behaviors such as expressions of sadness, social withdrawal, psychomotor retardation, apathy, and nonverbal body language like facing away from people or crying. However, at times it can be masked with seemingly opposite feelings and behaviors such as agitation or restlessness, or can be disguised by *somatic equivalents*, physical symptoms that are the only observable manifestations of a depression. It is necessary to be aware of and alert for the myriad ways this emotional reaction can be manifested.

Anger and Hostility

Anger and hostility are experienced by both the bereaved and the dying. They are expressed in many ways: negative verbalizations, aggressive behavior, sarcasm, negativity, obstinacy, passive-aggressiveness, withholding, withdrawal, jealousy of others, and stinginess are a few. It is perfectly reasonable that the patient be angry. She is being deprived of a future while so many others are allowed to live on; she must give up everything and everyone in life; she is being tortured by pain in the little amount of time remaining; her religious belief has not halted her illness; and people react strangely to her now that they know she is dying. More often than not, these angry feelings cover up the more painful ones of grief and anxiety. Following the initial shock, disbelief, and denial of learning of a terminal illness, and after the often unanswerable question "Why me?" has been asked, it may take very little to disturb the patient. Since there is the very natural and understandable feeling of anger at the thought that death will come soon, and since the source of this feeling cannot be extinguished, the terminally ill patient is very likely to displace these feelings on anyone and anything available. Frequently those people who are the most accessible will be the targets of the patient's displaced anger.

This can prove to be an extremely difficult and taxing time for family members and caregivers. It is a demanding task to care for someone who is abusing you, and it is not unusual to feel anger in return. When this occurs, it becomes difficult to respond therapeutically. It may seem easier to avoid the patient. This avoidance is usually noticed by the patient and may contribute to the escalation of aggressive behavior as it engenders further feelings of loss of control, anxiety, grief, and anger at being in the situation.

Until the patient's aggressive feelings drain off to some extent, the best therapeutic approach is to recognize that the anger and hostility are natural and appropriate reactions. They are also very much symptoms of the underlying fear of death. If they can be tolerated as such, and are not reacted to with counter-hostility and anger, the patient will be able to calm down. Effective interventions will address the anger, hostility, grief, and anxiety that are present underneath the patient's aggressive behavior. They also will offer appropriate physical, as well as psychosocial, outlets for discharging the aggression (e.g., pounding a pillow, playing a sport). As in other instances of human aggression and anxiety, physical release of tension is most therapeutic. It addresses the physical effects of the individual's emotions. This therapeutic approach is too often overlooked. It should be remembered that minds and bodies are hooked up together; we can often pay effective attention to the ills of one by using the avenue of the other.

It is important to identify those emotions, thoughts, and fears that cause and/or fuel the behavior. The patient should be assisted in dealing with them directly. This is similar to the identification of the component fears of death that contribute to the patient's global anxiety. When the causes of the aggressive behavior are specified the patient can cope with them more effectively than if she tried to confront them en masse. Only when the real concerns are known can they be responded to effectively.

> *Case Example:* Tom was a busy executive who headed up the marketing division of a national company. He was a high-powered individual, accustomed to giving orders and getting his own way. Consequently, when he was hospitalized with a brain tumor, he reacted quite poorly. He became verbally abusive to his caregivers and his demands never ceased. The staff would look for any way possible to avoid having to go into his room.
>
> Finally a psychologist was called in to consult with the nurses around management of the patient. In talking with him it became clear that, in addition to the natural reactions to loss and impending death, the lack of control and the absence of people and tasks to manage especially fueled Tom's rage. The nurses were advised to search for all possibilities to give Tom a chance to make decisions, even about trivial matters. One of them also solicited his advice about a financial decision she was making. Although the interventions were not elaborate, Tom's aggressive behavior diminished rapidly. As a result, he was not avoided by the staff anymore. This further reduced his hostility towards them. Although Tom still sustained feelings of anger about his illness, the intensity of it was markedly reduced by identifying the issues contributing the most to his feelings and then intervening to address them specifically. The staff tried to minimize his losses, while striving to maximize opportunities to support his self-esteem.

Although aggressive feelings will continue to arise at other times in the future, usually they will not be as intense as at the time of diagnosis and shortly thereafter. The patient needs to be allowed to express anger and hostility without being judged or made to feel guilty. Although in some cases gentle but firm limitations will have to be put on the patient's expression of anger (e.g., patients cannot assault the doctor who rendered the diagnosis), the release of pent-up frustrations through verbalization of anger or some physical activity will diminish the aggression.

A cautionary point needs to be made here about the overuse of interpretation of the patient's feelings, especially anger. Although frequently the anger expressed by a dying patient relates to her approaching death, at times the anger will be a reality-based reaction to a present situation. It is important to investigate the sources of a patient's anger and not automatically assume it is a response to dying. An excellent illustration of this was provided by the chaplain who was asked to see a dying woman after she had

had an angry outburst over cold mashed potatoes at lunch time. The nurses were certain that this reflected some of her unexpressed feelings about her illness. Upon visiting the woman the chaplain found that she refused such interpretation and instead challenged him to stick his finger in her mashed potatoes. Indeed, they were stone cold—proving that there is a danger of overusing psychological models in this field (Doka, Note 14).

Guilt and Shame

Guilt and shame are frequently associated with illness and are especially intense with terminal illness. Guilt arises when people behave contrary to their ethical principles, fall short of their self-image, or violate their conscious or unconscious standards. It involves self-devaluation and fear of punishment. Evidence of guilty feelings may come from the patient's words or through behaviors that demonstrate self-punishment, withdrawal, self-sabotage, or attempts at expiation and making amends.

Many consequences of illness can produce guilt. The patient is aware of the pain he causes loved ones and the drain he is on their resources. He must depend on others as he increasingly loses self-reliance, self-control, independence, and productivity. Long-held unrealistic expectations, such as a need to always be strong, can no longer be sustained.

In the state of being terminally ill, the patient may fantasize many reasons for feeling guilty. It is not uncommon for a patient to believe that the illness is a form of retribution for past real or imagined offenses. He may search for "causes" of the terminal illness, such as retribution for marital infidelity. Relieving the guilt of the patient may do more harm than good if he is using guilty fantasies as a form of denial in disguise. To break this form of denial before the patient is appropriately ready to handle it could result in ruining all the feelings of hope the patient might harbor about doing something else to atone for offenses besides giving his life. Again, it is critical to understand what is behind each patient's reaction before intervening.

There are other reasons why the patient might have feelings of guilt. Angry feelings towards others not terminally ill (including health care personnel, who have much of the anger displaced onto them) often cause patients to feel guilty about their feelings. The emotions of envy and jealousy, so understandable given the patient's condition, also serve to produce guilt. The normal emotions of grief also may cause some people to feel guilty, such as the patient who feels guilty because he lost control and cried.

Many kinds of intervention can be used to alleviate guilt. The feelings can be normalized when appropriate. Participation in a mutual self-help group may show the patient that such feelings are common. Irrational beliefs or standards can be identified for the patient and relinquished by him. Losses that give rise to guilt can be minimized, and the patient can be helped to "forgive" himself for those changes that are out of his control, such as his inability to care for himself. He also can be encouraged to ventilate his feelings. Some of his guilt may be discharged by becoming involved in altruistic activities. Finishing unfinished business may also relieve past and present guilt. Caregivers can assist him in planning for future needs of the survivors, which may have worried him. Most importantly, he needs continued acceptance and respect.

Shame is closely allied to guilt. It is what people feel when they are observed in a situation in which they are not living up to their self-image. Feelings of shame and embarrassment are not uncommon in a patient who has been forced to be dependent due to illness, who experiences increasing helplessness, or who is not allowed to maintain any sense of control or, most importantly, a sense of dignity. It may result from involuntary exposure of private thoughts or feelings, especially when these are construed to be weaknesses or socially unacceptable wishes. Traditionally assumption of a patient role has made males in our culture uncomfortable and ashamed because it violates their image of themselves as men.

Shame may be present even when it does not seem to be, for it can be covered up by other feelings such as anger or overconfidence, or it can be overcompensated for by such responses as denial or aggression. It is important to be sensitive to this, especially when caring for patients who are disfigured or who require attention to private body parts. There is a need to convey respect and empathy when caring for them. "While our eyes see the mutilated part of the patient, our voice must communicate with him as a total human being. In this way we can provide the proper setting wherein the patient can face his deformation and still be convinced that he is accepted" (Verwoerdt, 1966, p. 87).

To some extent, all individuals who are terminally ill are in the same position. They are frequently placed in situations where they can feel shame for either physical or psychological deficits. Part of the patient role demands the giving up of much self-reliance, control, and autonomy. These things are exceptionally valued in our culture; when they are not possessed or exercised, people have strong feelings of shame. For this reason, since the nature of illness itself is so shameful, it is imperative that the terminally ill patient be treated with the utmost respect in this very trying situation. This ranges from respecting the patient's privacy while he is bathing to ensuring that he is given a choice in as many situations as possible, even in something as small as whether a backrub is given before or after medication. In addition the patient should not be placed in situations where his functioning will embarrass him. The same interventions suggested for guilt can also be used effectively with shame.

REACTIONS TO DEATH
ACROSS THE LIFE CYCLE

Each individual changes emotionally and cognitively throughout the life cycle; so too do her concepts of death and attitudes about it. This section will provide a brief overview of the identity tasks, conceptions of death, and issues of terminal status that commonly accompany the major developmental phases of life. Much of it will be based on the syntheses of Kastenbaum and Aisenberg (1972) and Pattison (1977). This knowledge is critical to an appreciation of the framework out of which the patient is operating. Like previous experience and cultural, religious, personality, and social attributes, developmental variables will influence the response to the threat of death or loss. All of these variables act together to shape the unique response of each individual.

The Individual Under 3 Years Old

The small child works on differentiating self from non-self. At this stage in life, the child requires the presence of significant others, usually parents, to maintain the sense of self and to provide constancy and security in the world. This world is primarily focused on body and parents.

The child is not cognitively able to grasp the abstractions of irreversibility, finality, inevitability, and permanence implied in the concept of death. However, children have definitely been exposed to experiences and behaviors that are relevant to death: periodic alternations of experience (separations, periodic routines); disappearance and return games (Peek-A-Boo); and things "all gone" (blowing out matches, flushing toilets).

The child of this age most fears separation from parents. When such a child is terminally ill, therapeutic intervention will facilitate the parents' constancy and closeness to the child. If parents are unavailable, for whatever reasons, a stable and reliable parent substitute must meet the child's need for love and help maintain the sense of being.

The Individual From 3 to 6 Years Old

This child is developing the capacity to think, reflect, inquire, and have self-control, initiative, and independence. This is the age of fantasy, daydream, and magical thinking. The child is very concerned with right and wrong, praise and punishment.

At this time the child begins to form an intellectual appreciation for death, but recognizes it not as final, but merely as a diminution of life. There is a belief that death is reversible or partial. Clear perceptions of death-related phenomena are possible, yet the intellectual framework to completely understand them is not yet present.

This child tends to view terminal illness as a punishment for real or imagined wrongdoings. The emotional reactions of parents are frequently misinterpreted as constituting anger or disappointment. The child becomes aware of what to say and not to say so that parents and others will not be frightened away. Separation from parents is still a critical issue. The child has much more of an idea that the illness is very serious than those who might erroneously try to hide the fact realize.

Therapeutic intervention will include providing honest and rational explanations to dispel magical thinking and incorrect interpretations about the nature and implications of the illness. The child will be allowed and encouraged to release the overabundance of emotions that have been aroused by the illness. There should not be too many changes in the environment or in the way the child has always been treated, since these changes may further contribute to a sense of insecurity. This caution applies to the older patient as well.

The Individual Who Is Grade School Age
At this age the child experiences life to the fullest extent possible: constantly doing, constantly acting, constantly experiencing. The child starts to define an identity through the all-important peer group and through a variety of accomplishments.

Death is understood as a common finality of all living things. Youngsters in this age group may personalize death in the form of a skeleton or Boogey Man. They may feel that their own death can be avoided. Toward the end of this age span, the adult concepts of death as final, universal, and inevitable are established.

As a terminal patient, this child fears death itself, and is afraid of pain, medical procedures, and mutilation. The body has performed those acts that have provided self-identity, and to have it ravaged, or to be unable to utilize it maximally due to disability or dysfunction, assaults the capacity to be a person. Effective intervention will offer the concrete details of proposed medical interventions and will maximize the child's capabilities to do that which can be done. The child should still be provided access to friends. Surprises should be kept to a minimum and development of alternative skills should be encouraged.

The Individual in Adolescence

Adolescents are intensely preoccupied with the self as they search to answer the question "Who am I?" A sense of respect for oneself as a unique human being deepens. There is a focus on the present and near future, with a rush and sense of urgency experienced as adolescents move from the present to the near future, eagerly awaiting the unfolding of identity. The distant future appears barren and the past is obscured.

Adolescents have an adult concept of death. Now that they are establishing their own unique senses of self and identity, they are particularly vulnerable to the threat of death. Inherent in the process of the establishment of identity is the realization that ultimately they are alone. The acute sense of individuality and aloneness of this age creates a particularly sharpened sense of personal mortality. The developing sense of self confronts a natural enemy in death, on the other side of the future.

"The affirmation, confirmation, and clarification of the adolescent as a unique and real human being may be the most important task in coping with dying at this age" (Pattison, 1977, p. 23). Death anxiety, in an adult form, is clearly apparent. There may be a particularly strong sense of anger at being deprived of life when on the threshold of tasting its fullness. As with all other patients, regardless of age, adolescents need to ventilate feelings, get answers to questions, and maintain self-control, security, and relationships with significant others.

The Individual as a Young Adult

This individual is finally experiencing the beginning of the fruition of past hopes and labors. Careers, families, and relationships are in bloom. The young adult focuses on nurturing them and experiencing their sweetness.

Death is an inevitable event to be found in the future. It is feared as a threat to the fulfillment of life's goals and tasks.

The dying young adult is filled with rage and anger for the interruption of her life at the moment of its fulfillment. There is frustration, rage, and a sense of unfairness and of being cheated. The individual struggles "to reconcile what might have been with what is" (Pattison, 1977, p. 24). The patient holds onto life more tenaciously than at any other age. The losses now are especially acute, as the patient will never see the promise of life for self and significant others (especially children) fulfilled.

Therapeutic intervention will focus on assisting the patient in working through as many losses as possible and in ventilating feelings. An important goal of communication and therapeutic intervention will be helping the patient to achieve an appropriate death. This is especially difficult given that the individual has both more to lose and less to look back upon than at any other time in adult life.

The Individual in Middle Age

At this point in life the individual is faced with the tasks of creating meaning and being productive and creative, and is concerned with future generations (Erikson's stage of "Generativity vs. Stagnation," 1950). There is a mellowing in personality, and the development of meaningful and ongoing relationships with spouse, children, and friends is important. Responsibilities and obligations to others are of the utmost concern. There is an ability to appreciate the more subtle aspects of life.

More intense awareness of aging and death is taking place and the individual is starting to "personalize death" (Rothstein, 1967). The middle aged have learned, at a deeper level, that they too can become older and die as they witness the death and debilitation of meaningful others. At first there is shock in reaction to this; then there follows accommodation, change in expectancies, and acceptance of its inevitability.

Dying at this time disrupts the individual's involvement with significant others. There is a concern over the responsibilities and obligations that will go unmet subsequent to death. Therapeutic intervention will assist the patient in working through losses and planning for those left behind. The person also may need to look especially at the meaning of her life and what she has left behind.

The Individual in Old Age

The individual of this age looks back upon life and reflects upon its experiences. There is an attempt at an emotional integration of all the aspects of one's life, with the construction of meaning and acceptance of one's one and only life as something with dignity and uniqueness that could have been lived in no other way (Erikson's stage of "Ego Integrity vs. Despair," 1950).

It is a gross exaggeration to say that the elderly are all at peace with their coming death. Some are and some are not. The elderly do appear to see death as an important issue, one they often think about and for which they make plans.

All the issues previously discussed about dying patients are equally pertinent to the elderly terminal patient. It is an error to assume that advanced age precludes the normal difficulties inherent in facing death. Therapeutic intervention should continue to facilitate an appropriate death for the aged individual. Significant others may not be able to be supportive because of disabilities due to old age. Additionally, support may not be as forthcoming due to the erroneous assumption that all elderly people are prepared for their own deaths, since they have lived full lives. In such cases external support from caregivers may be necessary.

EXERCISE VI

Personal Fears of Dying

Anxiety about death can be made more manageable by breaking it into its component specific fears. Look at each of the specific fears listed here related to the experience of dying. Check the box that indicates the amount of fear each one generates for you.

	Have no fear of it	Have a mild fear of it	Have a moderate fear of it	Have a major fear of it
Fear of the unknown			✓	
Fear of loneliness				✓
Fear of loss of family and friends		✓		
Fear of loss of self-control		✓		
Fear of loss of body parts and disability		✓		✓
Fear of suffering and pain			✓	
Fear of loss of identity			✓	
Fear of sorrow		✓		
Fear of regression			✓	
Fear of mutilation, decomposition, and premature burial				✓

If your greatest fears happened, how would they affect you?

Are there any similarities between the fears listed here and the personal feelings about death discussed in Exercise I? If so, what? Why?

In what way do these fears influence your life? Your work? (Do they hinder your work or lifestyle? Do you try to overcompensate for them? Do they motivate you positively or negatively?)

What, if anything, are you doing about these fears now?

How could you cope more effectively with these fears?

Which of these fears are most difficult for you to respond to in a dying patient? Why?

Do any of these fears interfere with your being able to respond to a dying patient? Which ones? Why?

How could you cope more effectively with these fears in order to be more helpful to dying patients?

CHAPTER 10

The Dying Patient's Coping Mechanisms

In the process of coping with the stress of dying all patients employ ego-coping mechanisms. Previously these were called *defense mechanisms,* but that term unfortunately came to mean an evasive denial or avoidance response that allowed the individual to "run away." They have been misinterpreted as being bad or unhealthy, but they are adaptive when used appropriately. In fact, the lack of ability to use appropriate defense mechanisms when confronted with stress and threat has long been a hallmark of emotional illness. Consequently, this term has been supplanted here by the more positive *coping* (or *ego-coping*) *mechanisms,* which more accurately describes their purpose.

It is our responsibility as caregivers to support those responses that help the patient cope. They are crucial to the patient's survival in the face of imminent demise, and do not imply weakness. Thus, several determinants should be considered before evaluating a patient's responses as nontherapeutic:

> The patient's responses to life-threatening illness may be considered maladaptive if the reactions are stronger than the danger warrants, if they persist when the threat no longer exists, or if the appropriate responses to danger are lacking. . . . The major behavioral criteria of a significant emotional complication in a patient with cancer or chronic disease are when the emotional reaction 1) prevents him from seeking or cooperating with indicated treatment; 2) significantly increases the pain and distress of the illness; 3) interferes with effective functioning in the vocational, social, and familial spheres; 4) results in a disorganization of his personality with the appearance of psychiatric symptoms. (Schoenberg & Senescu, 1970, pp. 222-223)

A fifth determinant is the depletion of the patient's resources and weakening of his resistance by the responses (Verwoerdt, 1966).

These points should be kept in mind with regard to the ego-coping mechanisms of dying patients (Pattison, 1978):

- *All* people involved with dying experience high degrees of stress—patients, families, friends, *and* caregivers. Everyone utilizes some coping mechanisms.
- During the acute crisis stage of dying more primitive and immature coping mechanisms are commonly used. Frequently these are quickly discarded as the patient and family progress to more mature coping mechanisms. Thus, concern should be less for the moment than whether the dying patient is able to move on to more adaptive mechanisms following the passage of the acute crisis.
- The living-dying interval is a time of repetitive stress. The dying person is physically ill, and this drains him of his psychic energy. Consequently, he may lack the energy for the effective use of coping mechanisms and his range may become more limited. For example, because of physical disability he may not be able to engage in physical activities that once helped him cope by discharging emotion.
- Coping mechanisms are related both to the stage of the life cycle and the stage of the living-dying interval that the patient is in. In the initial acute phase there are likely to be transient maladaptive coping mechanisms. In the chronic living-dying interval coping mechanisms normal to the developmental stage of the patient can be expected. In the terminal phase, typical coping mechanisms recede and tend to be replaced by isolating mechanisms, withdrawal (often misinterpreted as depression), and increasing detachment.

There are three groups of coping mechanisms used by dying patients as they struggle to contend with the approach of death: retreat from the threat of death and conservation of energy; exclusion of the threat of death or its significance from awareness; and attempts at mastery and control of the threat of death. There can be various degrees of overlap between individual mechanisms or groups of mechanisms. The following discussion of these mechanisms is adapted heavily from the superb work of Adriaan Verwoerdt (1966).

RETREAT FROM THE THREAT OF DEATH
AND CONSERVATION OF ENERGY

The main mechanism that allows retreat from death is regression; when it does not offer sufficient protection, the patient may then give up.

Regression

The psychological definition of regression is an "ego-defense mechanism in which the individual retreats to the use of less mature responses in attempting to cope with stress and maintain ego integrity" (Coleman, 1972, p. 772). This is essentially what happens to the patient who must come to grips with the overwhelming stress and anxiety of impending death. For the terminally ill patient regression to proper levels is both necessary and therapeutic. Regression in the terminally ill individual includes restriction of interest in the external world, egocentricity (excessive concern with the self rather than others), dependency upon others for need gratification, an altered time sense, and hypochondriasis (preoccupation with bodily needs).

As the structure of life becomes more restricted as a natural consequence of the illness, it leads the terminally ill patient into a personal and social setting resembling childhood. Many times caregivers get disgusted with patients who act like children. The pressure of their own death and its implications for the rest of their time here have forced these patients to turn their backs on today to seek the yesterday where the world was a more secure less anxious place in which to live. Egocentrism, dependency, and more immature methods of coping often result.

Patients are driven into an increasing preoccupation with self, since their illness requires it and their social and physical worlds are diminishing in size. The satisfaction of basic physiological needs and the absence of pain and discomfort begin to take precedence over social needs. This egocentricity, however, carries with it a liability. Since the patient has reduced the scope of the world and become more interested in himself, he is less capable of making reliable judgments about what is happening. The ego's reality-testing function is hampered. (However, it is still incorrect to assume that the patient should not be consulted in decision making. It is critical to give the patient as much control as possible.) Consequently, the patient feels insecure and the need for continuous reality-testing arises. Much disturbing behavior can be interpreted as attempts by the patient to see just where he stands with other people.

Dependence upon others is a regressive characteristic stemming from the patient's egocentricity, disengagement, and withdrawal from previous role activities and independence. Anyone who is the victim of a chronic illness that necessitates prolonged and repeated hospitalization or reliance on others is inevitably placed in a position of dependency that causes him to feel helpless and childlike.

Reactions to these feelings can be numerous. The patient may feel guilt due to his lack of independence and productivity, two attributes highly valued in our culture. He is often uncomfortably aware of his increasing dependence upon others and may react to this with hostility and resentment, frequently covering up a sense of inferiority and shame. This is obviously a very anxiety-provoking situation, since to lose control over many aspects of one's life is to surrender pride and self-esteem. It is not something that the ego can take lightly.

The phenomenon of regression is therapeutic when it enables the patient to relinquish some independence in order to receive treatment and assists the patient in accepting some restrictions. It aids the formation of the caregiver-patient relationship, in which there necessarily will be some dependency on those who are responsible for care (in some end-stage cases, almost akin to a parent-child relationship). If the patient refused to submit to the natural regressive tendencies to become less independent and relinquish some self-control, he would become isolated without being able to accept the help and support of others. However, regression can be detrimental when patients' egocentric and dependent behaviors make them a problem to caregivers and, ultimately, to themselves. This occurs when the defense of regression is out of proportion to the disabling effects of the illness. Therefore, caregivers must support regression when it is healthy, but must avoid encouraging it prematurely or too completely. It should be appropriate to the particular phase of the illness that the patient is in.

The most effective method of handling patients who are having difficulty surrendering their autonomy is to treat them with a combination of gentleness and firmness. Arbitrary limits that are set without respect for patients cannot afford them any peace of mind. But when limits are established and explained to patients, and those limits are consistently maintained with empathic firmness, patients feel secure in the knowledge that their caregivers are looking out for their best interests, not only by treating them with respect, but also by saving them from more possible pain. Although this may seem analogous to the way a concerned parent might handle a child, the patient should never be treated as less than an adult. No matter how far they regress, patients still need to preserve their dignity.

As regression deepens, dependence upon the familiar and established order appears to extend to routines and inanimate objects. Patients need to have predictable order and schedules on which they can depend for security and a sense of control. If there are any variations from the routine, they are apt to become very anxious. For this reason it is quite important to structure activities to preserve the status quo and render the impression of stability. This also applies to inanimate objects. A misplaced toothbrush can be a catastrophe for the terminally ill patient. Just like the neurotically compulsive individual, the terminally ill patient derives security from the precise ordering of the world. In this way he can still have some control.

An important characteristic of the individual's regression is an altered time sense. The time sequence of the regressed patient is different from that of the adult who is not terminally ill, and must necessarily be so. Instead of looking forward to the future in months and years, which to the fatally ill individual is extremely anxiety-provoking since it contains only death, the patient becomes as a child and takes the future on a day-to-day basis. This relieves some of the anxiety and creates a situation in which some hope can be reactivated. The patient is given a refuge in which the possibility of planning and action can be maintained. For this reason it is helpful to have patients have some small task to accomplish or activity to do each day so that there is something that they can look forward to and that will provide a reassuring sense of continuity. A walk in the garden, a birthday party for another patient, a chance to try on a new robe and put on make-up for a long-awaited visitor—all of these things give the patient something to strive for and to mark time with. They engender feelings of accomplishment and control, and support and foster the continuity of the patient's self-image. The beneficial effects of having something to look forward to also suggest that we as caregivers should attempt to make regularly scheduled visits to patients.

The hypochondriasis and egocentricity of the regressed patient are closely related. Due to lack of other stimulation and the nature of the condition, the patient becomes engrossed in the physiological manifestations of the illness and eventually withdraws from many external happenings. Sometimes this becomes so pronounced that the patient is a problem because of constant somatic complaints. Such a patient may be regarded as a nuisance, which is unfortunate because his real needs, hidden by these behaviors, may be ignored.

It is important that the terminally ill patient regress to a state of dependency and to some earlier modes of adaptation if ego-integrity is to be sustained in the face of imminent death. The degree of regression will vary from case to case. Two clinical examples of dramatic regression follow.

> *Case Example:* Ruth was the 64-year-old mother of six adult children. She was an independent woman who knew her own mind and acted on it. Ruth was a loving, nurturing mother, as well as the matriarch who held the position of power in the family.
>
> In the last 2 to 3 weeks of her life, when she was hospitalized for the final time, she started requesting that her children feed her whenever they came to visit. This was something she would never have asked previously and was a task she

could, in fact, accomplish by herself when they were not around. She became increasingly demanding and whiny whenever they were present. If they did not comply with her wishes she asserted that they did not love her. In the last week of her life she slipped in and out of consciousness. When she was semi-conscious she would call for her own mother, long deceased. She needed to be held and nurtured as she had held and nurtured her own children and as she had been comforted by her own mother.

Case Example: Paul was a 58-year-old man dying of cancer of the liver. As a child he had had a severe problem with stuttering. It was a handicap he had fought arduously and he was ultimately successful in overcoming it. Now, in his final weeks, the stuttering returned. It was determined not be the result of any neurological involvement. The recurrence of his childhood affliction greatly troubled and stressed Paul. He became disconsolate and started to withdraw. The staff noted that he began behaving exactly like a stuttering child who is overly shy, timid, and lonely—the same behaviors that had marked Paul's experience over 50 years before.

Giving Up

Giving up is not a coping mechanism per se, but the end result of regression and other coping mechanisms failing to offer enough protection. "When the patient sees no way out and the future appears totally bleak, passive surrender to fate may be the only way to escape overpowering anxiety, and so the patient blends in with his hostile environment [Meerloo, 1962]. Clinically, giving up can be seen as the apparent abandonment of all spirit and loss of sense of personal control and intactness of self [Engel, 1962b]" (Verwoerdt, 1966, p. 59).

The importance of preventing this surrender cannot be stressed too much. Studies on the crucial significance of hope in maintaining survival reinforce this. Cannon's (1942) investigation of voodoo death, Frankl's (1963) description of concentration camp survivors, and Richter's (1959) work on the phenomenon of sudden death in animals and man all contribute to the evidence of the necessity of hope and the will to live if the organism is to maintain life. In terminally ill patients some dimension of hope must be protected, not only to support survival, but to provide as much meaning and life as is possible in the remaining time.

Verwoerdt (1966) suggests several ways in which hopelessness can be prevented. First the caregiver must find out whether the patient privately fears reaching the point where she will relinquish hope or be overcome by terror and, if so, what these fears are founded upon. Verwoerdt notes that patients may intuitively fear giving up and use defenses to keep themselves from recognizing the full impact of what is happening to them. They will tend to vacillate between expressions of despair and hope, using the hope to bolster their defenses. By ascertaining the fears contributing to the patient's worry over giving up, the caregiver can determine where the patient requires the most support and respond to these needs. Second, optimal regression can be encouraged to combat hopelessness. Although the patient lacks a future of months and years, an increased focus on day-to-day living can maintain hopes and pleasant expectations. Parenthetically, Verwoerdt points out that the day-to-day interval should not begin with the morning of one day and end with the evening. The evening, with its darkness and diminished external stimulation, is often anxiety-provoking for dying patients. Therefore, it is helpful to portray the daily span as reaching from the present day into the succeeding day, cushioning the lonely night on both sides with hopeful expectations and making tomorrow seem not so remote. Finally, it is critical to provide regularly scheduled, specific activities each day that the patient can look forward to, such as daily scheduled visits or repeated daily routines like bathing, working, or getting a nightly backrub. Brief, frequent visits by friends, family, and caregivers are the best morale boosters. (See "Acceptance, Withdrawal and Detachment, and Hope" in Chapter 11 for more on this topic.)

EXCLUSION OF THE THREAT OF DEATH OR ITS SIGNIFICANCE FROM AWARENESS

Coping mechanisms that fall within this group are repression, suppression, denial, rationalization, depersonalization, and projection and introjection.

Repression
The use of repression by the terminally ill patient facing imminent death is not surprising. Faced with the extreme stress of this situation, the patient forces the anxious thoughts and feelings about the condition into the unconscious. She attempts to exclude from conscious awareness intolerable thoughts of death and its significance. Through this struggle the patient attempts to maintain an emotional equilibrium.

It is probable, however, that this mechanism of repression is only useful for the patient to a limited extent since the symptoms are a constant reminder of the condition. The failure of repression to function adequately necessitates the emergence of auxiliary mechanisms aimed at exclusion of the threat from the patient's awareness: suppression, denial, and rationalization.

Suppression

In contrast to repression, suppression is the conscious attempt to dismiss anxiety-provoking thoughts from awareness. This is often accomplished through engaging in some kind of diversionary activity pushing the anxious feelings out of consciousness by being busy with something else. For example, when patients are in the presence of others, they may resort to excessive talking or sleeping to keep dangerous thoughts at bay and to keep others from speaking of stressful matters. They may fill their time with sewing or playing solitary word games and shut out the world and their anxious thoughts.

Diversionary activities become more difficult to sustain as the fatally ill patient deteriorates. Suppression becomes weakened through the increased idleness and passivity inherent in the bedridden state. Nighttime is especially trying for patients. The lack of sensory input and the horizontal position in bed deprive them of possible diversions and leave them alone with their anxious thoughts. (This may be one of several reasons that the majority of hospital deaths occur during the night.) To combat the stress that the night poses, patients may frequently get out of bed and move around their rooms.

It is extremely important to recognize that suppression is often necessary to the patient and should be supported instead of discouraged. No one can continue to contemplate the issues posed by terminal illness without adequate respite. "When nothing is to be gained from a therapeutic standpoint by encouraging expression of the patient's thoughts and feelings, he should be supported in his attempts to relegate fears to the back of his mind" (Verwoerdt, 1966, p. 64).

Misinterpretation of recent literature in the field has prompted some caregivers to feel that they must constantly bombard dying patients with questions and experiences, forcing patients to discuss their terminal condition and its implications. As will be discussed next with respect to denial, it is necessary and important to allow patients to have some distance from the ever-present threat of their own demise.

Denial

The defensive process of denial occurs to a greater or lesser degree in all patients with terminal illness. It is a form of avoidance that temporarily negates or pushes into the unconscious painful and intolerable thoughts and stimuli. The process consumes energy and alters reality but, at that moment, makes life more bearable for the patient (Schoenberg & Senescu, 1970). It is another way to gain a respite from the continuous contemplation of the threat of death.

Most terminally ill patients exhibit several types of denial over the course of the illness. Weisman (1972a) differentiated three types. Type I is a denial of the specific facts of the illness. For instance, the patient may insist that the tumor in her neck is only a swollen gland. Type II is the denial of the implications and extensions of the illness. In this case the patient acknowledges the seriousness of the illness, but denies that it will end in her death. Type III is the denial of extinction. Although the patient accepts the diagnosis and its implications for taking her life, she still does not expect that *she* will die from it. Besides denying the illness, patients may also deny concerns and problems associated with the illness (e.g., they may deny fear of wasting away like someone they knew did), and their own emotional reactions to it (e.g., they may become hypomanic to cover up feelings of depression).

Anyone who values life at all wants to deny death. "Evasion, avoidance and denial of death all have a rightful place in man's psychic economy. Man has a legitimate need to face away from death, and in truth, who is to say that under certain conditions this may not be salutary?" (Feifel, 1971, pp. 11-12). Yet denial has been much misunderstood. According to Lazarus (1981), denial has traditionally been viewed as a self-deception, a distortion of reality considered tantamount to mental disorder. Yet, in everyday life people do create their own realities; there are ambiguities in judging reality; life is hard to carry on without some illusion or self-deception; and we all share some collective illusions (e.g., our society is free, moral, just; successful people work harder, are smarter, more favored by God than others). Consequently, denial "can be both adaptationally sound *and* capable of eliciting a heavy price" (p. 53).

Most forms of denial should be respected and supported. Recent misperceptions of the literature implying that denial is counter-therapeutic and always needs to be broken are grossly incorrect. If denial serves to hold the integrity of the individual together, then it is therapeutically useful.

> The emotional defenses of a patient should be respected unless there is clear evidence that the advantages of breaking down a patient's defenses outweigh the advantages of maintaining them. Confronting the patient with evidence that he is dying may precipitate a reaction which can cause further depression, emotional disorganization, or further withdrawal from reality. Sudden disclosure of evidence may stimulate even more denial and make the patient less accessible. (Schoenberg & Senescu, 1970, p. 231)

Denial functions as a buffer to the shocking news of a terminal illness, giving patients time to collect themselves and mobilize other, less radical defenses. Those who want and need to deny the fact that they are dying will find a way to do so even if they have been told the true condition of their illness. It has been argued that is some cases people should not be told their illness is terminal because they will not be able to deny their illness long enough to mobilize their defenses. However, a patient who does not want to hear the diagnosis, won't.

Many times patients know the true nature of the illness, but are not able to admit it. They may go "doctor hopping" in hopes of finding a physician who will say they are not dying. This kind of denial serves two important functions. It first renders the threat less real because it is not verbally addressed and brought out into the open. The threat still retains some qualities of the imagined or possible. If the patient refuses to talk with the caregiver about the illness, it then also allows the threat to be suppressed to decrease anxiety.

During the illness denial may be intermittently employed when the patient is confronted with anxiety that becomes too overwhelming. It is usually only a temporary defense, since it is difficult to maintain it completely in the face of illness, a constant reminder of the truth.

In the living-dying interval patients will vacillate between denial and acceptance. The vacillation reflects the changes in the patient's ability to cope with reality at any given time; the conflicts that sometimes arise between reason and emotion; the fact that awareness is not an all-or-nothing concept; and the patient's need for a pause in the contemplation of his own death and an opportunity to focus on aspects of living as well as dying.

Patients can also deny and accept at the same time. For example, although a patient may intellectually accept and confront the fact that she is dying, she may deny some aspect or implication about the death that is too painful to face. She may admit that she is dying, but refuse to believe that she is sick enough to have the physician notify the children in order to say good-bye.

> Many seriously or terminally ill patients maintain a subtle equilibristic balance between realistic acceptance of death and its simultaneous rejection . . . . this counterpoise seems to serve adaptational needs of the patient, allowing him to maintain communal associations and yet organize his resources to contend with oncoming death . . . . both acceptance and rejection of death can coexist within the same person, with acknowledgement and manageable fear generally dictating verbal or conscious considerations while denial and dread rule the "gut" level reactions. (Feifel, 1971, pp. 7-8)

There are different degrees and combinations of denial and acceptance within each individual that will vary over the living-dying interval. Therefore, it is best not to try to completely eliminate denial and foster absolute acceptance of death, but to respond to the ongoing process of both in the patient (Pattison, 1978).

Although denial is probably unavoidable in the course of a fatal illness, and may even be conducive to good adjustment, extreme denial is highly detrimental. It can become physically and psychologically self-destructive. Physically, patients can destroy themselves if they refuse to accept their conditions and neglect doctors' warnings and prescriptions. Psychologically, patients can destroy themselves if they refuse to drop their major denial. They slowly work themselves into a corner where they will eventually have to turn around and face the threat all at once. In addition, they will probably be unable to effectively use their remaining time to finish unfinished business. For them to do this would be to admit that they are dying.

In 1981 Lazarus discussed the costs and benefits of denial. He noted how various types of denial, such as certain kinds of self-deceptions and illusions people live by, are "important. . . for mental health. . . . such working fictions have been regarded as useful not only in maintaining morale, but also in aiding effective adaptation" (p. 64). After reviewing the studies on the effects of denial and denial-like processes, Lazarus formulated five principles about the adaptational consequences of denial:

- *Principle 1*. Denial can have positive value under certain conditions and negative value under others. When denial undermines actions required for adaptation to stress (e.g., a diabetic not taking insulin), it is destructive. In circumstances where direct action is irrelevant to the adaptational outcome, denial is not damaging and may even be valuable by reducing stress and allowing the individual to address other matters.
- *Principle 2*. When a given stress must be encountered repeatedly, denial prevents ultimate mastery of the stress by keeping up the patient's morale and thus reducing the incentive to deal with the stress.
- *Principle 3*. Denial is time-related. It may be quite helpful in the initial stages of coping with stress, when the individual's resources are insufficient for coping in a more problem-focused way.
- *Principle 4*. Some kinds of denial are dangerous, while others may be of considerable value. Denying fact, what is clearly known and unambiguous (e.g., the illness), is more harmful to adaptation than denying what is uncertain (e.g., the implications of what happens after death). If the object of denial is unclear, uncertain, or ambiguous, the denial can be more easily sustained.

- *Principle 5.* In cases where denial is partial, tentative, or minimal, it is less pernicious and often quiet useful.

Hyland (Note 15) has described *adaptive denial*, in which the
patient is well aware of the illness and its implications, but chooses
to focus on the strengths and opportunities remaining rather than
dwell on the unpleasantness. Other research suggests that this fosters optimism and enhances coping, and is a process that should
be encouraged (Lazarus, 1981; Weisman & Worden, 1975).

Rationalization

Rationalization, which is one of the most common of all coping
mechanisms, "represents a kind of reasoning whereby true causal
relationships are not recognized, minor aspects of a situation are
emphasized out of proportion or major aspects minimized so that
the central context is not perceived, or a nonattainable object or
situation is devalued" (Verwoerdt, 1966, p. 66). Aspects of the
threat of death can then be explained away so as to deny its existence. For example, a patient may minimize the symptoms of
pain as gastrointestinal problems instead of recognizing and ad-
mitting that the pain is symptomatic of the fatal illness. Rationalization may also be seen in the patient's devaluing a particular
loss to prevent grief, or devaluing her own feelings (e.g., "It doesn't
really matter to me that I will lose my leg") to make them more
manageable.

Depersonalization

This defense is a very maladaptive one that operates through
a blurring of the ego boundaries. In this process, the stress that
the patient has to endure causes the boundaries of the ego to become less differentiated from external reality. Usually, when these
boundaries are intact and clearly differentiated, the person feels
intact and the external reality is perceived as being "something
out there." The self has a feeling of sameness. However, when the
boundaries become blurred because of stress, the distinction between the internal self and the external reality is not readily apparent. There is a feeling of unreality, and self loses its sense of
identity. Patients feel as if they are detached and standing outside
of life, observing it as onlookers or as if they are in a dream. Everything around them seems foreign and strange. They manifest symptoms of dissociation, wherein they feel that their experiences, and
indeed sometimes their own bodies, are not part of them. They
may feel "mechanical." In this way they distance themselves from
their painful feelings. "The defensive function of depersonalization
lies in the patient's feeling that 'this experience does not belong to
me, has nothing to do with me, so there is no cause for alarm'"

(Verwoerdt, 1966, p. 68). It is another way to deny the fact that it is the person herself who is, in fact, dying.

The defense is used most frequently at the time of diagnosis, and the reaction is usually brief. Verwoerdt (1966) provides an example:

> One patient, an intelligent businessman with Hodgkin's disease who was told his diagnosis in a rather straightforward manner by his physician, described his initial reaction as follows: "I could hear the doctor talk, but his voice seemed to come from very far away . . . his words echoed back and forth in my head. As he spoke to me, I saw his face in a mist . . . and the thought occurred to me that Hodgkin really was an odd name." (p. 68)

Verwoerdt goes on to note that patients with acute depersonalization can be helped by rest or sedation, or by reestablishment of contact with reality through familiar enjoyable activities that lessen the impact of the traumatic stimulus prompting the depersonalization.

Projection and Introjection

"Projection is the mechanism by which one externalizes one's own undesirable condition, thoughts or feelings by ascribing them to others, and introjection is the reverse process—that of attributing phenomena which originated in others to oneself" (Verwoerdt, 1966, p. 68). Like dissociation, these processes involve a blurring of the ego boundaries.

In introjection, what occurs in the external world is perceived to have originated within the patient. For example, the fact that a tumor is malignant is perceived by the patient as being something he came up with himself, and not something told to him by the physician. Therefore he does not have to confront it as he would if it came from outside of himself. It can be more easily denied. The patient can alter the objective character of information coming from the outside world, especially the diagnosis and all of its implications.

For projection to get to the point where it results in the patient's ascribing the illness to other persons, the patient has to be psychotic from emotional disorder or organic brain syndrome. It is more frequently manifested in the patient's projecting the cause or symptoms of the illness from within himself outward onto someone or something else in the environment. It is a way of finding a scapegoat. It also distances him from guilt and removes the cause of illness from within himself. For example, a patient who experiences a spontaneous femoral fracture secondary to the disease process may blame it on mishandling by orderlies. Verwoerdt (1966) notes, "It was as though he were saying: 'It is nothing inside of *me* which is destroying me; it is *you* outsiders who are responsible.' Such forms of projection obviously coexist with feelings of hostility in the patient and eventually engender similar feelings in the medical personnel, who exhibit a very natural disinclination to be unjustly attacked" (p. 69).

We need to identify the serious psychopathology of projection, recognize it as a symptom, and help the patient find less destructive ways of coping with his basic anxieties. This mechanism tends to create interpersonal problems. The patient projects and blames others, often with great hostility, and angers those around him. However, to react to the patient with hostility, become condescending, argue, or try to correct his misconceptions will not be therapeutic. We should neither oppose nor side with the distortions; rather we should be neutral, offer the patient opportunities to express his anger and hostility, and perhaps, in a nonjudgmental way, question why the patient thinks or feels as he does and ask what he would need to correct the problem. Then, very gently, misconceptions might be corrected, with assurances of future efforts to minimize the patient's discomfort. A policy of acceptance without retaliation and of genuine concern for the patient may demonstrate to him that his hostility and irrational fears are groundless; this may reduce the need for such a defense, defuse the anger accompanying it, or relegate it to a face-saving device with the tacit acknowledgment between patient and caregiver that feelings are different deep down inside (Verwoerdt, 1966).

MASTERY AND CONTROL OF THE THREAT OF DEATH

Ways of coping that are attempts to master and control death include intellectualization, obsessive-compulsive mechanisms, counterphobic mechanisms, and sublimation.

Intellectualization

This coping mechanism isolates feelings from thoughts. Very simply, patients become observers of their own condition and do not permit their emotions to become involved. Such patients often appear intellectually preoccupied with their illness and somewhat detached from it. They try to allay feelings of anxiety by distancing themselves through intellectual and cognitive acts.

If intellectualization is carried on in moderation, it can give the patient a sense of predictability, control, and hope. For instance, some knowledge of the illness may allow the patient to more effectively cope with its progression, since she knows what to expect. Reading about or discussing the illness also may help the patient envision herself as contributing to society through the knowledge that she may help provide research on this fatal illness. By giving death some meaning, the patient may be able to accept it with more equanimity. On the other hand, if the patient becomes too involved in reading about the development of the illness, she may become anxious, anticipating losses and events that may never arrive. Some patients have even become highly distressed over the fact that their illness had not run its course in the time allotted. If the patient consistently denies feelings by the use of intellectualization, or causes premature anxiety over losses to be encountered later in the illness, then the defense is counter-herapeutic.

The emotions and concerns beneath the intellectualization can sometimes be reached by asking how the patient feels and by inquiring about her reactions to the issues being intellectualized. Talking about expectable feelings can help normalize them. Very gentle confrontation or interpretation of the patient's avoidance of feelings may open avenues for discussing them. We should be wary of fostering intellectualization through the use of distancing jargon and avoidance of direct communication with the patient.

Obsessive-Compulsive Mechanisms

Obsessive-compulsive mechanisms rely heavily on intellectualization and isolation of feelings from thoughts. Compulsive rituals and concerns may emerge as attempts at mastery and control of the illness. If these compulsions are not carried to extremes and do not constrain the patient's personal sense of freedom, they can be therapeutic, as they provide the patient with a sense of predictability, order, security, and control. Like the obsessive-compulsive neurotic, the patient orders her world to reduce anxiety. It gives her something she can control, since she cannot control the fact that the illness progresses and death awaits. An example of this is the patient who requires a structured and fixed daily routine in order to function throughout the day.

Counterphobic Mechanisms

These mechanisms represent an attempt to master the threat by moving into the dangerous area itself. Patients who employ such coping mechanisms feel the need to disregard imposed restraints and to assert that they are the masters of the threat and not vice versa. For instance, the patient who repeatedly drinks alcohol despite the doctor's orders to the contrary is actually trying to beat the threat of death. For such patients it is an attempt to assert that they still have control. In many cases denial, rebellious protest, and overcompensation are associated with counterphobic mechanisms. Additionally, many patients combine them with intellectualization and isolation of affect in an attempt to master the threat intellectually.

Counterphobic mechanisms may require gentle confrontation or interpretation and possibly a questioning of the patient's purpose in order to help him identify the underlying need for control and desire to deny (e.g., "I wonder why you keep doing what your doctor has forbidden"). However, it must be recognized that for some patients this type of mastery is the only way they can cope with the stress and maintain their integrity. This is especially true with people who have characteristically asserted themselves through rebellion. Although such activities may shorten their lives, it is more important to them that they respond in this fashion. Otherwise, they feel they have capitulated. This can be very difficult for family and caregivers to watch. Hopefully, if patients are supported and encouraged to have control and choice in other areas, there may be relatively less of a need to act-out to assert control. Appropriate sublimation and suppression can be encouraged to offer the patient some therapeutic distance from the threat.

Sublimation

This is a coping mechanism by which the individual channels unacceptable thoughts and feelings into socially and personally acceptable ones. In this way an outlet is provided for them. If a terminally ill person is very angry at the way he was treated by his physician, he may go and release his aggression through watching a boxing match or hitting golf balls. Often patients may direct their anger at being stricken with cancer into expending energy by working for organizations such as the American Cancer Society. We should support the healthy use of this mechanism.

CHAPTER 11

Caring for the Dying Patient

In the terminal illness of any patient, the relationship sustained with caregivers is extremely important. The patient has to have great faith in us, as she is literally placing her life in our hands. We become central figures in her life. She will ultimately enter into some sort of dependency relationship with us that will make it easier for us to provide the care she needs and for her to respond to it and accept the necessary amounts of loss of self-control and autonomy.

One of our ideal goals should be to not only allay the physical suffering of patients as best we can, but also to help them prepare "for recognition and acceptance of this reality of life [death] so that they can undertake their last task in life with credit and dignity" (Verwoerdt, 1966, p. 6). We function in many roles for terminally ill patients. We may serve as medical caregivers, confidants, advisors, counselors, and therapists. Our presence can bring comfort and reduce anxiety. We have the power to structure schedules and surroundings so patients have a sense of security and control over life and their environment. If we have a non-judgmental, warm attitude, we can elicit the feelings and thoughts they need to communicate. And we can support their self-esteem by asking for their opinions in matters that directly concern them and in which alternatives have to be chosen. As Verwoerdt (1964) notes, performing these activities is supporting a regimen that functions as an "ego prosthesis," an artificial ego that gives patients emotional support.

Of all the needs of the dying patient, the three most crucial are the needs for control of pain, preservation of dignity and self-worth, and love and affection (Schulz, 1978). In a quite unique way, we have a special capacity to address those needs.

267

ACCEPTANCE, WITHDRAWAL AND DETACHMENT, AND HOPE

Acceptance, withdrawal and detachment, and hope are three issues that arise repeatedly in working with the terminally ill. The issue of the acceptance of death by the dying patient has recently been much debated. Some clinicians and researchers have taken the position that the goal of therapeutic intervention with a terminally ill patient is to facilitate the acceptance of death. Many others question this goal and wonder whether it has been established for the sake of the patients or for those working with them. Obviously, it is easier on all those concerned if a patient can accept death with equanimity and peace.

Those who question this point out that it is natural to want to fight the fact that we must die. They cite the Dylan Thomas exhortation "Do not go gentle into that good night. . . . Rage, rage against the dying of the light." They contend that it is possible for a patient to experience a good death without having come to this state of acceptance and its implied resignation.

A more appropriate description of what therapeutic attempts should facilitate has been provided by Humphrey (Note 16), a nurse with a long-term, clinical involvement with the dying. She notes that in actual clinical practice true acceptance (in the sense of the phase articulated by Elisabeth Kübler-Ross in *On Death and Dying* [1969]) is seldom witnessed. Instead, what seems to occur is a realization of the inevitable. A patient may still not be willing to go or be at peace with the fact that death will happen, but can take the view that, for whatever reasons, the time has come. Accompanying this is the acceptance of death as a natural part of life and a fulfillment of the cycle of existence. Although the patient may not be at peace with the fact that all that is loved must be lost, she is at peace with not denying that the loss will occur.

The issue of withdrawal and detachment is important because it has implications for treatment. Throughout this book it has been asserted that dying patients need continued and rewarding interaction with others. There is a clear mandate for family, friends, and caregivers to make sure that abandonment, so frequently a part of the dying patient's experience, does not occur. However, there is a time, very close to death, when the patient starts to markedly restrict involvement with reality and the outside world. (See "Anxiety" in Chapter 9 for more on this topic.) This is not to say that this had not been occurring to a lesser extent throughout the entire dying process. Indeed, the patient has been slowly loosening the ties that bind, gradually moving towards a state of detachment and separation from that which must be left behind. At a point close to death, however, this now occurs with those closest to the patient and with whom the patient has still continued to be emotionally involved.

Humphrey (Note 16) makes the analogy that the experience of the dying patient in close proximity to death is similar to that of the woman in labor. Initially, when the process begins, the woman has an increased awareness of all that is going on around her. As she gets closer to birth, however, nothing and no one else really matter as she concentrates on the moment. A similar withdrawal and detachment occurs with the dying patient. The patient becomes involved in making the transition, in passing through a portal through which the journey must be made alone. In a sense, at the very end of life, the patient is not all here. It is as if the dying person had one foot in another world. The outward appearances signal that the patient has become introverted and withdrawn from the last ones she has been involved with on this earth. Frequently this is the family.

At this point there is a shift in the emphasis for care. No longer is the patient the one who requires the support; rather, it now becomes the loved ones. They may interpret the patient's turning away as rejection. They need to be helped to understand that this is not a rejection of them, but rather that all the patient's energies are now directed towards going where they cannot go. The patient's self-involvement is not a statement of lack of love, but a natural part of the process of death through which everyone passes. Intervention must be aimed at supporting the family at this time, for the withdrawal and detachment may be difficult for them to accept, especially if they sense it as desertion.

Usually this last decathexis occurs in the very final hours of life. This needs to be differentiated from some of the other gradual detachment that already has been occurring throughout the dying process. Up until this point it is still important to have significant loved ones around and to avoid the pitfall of abandoning the patient prematurely. Even at the very end, when the patient is withdrawn, it may be very meaningful to have a sense that the loved ones are still there. It must be repeated—one of the worst fears of any individual is to be left to die alone.

The third issue deals with something that has been present from the moment of diagnosis: hope. The type and quality of hope will change throughout the course of the individual's terminal illness. Initially the hope is that the diagnosis will be proven incorrect. This changes, upon confirmation of the diagnosis, to the hope that there will be a cure or some miracle that will enable the patient to escape death. Later, this hope is transformed to a smaller scale and the patient hopes that life will be optimal, albeit limited (e.g., with a minimum of pain and disruption of life). Smaller hopes related to everyday life and activities, referred to by Worden as *mini-hopes*, may remain until the end (e.g., hope that symptoms will be minimal on the day the grandchildren visit).

Some degree of hope persists through all the phases of dying, through the emotional reactions, grief, and defenses. Frequently it is this hope that sustains the patient through suffering. When all hope becomes lost there is a psychological and then a physical surrender to the environment. Previous investigations of the survivors of concentration camps illustrate that the most torturous conditions can be survived if the individual has hope, and that the relinquishment of such hope is rapidly followed by death.

Fortunately, hope depends less on the patient's perception of futurity than on her perception of self-worth and effectiveness.

> Hope, however, is not dependent upon survival alone. . . . Hope means that we have confidence in the *desirability* of survival. It arises from a desirable self-image, healthy self-esteem, and belief in our ability to exert a degree of influence on the world surrounding us. . . .
>
> Hope is decided more by self-acceptance than by objects sought and by impractical aspirations. . . . Foreshortened life does not in itself create hopelessness. . . . More important is our belief that we do something worth doing, and that others think so, too. Thus, people lose hope when they are unable to act on their own behalf and must also relinquish their claims upon others. (Weisman, 1972a, pp. 20-21)

This means that we can support the patient's hope by helping her retain control, dignity, and self-esteem. Some ways we can do this are suggested by Verwoerdt (1966): focusing on the present and what is immediately ahead rather than on an uncertain future; emphasizing remaining potentials and abilities; and structuring events in the patient's daily life to render a sense of predictability and continuity, while fostering opportunities for specific accomplishments that bring the patient satisfaction. Each patient should have things to anticipate, such as a weekly chess game with an off-duty caregiver. Those patients with a very bleak and empty future can be encouraged to reminisce about previous joys and fulfillments. An expression of interest in such memories is usually quite welcome and heartening to the patient.

Hope is an essential requirement for existence to continue, for the threat of demise to be confronted, and for life's meaning to be sustained. Hope must never be destroyed. The transmission of diagnoses and discussions with patients must never preclude the patient's being able to hang on to some hope, however tenuous. A patient can hear a terminal diagnosis and still have hopes for the type of life remaining.

REQUISITES FOR WORKING
WITH THE DYING

There are some necessary prerequisites for those wishing to work with dying patients (Knott, Note 17):

- A personal confrontation with death in the sense of having started to come to grips with one's own mortality. This can never be done completely, but the issue needs to have been addressed.
- An understanding of the grief process and an appreciation for the total experience of the dying patient.
- Effective listening skills and the ability to respond appropriately. This attending behavior will be nonverbal as well as verbal.
- A commitment to giving part of oneself to the dying person and to working with families after death when appropriate.
- A knowledge of one's own personal limits, knowing when there is a need to get away from death and how to avoid burn-out.

Personal attitudes can influence effectiveness in working with the dying. It is necessary to be realistic about what can be done for dying patients, and to control personal fears about death and dying individuals.

Maintenance of a Realistic Perspective

One of the least discussed yet most critical issues involved in the care of the dying pertains to our own expectations for death and dying. These expectations influence our actions and emotional responses, which in turn impact upon dying patients.

At the time of this writing many professional caregivers, even those trained specifically to work with the terminally ill, continue to sustain grossly inappropriate expectations of death and themselves. The trend in today's literature and art, and in too many professional discussions about death and dying, is to view death in a romantic fashion. There is a belief that if the "right" things are done, a beautiful, serene, accepted death can be ensured in which all business will be finished and the exit will be made gracefully after well-articulated good-byes.

Many caregivers espouse this view. Full of ardor and zeal, they seek to passionately bring the "beautiful" death to their patients. They have read about society's previous reluctance to address the dying and want to rectify the cruelty with each terminally ill patient they meet. There is a determination to get patients to reveal their innermost feelings and fears about death, even if they don't want or need to.

Although armed with good intentions, and more than passing knowledge about death and dying, these caregivers are poorly equipped for what they inevitably must confront. For death, in far too many cases, is not romantic. It is not graceful. It is not beautiful. In fact, death stinks—literally and figuratively! It is clammy, too. It can sound bad, and it often is ugly.

The disillusionment that confrontations with death may bring is often compounded when it is recognized that frequently people die angry or hurt, without emotional closure. Death-bed reconciliations are more rare outside of the movies than one might be given to expect. And unfair as it seems, money can make a difference in how people are able to die. Sometimes the good wins out—sometimes death does. "Fairness" and "justice" become words devoid of meaning. "Why" seems to be completely unanswerable.

Unrealistic expectations can predispose these caregivers to professional burn-out. They also steal from dying patients the emotion, the warmth, and the outgoingness of their caregivers. The discovery that death is not necessarily "beautiful" ends up hurting the patients as much as the professionals.

Some caregivers have inappropriate expectations not only about death, but also about their own capabilities. Because they care, they want to take away pain. They want to make things better and fix the problem. However, the dilemmas that dying people are in cannot be fixed—they can only be coped with, accommodated to. The pain of loss cannot be taken away; it can only be assuaged.

It is one of the most difficult things in the world to do: to sit and listen while another's heart is breaking with grief, to hold the hand of a dying patient who cries silently while staring into space. The gift of presence, the gift of being with those in pain, is the only gift that we can give. It is the sole armor patients have against the anguish. The very most that we can do for dying patients is to make it better, with our presence and concern, than it would be if we were not there. We can strive to facilitate emotional expression and ventilation, which have been demonstrated to be therapeutic, but we cannot "do" anything that can get rid of the psychic pain of impending loss and death.

The major problem for many caregivers is that they are trained to "do," to find the correct technique, to perform the proper action. They can become bitterly frustrated when they find themselves in situations for which no action can bring the desired response of relief from suffering. They often feel that they have failed. Even though palliative medicine emphasizes "care" instead of "cure," many of the practitioners of palliative care maintain the "cure" mentality deep in their hearts. They still search for the correct thing to "do." They need to become accustomed to the discomfort generated by not "doing" anything for those patients who are at the point of being past cure. This does not mean that things are not done to promote patients' comfort; rather, it is a recognition that activity is directed toward care—both physical and psychological—and that psychological pain cannot be taken away by "doing." It is necessary for caregivers to learn to "Just be, don't do." "Doing" will be ineffective and will only serve to take a caregiver's real gift, his presence, away from the patient. Each caregiver has to realize that he is the most valuable and effective tool he possesses, or he will be doomed to failure because of his unrealistic expectations.

In summary, we must be realistic about what death is really like at times. We also must develop appropriate expectations about what we can and cannot do for dying patients. When all else has been done and the patient is dying, it is best to heed Kalish's (1981) reversal of a famous cry: "Don't just do something, stand there!" The lack of appropriate expectations and a realistic perspective about death and ourselves will result in emotional and professional reactions that will render us less effective to the patients we desire to serve.

To begin forming a new picture of your personal beliefs about death and dying patients, complete Exercise VII at the end of this chapter.

Avoidance of Withdrawal From the Patient

Just as some caregivers are anxious to talk with and do things for the dying patient, others feel so uncomfortable that they draw away from the patient. Arteberry (1967) writes that caregivers experience a sense of frustration, fear, and uneasiness when they are caring for dying patients. They then tend to isolate themselves emotionally from the patient in an attempt to avoid facing their own death anxiety. This is easily perceived by patients and contributes to the loneliness and alienation frequently felt. Similar reactions are observed in friends and relatives, who may eliminate their social contacts when the patient most needs them. All too often these excuses are given: "I just don't know what to say"; "Maybe I should just leave her alone"; "It won't make any difference if I don't visit her in the hospital." This is sadly unfortunate, for patients do not want to be abandoned when they are in their hour of greatest need and they certainly do not want to be considered hopeless cases.

Some patients experience social death long in advance of their actual demise. Due to illness they frequently are nonproductive, out of control, physically unattractive, and anxiety-provoking to others, all attributes that are poorly tolerated in our society. They become socially devalued and are frequently avoided. This causes further self-disparagement, anger, and grief in patients.

Sensing the avoidance and discomfort of others, patients may adopt styles of speaking and relating that minimize their threat to others and hopefully keep others from leaving them. The price they pay to forestall abandonment is often high—the relinquishment of honest communication that could reduce their own personal distress. It is a trade-off to escape rejection and isolation, one of the greatest fears of all dying individuals.

Professional caregivers, as well as the patient's acquaintances, employ a variety of defenses to avoid confronting their own personal death anxiety generated by the patient, as well as their own frustrated desires to take away the pain of loss and cure the disease. At times these are cloaked in an expressed desire to "protect" the patient from the knowledge of diagnosis, which also serves to protect them from having to deal with someone who is in pain from having to face loss and death.

There are four types of possible interactions and awarenesses between dying patient and caregivers (Glaser & Strauss, 1965). In a *closed awareness context* caregivers are aware of the patient's condition but keep this information from the patient. A *suspicion awareness context* is present when caregivers know the truth and the patient suspects that she is dying. She simultaneously wants to discover the truth and desires to avoid it. The *mutual pretense awareness context* is one in which caregivers and patient are aware of the illness and its implications, but pretend they are not. An *open awareness context* is one in which there is shared knowledge, information, and communication about the patient's dying.

In the first three awareness contexts the dying individual is robbed of the intimacy of genuine communication. At least one or both of the parties involved must conceal the truth—an act that cannot foster closeness or further communication, generating further loss for the patient. Even if caregivers can hide the truth and avoid honest confrontation with the patient, it often exacts a high price in discomfort and anxiety. These emotions may encourage them to withdraw further from the patient to reduce their stress. Only the open awareness context allows for interchange without the anxiety that accompanies withholding truth or pretending. It facilitates the patient's finishing unfinished business and grieving losses, while it promotes continued interaction and conditions for an appropriate death and allows significant others to be open with the patient as well.

Professional caregivers and social acquaintances are not the only ones who may distance themselves from dying patients. Even those most close to the patient may sustain the same desire. It is not easy to watch a loved one wither away. The pain of watching the patient struggle to give up the world and the self can become unbearable; and the sights and smells of terminal illness can be repelling, bringing guilt and shame at the revulsion felt. (See Chapter 12 for more on this topic.)

Like professional caregivers and friends, close loved ones need to be aware of how critical it is to maintain relationships and communication with the dying patient. During most of the living-dying interval, the patient requires ongoing social and emotional support. This support helps the patient to feel worthy and valued and to adapt as successfully as possible to the illness and the dying process. Caregivers and loved ones alike need to keep in mind that the patient, although dying, is also still living. This attitude should be communicated to the patient through both words and behavior.

Support should continue even up to the time just prior to death, when it is important that the dying patient receive "permission" to die from her closest loved ones.

> First, the dying person needs to receive permission to pass away from every important person he will leave behind. . . . At first it might seem strange to insist that the dying need permission to do the inevitable. . . . But patients who feel any degree of human closeness or of responsibility to others, who had love in their lives and people near who needed them, require permission if death is to be peaceful. There is no other way to still feelings of guilt for going, for copping out on life, for becoming an emotional and financial burden and for that feeling of horrible helplessness inside.
>
> Reasonably sensitive persons know well and feel deeply the pain and sorrow their death will cause. They feel guiltily responsible even when they know logically they are not. Each tearstained face, each wringing hand, each look of futility, pushes buttons of guilt inside a patient who cares. Always before there was a way out of guilt, an apology or explanation, a promise not to fail again, an act of special kindness in reparation. Because when dying there is only a single and unacceptable solution, permission becomes essential. (Kavanaugh, 1974, pp. 75-76)

This is not to say that the loved ones around the dying patient do not feel or express some anger or sadness. What giving permission to die means is that, despite the pain and the grief that will ensue, loved ones can let the death happen and allow the peaceful transition of the patient. While they can share their sorrow and their concerns about the loss with the patient, they will not attempt to hold her by making her feel guilty for leaving, underscoring their dependence on her, or refusing to acknowledge her imminent death. At the end, she will not be made to feel cruel for leaving her loved ones, but will be allowed to quit the struggle after the battle has been fought as valiantly as possible. Such permission to die need not be spoken aloud or addressed explicitly. It is conveyed in the ability of each loved one to cope with the patient as a person and to accept the reality and needs of the situation and of each other. Dying with the permission of loved ones can make the death more appropriate and peaceful.

> My guess is that the smile or look of peace reflects a satisfaction limited to men of any creed who died in peace. They expired without earthly strings of any kind choking their hearts and they realized that they had bequeathed no strings to choke the hearts of those they left behind. (Kavanaugh, 1974, p. 79)

The importance of ensuring that the dying patient feels supported and accepted cannot be stressed too much. One of the greatest fears of the dying is that they will be left alone. Ironically, this is one of the easiest problems to resolve in the entire dying experience. While we cannot take away the pain of loss, and we are unable to make death disappear, we most definitely *can* make sure the patient is not abandoned, isolated, or made to feel unacceptable. Exercise VIII at the end of this chapter can help in grasping what a dying patient is experiencing and how we can be supportive.

COMMUNICATION WITH THE DYING PATIENT

Communication with a terminally ill patient can be directed towards three sets of therapeutic goals on three levels (Verwoerdt, 1966). The first level is the illness and its symptoms. The goals are to promote the patient's cooperation and encourage him to mutually work with caregivers to follow through with recommended therapeutic procedures. The second level is the patient's awareness of and psychological reactions to his disease and impending demise. Communication here is meant to help the patient protect and maintain his emotional equilibrium and achieve an optimal degree of awareness of the seriousness of the illness, while also preventing or treating emotional distress and supporting the use of effective coping techniques. The final level focuses on interactions between the patient and those around him. It is directed towards assisting his adjustment to the sick role and avoiding emotional problems resulting from disturbed communication. Verwoerdt discusses the perspective that must be maintained in communicating with the dying patient:

> From a practical, clinical point of view, it is safe to assume that patients in any stage of fatal illness are anxious, unless there is good evidence to the contrary. And, in keeping with the goals of therapeutic communication, it is a general principle to avoid making the patient more anxious, since increased anxiety necessitates either additional coping mechanisms or an increase in avoidance mechanisms, both of which are likely to result in maladaptive

behavior. The principle of "first, do not harm" is a cardinal rule: the patient's defenses should never be heedlessly stripped away. (p. 29)

Dying patients try to communicate in a number of different ways. Kübler-Ross (1974) has discussed this in terms of dying children, but her conclusions are equally applicable to dying adults. She believes that dying patients communicate using three "languages": plain English, symbolic nonverbal language, and symbolic verbal language. In the first language the message of the patient is directly articulated on a conscious level. In the second language, dying patients reveal their concerns, thoughts, and needs through overt behavior. Physically ill patients often utilize nonverbal communication to convey messages out of fear that if those messages were communicated directly in plain English they would not be responded to, which would be too painful for the patients to cope with. Consequently, dying patients may repeatedly make requests of caregivers in order to secure their attention, instead of directly asking them to sit down and talk for a while. (This may be done without conscious intent on the part of the patient.) The third language is a symbolic verbal language, which Kübler-Ross feels is used by the neediest patients. A message is verbally given, but its true meaning is hidden behind symbols. For example, a patient who is facing leg amputation may talk about having seen horses with broken legs destroyed. An astute caregiver would sense and pursue the fears and concerns obviously underlying the patient's discussion.

Three kinds of possible caregiver-patient relationships are described by Szasz and Hollender (1956). Though originally they were seen in terms of the severity of illness to which each was appropriate, here they are examined for their effects on communication. The major variables are the degree of participation and feeling of autonomy on the part of the patient. The first is the *activity-passivity relationship*. In this relationship the caregiver assumes the authoritarian role and the patient feels no autonomy. He tries to please the caregiver. This is the poorest type of relationship for diagnostic interviewing and data-gathering, to say nothing of treatment. The second type of relationship is only slightly better. In the *guidance-cooperation relationship* the caregiver still functions as the authority figure; however, the patient feels a little more autonomy and participates a little more actively than in the first relationship. Although it is better than the activity-passivity relationship, there continue to be problems arising out of the patient's desire to please the caregiver and the resulting inhibition of relevant information. The third relationship, the *mutual participation relationship*, is the most desirable for interviews and for the management of chronic illness. In this relationship the patient is actively involved and

feels autonomous and appropriately responsible for his own behavior and the outcome of the relationship. This is fostered by a
reasonable moderation of the caregiver's authority. Such a relationship allows the widest range of relevant material to be disclosed and is associated with the most successful treatments. This
is the relationship for which we should strive.

Communication Guidelines

The initial communication of diagnosis must be conducted pa-
tiently, with honesty, sensitivity, gentleness, and tact, and without
the destruction of the patient's hopes. Human compassion is a
necessary requirement. Hogshead (1976) makes the following suggestions:

- Keep it simple; don't go into too many details or technical-
  ities. The patient often has a difficult enough time struggling
  with the emotional impact of the news. Keep the message
  clear. You must be careful not to deal with your own apprehension or uneasiness by becoming too verbose.
- Ask yourself, "What does this diagnosis mean to this patient?" Different patients assign different meanings to what
  they have been told based on previous experience and preconceptions about the disease and its consequences. Try to
  understand what the illness means to the patient psychologically. You may have to correct some misconceptions. Make
  sure the patient has intellectually understood the nature of
  the diagnosis. If he has not comprehended it, find some methods to gradually educate him.
- When possible, take into account the person's background
  and personality when deciding how to break the news. It is
  easier if you already have some relationship with the patient
  and some understanding of his background and possible reactions.
- Don't deliver all the news at once. Try not to overload the
  patient at the first sitting. Full disclosure may need to be
  spread out over several sessions. It may take the patient a
  while to absorb all the information and its implications. Take
  your cues from the patient. He will let you know verbally or
  nonverbally how much he is able to take at a given time. The
  patient does have a right to all the information he is able to
  handle. Make sure your assessment of what the patient can
  handle truly reflects the patient's abilities, not your anxiety
  or desire to protect.
- Wait for questions. Some caregivers either deluge the patient
  with information or breeze in and out of the room—in both
  cases trying to avoid questions from the patient. This is distinctly unhelpful for the patient. His questions can provide
  valuable information about his thoughts, concerns, and feel-

ings. Allow adequate pauses to give the patient time to formulate his questions. Often such questions will yield the best information on what steps to take next.

- Do not argue with denial. Denial serves an important defensive function and must be respected. At this juncture it suffices that the patient has been directly informed of the diagnosis. If he chooses to deny it initially, do not try to argue against it. The patient will "hear" the message when he can accept and deal with it. Indeed, the outward denial may only be a façade. It is not uncommon for patients to later reveal that they knew the diagnosis to be true, but wanted to avoid hearing it aloud. This is why continued consistent communication with caregivers is so critical—it may only be through repeated contacts over time that the patient can feel safe and secure enough to drop the denial.
- Ask questions yourself; ask the patient what he has been told and understands about the nature and implications of his illness. You may be surprised at what you discover. This is another excellent way of assessing the patient and a very reliable way of making sure you have effectively delivered your message. Too often we believe we have gotten our point across, but it has not been received as we thought.
- Do not destroy all hope. Even the most malignant diagnosis can be conveyed with an accompanying glimmer of hope (e.g., "In most cases. . ." or "While the remaining time appears to be short, we can keep you comfortable. . ."). (See "Acceptance, Withdrawal and Detachment, and Hope" in this chapter for more on this topic.)
- Do not say anything that is not true. That would be the cruelest blow of all.

In fatal illness the patient, after being informed honestly of the diagnosis and its meaning, should set the tempo for becoming increasingly aware of the nature of the illness and its implications. Timing is critical. Gradual release of negative information is not only more effective, but allows the patient to begin to anticipate and prepare himself for the full impact of the news. Too much too soon can end in disaster, forcing the patient into a corner in which extreme defenses must be used. However, withholding information too long can result in loss of faith in the caregiver and, if the patient feels deceived or overprotected, may establish a mutual pretense that robs the patient of needed opportunities to talk honestly with his caregiver. The patient is apt to feel that he is being treated like a child or that the caregiver cannot deal with the information. Trust and respect in the relationship will deteriorate. Thus, a balance must be struck between disclosing all the necessary information and allowing the patient to adapt at his own pace.

On occasion patients will repeat the same or similar questions. This may reflect their fluctuating ability to absorb information due to their anxiety. It also signals the need for continuity of care with the same caregivers, especially those who gave the diagnosis.

A set of guidelines for communicating about treatment with the dying proposed by Krant (Note 13) for physicians provides some good suggestions for all caregivers.

- Deliver and interpret the technical information necessary for making decisions. Make sure patients understand what they have been told. Too often we hide behind medical terminology and jargon. Although we may have technically delivered appropriate information, for all intents and purposes the patients have not been truly informed since they do not comprehend. At times it is done to avoid having to deal with their reactions; this is an unhealthy and unfair game. Check out patients' perceptions if there is some doubt as to how much they comprehend.
- Facilitate meaningful discussion within patient and family limits. Ask questions to determine what they understand, and provide a climate in which they can voice their questions, concerns, and fears. Encourage patients and their families to discuss alternatives and their consequences. Such communication can foster closeness between patient and family and between caregiver and the patient-family unit. Thoughts and feelings expressed now can prevent guilt from arising later on.
- Be alert to the values of the patient and family. Without an appreciation of these values, there cannot be the kind of understanding that will allow the effective and meaningful communication of information and intervention. This may profoundly influence treatment compliance and intervention results. For example, a caregiver might tell a patient to resign from his job and stay home after hospital discharge, thinking that this would make the patient feel better. However, if the patient and his family saw working as a prerequisite for self-esteem, this might lead to many problems: the patient might go back to work and deceive the caregiver; he might stay home and become depressed; or the family might treat the patient as if he were already dead because he did not work. If the caregiver had been aware of the family's values, some kind of accommodation might have been made that allowed the patient to work in a limited way.
- Avoid undermining the patient's right to determine his own fate. All attempts must be made to ensure that as much control as possible remains in the hands of the patient. It is the patient's life and the patient's death. This fact must be rec-

ognized explicitly. Even if we disagree with the patient's choice, we must respect the patient's right to choose.

- Provide a working team to plan holistic care of the patient and to facilitate the patient's understanding, control, and communications. One professional cannot possibly meet all the diverse needs of the terminally ill patient. Consequently, there must be a working team of professionals to ensure that all the aspects of the patient's life are cared for: physicians, nurses, clergy, psychologists, social workers, dieticians, physical therapists, occupational therapists, pharmacists, volunteers, and others, as appropriate to the patient's care. The patient and his family should always be included in this working team. Their inclusion gives them a sense of control in the planning process and allows them to express how the treatment directly affects them.

  With a team approach, an effective, individualized program can be planned for the patient. Communication between professionals is enhanced, and options can be explored jointly, with input from the appropriate people. Everyone has access to the same information and can see the treatment as an integrated whole, preventing misunderstandings and contradictory efforts. (See "Assistance With the Practical Considerations of Dying" in this chapter for more on this topic.)

Several other guidelines may help when communicating with the dying patient:

- When normalizing feelings, make sure it does not appear that you are minimizing them.
- Listen to the patient. He will tell you what he needs to have done.
- Ask what questions are on the patient's mind. Many times the patient is afraid to ask or to reveal all of his concerns to you. Legitimize this fear and ask about it straight out. In particular, if death is not addressed at all, and you are sure the motivation to talk about it is not solely your need to, then you may want to gently question the patient about it.
- When the patient is attempting to investigate an emotionally charged area, make sure you know what he is "really" asking by requesting clarification and reflecting back the statement that exists under his question.
- When a patient is communicating vaguely, help him communicate more clearly by asking for clarification or by summarizing and asking him to confirm whether what you have said is accurate.
- When appropriate, acknowledge the difficulties of terminal

illness. Do not try to minimize the situation. However, never force the patient to confront it if he does not want to.
- Make sure you are talking about the same issue as the patient. At times issues may sound similar, but actually be quite different. Always check out your understanding with the patient and ask for feedback.
- Recognize incongruities between your verbal and nonverbal behaviors, and ascertain what you are really conveying.
- Try to capitalize on those times that the patient is willing to talk, even when it is inconvenient for you.

Counseling the dying patient is the most nondirective form of assistance there can be. All cues must be taken from the patient. It is important not to force communication. If the patient does not wish to communicate at a particular time, he needs to know that this is acceptable and will be respected. Indicate your willingness to return at another time, when he may feel more comfortable. The most important way in which to help is to be available to listen actively, nonjudgmentally, and with acceptance, allowing the patient to express emotions and feelings without fear.

> If patients sense that you can talk about dying whenever they are ready to talk about it, they will indeed call you. You can then do in five or ten minutes, maybe at 3 a.m., more than you do in ten hours during the daytime when it is convenient for you. This is one of the biggest problems: patients cannot talk about dying when it is convenient for us! Usually in the middle of the night when it is dark and quiet and all their defenses are down, it suddenly hits them that they are dying. Then they should have a friend who walks in, sits down and listens to them. (Kübler-Ross, 1974, p. 23)

Therapeutic Communication Skills
Therapeutic communication expresses respect for the patient, maintains realistic hope, and offers appropriate reassurance and support. Support can be conveyed through statements of comprehension ("I understand"), empathy ("That must have been very upsetting"), or a brief summary of what the patient has just said (Enelow & Adler, 1979). However, supportive words without an accompanying supportive attitude will ring hollow and fail to provide comfort; reassurance that is unrealistic or given merely to calm a patient will not work. Stating that "Everything will be fine" when this is untrue will only increase the patient's anxiety and violate his trust in the caregiver. It is far better to give reassurance in a limited way that is consistent with the facts; for example, "Although you must have an amputation of your leg to protect you from the spread of cancer, there is still much that can and will be

done to help you maintain your mobility and independence. You can make it." Such reassurance is communicated by words and acts that restore the patient's sense of well-being, worthiness, or confidence (Enelow & Adler, 1979). Therapeutic communication will also require careful attention to what the patient expresses verbally and nonverbally. Interpretations or summaries of the patient's thoughts and feelings should always be carefully checked out with the patient for their accuracy and their effect on him.

To communicate therapeutically, two kinds of skills are important: attending behavior and methods of facilitating communication.

Attending Behavior

Behavior that indicates we are listening to the patient is *attending behavior*. It includes appropriate eye contact, attentive body language, and verbal following. (Ivey & Gluckstern, 1976).

Eye contact is especially important for dying patients, since they may receive numerous messages of rejection from other members of society. This is particularly true with patients who have suffered disfiguring illnesses. We need to have frequent, varied eye contact with our patients. Some interesting information can be gained about ourselves by paying attention to those points at which we break eye contact with patients. Often this occurs when we are unsure of ourselves or when we are discussing something difficult with the patient.

A unique problem in communicating with physically ill patients is that the caregiver is usually standing up while the patient is typically lying down in bed. This accentuates the patient's feelings of regression and being out of control, dependent, and helpless. We need to be sensitive to the literally "one down" position the patient is in, and one of the most effective methods of enhancing our sensitivity is to go through the following exercise:

> Lie on the floor on your back. Attempt to have a conversation with someone while she is standing up looking down at you. Hold this conversation for 5 minutes. What are your reactions? Do you feel in control? Adult-like? Independent? How easy is it to communicate from this position?

Such an exercise will probably suggest that in terms of attentive body language the following cues are important: a relaxed posture; a slight leaning forward of the body; encouraging gestures (e.g., head nodding); interested facial expression; a warm, animated tone of voice; and appropriate closeness to the patient. Many times these nonverbal accompaniments to our verbal behavior are missing and the incongruence is easily perceived by the patient. The caregiver who speaks with the patient from the hallway, who does not approach the bed or look into the eyes of the patient, will signal anxiety and/or unconcern to the patient despite any contrary verbal message. The exercise just described makes it strikingly clear that we need to show our attentiveness in nonverbal as well as verbal ways. For instance, we can choose to sit in a chair close to the patient's bed in order to minimize the physical distance between us and the emotional distance it implies. We can show we are concerned about communicating with the patient by making effective plans to ensure undisturbed time for communication. This may be built into the staff schedule or planned for individually. By informing other staff and requesting privacy, by putting a "Do Not Disturb" sign on the door, or by drawing the curtain around the bed, the message is conveyed that quiet and privacy is desired—a message that informs the patient of our concern, respect, and interest in him. When appropriately used, touching is a very effective means of communication. Later on in the illness, when strength for or interest in verbal communication has dwindled, touching is particularly important. The hand that is held, the arm that is patted, the tear that is gently wiped all indicate our attending behavior as well as our concern and care.

A third type of attending behavior is verbal following. In verbal following the listener says something to the patient that demonstrates that she has been listening and paying attention. We can show that we have been following the conversation through accurate reflection of what the patient has said and expressed nonverbally. All of our comments should pertain to the topic of the patient's conversation.

Methods of Facilitating Communication

The ways to facilitate communication discussed here include reflection of feeling; paraphrasing and summarizing; the use of minimal encouragers; the use of open-ended versus closed questions; the elicitation of the patient's own thoughts on a topic or question; therapeutic silence; and appropriate self-disclosure.

Reflection of feeling means accurately restating the feelings expressed implicitly or explicitly through the patient's communication. This is often helpful for the patient because it allows him to more clearly identify the emotions that may be camouflaged by intellectualization in what he says. Reflection of feeling allows us to help the patient verbalize and clarify difficult emotions and give the patient "permission" to express these feelings, with a recognition that such expression is acceptable and even therapeutic. Many times it affords a perfect occasion to normalize emotions patients may have been uncomfortable in sharing. This process involves two steps. We must first, through the process of empathy, identify the patient's feelings, then formulate a response to reflect this back to the patient (White, Kunz, & Hogan, 1981). Such feedback would include phrases such as "It seems you are feeling . . ."; "I sense that you feel . . ."; or "The feeling underneath all this appears to be one of. . . ."

Paraphrasing involves communicating back to the patient the essence of what he has said. It involves reflecting cognitive content rather than feelings. For example, the patient might say, "I don't like the fact that I am supposed to give up smoking. After all, I've been smoking two packs a day for 30 years and I just don't know how I would ever be able to quit." We might respond with the paraphrase "You're not sure you can give up such an ingrained habit" or the reflection of feeling "You seem worried that you'll be unable to give up cigarettes." As with reflection of feeling, paraphrasing demands that we determine and identify what was communicated and then restate it back to the patient. This allows us to communicate to the patient that what he has said is understood; to help the patient recognize what was said; to receive information about the accuracy of our perceptions; to focus the patient's attention and give direction to future communication; and to give the patient the opportunity to correct any misunderstanding or modify what was said (White et al., 1981).

Summarizing aims to help the patient pull his thinking together by reviewing the essence of his communication over a period of time. The main themes, critical elements, and important patterns or issues are restated for the patient to help him see the situation more clearly. Summarization can also be used to show we are paying close attention; to get feedback from the patient; to encourage further discussion on the topic; and to close a particular discussion topic or terminate a session (White et al., 1981).

Whenever we use any type of reflection, paraphrasing, or summarizing, we must understand that the patient may disagree with our interpretation. We should evaluate this disagreement to determine if it comes from an honest difference of opinion, or from the patient's denial or lack of awareness of his own feelings and thoughts. We must remain nondefensive in the face of rejection of an interpretation and, instead, view the conflict of opinions as a situation that can lend further information about the patient. If such an attitude is not possible, we need to seek help in clarifying our own problems in these areas.

Minimal encouragers are brief utterances indicating to the patient that his communication is being followed and should continue. Examples include "Oh?"; "Um humm"; "Then?"; "And?"; "Tell me more"; the repetition of one or two key words; and a simple restatement of the exact words of the patient's last statement. Nonverbal encouragers include a head nod, leaning closer, and an interested facial expression. At times, simply being silent will encourage further communication.

Open-ended questions provide a better opportunity for communication than closed questions. They provide a more open invitation to talk and do not limit the patient's response options. Examples of closed questions would be "Do you feel well?"; "Is your marriage good?"; "Are you going home for the weekend?" The same questions could be asked in a more open-ended fashion to obtain more information: "How do you feel?"; "Could you tell me a little about your marriage?"; "What are your plans for the weekend?" There are some times it is advisable to ask closed questions: when discrete information (e.g., medical history) is required; when the patient is anxious or nonverbal and needs to be encouraged to talk; when the caregiver needs the patient to focus on a particular point; or when the interview needs to be moved from a deeper level to a more superficial one (e.g., "closing down" the interview) (White et al., 1981).

All questioning should be conducted so as to minimize defensiveness on the part of the patient. "Why" questions frequently imply some sort of blame or reproval. They tend to put people on the spot. They are better restated as "what," "how," or "could" questions. Questions that imply answers, or are leading in some way, are to be avoided: "You do want a television in your room, don't you?"; "Of course you will want a visiting nurse, won't you?" This not only puts pressure on the patient to give the "correct" answer, but it also fails to respect the patient as an adult capable of making his own decisions. This type of questioning is to be avoided at all costs.

The last caveat about questions has to do with providing adequate response time. There is nothing so frustrating as the person who asks a question then fails to wait to receive the answer before continuing on. Allow the patient enough time for reflection and formulation of a response. This is especially true for those patients whose energies have been depleted by illness. They may need a longer response time.

Eliciting the patient's own thoughts on a topic or question, while an obvious way to encourage communication, is frequently neglected. It is not uncommon for caregivers to assume that the patient cannot be consulted and consequently gear their communication towards the family, even in questions of medical treatment that clearly affect the patient more than anyone else. At times this represents the fact that in the caregiver's mind the patient has already died as a competent, rational, decision-making adult. This is seen when questions are addressed to family members over the patient's bed when the patient is still fully alert and competent.

The message to the patient is excruciatingly clear—he is already considered to be less than alive. We must be mindful of any tendency to "bury" the patient prematurely. Whatever modes of communication are available must be attempted with the patient.

Silence can be as meaningful as words. In constructive amounts it can convey acceptance and support, indicate our interest in and time for the patient, and prompt further discussion. At times, when accompanied by a shrug of the shoulders or a nod of the head, it can convey a message that may be too painful or shocking to put into words. The key to the therapeutic use of silence is knowing when and how much silence to employ. Silence occurring too early in a relationship, before the patient and caregiver know each other well, may leave the patient wondering what is expected of him or may be interpreted as rejection, aloofness, detachment, or avoidance. Too much silence can become uncomfortable and anxiety-provoking. In later stages of the illness, when energy for conversation may be depleted and we recognize that our presence alone is therapeutic for the patient, shared silence may be meaningful, reassuring, and comforting to the dying individual.

Self-disclosure involves sharing personal thoughts, feelings, attitudes, and experiences with the patient in an effort to help that patient. Used judiciously and appropriately, such self-disclosure can bring us closer to the patient; can further the patient's own exploration and discussion of a subject; can provide the patient with feedback about his affect on us; and can offer additional data in helping a patient understand something or in making a point. Effective disclosure depends on suitable timing and content. Self-disclosure can have strong and, at times, unintended effects (White et al., 1981). Thus any self-disclosure should be related directly to the patient's situation and utilized only after determining that the situation has been correctly identified. In order to monitor the timing, content, and necessity for the self-disclosure, White et al. suggest asking "Am I wanting to reveal this for the patient's needs or for my own needs?" The disclosure should be relatively short and to the point in order to avoid shifting the focus away from the patient. It also should reveal information only at a level of intimacy that is comfortable for the patient and ourselves. Asking the following questions before disclosing will help: "How will I feel later about having disclosed these feelings and experiences to the patient? How might such revelations affect my feelings toward the patient?" Despite these caveats, the prudent use of self-disclosure can be most therapeutic with dying patients. This is especially the case when it conveys to the patient that your conversation is between two alive human beings who can trust and respect one another enough to share meaningful personal information with each other.

There are three other facets of communication with the terminally ill patient. These are geared more towards intervention and are less nondirective than the ones previously described. They include confrontation, interpretation, and problem-solving.

Confrontation involves making the patient aware of something that he may be unaware of or avoiding. Contrary to popular opinion, it is not a hostile attacking or accusatory act. It should be constructive and reflect sympathetic interest in the patient. In their classic work on medical interviewing, Enelow and Adler (1979) noted that confrontations must be based only on what has been observed; there must not be inferences about the patient's feelings or motives. The patient's response to the confrontation will provide additional useful information. Other points made by Enelow and Adler about confrontation include that it should not be formulated as a question—for example, "Why are you uncomfortable?"—because of the problems discussed before with regard to "why" questions and because it usually assumes that the observation is correct. Instead it is much more advantageous to state "You appear to be a little uncomfortable." They believe that confrontation is useful in situations in which the patient's nonverbal behavior communicates something the patient is not addressing (e.g., the patient who looks depressed but is talking about other matters); the patient's nonverbal behavior is expressing emotion (e.g., the patient appears angry because he is scowling and banging his fist on the table); the patient's verbal and nonverbal behaviors are clearly incongruous (e.g., the patient speaks about very sad things in an indifferent manner); and there are inconsistencies in a patient's story. White et al. (1981) delineate the following goals of confrontation; to help the patient explore issues that cause painful and conflicting emotions; to reveal inconsistencies, discrepancies, and conflicts; to identify defenses for the patient; to aid the patient in analyzing his own behavior and feelings and to accept responsibility for them; and to allow us to demonstrate concern. Their four guidelines for effective confrontation are as follows: do not accuse, attack, or punish the patient; use confrontation only when trust and empathy have been established between yourself and the patient; confront only those specific, concrete behaviors that the patient can change; and tailor your confrontation to make the best possible use of the patient's strengths. To this should be added the caution that too much confrontation, even when conducted in the most therapeutic manner possible, can become counterproductive.

Interpretation is "the act of renaming or redefining 'reality' (feelings, attitudes, behavior, situations) from a new point of view" (Ivey & Gluckstern, 1976, p. 106). It is a creative act requiring the ability to break a mind set and look at a situation from a new and different viewpoint. In the clinical situation it means taking the information that the patient reveals and, with a new frame of reference, giving it a different interpretation. The purpose is to provide the patient with a novel perspective in order to increase insight, understanding, and awareness, and to promote alternative ways of perceiving a particular situation. Used with care it can gently move the patient to greater emotional health by increasing his ability to cope with his illness. An idea does not have to be profoundly psychoanalytic or dramatic to qualify as an interpretation. For example, after a patient found himself being gruff with visitors, he wondered aloud to his caregiver why he acted this way. The caregiver hypothesized that perhaps the patient acted gruff to cover up his feelings about being dependent on people to visit him and to hide from people the fact that it meant so much to him when they did come.

Problem-solving is not technically a communication skill but is included here because a large amount of communication with the terminally ill is directed towards the resolution of problems. Modifying the model proposed by White et al. (1981), the following steps are suggested:

- List the problems that need attention and then prioritize them. Begin with a problem that is fairly easily solvable.
- Define a "workable problem." Such a problem will be specific and narrow enough to address successfully. The desired change must be outlined.
- Analyze the problem by listing the factors that are working for and against change of the problem.
- Explore the alternative ways of promoting the desired change. This usually involves making a force working for change stronger or a force working against change weaker. Gather information on each alternative, and test each one for practicality and workability.
- After reexamining the goal in light of the alternative choices, develop and implement a plan of action.
- Provide opportunities for feedback and follow-up.

The following case examples demonstrate effective problem-solving.

Case Example: Marge was a 42-year-old housewife who had cancer of the tongue and roof of the mouth. She had been resected and consequently had major difficulty in swallowing and often choked violently. In addition she had trouble speaking clearly, her features were drastically altered by surgery, and she had to use an emesis basin repeatedly because of the salivation difficulty.

The problem to be resolved was that Marge wanted to attend her 15-year-old daughter's confirmation. She knew she would never live to see her daughter's next birthday, so the confirmation was quite special to Marge. The forces working for Marge's attending her daughter's confirmation included her strong motivation and desire to go; her family's support for her being there and lack of concern about embarrassment; and the priest's willingness to make adjustments in the ceremony to accommodate her problems. Forces working against Marge's attending were the physical problems she had, which could eventuate in her choking; the negative social reaction that could be expected from some people; and the distance of the church from her home.

The caregiver called a family conference, the priest was conferred with, and the visiting nurse was consulted about the practical matters pertaining to physical management, transportation, and the use of the portable suction machine. As a result, Marge was able to be present at the confirmation with the suggested arrangements to accommodate her disabilities. She was seated with her family in the rear of the church with a suction machine nearby. The ability to be there greatly enhanced her feelings of self-esteem, mastery, and continued involvement with her family.

The second case illustrates how even the best plans may need to be altered to accommodate the continuing changes caused by illness. What initially seemed feasible required compromise if the problem was to be resolved. What is significant is the fact that, although the patient's desire was not entirely fulfilled, the caregiver refused to give up. A healthy compromise was reached that permitted partial realization of the goal.

Case Example: Gert was a 45-year-old woman bedridden with ovarian cancer and gross metastases. She had severe edema of the legs and was mobile only in a wheelchair. She, her husband, and her three children lived in a poor part of the city where they were very active in the only French-Canadian church community within an Italian district. They were very ethnically oriented in all areas of their lives.

Gert's 25th wedding anniversary was approaching and it was a special and shared goal with her husband to renew their wedding vows in their church a block from their home. An entire plan was developed that entailed wheeling Gert to the church in her wheelchair where the vows would be renewed. This was to be followed by a small reception at their home.

However, as the date of the occasion approached, Gert became increasingly weaker. Her husband became progressively more unsure about the plan as he contemplated the social reaction arising from wheeling his sickly, emaciated wife down the street in a wheelchair. Consequently, the original plan was no longer feasible.

The caregiver decided to try to salvage at least part of the patient's goal. Although she recognized that it was impossible for Gert to renew her vows in her beloved French-Canadian church, the caregiver searched for alternative ways of providing a ritual that would be meaningful to the family. A priest was consulted and special permission was received to have a mass said in Gert's home, involving a ceremony for the renewal of wedding vows. A small and intimate reception followed. This allowed Gert to achieve a major portion of what she desired.

It is vitally important to remember that there is no way for the patient to "solve" the problem of dying. However, there are ways in which we can share the attendant feelings and fears of the patient. Through open and sensitive communication with the dying patient we not only facilitate the expression of emotion, but we also affirm that the patient is a living human being we still support and care about.

GUIDELINES FOR INTERVENTION WITH THE DYING PATIENT

At this point, many individual suggestions have been made for intervening with the dying patient. The following guidelines may be helpful in choosing interventions and developing treatment programs for care.

Standards for Care of the Dying

In 1978 the International Work Group on Death, Dying and Bereavement disseminated the document "Assumptions and Principles Underlying Standards for Terminal Care" (International Work Group, Note 18). Up to that time there were no explicit and recognized standards for treatment for the dying. The work group had noted the unwritten, unofficial assumptions and practices that had previously governed care of the terminally ill. At the time, the "good" death in the typical medical facility was judged by the following implicit standards:*

1. The good or successful death is quiet, uneventful. Nobody is disturbed. The death slips by with as little notice as possible.
2. Not too many people are around. In other words, there is no "scene." Staff does not have to adjust to the presence of family

*From "Toward Standards of Care for the Terminally Ill Part II: What Standards Exist Today?" by R. Kastenbaum, *Omega*, 6(4), 1975, Reprinted by permission.

and other visitors who have their own needs and who are in various kinds of "states."

3. Leave-taking behavior is at a minimum.

4. The physician does not have to involve himself intimately in terminal care, especially as the end approaches.

5. The staff makes few technical errors throughout the entire terminal care process, and few mistakes in "etiquette."

6. Strong emphasis is given to the body, little to the personality or spirit of the terminally ill person in all that is done for or to him.

7. The person dies at the right time, i.e., after the full range of medical interventions has been tried, but before a lingering period has set in.

8. The staff is able to conclude that "We did everything we could for this patient."

9. Patient expresses gratitude for the excellent care received.

10. After patient's death, family expresses gratitude for the excellent care received.

11. Parts or components of the deceased are made available to the hospital for clinical, research or administrative purposes (i.e., via autopsy permission or organ gifts).

12. A memorial (financial) gift is made to the hospital in the name of the deceased.

13. The cost of the total terminal care process is determined to have been low or moderate: money was not wasted on a person whose life could not be "saved." (p. 289-290)

These standards were clearly unacceptable. The assumptions and principles in Table 1 (International Work Group, Note 18) have been proposed as appropriate for guiding the care of the terminally ill.

TABLE 1

Assumptions and Principles Underlying Standards for Terminal Care

There is agreement that patients with life-threatening illnesses, including progressive malignancies, need appropriate therapy and treatment throughout the course of the illness. At one stage, therapy is directed toward investigation and intervention in order to control and/or cure such illness and alleviate associated symptoms. For some persons, however, the time comes when cure and remission are beyond the capacity of current curative treatment. It is then that the intervention must shift to what is now often termed "palliative treatment," which is designed to control pain in the broadest sense and provide personal support for patient and family during the terminal phase of illness. In general, palliative care requires limited use of apparatus and technology, extensive personal care and an ordering of the physical and social environment to be therapeutic in itself.

There are two complementary systems of treatment, which may often overlap. One system is concerned with eliminating a curable disease and the other with relieving the symptoms resulting from the relentless progress of an incurable illness. There must be openness, interchange and overlap between the two systems so that the patient receives continuous appropriate care. The patient should not be subjected to aggressive treatment that offers no real hope of being effective in curing or controlling the disease and may only cause the patient further distress. Obviously, the clinician must be on the alert for any shifts that may occur in the course of a terminal illness that make the patient a candidate for active treatment again. Patients suffer not only from inappropriate active care but also from inept terminal care. This is well documented by studies that only confirm what dying patients and their families know first-hand. The following principles have been prepared as an aid in delineating standards of care for those who have initiated or are planning programs for the terminally ill.

GENERAL ASSUMPTIONS AND PRINCIPLES

Assumptions	Principles
1. The care of the dying is a process involving the needs of the patient, family and care-givers.	1. The interaction of these three groups of individuals must constantly be assessed with the aim being the best possible care of the patient. This cannot be accomplished if the needs of family and/or care-giver are negated.
2. The problems of the patient and family facing terminal illness include a wide variety of issues—psychological, legal, social, spiritual, economic and interpersonal.	2. Care requires collaboration of many disciplines working as an integrated clinical team, meeting for frequent discussions with a common purpose.

Standards for Terminal Care (cont.)

Assumptions	Principles
3. Dying tends to produce a feeling of isolation.	3. All that counteracts unwanted isolation should be encouraged. Social events and shared work that include all involved should be arranged so that meaningful relations can be sustained and developed.
4. It has been the tradition to train care-givers not to become emotionally involved, but in terminal illness the patient and family need to experience the personal concern of those taking care of them.	4. Profound involvement without loss of objectivity should be allowed and fostered, with the realization that this may present certain risks to the care-giver.
5. Health care services customarily lack coordination.	5. The organizational structure must provide links with health care professionals in the community.
6. A supportive physical environment contributes to the sense of well-being of patients, of families and of care-givers.	6. The environment should provide adequate space, furnishings that put people at ease, the reassuring presence of personal belongings and symbols of life cycles.

PATIENT-ORIENTED ASSUMPTIONS AND PRINCIPLES

Assumptions	Principles
1. There are patients for whom aggressive curative treatment becomes increasingly inappropriate.	1. These patients need highly competent professionals, skilled in terminal care.
2. The symptoms of terminal disease can be controlled.	2. The patient should be kept as symptom free as possible. Pain should be controlled in all its aspects. The patient must remain alert and comfortable.
3. Patients' needs may change over time.	3. Staff must recognize that other services may have to be involved but that continuity of care should be provided.
4. Care is most effective when the patient's life-style is maintained and philosophy of life is respected.	4. The terminally ill patient's own framework of values, preferences and outlook on life must be taken into account in planning and conducting treatment.
5. Patients are often treated as if incapable of understanding or of making decisions.	5. Patients' wishes for information about their condition should be respected. They should be al-

6. Dying patients often suffer from helplessness, weakness, isolation and loneliness.

7. The varied problems and anxieties associated with terminal illness can occur at any time of day or night.

lowed full participation in their care and a continuing sense of self-determination and self-control.

6. The patient should have a sense of security and protection. Involvement of family and friends should be encouraged.

7. Twenty-four-hour care must be available seven days a week for the patient and family where and when it is needed.

FAMILY-ORIENTED ASSUMPTIONS AND PRINCIPLES

Assumptions

1. Care is usually directed toward the patient. In terminal illness the family must be the unit of care.

2. The course of the terminal illness involves a series of clinical and personal decisions.

3. Many people do not know what the process of dying involves.

4. The patient and family need the opportunity for privacy and being together.

5. Complexity of treatment and time-consuming procedures can cause disruption for the patient and family.

6. Patients and families facing death frequently experience a search for the meaning of their life, making the provision of spiritual support essential.

7. Survivors are at risk emotionally and physically during bereavement.

Principles

1. Help should be available to all those involved—whether patient, relation, or friend—to sustain communication and involvement.

2. Interchange between the patient and family and the clinical team is essential to enable an informed decision to be made.

3. The family should be given time and opportunity to discuss all aspects of dying and death and related emotional needs with the staff.

4. The patient and family should have privacy and time alone, both while the patient is living and after death occurs. A special space may have to be provided.

5. Procedures must be arranged so as not to interfere with adequate time for patient, family and friends to be together.

6. The religious, philosophical and emotional components of care are as essential as the medical, nursing and social components, and must be available as part of the team approach.

7. The provision of appropriate care for survivors is the responsibility of the team who gave care and support to the deceased.

Standards for Terminal Care (cont.)

STAFF-ORIENTED ASSUMPTIONS
AND PRINCIPLES

Assumptions	*Principles*
1. The growing body of knowledge in symptom control, patient- and family-centered care, and other aspects of the care of the terminally ill is now readily available.	1. Institutions and organizations providing terminal care must orient and educate new staff and keep all staff informed about developments as they occur.
2. Good terminal care presupposes emotional investment on the part of the staff.	2. Staff needs time and encouragement to develop and maintain relationships with patients and relatives.
3. Emotional commitment to good terminal care will often produce emotional exhaustion.	3. Effective staff support systems must be readily available.

Standards for Hospice Care

The National Hospice Organization (1981) has defined the hospice program of care and its philosophy, and outlined standards and principles for hospice care. As defined, "a hospice is a centrally administered program of palliative and supportive services which provides physical, psychological, social, and spiritual care for dying persons and their families" (p. 2). The program includes:

- Offering of services by a medically supervised interdisciplinary team made up of professionals and volunteers
- Availability in both the home and an inpatient setting
- Provision of home care on a part-time, intermittent, regularly scheduled, and around-the-clock on-call basis
- For the family, availability of bereavement services
- Admission on the basis of patient and family need

The hospice philosophy is to affirm life. Hospice programs exist to give support and care to the terminally ill so they may live as fully and comfortably as possible. Death is seen as a normal process, and hospice programs neither hasten nor postpone death. It is hoped that through care and the availability of a community sensitive to their needs patients and their families will be able to satisfactorily prepare themselves mentally and spiritually for death.

In Table 2 the standards and principles of hospice care are shown.

TABLE 2

The Standards and Principles of a Hospice Program of Care

The Standards of a Hospice Program are based on certain principles of human behavior and health care. For the purpose of this document the standards have been organized into four categories, which constitute a general framework in which to view Hospice care as a response to the needs of patients and families. The four categories are

A. Basic Principle Underlying Hospice Care
B. The Nature of Hospice Care
C. The Patient and Family
D. The Hospice Program

A. *BASIC PRINCIPLE UNDERLYING HOSPICE CARE*
One of the tenets of Hospice is the belief and recognition that dying is a normal process whether or not resulting from disease. Every aspect of Hospice care and program development emanates from and is guided by this tenet.

No.	Standard	No.	Principle
1	Appropriate therapy is the goal of Hospice Care.	1	Dying is a normal process.

B. *THE NATURE OF HOSPICE CARE*
Appropriate therapy is a goal of Hospice Care, therefore, it is necessary to define that which is appropriate within a given situation. With the recognition that death is inevitable as the final moment of the natural course of human life and that the terminal phase of the disease process is irreversible, it becomes possible to establish goals for caring and interventions to achieve the palliation of the accompanying concerns and distressful symptoms of the process of dying.

No.	Standard	No.	Principle
2	Palliative care is the most appropriate form of care when cure is no longer possible.	2	When cure is not possible, care is still needed.
3	The goal of palliative care is the prevention of distress from chronic signs and symptoms.	3	Pain and other symptoms of incurable disease can be controlled.
4	Admission to a Hospice Program of care is dependent on patient and family needs and their expressed request for care.	4	Not all persons need or desire palliative care.
5	Hospice care consists of a blending of professional and nonprofessional services.	5	The amount and type of care provided should be related to patient and family needs.

Standards for Terminal Care (cont.)

No.	Standard	No.	Principle
6	Hospice care considers all aspects of the lives of patients and their families as valid areas of therapeutic concern.	6	When a patient and family are faced with terminal disease, stress and concerns may arise in many aspects of their lives.
7	Hospice care is respectful of all patient and family belief systems, and will employ resources to meet the personal philosophic, moral and religious needs of patients and their families.	7	Personal philosophic, moral, or religious belief systems are important to patients and families who are facing death.
8	Hospice care provides continuity of care.	8	Continuity of care (services and personnel) reduces the patient's and the family's sense of alienation and fragmentation.

C. *THE PATIENT AND FAMILY*

The patient and family are the raison d'etre for Hospice programs. Patient and family participation in the decisions and care giving, to the maximum extent possible, should enable the patient and family to live according to their "style" and with the dignity and respect due all human beings until the moment of the patient's death.

No.	Standard	No.	Principle
9	A Hospice care program considers the patient and the family together as the unit of care.	9	Families experience significant stress during the terminal illness of one of their members.
10	The patient's family is considered to be a central part of the Hospice care team.	10	Family participation in care giving is an important part of palliative care.
11	Hospice care programs seek to identify, coordinate, and supervise persons who can give care to patients who do not have a family member available to take on the responsibility of giving care.	11	Not all patients have a family member available to take on the responsibility of giving care.
12	Hospice care for the family continues into the bereavement period.	12	Family needs continue after the death of one of their members.

D. *THE HOSPICE PROGRAM*

A Hospice Program is designed to achieve the goals of the patients and families for whom the program exists through the provision of appropriate palliative care. The program has a number of components, each of which makes Hospice care possible and is aimed at ensuring quality care. The components of a Hospice Program are identified in the following standards.

No.	Standard	No.	Principle
13	Hospice care is available 24 hours a day, 7 days a week.	13	Patient and family needs may arise at any time.
14	Hospice care is provided by an interdisciplinary team.	14	No one individual or profession can meet all the needs of terminally ill patients and families all the time.
15	Hospice programs will have structured and informal means of providing support to staff.	15	Persons giving care to others need to be supported and replenished in order to continue to give care.
16	Hospice programs will be in compliance with the Standards of the National Hospice Organization and the applicable laws and regulations governing the organization and delivery of care to patients and families.	16	The need for quality assurance in health care requires the establishment of standards for practice and program operation.
17	The services of the Hospice program are coordinated under a central administration.	17	Optimal utilization of services and resources is an important goal in the administration and coordination of patient care.
18	The optimal control of distressful symptoms is an essential part of a Hospice care program requiring medical, nursing, and other services of the interdisciplinary team.	18	Attention to physical comfort is central to palliative care.
19	The Hospice care team will have: a. medical director on staff b. physicians on staff c. a working relationship with the patient's physician.	19	Medical care is a necessary element of palliative care.

Standards for Terminal Care (cont.)

No.	Standard	No.	Principle
20	Based on patient's needs and preferences as determining factors in the setting and location for care, a Hospice Program provides in-patient care and care in the home setting.	20	The physical environment and setting can influence a patient's response to care.
21	Education, training, and evaluation of Hospice services is an ongoing activity of a Hospice care program.	21	There is a continual need to improve the techniques of palliative care and to disseminate such information.
22	Accurate and current records are kept on all patients.	22	Documentation of services is necessary and desirable in the delivery of quality care.

Objectives for Intervention

General objectives for care are needed to provide the rationale for specific interventions that are undertaken. The following objectives for treatment of the dying patient are suggested. They have been synthesized largely from the work of Weisman (1972a; 1972b; 1975; 1977).

- *Safe conduct for the dying.* A primary objective of treatment is the alleviation of emotional suffering due to the personal crisis of dying. The patient must be helped to cope psychologically and socially. This concept is captured in the phrase "safe conduct," which refers to two things: the behavior of the caregiver, which must be cautious and prudent; and the feeling of safety and security generated in the patient by the caregiver's guidance through the perilous course of dying. During the illness the caregiver will work to reduce the patient's anguish and loneliness and relieve some of the distress of the patient's family. There will be attempts to continuously engage significant others and caregivers with the patient and her treatment. At the end, the caregiver will be there to intercede, interpret, and be with the patient. Throughout the illness he will behave compassionately and act to prevent the dehumanization of the patient.
- *Significant survival and dignified dying.* Significant survival means realizing the value in what we are and do. The caregiver who seeks to offer safe conduct tries to enable the dying patient to find significance in the last phases of living. More than solely relieving suffering, he looks for what was significant to the patient during earlier and healthier days to recall

the sense of well-being and self-esteem. Although those things that are significant may not be able to be experienced as they have been in the past, their remembrance, along with the experience of dignity in dying and the maintenance of as much self-control as possible, make the dying patient's survival significant to her. Oscillations between sickness and capability then can be accepted without loss of self-esteem.

Dignified dying is afforded to the individual when she is continually regarded as a responsible person who is capable of clear perceptions, honest relationships, and purposeful behavior, despite physical decline and disability. She is allowed dignity, relief, and privacy, while demoralization, emotional neglect, and infantilization are avoided. The individual is treated as a living person, despite the fact that she is dying.

- *Appropriate death.* A death that one might choose for oneself is an appropriate death. It is not necessarily an ideal death, but one that is experienced as consistent with an ego-ideal. The continuity of important relationships is preserved or restored. Appropriate anticipatory and reactive grief is resolved. The dying person's conflicts are reduced or relieved. There is an absence of suffering and an exercise of all feasible options within physical limitations. The individual will die with a sense of dignity and will have been provided safe conduct. (See "The Concept of Appropriate Death" in Chapter 8 for more on this topic.)

In order to further these three objectives Weisman (1972b) makes a number of clinical suggestions:

- Accept the terminal patient according to what he would be like *without* the illness and disease. Otherwise we may fall victim to a tendency to confuse the person of the patient with the disease, lesion, or symptoms.
- Make allowances for the deterioration and disability caused by illness. But this should not mean supporting regressive defenses.
- Permit, encourage the patient to talk about how illness has changed him. But emphasize the person who is sick, not disease in the abstract.
- Be sure that you understand the difference between disease, fatal sickness, and the sickness until death (terminality itself).
- Ask about the people, possessions, and pursuits that meant the most during the patient's healthy life. This includes both factors that supported his ego ideals and self-esteem, and factors that made him feel discouraged, demoralized, or defeated.

- Preservation of the highest practical communication and behavior also preserves self-esteem. This is even more important than the fact of illness itself.
- Monitor your own feeling: You are not immune to denial, dissimulation, antipathy, and fears of personal annihilation. Do not be ashamed to admit that caring for the dying is, itself, exposure to endangerment. Therefore, do not hesitate to enlist the assistance of significant key persons, and other kinds of support.
- Safe conduct requires acceptance, clarity, candor, compassion, and mutual accessibility.
- Time your confrontations to meet what is relevant to the moment. Do not rush to talk about death or to underscore the gloomiest side of the illness, nor should you persist with empty optimism when facts no longer justify it.
- Unless a patient's physical condition and state of consciousness have compromised his judgment, do not exclude him from decisions and information about the illness.
- While we do not allow the family to make decisions for the patient, we encourage decisions with the patient, since he will yield control to others as the illness progresses.
- Do not hesitate to assess the specific changes that death will bring to the family. The optimal attitude toward the terminal situation is one of compassionate objectivity. A [caregiver] who is stringently clinical is scarcely a [caregiver], but a technician. If he becomes a surrogate mourner he is not very helpful, since he displays his helplessness. The therapist remains sufficiently detached to be the intermediary between family and other professional staff, without usurping the prerogatives of either.
- Help survivors to accept the inevitable death, but do not force a theory of bereavement and mourning upon anyone. In addition to bereavement, families may need help with the practical problems of readjustment to an altered life.
- Recognize signs of iatrogenic distortions and psychosocial complications that the terminal situation creates. False hopes, displacement of interests to the illusory or to the trivial, withdrawal of personal concern, and premature burial are but a few signs of iatrogenic problems. (pp. 170-171)

In developing therapeutic interventions with dying patients it is important to have an appreciation for exactly what they think and feel. Many patients have had prior experiences with the loss and death of family and friends, and these experiences have left them with fears, expectations, and misconceptions. Each patient also operates out of a unique combination of cultural, social, and personal value systems, and has special needs and fears. Along with personality characteristics and factors specific to the illness, these elements must be taken into consideration when determining how to be helpful to the dying. An accurate assessment of each of these elements must be conducted before intervention can begin, in a manner much like a differential diagnosis. The unique needs and issues of each patient must be ascertained. Without such an assessment, clinical intervention may be ineffective, or even counterproductive.

It is important to bear in mind that as circumstances and the illness cause changes, the patient changes as well. A process, as opposed to a static, perspective is necessary throughout the entire illness. It must also be remembered that all dying patients are not alike merely because they all have terminal illnesses. If these points are observed, we can avoid the pitfalls of lumping all patients together and of thinking that one assessment of the patient is all that is required. Each patient should be treated as an individual, with the recognition that her needs, fears, hopes, expectations, and concerns will change over the course of the illness. This will require new adaptations from her and new responses from us. Continuing reevaluation is mandatory.

Providing Control to the Dying

Throughout the entire dying experience the individual is forced to confront a loss of control. She is powerless to stop imminent death and the preceding deterioration, nor can she stay the losses that befall from the moment of diagnosis until the time of death. In the effort to provide support and assist the patient in dealing with her feelings and experiences there is no more superior intervention than providing the patient with control. It is this that will enable her to combat the assaults to her self-esteem and nourish her remaining hopes.

Patients can be given control by offering options and choices and through education and information (Kastenbaum, 1978). Wherever and whenever possible the patient is given choices. Early in treatment these are wide in latitude. The patient may decide about continuing to work or taking a long-awaited voyage. Later on, choices become more restricted, due to the limitations imposed by the illness. However, some amount of decision-making is still available to the patient, although clearly diminished in scope. The options may now revolve around preferences for diet, medications, activities, and visits from significant others. Education and information about the illness also enhance the sense of control. Just as caregivers find solace and control by calling on their knowledge and expertise, so too will the patient find assistance in seeking mental control over her suffering and illness. Patient education results in a more actively participating patient who feels more in control because she is involved in the process and knows what to expect. The fear of the unknown is reduced and the anxiety, helplessness, and apathy of ignorance disappear.

Four measures to encourage self-control in patients have been suggested by Verwoerdt (1966). First, the patient's needs can be anticipated and provisions can be made to satisfy them before they become acute. This reduces the number of times that the patient is reminded of her inability to avoid pain and minister to her own needs. Next, the patient who still has a measure of energy reserves can be provided with mobility and diversion. This supplies both helpful distraction as well as a sense of mastery to the patient. When active mobility is not possible, physical therapy through massage and passive exercises furnishes healthy stimulation. Whenever possible, a wide variety of appropriate stimuli should be provided to break the monotonous boredom of invalidism: auditory and visual stimulation from radio or television; intellectual stimulation through reading; social stimulation through visits with friends and family. The key to this is to gear the intervention to the sensory abilities and tolerances of the patient and not overload her. A third measure that can be taken is setting up a regimen that functions as an ego-prosthesis. Basically this means structuring the patient's environment and schedule in a regular, reassuring, and consistent manner. This assists the stressed ego by limiting demands for adaptation and increasing the feeling of mastery. Unavoidable alterations must be explained in advance to the patient so she may prepare for them. Finally, the patient should be encouraged to care for herself as much as possible. This reduces feelings of diminishing control and lack of mastery. Whenever a patient can complete all or some portion of a task independently, she must be allowed to, even though it may not be expedient in terms of time. Self-care, self-reliance, and independence are hallmarks of the healthy, fully functioning adult and must be approximated as closely as possible for the dying individual.

If the patient's sense of control diminishes and is not attended to by caregivers, patients may attempt to obtain control through defensive maneuvers or acting-out, or develop anxiety, depression, and a devastating sense of helplessness. However, the amount of control desired will vary from patient to patient. Assessment will be required to determine the appropriate intervention in each case. (See "The Patient's Struggle for Control" in Chapter 8 for more on giving control to the dying patient.)

Therapy With the Dying

At times therapists are confused as to how to approach the dying patient. Is clinical thanatology (working with the dying) similar to traditional psychotherapy? If so, in what ways are they similar? Different? The issue has been well examined in a seminal article by Shneidman (1978). In it, he described specific characteristics of working with the dying.

- *The goals are different.* They are more finite because of limited time. Deep insight is not the goal. "The goal, as one fights the clock and the lethal illness, is to *will the obligatory;* to make a chilling and ugly scene go as well as possible; to give psychological succor; to permit the tying-up of loose ends; to lend as much stability to the person as it is possible to give" (p. 210).
- *The rules are different.* Because of the foreshortened future the usual rules for psychotherapy are modified and establishment of the patient-therapist relationship is swift. The intensity and depth of that relationship permits a degree of transference and countertransference neither sought nor tolerated in any other professional relationship.
- *It may not be psychotherapy.* While it has some of the elements of traditional psychotherapy, there are other elements that are usually not incorporated in traditional psychotherapy (e.g., normal conversation). There is no movement towards specified goals, such as the termination of psychotherapy, but a process and relationship that continue until interrupted by death.
- *The focus is on benign intervention.* The therapist is often active in the patient's interest. He may interpret, advise (when he is asked), interact with other health care personnel, arrange for social work services, and generally act as the patient's ombudsman. There is no therapist façade or detachment.
- *No one has to die in the state of psychoanalytic grace.* The therapist must realize that few, if any, people die with all their complexes and neuroses worked through. His expectations for success must reflect this.
- *"Working through" is a luxury for those who have time to live.* "Everyone dies more or less in a state of psychological intestate" (p. 212), leaving behind some loose ends. The goal for the therapist is to help facilitate as much of an appropriate death as possible. People tend to die either too soon or too late and consequently all issues will not be resolved.
- *The dying person sets the pace.* Since it lacks the specific substantive goals usually found in psychotherapy, the emphasis of thanatology is on the process and the therapist's presence. All cues are taken from the patient, who directs the pace and chooses the topics.
- *Denial will be present.* Throughout the dying process denial

will sometimes be present. It is expectable and probably psychologically healthy that such respite is taken. Therapists must be prepared for it to surface and should allow it.

- *The goal is increased psychological comfort.* All interventions are undertaken to increase the individual's psychological comfort. This alone is how success can be measured. A grim situation will become grimmer, and the therapist cannot stop the inevitable, but he can work to increase the patient's psychological comfort in the midst of the inexorable and to keep some dimension of hope alive until the end.

- *The therapist must relate to nurses and doctors on the ward.* Whether in or out of the hospital setting, no therapist should relate to a dying person alone. There needs to be an integration of treatment with other health care personnel. The therapist is responsible for informing them of the patient's state, condition, and needs, and of the guiding concepts that underline this particular therapist-patient relationship.

- *The survivor is a victim, and may eventually become a patient if not supported.* Recognizing the high rates of morbidity and mortality of survivors, postvention—working with survivors—should be part of the health care system. The therapist should become acquainted with the person who will be the main survivor early in his work with the dying patient. He ought to establish rapport with that individual and have an explicit understanding that he will see the survivor in both the premourning stages and, in decreasing intervals, for a year or so after the death.

- *Just as the role of transference is paramount, countertransference bears careful watching and a good support system is a necessity.* The therapist must recognize that this work breeds bereavement, anguish, and a sense of impotence as he is made vulnerable through investment in the patient. Effective support systems and periods of working with other populations are suggested.

Treatment of the dying patient should focus on assisting the individual to find or maintain meaning and value in his life despite the limited span of time left to live. The focus should be neither on mental pathology nor preparation for death, but on finding personal strength and remaining potential (LeShan, 1969). It should be planned to

assist the patient by enabling him to live at his highest level of functioning in all spheres of behavior, so that he may maintain gratifying relationships, continue activities, and approach death with a positive self-image. (Schoenberg, 1970, p. 249)

Too often it is felt that death must be the sole topic of conversation with the dying patient and the focal point from which all interactions originate. The danger here is in losing the person while paying attention to her dying. Even after the diagnosis of a terminal illness there are still goals that can be accomplished, conflicts that can be resolved, meanings that can be found, hopes that can be realized, relationships that can be started or brought to fruition. A dying patient will want to talk about matters other than death. If openness is encouraged, the patient will learn that when she needs or wants to discuss an important issue, fear, or concern— whether about death or other topics—the caregiver will be willing and present to do so.

Intervention, in summary, should attempt to achieve what Pattison (1969) terms "healthy dying." He has suggested six guidelines to use in reaching this goal:

1. Sharing the responsibility for the crisis of dying for the patient so that he has help in dealing with the first impact of anxiety and bewilderment.
2. Clarifying and defining the realities of the day-to-day existence which can be dealt with by the patient. These are the realities of his life.
3. Making continued human contact available and rewarding.
4. Assisting in the separation from and grief over realistic losses of family, body image, and self-control, while retaining communication and meaningful relationships with those who will be lost.
5. Assuming necessary body and ego functions for the person without incurring shame or depreciation, maintaining respect for the person, and helping him maintain his self-respect.
6. Encouraging the person to work out an acceptance of his life situation with dignity and integrity so that gradual regression may occur without conflict or guilt. (p. 14)

PAIN MANAGEMENT

Pain is determined by both physiological and psychosocial factors, and both must be addressed in the establishment of an effective pain control program.

First, there must be a recognition of the differences between acute and chronic pain. Lipman (1980) describes acute pain as existing on a continuum, from mild to moderate to severe. Most people have experienced acute pain at some time in their lives. It usually resolves fairly quickly and is rationalized as being inevitable in life. Individuals are encouraged to bear it stoically and medication for it is usually dispensed on a *p.r.n.* (as needed) basis as sparingly as possible. In contrast, chronic pain fails to resolve quickly. Rather than lying on a linear continuum, Lipman describes a circular continuum from aching to agony. The patient may experience only a dull ache on one day, and then excruciating agony on the next. It shifts back and forth. Chronic pain is difficult to rationalize because it seems meaningless and is not associated with the healing process. There are three dimensions to chronic pain: the physical; the psychological, as such continued pain produces anxiety, depression, and insomnia; and the social, as with the persistance of pain the patient's psychological reactions can cause her to become hostile and alienate others, leading to loneliness.

Each patient's unique pain experience must be assessed. The following parameters should be included (Donovan, Burns, Daley, Dietz, Faut, Gardenhire, Ivantic, McGuire, Steinweg, Wangler, Wright, & Yuska, 1981):

- *Physiological signs of stress (e.g., vital signs, nausea, muscle tension).* These are not necessarily good measures of chronic pain, but can indicate medication side effects and accuracy of dosage.
- *Patient responses to inquiries about pain location, duration, intensity, chronology, and aggravating factors.*
- *General observations of the patient.* In acute pain the patient may thrash or evidence postural changes. She may display facial grimaces. In chronic pain these behaviors do not help and it is more characteristic to see postures indicative of withdrawal, lack of facial expression, apathy, depression, and immobility.
- *Observations of the patient's interactions with others.* In severe pain, interactions are often very limited. In mild-to-moderate pain, interactions with others and distractions may be utilized to take the patient's mind off the discomfort.
- *Determination from patient interview of those methods of relief that have successfully reduced pain and stress in the past.*

The patient's own desire for level of pain control must also be established. There are some patients who want to experience their own pain. Some are willing to tolerate certain medication side effects in order to receive a particular degree of relief; others are not. It cannot be assumed that all patients have similar desires for pain control or that they experience the same pain or feel pain in the same way.

There must be an understanding of what pain means psychologically to the patient. For example, some patients think it is shameful to admit to it; others think it constitutes punishment. We also need to appreciate that the memory of previous pain may significantly affect the patient's anticipation of future pain and feelings about and tolerance of present pain.

As with other aspects of dealing with people under stress, we must try to discover how the patient has coped with pain in the past and identify what personal coping mechanisms the patient finds useful in dealing with pain. McGrory (1978) discusses the importance of supporting and capitalizing on the patient's preferred coping methods. Although written for nurses in institutions, her words are equally instructive for caregivers in other settings.

> Some clients in pain want to pray, pace, moan, or rock. By learning clients' own coping behaviors and allowing them to use them, nurses permit the clients to feel more in control of themselves and their environment, reduce anxiety, and maybe even reduce the subjective feeling of pain: it does not hurt as much. (pp. 65-66)

The control of physical distress must prevent fear and tension over future pain, as well as ameliorate current pain. Patients need to know they can expect pain control. Saunders (1975) articulates what has come to be current hospice policy: medications must be administered on a schedule that will prevent pain from recurring. In this manner less medication will be needed than on a p.r.n. basis, since once the pain is permitted to take hold it will require a larger dose for control than it would have for the prevention of it. (This is one of the major reasons why the fear that terminally ill patients will become addicted to medication unless used sparingly has been proven to be groundless.) Additionally, the patient will not have to be placed in the dependent position of requesting relief and will be spared the anxiety related to the fear that the medication will not arrive in time or work soon enough. The typical pain-anxiety-pain cycle of "the medicine will be wearing off soon and I'll still have to wait another hour for my pill and by then the pain will be killing me" is broken. This anxiety in and of itself has been shown to increase the intensity of the patient's pain (McCaffery, 1979).

It is important to always instruct the patient and family in what the medication is, how it works, how to use it, and what the side effects may be. If the patient is to stay at home, initial monitoring of dosage is essential, and the patient will need to be assisted in discovering how to titrate her medications to meet her needs and desires. The patient may have specific fears or concerns about taking medication and these must be ascertained. Some patients may be afraid the medication will cause them to lose control; others may fear being drugged and unaware. Appropriate reassurance and individualized tailoring of the medication protocol will take care of these concerns and enhance the efficacy of pain management.

In addition to the pharmacological methods of alleviation of pain, there are a number of cognitive-behavioral strategies that have been developed to reduce pain. Most of them have the advantage of returning control to the patient, who takes an active part in the reduction of symptoms.

In their excellent work *The Challenge of Pain*, Melzack and Wall (1983) survey the literature and conclude that it is unequivocal that psychological factors play an important role in pain perception and response. They also find that psychological approaches to pain relief have varying degrees of efficacy. Although they feel that a substantial amount of research is needed before it can be stated with certainty that one method is more effective than another, they feel that these nontraditional approaches can help when more traditional ones fail, especially to reduce pain from unbearable to bearable levels. Briefly, here are some of the psychological methods available.

• *Operant-conditioning techniques.* These methods are based on learning theory, focusing on the fact that complex patterns of behavior can be modified through the manipulation of reinforcement and punishment. Advocates of these methods note that people are often reinforced for having pain. They get attention and sympathy; they are excused from jobs; they can avoid people they dislike; they can get medication; they can receive financial compensation without working; and they are often treated with a degree of respect they never received when they were well. Consequently, the pain and other behavioral patterns associated with it are reinforced. The task of the behavioral therapist is to remove the reinforcements and to induce the patient to resume normal behavior patterns. Fordyce (1976) provides a model for this in his description of procedures utilized to retrain the patients who suffer chronic pain. Patients are hospitalized for a prolonged period and all pain behaviors are ignored. Physical activity is reinforced, medication is reduced, and alternative behaviors are socially reinforced. There also are other models employing simpler methods. They utilize the same principles but are briefer.

• *Biofeedback.* This is the procedure of gaining voluntary control over biological activities (e.g., brain waves, blood pressure, heart rate) through the feedback of biological signals from sensitive electronic equipment monitoring these functions. Using feedback, the person is taught to relax or use other stratagems to reduce or increase these biological functions. Implicit in the procedure are other psychological variables that would reduce pain: distraction, suggestion, relaxation, and a sense of control.

• *Hypnosis.* The mechanisms of hypnosis and self-hypnosis are extremely complex and often debated. Some theorists maintain that it is a special and unique state of consciousness. Others propose that it is nothing more than compliance to suggestions made by others. Nevertheless, it has been demonstrated to be useful in allowing some patients to achieve control over some kinds of chronic pain.

• *Relaxation techniques.* As a procedure relaxation is an essential component in most forms of therapy for pain and a basis for most meditative practices. It induces a subjective state of well-being and has been shown to produce positive physiological changes such as decreased metabolism and lower blood pressure and respiration.

• *Cognitive coping skills.* The most common strategy for coping with pain is the distraction of attention. Thinking an absorbing thought or conjuring up pleasant imagery distracts attention from the painful stimulus. Some strategies for coping are as follows: (1) imaginative inattention, in which the patient is trained to ignore the pain by evoking imagery that is incompatible with pain, e.g., imagining herself on a beautiful beach; (2) imaginative transformation of pain, in which the patient is instructed to interpret the subjective experience in terms other than "pain," e.g., transforming it into a tingling sensation or minimizing the experience; (3) imaginative transformation of context, in which the patient is trained to acknowledge the pain but to transform the setting or context, e.g., the man with a sprained arm pictures himself as a fighter pilot who has been shot in the arm while defending his country; (4) attention-diversion to external events, in which the patient focuses attention on environmental objects, e.g., concentrates on the cracks in the wall; (5) attention-diversion to internal events, in which the patient focuses attention on self-generated thoughts, e.g., mental arithmetic, composing a song; and (6) somatization, in which the patient is trained to focus attention on the painful area in a detached manner, e.g., the patient analyzes the pain sensations as if preparing to write a magazine article about them (Tan, 1980).

• *Multiple convergent therapy.* It has been found that two or more procedures in combination may effectively control pain. For example, adding biofeedback to hypnotic training can significantly reduce pain (Melzack & Perry, 1975). Similar results have been obtained when alpha-biofeedback is paired with a procedure known as stress-inoculation training (Meichenbaum & Turk, 1976). In this procedure patients are given information that provides them with an understanding of pain and the stresses that accompany it and are trained in a variety of coping strategies (e.g., relaxation, distraction, imagery techniques). They are allowed to choose the ones they prefer, and then rehearse the use of the strategies while they conceptualize the pain and stress at each phase of the total pain experience. When this procedure was preceded by alpha-biofeedback training it produced significant reductions in pain compared to the stress-inoculation technique by itself (Hartman & Ainsworth, 1980). As in the Melzack and Perry study, it was assumed that the addition of biofeedback facilitated pain reduction by providing the additional elements of distraction from the painful area, relaxation, suggestion that the pain would diminish, and sense of control necessary for patients to achieve greater pain relief.

• *Training procedures.* Several procedures have been developed to teach pregnant women how to cope with labor pain, one of the most severe forms of pain. Lamaze training (Lamaze, 1970) and Childbirth Without Fear (Dick-Read, 1944) are two of these methods. These techniques include the provision of detailed information about childbirth so the mother-to-be is prepared and experiences less anxiety; relaxation training; coping strategies to distract attention from the pain; and breathing exercises to enhance relaxation, distract attention, and aid in the process of giving birth.

• *Psychotherapeutic intervention.* Psychological intervention has been found to decrease conflict and emotional states that have contributed to the experience of pain.

According to Melzack and Wall (1983), there are advantages and disadvantages to each technique, depending upon factors such as the type of pain, the source of pain, and the environmental and psychological variables that influence pain including:
• Cultural determinants
• Pain thresholds
• Past experience
• Meaning of the situation
• Attention, anxiety, and distraction
• Feelings of control over pain
• Suggestibility
• The patient's personality and conflicts

They feel that psychological approaches can have powerful effects on pain, but are concerned about the lack of evidence offered by proponents of some of these methods, and by the limitations of some of the procedures. Nevertheless, "the field is young and growing rapidly. It holds great promise as an approach by itself or together with the powerful yet simple methods of sensory modulation that we are also just beginning to understand" (p. 355).

Other aspects of the patient's pain must be evaluated and attended to as well as the physical. Woodson (1978) believes there are four aspects of pain, which may each occur alone or in combination: physical pain; psychological pain; social pain (e.g., social withdrawal of loved ones); and spiritual pain (e.g., feeling estranged from God). "The task of the skilled clinician in alleviating pain is to tease out through careful observation and examination of the patient specifically which of the four components of pain are present, active, in what combination, and to what degree. Once the combination has been determined, then the *appropriate* combination of intervention strategies can be initiated" (p. 366). Obviously attention must be paid to the psychosocial aspects of pain—they are what causes suffering and they profoundly impact on physical pain. Just as psychosocial pain can exacerbate physical pain, so can physical pain interfere with interactions to cause psychosocial pain. To overlook these aspects is to incompletely address the patient's pain and suffering. (See "Suffering" in Chapter 8 for more on this topic.)

There are certain attitudes towards patients in pain that are nontherapeutic and contribute to their further emotional and physical pain. The following attitudes should be avoided (Donovan et al., 1981):

- Patients do not have pain unless there is a proven organic basis (Hackett, 1971).
- The caregiver can judge when patients have pain and the degree of its intensity.
- The acute pain model can be used to evaluate chronic pain (Hackett, 1971).
- High pain tolerance should be rewarded and low pain tolerance should be frowned upon.
- Patients should respond to pain in the same way the caregiver does.
- Patients who watch the clock and ask for medication are addicted.
- Narcotics given regularly around the clock for several days will enhance patients' chances of becoming addicted.
- Withholding narcotics will help prevent addition.
- When an analgesic is ordered p r.n., it should be given only when the pain is severe (McCaffery, 1979).

ASSISTANCE WITH THE PRACTICAL
CONSIDERATIONS OF DYING

In addition to physical, psychosocial, and religious problems, terminal illness also brings up some very important practical considerations. If we want to be truly helpful to the terminally ill patient, we will look for ways to assist her and her family in attending to practical matters in order to ameliorate anxieties about events occurring after death (e.g., What will happen to the body? In what financial condition will survivors find themselves?) and to support the patient's sense of control before it.

Two studies have addressed these issues. Kalish and Reynolds (1976) found that the dying patient is quite concerned with the circumstances and grief of those left behind. Koenig (1968) surveyed 60 terminally ill patients and discovered that, in addition to needing help with problems related to the illness and its emotional strains, patients desired assistance with financial problems, changes in social and sexual relationships, and difficulties in dealing with the hospital such as insufficient knowledge about the system, or inadequate information about treatment. Both these studies illustrate the need to focus on practical matters since they can affect the patient as much as the more global psychosocial reactions to the illness.

Networking can help in dealing with the concerns of the dying and their families, beginning with the formation of an interdisciplinary team for each patient. The team usually involves the patient and her family, physicians, nurses, psychologists, social workers, clergy, pharmacists, volunteers, and representatives of other professions involved in the care of the dying patient, such as dieticians and physical and occupational therapists. In the case of children it would also involve schoolteachers. With an interdisciplinary perspective many potential practical problems can be addressed prior to their becoming full-blown issues. If members are chosen carefully and communication is open, an interdisciplinary team can provide invaluable assistance to the patient and render peer support and opportunities for debriefing and ventilation of emotions to caregivers. However, in practice most teams are not carefully chosen to reflect the patient's needs. They are usually thrown together by chance, if they are put together at all. Communication among members may be minimal at best, despite the fact that this is one of the primary reasons to convene an interdisciplinary team. (See "Communication Guidelines" in this chapter for more on this topic.)

Many practical issues during the illness of the patient can be dealt with by the social worker or social service personnel. These include assisting the family with insurance and other financial programs so they can maintain adequate financial resources. One of the things that is most often overlooked in the care of the dying is the astronomical cost of terminal illness. (See "Financial Issues" in Chapter 8 for more on this topic.) Finances are soon depleted and assistance may have to be sought from agencies or institutions. This may decrease the patient and family's sense of pride, dignity, and self-control. The social worker is often in an ideal position to help the family in this regard, both with the financial details and the emotional reactions that must be dealt with.

Additionally, the social worker or other professional caregiver can provide information on how to most efficiently handle the bureaucracy of the institution. Cutting through red tape, learning how to manage institutional business procedures, and, very importantly, understanding how to most effectively communicate and deal with busy staff are all invaluable tools that can decrease many of the anxieties of the dying patient. The social worker can also identify for the patient social resources (e.g., cancer support groups), practical resources (e.g., names and locations of stores that offer prostheses and supplies), and economic resources (e.g., referrals to organizations that may assist in the cost of medications or wigs).

The patient can also be helped to identify ways of leaving her mark behind in the time remaining. To do this the caregiver can ask the patient how she desires to be remembered and help her find ways to keep her memory alive For example, letters can be written or videotapes made for young children who will be left behind; an endowment in the patient's name may be established at the patient's alma mater; precious possessions may be bequeathed to certain loved ones; unfinished business can be completed with significant others; a cemetery headstone can be chosen. This allows the patient to provide for survivors, assuage any guilt she may feel, leave remembrances of herself, and have a sense of control after the death that reduces anxieties both in the present and for the future (Leimberg, Note 19). It is especially meaningful for the patient to plan the distribution of her worldly goods, for property is an extension of the self. Since the person is immortalized both through her gifts and the act of presenting them, estate planning and the disposition of possessions is an important task that caregivers should support. Families will rarely bring it up, as they fear being perceived as insensitive and greedy.

Another area in which patients require assistance is identifying those financial and business affairs that must be attended to in order to protect survivors. An attorney may be consulted in order to write a will and establish trusts. Tax planning can be done and business shelters set up with the help of an accountant, and an insurance agent can advise how settlements may be most helpfully disbursed. Agencies such as the Social Security Administration and the Veterans Administration can be contacted for information regarding benefits. City, state, and federal civil service benefits, and sources of compensation from trade union, fraternal, or business/professional organizations also can be investigated. Bank officials can be conferred with to secure safety deposit boxes and establish long-term financial accounts.

In terms of planning for the rites and rituals that will mark the death of the patient, clergy and funeral directors can be most helpful. Funeral preplanning is becoming increasingly popular. It is a way in which the dying patient can be assured that matters will proceed as she would like. Because it allows the dying person an opportunity to express her preferences, it releases the family from possible guilt later, when decisions would have had to have been made. It also can alleviate some of the concerns of the dying patient about the unknown process following the death. For example, it may be comforting to a dying patient to know that she will be cremated as she wishes instead of having to confront an old personal fear regarding decomposition following earth burial. (See "Funeral Preplanning" in Chapter 7 for more on this topic.)

We can offer much assistance by gathering these professionals and providing resource information that enables the dying patient and family to cope with the practical considerations of terminal illness and impending death. The helpfulness of such endeavors cannot be underestimated. The peace of mind that dying patients can receive from taking care of these matters is invaluable in reducing some of their ongoing stress.

SPECIAL CAREGIVERS

Two types of caregivers are often overlooked in planning care for the terminally ill: the clergy and ancillary staff. However, each of them is in a unique position to help the dying patient in ways other caregivers cannot.

The Clergy

Since ancient times there has always been a select group of people who have been dedicated to helping members of the community deal with spiritual matters. Whether shamans, magicians, druids, or priests, these individuals have helped to interpret and explain metaphysical matters to the populace and assisted them in developing meaning in their lives. They have offered philosophies to enable believers to transcend the heartaches of life on earth. Religious faith can help to sustain people through the crises of life in many ways (Jackson, 1963):

- It helps them control their fears and anxieties by revealing not only the tragedy and sorrow of life, but also its blessings and rich experiences.
- It emphasizes those events in the history and experience of humanity that make life seem more understandable and give people a sense of changelessness in the midst of change, of the eternal in the midst of time.
- It helps them to turn their best thoughts and feelings into constructive action. Those of faith are inspired to act as they believe, to fulfill their aspirations in life.
- It allows them to transform the tragic events of life through the direction of its hope and the power of its love.

- It leads to deeper sensitivity of the spirit, higher aspirations of service, and a firmer conviction that the cosmic purpose is best understood as creative goodness. Therefore, although grief is painful and disappointing, it does not lead to despair.
- When it contains a belief in immortality, it relieves some of the guilt and sorrow that would be present if it were thought that at no point in time or eternity could wrongs be righted or injustices rectified.
- It highlights tradition, giving people a longer view by allowing them to tie present sufferings to time-honored sources of spiritual strength, and thus transcend current pain.
- It gives courage in the present and direction for the future.
- It moves attention away from death and tragedy, not by denying them, but by fitting them into a larger perspective.
- Through community religious rituals, it provides evidence of group strength and comfort, and recognizes the dignity of life and the validity of the feelings prompted by facing death.

The spiritual dimension still is crucial in the lives of many people in our society; yet it is often disregarded as an element of the person that needs to be addressed. It has been ignored by many mental health clinicians who, although they probed every other aspect of an individual's life experience and beliefs, would neglect the spiritual and religious beliefs, values, and experiences of their clients. In the practice of medicine, the spiritual dimension of the patient usually was not considered since it did not fit into the technological discipline, could not be analyzed or dissected scientifically, and did not meet the criteria of the medical model. However, the wise caregiver has always recognized that the patient's belief system is a critical determinant in maintaining well-being and the ability to resist disease.

When Dr. Cicely Saunders publicized the need for hospice care in the 1960s, she reminded the medical community of the importance of attending to the spiritual dimension of the dying patient. For individuals fortunate enough to be involved in the hospice care system (whether institutionally based or part of a home-care program), the maintenance of an interdisciplinary health team perspective, containing a member of the clergy, is part of the health care plan. While there also is an acknowledgment of the spiritual side of the patient in acute care settings, there appear to be more problems in putting the interdisciplinary health care team into full practice. While teams may exist, they often do not function practically for the patient. Consequently, the cleric is often informed too late of the proximity of the patient to death.

Prior to the reforms in death awareness in the 1950s and 1960s, clergy were traditionally considered the gatekeepers of death (Mills, 1977). As society became more secular, pluralistic, and mobile, and advances in medical technology changed attitudes towards caring and curing, all issues surrounding terminal illness came increasingly under the purview of medical personnel. Clergy generally welcomed the involvement of other professionals in the crisis of death; however, they started to find themselves relegated to positions further and further away from the dying patient. There developed a reluctance on the part of individuals to call on the clergy (Freund, 1977). Many medical personnel and family members believed that the clergy only wanted to extract some form of confession or conversion from the dying patient. It was often felt that a cleric would utter platitudes, rattle prayers, or subject the dying person to meaningless rituals that could do little good. For some people, the arrival of the cleric on the scene signaled defeat, when all else had been exhausted and nothing else could be accomplished.

Freund notes, however, that there are many contributions that a cleric can make. He may assist the patient to accept the reality of the illness and its implications, facilitate healthy emotional expression, and point out the unrealistic aspects of inappropriate guilt or shame. But the most unique contributions he can make center around the dying person's spiritual needs. There are three major spiritual needs to which the cleric must minister (Doka, 1983). First is the search for meaning in life. Failure to find such meaning can create a deep sense of spiritual pain, as individuals may feel their lives have meant nothing. The cleric can help the dying find time for personal reflection and assist them in finding significance in their lives. The things they've done, the events they've witnessed, the history they have experienced can all be fruitful areas for exploration. Religious belief systems can provide a sense of purpose and forgiveness for oneself and others. The second need is to die appropriately. Besides feeling as if they have lived meaningfully, individuals must believe they are dying meaningfully as well, in ways consonant with their own self-identity. Through empathic listening the cleric can allow the dying the opportunity to interpret their own deaths and hence have a framework for understanding their demise and a theology for their suffering and pain. They can also be assisted in deciding the manner in which they choose to die. Discussing the death with a significant other can facilitate their preparation to die as they have lived. Third, there is the need to transcend death. Religion (as other belief systems) can provide critical reassurance of immortality. Continuity may be manifested through rituals, or through the presence of children, grandchildren, and other family members. The dying can be allowed to keep treasured possessions at hand and can, in general, be treated in a dignified manner that emphasizes their individual significance.

The clergy can also work to clear away problems that interfere with spirituality. During the dying process six possible obstacles to the spiritual well-being of individuals can appear (Attig, 1983):

- *Intolerance of patients' beliefs or proselytizing by the clergy or other caregivers.* It is critical that all caregivers recognize and permit alternative beliefs to their own.
- *Potentially inhibiting factors blocking the full and meaningful expression of spiritual values or the exploration of spiritually pressing questions.* Such factors might include restricted access to spiritual leaders and counselors; limited space and privacy; medical procedures that reduce lucidity or ability to express thoughts; or discouragement of exploration of spiritual territory that is thought to be too painful for the patient to face. In all of these cases the cleric or other concerned caregiver can

  at least minimize the hindrances and perhaps take positive steps to circumvent or overcome the obstacles to spiritual functioning, e.g., by providing access to spiritual guides or community members, making space available, promoting at least temporary lucidity, compensating for reduced expressive functioning and encouraging exploration of difficult questions. (Attig, 1983, p. 10)

- *Underappreciation of the value and power of their beliefs by the believers themselves.* The dying sometimes fail to see how their beliefs speak to their current circumstances. The cleric who is skilled in helping them see the connections so that they may be sustained by their beliefs will provide invaluable aid.
- *Lack of conviction on spiritual matters.* In this case the cleric will encourage and support the exploration of spiritual issues of meaning so individuals can discover or develop for themselves sustaining convictions that are congruent with their values and lifestyle.
- *Dominating emotions such as anger or guilt that are rooted in the beliefs of the dying.* Emotions may control the exploration of underlying spiritual values and may inhibit questioning. In order to facilitate spiritual development the cleric must overcome the resistance that allows these emotions to dominate and gently, but firmly, invite, encourage, and support the exploration of the validity of the beliefs that form the bases of the emotions.
- *Convictions that are clearly dysfunctional.* Such convictions must not be judged as dysfunctional merely if they contradict those of the cleric or serve a function he finds undesirable. This judgment must be based on the perception that the belief is contributing to the disorientation of the person or clearly undermining the person's ability to make the expe-

rience meaningful. Encouraging the exploration of alternative interpretations of the beliefs in question or alternative beliefs compatible with the person's values and lifestyle is appropriate and respectful. The imposition of the cleric's own alternative beliefs is inappropriate.

Several writers have described the roles that the clergy must integrate and the levels of interaction on which they must relate. Worden (1972) sees four roles a cleric may play: the personal role, in which he deals with another individual on an interpersonal basis; the professional role, in which he is involved in relating to others as a cleric per se; the sacramental role, in which he dispenses the sacraments; and the role of theologian, where it is his task to theologize about issues such as pain, evil, and dying. "In all of these roles his main goal is to help preserve the quality of life, even for the dying patient" (p. 365). There are also four levels of interaction between the cleric and the dying individual, as named by Cassem (1972): the interpersonal level, sharing another human being's experience of life and the human condition of dying; the psychological level, recognizing and at times sharing insights about underlying dynamics; the religious level, serving as an expert in matters such as liturgy and scripture; and the theological level, assisting the dying person to find and articulate personal beliefs in the face of death. This theological level brings the cleric back to the interpersonal level, since pat formulas cannot be given to the dying. On this level the cleric and the dying patient must search together in an open human sharing as they seek the meaning with which life can transcend the presence of death.

In our society, *Aesculapian authority* is bestowed on the cleric (Moss, 1976). This type of authority has three parts: the religious and allied knowledge the cleric is presumed to have (sapiential authority); the assumption that his actions and decisions are for the good of people (moral authority); and his role in the religious realm involving the mysterious and the unknown (charismatic authority). Moss suggests that even though all authority has diminished somewhat in our society, the cleric is still bestowed with Aesculapian authority in moments of acute grief and during the accompanying funeral and mourning rituals. Its vestiture in clerics at the time of crisis can be helpful to the dying and bereaved by providing direction and a sense of order.

Clergy often have the unrealistic role expectation that they should understand, and be able to withstand the inexplicable and sorrowful parts of life. Yet ordination does not completely prepare the clergy for or exclude them from the normal human anxieties that are aroused when dealing with death. Reeves (1976) discusses the three ways in which the clergy tend to handle their own discomfort: (1) they cultivate objectivity and shield themselves against emotional involvement; (2) they utilize ritual to distance themselves; and (3) they exercise doctrine as a defense against the inability to answer the anguished cries of "Why?" from the bereaved. Flesch (1976) studied the failures in the ministry of the bereaved and felt that they could be classified into the following categories: (1) failure in heart, in which the cleric fails to be understanding, kind, and accepting of the bereaved; (2) failures in mind, in which the cleric fails to understand the grief experience and implications of bereavement; and (3) failures in role, in which the cleric fails to listen to the questions of the bereaved nonjudgmentally and to provide appropriate assistance in finding meaning in death.

This last failure is one that has resulted in the rejection of the cleric and his role by many mourners. Too often the clergy are motivated by their own anxieties and desires to be helpful, leaping to silence diatribes against God and answer questions that are best left unresponded to in the moments of anguish of grieving people. Clearly, as a representative of a religious philosophy, the cleric has much to offer, but timing is crucial. A religious philosophy put forth to answer existential questions too early may not only not assuage the grief of the individual, but may push that person further from the meaning and comfort that is intended.

> Certainly, maintain some degree of objectivity, and be ready, when it is time, to offer prayer or interpret the teachings of the faith. *When it is time*—but until it is time, he must hold his peace, accept the discomfort and pain as his share in his parishioners' experience of loss, be to them one who feels with and understands their feelings, and helps them express even the worst of them, saying, in effect, by his supportive presence, that God, too, feels and understands. (Reeves, 1976, p. 190)

Ideally, clerics will first of all be concerned caregivers. They will support patients with their presence, and be honest in their responses. If they are unable to answer patients' questions, they will say so; when appropriate, they may even share the process of searching for answers with patients. They will try to transcend their own fears and concerns, and be nonjudgmental and accepting. Religion should be used to comfort patients; when it cannot bring solace, compassion and care must take its place. Clerics should work to provide the best transition and safest passage to death. Whether this is done through the use of ritual, interpretation of religious tenets, involvement in the community, prayer, or the gift of human caring and presence is a moot point. The issue is that they do what is necessary to meet the human, including religious, needs of the patient, and be flexible enough to do so in comfort.

The clergy are in a special position to meet patients' spiritual and psychosocial needs. As they become more appropriately trained to deal with issues of mental health and the normal crises of life, including death, they will be in an especially advantageous position to serve on the interdisciplinary team ministering to the dying patient and the bereaved.

The Ancillary Staff

In the health care system, most notably in institutions, the dying patient is exposed to a number of ancillary staff in addition to the primary caregivers. Some of the staff will be directly involved in medical functions pertaining to the dying patient (e.g., blood technicians, x-ray technologists, inhalation therapists), while others will be involved in such diverse duties as maintenance, housecleaning, and volunteer work. Frequently the patient is exposed more to these ancillary staff members than to the primary caregivers, and the time spent in contact with them may have a profound impact upon the dying patient. If we are to make the patient's last days as comfortable and fulfilling as possible, ancillary staff should be given some measure of training on how they may affect the dying patient and how their presence relates to the patient's needs and experience.

Ancillary staff may be uniquely effective at communicating with some dying patients because of their lack of professional façade. They may seem to be more approachable and familiar to these patients than other caregivers. Administrators in health care systems need to recognize the possible influence of these individuals upon the terminally ill. If the staff's sensitivity can be sharpened, they may be in uniquely advantageous positions to ameliorate the ordeal of terminal illness through their understanding and also through presence.

Professional health caregivers can model effective interventions with dying patients for ancillary staff and can informally educate them to the needs of dying patients. With the help of ancillary staff, caregivers can come closer to achieving their goal of a dignified and appropriate death for the patient with continued treatment as a living, as well as dying, human being.

EXERCISE VII

Your Attitudes Towards Working With the Dying

We *all* entertain preconceptions about dying. It is important to recognize our unconscious and conscious attitudes and expectations about dying patients in order to be more responsive to them.

As honestly as possible, list some of the expectations you have about dying patients (they should all talk about their illness, or make peace with their families prior to death).

What do you like most about dying patients?

What do you like least about dying patients?

How do your attitudes affect your work with the dying, positively and negatively?

What are the struggles you have in your work with the dying?

How do you cope with people who lack positive characteristics because of their dying (they are not pretty, productive, independent)? What reactions does this arouse in you?

How do you deal with your reactions to these unfavorable characteristics of dying patients?

In what areas do you need more work?

It is not uncommon to wish we could take away the pain from the dying and bereaved. Unfortunately, we cannot. How do you control the urge to "do"?

EXERCISE VIII

Sensitizing Yourself to the Experience of the Dying Patient

Imagine that you have been diagnosed as having a terminal illness. You have been thrust into a strange new medical world of treatment regimens, medical jargon, medications, doctors, and hospitalizations. It is like being a stranger in a foreign country without being able to speak the language. How do you feel? What do you do? Who can serve as translator?

List those things you value most about yourself. Would these things be changed by your being terminally ill? If so, what could be done to minimize this?

Name those things that are very reinforcing to you. They could be physical objects (food, art), social stimuli (recognition, love), or activities (walking outdoors, playing football). How do you get these things now? From whom do you get them? Would your ability to get them be changed by your being terminally ill? If so, what could be done to minimize this?

Note those ways in which you have been productive in society. Include your paid work, volunteer work, home life, and social support to others. Would your ability to continue your productive activities be changed by your being terminally ill? If so, what could be done to minimize this?

What would be the hardest things to give up in your illness? What could be done to help you with these?

What would you most want or need from your caregivers?

CHAPTER 12

The Family of the Dying Patient

Since the early 1950s there has been a considerable shift in emphasis in psychiatry and psychotherapy away from an individual-oriented perspective focusing on intrapsychic process to a family systems orientation concerned with the interrelationships of family members. The family constellation is currently perceived as a unit, a system in which the sum is more than the total of its parts. As a system, it operates under the same conditions as does any system: anything that affects the system as a whole will affect the individual members, while anything that affects the individual members will necessarily affect the family as a whole. Like all systems, the family system struggles to maintain its homeostatic balance and equilibrium. To do this families develop specific roles, rules, communication patterns, expectations, and patterns of behavior that reflect their beliefs, coping strategies, system alliances, and coalitions. These work to keep the system consistent and stable.

All families have distinct and characteristic styles. Each one is unique in where it falls on the continuum of a number of variables. The five most salient dimensions are communication patterns; boundaries between individual family members and between the family as a whole and the rest of the world; role flexibility within the family; subsystem alliances within the family; and family rules. Communication patterns in families run along continuums of openness or closure; directness or indirectness; verbal or nonverbal content; acceptance or prohibition of the expression of feelings; congruency or incongruency of verbal and nonverbal behavior; and validating or disqualifying messages. Boundaries are the rules defining who interacts or has contact with whom and how; their function is to protect the differentiation of the system and its members (Minuchin, 1974). Boundaries also define the degree of emotional symbiosis that exists between members and how independent and separate their identities are from one another. Boundaries between family members and between the family as a whole and the rest of the world lie along a range from flexible to rigid, permeable to impenetrable, and enmeshed to disengaged. In families, roles may range from degrees of flexibility, which allows one member's role to be assumed by another, to inflexibility, where roles are so rigidly assigned they cannot be reassigned. Subsystems are the special relationships or alliances that exist between two (i.e., a dyad) or more (i.e., a coalition) family members. They are not necessarily static; they shift depending upon the needs of the individuals and system and the demands of the situation. Family rules govern and regulate family life and the experience of its members, as well as the beliefs, attitudes, and behaviors that are accepted or prohibited in the family. They range on a continuum of being overt or covert; growth producing or reducing; and up-to-date or out-of-date.

In general, families can be conceptualized as open systems if they have direct, clear, congruent communication in which family members have full freedom to communicate anything; flexible boundaries and roles; balanced subsystems allowing appropriate interaction; overt, up-to-date rules; and an acceptance of change as normal and inevitable (Satir, 1972). In contrast, closed systems have communication that is restricted in which comments are indirect, unclear, or incongruent; enmeshed boundaries in which family members lack appropriate differentiation and are overly involved with and dependent on each other; inflexible rules; subsystems that inappropriately isolate, enmesh, or create unbalanced access to power; and rules that are covert, out-of-date, and too inflexible to allow change, meet members' needs, or permit growth. There is a desire to avoid change (Satir, 1972).

When an individual is terminally ill and cannot fulfill assigned roles or obligations in the manner that has become expected, there is a shift in the homeostatic balance of the family. One element has been changed and consequently the entire family system is thrown into disequilibrium, with a consequent demand for adaptation. The emotional energy of the family is directed towards reestablishing balance in the system. This will affect not only the system as a whole and its individual members, but also the various subsystem dyads and coalitions that existed within the family. Power, responsibilities, and roles will be reassigned as a consequence of the family system's struggle to reestablish stability in the face of a changed situation. The characteristics of the family previously mentioned determine how it will respond to any demands for change. These characteristics must always be considered when evaluating the potential for adaptive change and planning interventions to facilitate change or maintain some level of functioning in the family.

FAMILY PROBLEMS

Unique problems arise for a family when a member of that family is dying. These problems additionally stress individual family members who already are trying to cope with the process of losing their loved one.

The family is removed from homeostatic balance some time in advance of the actual death of the patient. The disruption begins long before, often at the time of diagnosis. Communication becomes more difficult, as family members differ in their rates and degrees of acceptance of the diagnosis and their responses to its threat. Expectations must be radically altered with the recognition that a member of the system will no longer function normally within that system and will eventually not be a part of it. This precipitates demands for family adaptation and change, causing stress reactions in individual family members and the family as a whole.

There are some unique reasons for the additional stress occasioned by the threat of loss of a family member in America. As a result of a series of sociological changes in our society—industrialization, urbanization, increased social mobility, increasingly rapid social changes, and the increase in technology—there have been corresponding changes in the family as an institution. Family integration and primary group interactions have declined, and the extended family of the past has been replaced by today's more isolated nuclear family. This family, with fewer resources for interpersonal support due to geographical and social distance from family and other primary groups, is limited in its ability to meet all the needs of its members. Consequently, familial tasks have been delegated increasingly to society, making the family dependent on society for many more supportive functions than before. It is now much more vulnerable to stress and less able to provide for family members.

The death of a family member causes a greater psychological impact in American culture than in other societies (Volkart, 1957). This is because of the more intense emotional involvement fostered by the limited range of interaction possible in the American nuclear family. In those societies where psychological involvement is spread out over more individuals and the extended family is the norm, others besides the biological parents are actively involved in childrearing and emotional involvement is more dispersed. The death of a family member in these societies does not generate such intense emotions or have the same impact it would if family relationships were more exclusive. In the American nuclear family there also is a greater potential for ambivalence and hostility to arise as a consequence of a family member's death, since self-identification and personal dependency are rooted within the limited scope of interactions among family members. Even though family members are a major source of love and gratification, they are also sources of punishment, frustration, and anger. This necessarily leaves individuals with more negative and ambivalent feelings to contend with after a death in this society. Compounding this is the small family system's tendency to breed overidentification and overdependence. Emotional attachments to particular people, as opposed to their roles, is the norm in the American family. All of this constitutes a situation of high vulnerability to stress for the individual in contemporary American society who is bereaved through the death of a loved one.

In their discussion on "The Family as a Matrix of Tragedy," Weigert and Hastings (Note 4) note that the individual family is the one institution vulnerable to *time death*, that is, it will gradually die with the death of the members. The passage of time will eventually end that specific institution, whereas other institutions (e.g., political, educational, religious, economic) will endure long beyond the lifetimes of specific individuals. This presents the family of the terminally ill individual with another loss. In addition to grieving for the potential loss of the loved one, there is also grief for the death of the family unit as it has existed in the past. Although the family will continue after the death, it will forever be changed by the irretrievable loss of the presence and role-fulfilling behaviors and functions of the deceased. For individual members there is also grief for the loss of the part of the self that existed within that family unit:

> From a symbolic interactionist and phenomenological viewpoint, it is theoretically necessary that a socialized self, invested in a particular biographical family, experience the sense of loss, not only of the other person, but also of that part of the self constituted by the relations which were anchored in that other person. The death of a father forever destroys that part of the interactional self which was son, and which is sedimented in the memories and role enactments mutually constituted by father and son. (Weigert & Hastings, Note 4, pp. 7-8)

Therefore the family of the terminally ill individual is not only coping with the realization that their loved one is dying and will eventually be lost to them, but also with the death of the family unit as it has been known. In addition, family members will lose their interactional selves in relation to the deceased. Consequently, this leaves the family in a position of coping with multiple grief experiences occurring simultaneously. While this situation may constitute a bereavement overload, leaving family members with profound feelings of loss, it is part and parcel of the experience and cannot be avoided. Compounding this is the very delicate balance that family members must try to maintain in remaining involved with the dying patient while simultaneously starting to decathect from her. Attempting to do this while enduring the uncertainty and anxiety inherent in terminal illness results in an acutely painful experience that continually saps the energy of family members already overburdened with their own feelings of anticipatory grief.

> During this time of stress the strength and resilience of family relationships are severely taxed. . . . The uncertainty about when death will occur leaves the family with the feeling of being in limbo, enduring the strains of current hardships while attempting to prepare for painful changes, knowing neither when these changes will occur nor exactly what sequence of events to anticipate. The family faces dual tasks that always are painful and sometimes make contradictory or incongruent demands. The family must care for the dying patient and continue to interact with him. Simultaneously, the total family attempts to prepare for the final separation that death will bring and for a future from which this family member, now the focus of everybody's concern, will be missing. (Arndt & Gruber, 1977, pp. 42-43)

Despite the particularly painful predicament that families of terminally ill patients are placed in, it is critically important to include them in the patient's treatment. Family members' reactions will influence the patient, as will the patient's influence the family, making the most effective intervention in this system one that treats the patient and family conjointly. Most clinicians and researchers agree that a caregiver cannot help a patient in a meaningful way if the family is not included to whatever extent is possible. The hospice movement has been instrumental in having the patient and her family regarded as the unit of care. Such integration allows for continued support of the patient and, hopefully, through continued interaction with loved ones, maintenance of her sense of identity, self-worth, integrity, and meaning. Additionally, it fosters opportunities for the patient and family members to complete unfinished business. Such experiences will minimize the likelihood of unresolved grief and decrease the amount of guilt and disorganization following the death. Many caregivers utilize the time during the illness of the patient to establish a relationship with the family that will continue after the death, in an attempt to prevent later problems in bereavement.

Despite the benefits of treating the family and patient as a unit, family members should not be expected to constantly remain with the dying person. Kübler-Ross (1969) points out that it is cruel to expect the constant presence of loved ones and that this puts a burden on them and on the patient, who both may need a respite from dealing with anticipatory grief. Many times family members will need to be given permission for "time out" periods to attend to their own needs or those of other family members. During the illness family members can be expected to experience guilt due to the normal ambivalence and lack of perfection in relationships, the resentment of resources spent on the patient, and the relief that they may feel because they themselves are not dying. Family members may respond to their guilt by putting all of their time, energy, and resources into the care of the dying patient. However, this can create additional problems and therefore needs to be monitored. Caregivers are in an excellent position to sensitively time interventions, allowing a break between the family and patient when both parties could benefit from it. For example, it is at times helpful to encourage family members to go home and rest, shower, and change, and then return to spend time with the patient. While this may be something that they require, family members may be reluctant to initiate this themselves. Giving them this permission can be helpful in preventing the emotional and social exhaustion that results, especially near the end of the illness when family members may be keeping a vigil with the patient. This does not mean it is not important for family members to be present; but even in the best of circumstances people need time away from each other and from the contemplation of threatening situations if they are going to continue to cope in healthy ways.

FAMILY TASKS AND REACTIONS

The family of the terminally ill patient is confronted with a series of tasks. While many of these pertain to the need to cope with the terminal illness of the family member, others reflect the family's vital need to continue to take care of itself. Again, it is a very delicate balance that must be struck by family members. Competing demands often leave people feeling guilty because there is never enough time or energy to attend as completely as possible to both sets of needs. When visiting at the hospital, they may be concerned about the children at home; and when at home, they may constantly wonder what is happening at the hospital in their absence. Nevertheless, the demands on the family continue:

> While providing care for the dying person and being immersed in the context of death, the family must continue to meet its members' needs, function as a social unit in society, and provide a structure for the growth and development of its members. The family must adapt to the many changes resulting from the dying person's illness, maintain its identity, and begin to provide for the adaptation to the ultimate loss of the person by reorganizing to continue its function after the family member's death. (Barton, 1977, p. 59)

The family unit must struggle to continue to perform those functions it is charged with providing to its members: nurturant functions, caring for both physical and psychological needs; relational functions, developing interpersonal abilities for relating to others; communicative functions, educating family members in verbal and nonverbal skills; emancipative functions, equipping family members to attain physical, emotional, and economic independence, along with the desire and ability to begin their own family; and recuperative functions, providing family members with a setting allowing them rest, relaxation, and reconstitution of energies for continued participation in society (Fleck, 1975). Depending on the illness, the role of the patient in the family, and the adaptive capabilities of the family, these functions will be more or less compromised during terminal illness and the family's adaptation to the impending loss of a member (Barton, 1977). Family members may begin to resent the emotional, economic, and time resources spent on the dying patient that deprive them of these resources to gratify their own needs. For example, children may resent the lack of attention they receive from a parent, or a spouse may be dissatisfied with the lack of intimacy resulting from a mate's exhaustion from caring for the dying patient. Recognition of such resentment, which actually is quite normal and understandable, can be extremely disquieting and guilt-provoking to family members. Caregivers can normalize these feelings and point out that they need not preclude positive feelings towards or further interaction with the patient and should not prompt overinvolvement with her in compensation for the guilt. Rather, these feelings should be acknowledged and ventilated. Those needs of the family members that must be met should be identified, and ways should be found to meet these within the constraints of the family's resources at the time. Often open discussion of the importance of balancing patient and family needs, along with appropriate gestures and reassurances that all are loved despite apparent inequalities, helps family members who feel neglected to manage their resentment by providing some of the security they need and acknowledging their feelings.

In addition to the sociological functions just discussed that must be maintained to some extent, there are a number of family coping tasks that must be undertaken during the terminal illness of a family member. These include denial versus acceptance of the illness; establishing relationships with caregivers; meeting the needs of the dying person; maintaining functional equilibrium; regulating affect; negotiating extrafamilial relationships; and coping with the postdeath phase (Cohen & Cohen, 1981).

Denial versus acceptance of the illness is an issue that underlies all others. Depending on the resolution of this process, there will be other subsequent tasks for and reactions evidenced by the family. Cohen and Cohen (1981) note that reactions are so particularly intense at the time of diagnosis that some denial of reality is necessary for the continued effective functioning of the family. This denial is not a total distortion of reality, but rather an adaptive strategy whereby the family attempts to accommodate the news at a more tolerable pace to avoid extreme disequilibrium. Like the dying patient, the family system will respond to the terminal illness with a fluctuation between denial and acceptance. "A healthy balance between these strategies will enable the family unit to continue functioning with a sense of purpose and meaning while making necessary changes and accommodations to meet the needs of the dying member" (Cohen & Cohen, 1981, p. 186). The family's communication patterns will reflect the degree of denial or acceptance of the illness. Previous research has revealed that families that sustain open communication processes are better equipped to cope with the vicissitudes of the illness experience.

A second coping task required of the family of the terminally ill patient is establishing a relationship with health caregivers. It is a reality of the illness that family members will be required to learn how to be assertive, and how to express constructive anger and discontent with health caregivers, in ways that will not jeopardize either their future relationship with the caregivers or the care of the patient. Projection of anger onto caregivers, resulting from the helplessness and lack of control experienced due to the illness, needs to be kept to a minimum. Unfortunately, sometimes frustration with caregivers is expressed through noncompliance with medical advice. Family conferences with caregivers and family members have been found to be very helpful in alleviating family anxiety and cognitive distortions about the illness. Such conferences appear to reduce the family's distrust of medical staff and promote more open communication.

At times caregivers need to establish guidelines for the communication process, particularly when they are continuously besieged by family members for information. Of course, ideally someone such as the physician would be able to communicate with each family member as needed and desired, However, the reality of the situation is that time is often at a minimum, and in those instances when numerous family members request the same information, it may be better that one family member be appointed the spokesperson and other family members receive their information through him. Ongoing family conferences also will diminish the need for repetitive individual consultations and should be promoted wherever possible.

As the illness continues the family develops strategies for the task of meeting the needs of the dying person. Depending on the nature of the illness, the family may be required to adapt to a loved one who, though slowly dying, will go on living for an extended period of time. It is a myth that the patient linearly progresses on a downward course from the time of diagnosis until death. Although this would be painful, it would be relatively easier than what reality often presents: a living-dying interval in which the patient sometimes appears completely normal, allowing family life to be resumed as before, and at other times becomes severely ill, creating demands for major readaptation within the family system. In the living that the dying patient does before death, she must be treated by family members as a living person despite her diagnosis or decline towards death. This means that although the patient may be somewhat changed due to her confrontation with mortality, pain, or disease, in most cases she is still much the same person she was. In all probability, until a point relatively close to death, she will still expect to be treated as she always has been. For example, a mother may feel hurt if she is not asked to sign the report card for her son that she has always signed previously. The dying patient will still have the same preferences, hopes, and desires that she always had, and she will still need intimacy, enjoyment, productive work, and social and intellectual stimulation. The diagnosis of a terminal illness does not take away the human needs of the dying patient; if anything, it heightens them. Thus, the family must resist the tendency to socially bury the dying person prematurely. Fear and anxiety have often caused families to decathect too much, creating precipitous separations much too early in the dying process.

It also is important that families not allow their awareness of the patient's dying to be psychologically destructive to their relationship with her. They must balance relating to their loved one as a living person with recognizing and adjusting to the fact that she is dying. Family members should continue to relate to her in ways that evidence their concern, yet continue the ongoing relationship as it was previously sustained. They must be honest with the patient, and not be afraid to disagree with her simply because she is dying. Indeed, condescension or placation is demoralizing and infantalizing. This type of "protection" only serves to increase the patient's isolation and decrease her trust. It signals to her that she is already considered dead in many ways. Such a communication is often followed by the patient herself giving up hope.

Throughout the illness the family needs to grant the patient permission to experience the feelings generated by the illness, its accompanying losses, and the threat of impending death. This acceptance must be felt by the dying patient if she is to be comfortable enough to reveal her thoughts, fears, feelings, and hopes during the living-dying interval. If the patient does not receive this acceptance or fears that communicating certain things will result in her being abandoned, she learns to keep her feelings to herself and struggles with them alone. This robs her of the social support that is so critical when facing death. Therefore, to effectively love and support the dying patient, the family must give her permission to be as she is and to do and say what she must.

In order to meet the needs of dying patients, family members must be aware of what they are. The major responsibility of the family is to create an atmosphere in which the dying person will feel free to make her needs and wants known without the fear of incurring resentment or disapproval from family members. An open awareness context is helpful in this regard. Family members should not assume what the patient's needs may be, but instead ask the patient directly. They also must recognize that at times they will need to search outside of the family for support for the dying patient. For example, a confidant may be needed for the patient who is too embarrassed or threatened to discuss particular issues with family members, or a caregiver may have to assist the patient in dealing with embarrassing aspects of the illness, such as personal hygiene needs. If the family can be educated to understand the losses involved in a terminal illness, the members may be able to better anticipate and respond to the needs of the dying patient.

Meeting the needs of the patient is a very delicate situation for, with the advent of the illness and the results of its progression, the dying person has to relinquish roles, responsibilities, and functions to some extent. Not only is this painful for the patient, but it may result in a lack of contact with significant others, or may prompt some decathexis from the patient by them. For example, if a man can no longer attend father-son functions with his child, he may be replaced in this regard by an uncle. This obviously reduces some of the contact he has with his son. Something they shared together now is lost. While the uncle cannot replace the father, the son may start to depend on the uncle for certain things, or he may turn to his uncle with specific questions or concerns that he formerly would have addressed to his father. This does not mean he does not love his father, but it signifies that some of the father's roles are being assumed by another family member. This can be particularly painful for the dying person to witness and consequently family members and caregivers must make sure that only those roles are relinquished that necessarily must be. When roles are reassigned, the dying patient must be reassured of having continued value in the family system, and family members must take precautions to see that these changes do not result in the social or psychological death of the individual.

The family must balance support for the patient's increased

dependency with her continued need for autonomy. Too much of either can be countertherapeutic. While the surrender of autonomy is difficult for the patient, it makes the family suffer as well. Family members require support in coping with those processes that mark the decline towards death, without abandoning the loved one in order to avoid seeing it happen. It is particularly painful for family members to watch the loved one deteriorate and have to relinquish the roles and responsibilities that were once sustained. Their feelings of helplessness and lack of control are frequently defended against through a variety of coping mechanisms: denial, isolation of affect, sublimation, repression, reaction-formation, displacement, projection, introjection (Maddison & Raphael, 1972). To these, McCollum and Schwartz (1972) would also add avoidance, the conscious suppression of thought and associated emotion ("I don't let myself think about it"). They suggest the following four criteria for evaluating the role and value of these coping mechanisms:

- Are they expectable and appropriate at this time?
- Do they safeguard the individual against incapacitating anxiety and depression?
- Do they enable the individual to maintain need-fulfilling relationships with the patient and other family members?
- Do they interfere with the medical care of the patient?

Depending on the answers to these questions, a particular defense may be appraised as functional or dysfunctional for the individual in a given situation.

Maintaining a functional equilibrium is a major task for the family unit, and one that must be attended to throughout the illness. "The tasks during this phase center on preserving a sense of normalcy and routine while simultaneously making necessary role shifts and balancing the special needs of the dying member with the needs of other family members" (Cohen & Cohen, 1981, p. 194). Since the family as a system is out of balance and there is a demand for reorganization in order to reestablish homeostasis, there will need to be a redistribution of roles and functions within the family. This results from the decreased ability of the dying patient to participate and the alteration of that individual's behavior and emotional responses within the family system. The degree of role reorganization that will be necessary is a function of two variables: the number of roles held by the terminally ill patient and the types of roles she fulfilled (Vollman, Ganzert, Picher, & Williams, 1971). The role shifts that necessarily must occur put additional burdens on family members who are already quite vulnerable and overtaxed. For example, if the dying patient is the breadwinner, the economic support of the family must be undertaken by another family member. This may mean, for example, that one spouse will have to take a part-time job in order to supplement the family's reduced income as a consequence of the other's illness. This role change in itself will engender further changes in the family. There may be less time for the spouse accepting a new role to engage in childcare, nurturing of other family members, or relaxation. Role reassignments can be potentially harmful, as when a child is expected to assume parental responsibilities following the death of a parent or is assigned the identity of a deceased sibling. Thus reassignment must be done with consideration of such issues as the appropriateness of a given role responsibility for a specific family member, the member's preparation for and probable rewards in assuming the role, and the congruence of the new responsibilities with existing roles (Arndt & Gruber, 1977). New role assignments may constitute either secondary losses or secondary gains for individual family members. It is not uncommon for young adults to be robbed of their independence as they are expected to assume adult responsibilities earlier than anticipated. In some cases, however, the reassignment of roles allows individuals to receive recognition and/or responsibilities that may have been withheld and adds meaningful functions to their lives. In families where role reorganization does not occur, a malignant process of scapegoating may develop in the family's attempt to maintain homeostasis and to provide greater cohesion and unity to ensure the survival of the family. This unhealthy process allows family members to discharge the feelings created by the illness and threatened loss of the dying family member.

Of course, the dying patient who, of necessity, must change or relinquish her roles, will often have emotional reactions to these additional losses. The husband who resents the fact that the wife is now the breadwinner and the sibling who reverts to fierce competition with other siblings after she is diagnosed both exemplify some of the natural responses to the continued loss that takes place throughout the illness. Indeed, adjusting to the changes occasioned by the illness is often as difficult, if not more so, as adjusting to the illness itself. It is part of the accommodation to the continuous loss process, to which the dying patient and family have no choice but to adapt.

The regulation of affect is a tricky task for family members during the terminal illness of one of the family. The knowledge of the threat of death and potential loss intensifies the levels of emotion that are present. The remissions and relapses of the illness may bring about shifts in the type and intensity of emotions that the family experiences. With the presence of a dying individual, there may be modulation or suppression of negative feelings in order to eliminate potential stress. All too frequently these erupt in less appropriate ways at other times and can result in resentments that eventually undermine family cooperation. The expression of feelings must be balanced with the other adaptive tasks required of the family. Cohen & Cohen (1981) identify some therapeutic steps to encourage appropriate emotional expression:

> We have found that working with families to establish flexible communicational boundaries is the best safeguard against the dysfunctional behavior resulting from the inhibition of emotional expression under stress. This means predicting and anticipating with the family the emotional reactions they might experience, bringing out into the open any fears regarding consequences of affective expression, and helping each member to express feelings in an appropriate manner. (p. 199)

Negotiating extrafamilial relationships becomes a more difficult task when a family member is dying. This results from the family disruption that inevitably occurs during a terminal illness, leaving family members with little energy with which to maintain and nurture outside relationships. There is also the social avoidance that often arises as friends distance themselves due to the anxiety-provoking nature of the terminal illness or lack of knowledge of what to do to be supportive. Both these factors commonly result in family members lacking needed social support during this critical time, when extrafamilial relationships could replenish them and give them a respite from the family demands that are so burdensome. Frequently families have to take the lead in dealing with friends, who many times are interested in helping but do not know what to do. This may mean that family members must specify exactly what they need if their friends are to be able to respond and must learn how to assertively ask for what they desire. In particular, close friends of the dying patient should be encouraged to participate in her care. Such friends are often subject to many of the same stresses and emotions as family members.

Occasionally there are other problems with outside relationships. Family members sometimes are resentful over the good fortune of friends or feel that others cannot understand their plight. This can cause them to be unable to respond to the gestures that are made by concerned friends. There are also those outside the family who label any attempt by family members to relax and temporarily escape their burden as frivolous or uncaring. This only adds to the family's difficulties.

Just as the dying patient requires support, so does her family. Support groups for the terminally ill and their families have been found to be uniquely effective in helping individuals adapt to and resolve the unique difficulties of coping with terminal illness. These include Make Today Count, Can Surmount, I Can Cope, Candlelighters, and other hospital-affiliated groups or organizations devoted to mutual support.

Coping with the postdeath phase will be discussed in detail later in this chapter.

The main tasks of the dying patient's family can be synthesized into three aspects. First, the family must begin a joint process of anticipatory grief and finishing unfinished business with the dying member to prepare for the decathexis that must ultimately occur. Second, the family must accomplish the first task while supporting the dying patient and struggling to find ways to continue to live with her as fully as possible until the moment of death. The dying patient must be given as much control as possible, despite the ongoing process of relinquishing family roles and responsibilities. Third, the family must start to reorganize itself to maintain its stability following the imbalance fostered by the illness of the dying patient. It must ensure the continued survival of the other family members and commence the change process that must be completed following the death of the patient. This also entails grieving for the death of the family unit as it has been known to all of the family members.

EMOTIONAL RESPONSES OF THE FAMILY

Common emotional reactions have been referred to throughout the previous analysis of the problems and tasks of the family of the terminally ill patient. In this section they will be examined more specifically.

In addition to grieving for the loss of the loved one, the family member is also grieving for that part of himself that will be lost with the death of the loved one and for the family which will be forever changed. It is a strenuous time of indefinite duration that requires living with a certain knowledge that a major loss will occur, often with continuous pain, suffering, futility, and helplessness. The family struggles to cope with the impending loss until it becomes a reality and then must face the further crisis of bereavement (Maddison & Raphael, 1972).

Anticipatory grief refers to the process of normal mourning that occurs in anticipation of the death and its consequences. It is defined as "the total set of cognitive, affective, cultural, and social reactions to expected death felt by the patient and family" (Lebow, 1976, p. 459). The process of anticipatory grief has an inherent set of adaptational tasks for the family that must be addressed (Lebow, 1976):

• *Remaining involved with the patient.* This entails responding to what the patient is undergoing, and sharing with and including her in family experiences. The treatment goal is to maintain the patient and family relationship by facilitating open communication and interaction patterns to the extent the family style allows.

• *Remaining separate from the patient.* This task of individuation is almost the opposite of the first task. Here each family member must recognize his own separateness from the patient and learn to tolerate the awareness that the loved one will die while he continues to exist. Treatment will focus on supporting each family member's own identity and capabilities, helping him to differentiate his needs from those of the patient, and encouraging him to begin to plan for his future life.

• *Adapting suitably to role changes.* Each member must accommodate himself to the new demands within the family. Intervention is geared towards assisting the family to cooperatively reassign current responsibilities and anticipate future permanent changes, directing them towards restructuring their roles in mutually adaptive ways.

• *Bearing the affects of grief.* This requires managing the myriad feelings of anticipatory grief arising from both the current situation and past losses that have been revived by the grief. Interventions would include encouraging expression of feelings, providing support for coping with them, and being aware of the present situation's relevance to the person's past relationships and losses.

• *Coming to terms with the reality of the impending loss.* The family goes through a series of emotional reactions that leads them to the increased awareness and acceptance of the loved one's dying. Family members need to be able to anticipate a future without the loved one and to tolerate some thoughts of and planning for themselves in that future. The goal of the caregiver is to assist in reality testing and planning. This entails helping the family understand the implications of medical information; making practical plans for pre- and postdeath activities (e.g., patient care, burial plans); and encouraging repetitious recollection of events leading up to the illness and death to assist in the family's gradual adaptation to the shock of the loss.

• *Saying good-bye.* This is an acknowledgment that leave-taking is occurring. It may transpire through verbal or nonverbal, concrete or symbolic means. The goals of intervention revolve around helping the family recognize the end is near and prompting their good-byes by modeling the first farewell to the patient.

As these tasks are being completed, each family member hopefully will attempt to finish unfinished business with the patient. Expressing feelings, resolving past conflicts, tending to last wishes, straightening out misconceptions, and recollecting the mutual relationship will create the closure that makes the final separation more peaceful and bearable for family and patient.

While all emotions in response to the threat of the loss of the loved one are legitimately an aspect of anticipatory grief, the main ones are sorrow, depression, and anxiety. These are constantly being stimulated by the day-to-day suffering, changes, and physical separations that the illness imposes. Unfortunately, they can be exacerbated further by the distancing mechanisms that too often are employed by patient and family to avoid or attenuate the potential loss (Lebow, 1976).

Sorrow is the sadness, pain, and anguish that family members feel in their anticipatory grief over losing a loved one. Many individuals fear that they will be overwhelmed by this mental suffering. Because of this, they may distance themselves emotionally or physically from the dying patient (only further contributing to her sorrow) or they may overcompensate with aggressive or demanding actions to hide their true vulnerability. At times an attitude of indifference is used to camouflage the feelings. Sorrow and accompanying depression are difficult emotions for all individuals to contend with, especially when they are concerned about staying in emotional control. Therefore, these points should be kept in mind when dealing with these issues:

• Identify, legitimize, and normalize these feelings for family members, which will help reduce their fear of such feelings. Help families find ways other than distancing to cope with their sorrow, pointing out how distancing affects the patient. They must conquer their fear if they are to make good use of the remaining time with the dying person.

• Redefine terms such as "lose control" or "break down." Legitimize the sadness, anger, depression, and other uncomfortable feelings that are involved and acknowledge their intensity, but reframe the experiencing of them more positively (e.g., use terms such as "intense feelings," "emotional release").

• Point out to family members that crying or being intensely upset does not mean that one is losing control. Indicate that these are normal reactions that need to be expressed.

• Help family members realize that there are different norms in this situation. To experience intense emotion is normal and therefore, by definition, does not equal a loss of control.

• Assist family members in recognizing that it is those emotions that go unexpressed that will prompt "loss of control" responses. Emotions that are processed, even though they hurt, will not by themselves cause loss of control.

• Convey to family members the value of expressing a little emotion at a time. Encourage them to deal with painful emotions as they occur so that they will not accumulate and then contribute to an emotional explosion at a later time.

• Point out that just because their present feelings are intense and different from those they are accustomed to does not mean that these feelings cannot be controlled.

• Help family members to recognize that facing painful emotions does not have to mean being overwhelmed by them. Express the expectation that they will be able to bear the emotions, painful though they may be.

• Suffering is pain without meaning. To keep family members from being overwhelmed by their suffering, help them place it in a context of meaning for them. Point out that it is because they love the dying person that they hurt so much. Utilize a religious/ philosophical framework if this is in accordance with the individuals' beliefs.

• Try to encourage expression of feelings in private places that are comfortable and not threatening. Do not try talking in the hospital corridor; find a quiet, more isolated place.

• Give family members control. Tell them that you will respect their limits but convey to them the expectation that the processing of these painful emotions must be completed. Let them take this step by step. Frequently when individuals feel that they have control of a painful process they will be able to push themselves further than any caregiver ever could.

• Call sorrow what it is—hard, painful, "rocks you down to your soul." This helps normalize the reaction to these feelings and attenuates concerns about overreacting to them or losing control.

• Convey calm and reassurance to individuals who are experiencing overwhelming emotion. Do not become disorganized in the face of their outbursts, although appropriate empathy when their emotion subsides can be very heartening to them.

• If necessary, recognize the limits of individuals' coping capacities and gently facilitate closure in situations where they are becoming overwhelmed. This does not mean "protecting" them or not helping them to face reality; rather, it means modifying the experience to maximize their ability to cope with it and not be so inundated that they give up. For example, provide family members with information a little at a time if you observe that they can only tolerate upsetting news in small bits and pieces. They still must be given all the information, but it can be delivered gradually to prevent them from being overwhelmed all at once.

• Predict that, although it is painful now, it will not always be. Do not be a Pollyanna, but let family members know that their present reactions are expected and normal and that there is hope of reaching a time when there will be less pain.

• Most importantly, as with the dying patient, focus on enabling family members to experience the joys and pleasures that are available despite continued loss. Premature sorrow can detach them from the dying patient too soon, when there are still many satisfactions to be gained from the relationship.

Everyone expects family members who are mourning the anticipated death of a loved one to feel sorrow and depression. Less appreciated is the anxiety that they often feel when beset by the uncertain, sometimes mutually exclusive demands of the terminal illness. Continual changes and losses occur unpredictably in the patient, family, and themselves as the illness continues. They are called upon to decathect, yet stay cathected at the same time. They must grieve for what they are losing and will soon not have, while still having some of it. In addition, there are other reasons for anxiety (McCollum & Schwartz, 1972):

- The frightening sense of helplessness aroused when a loved one is endangered and the outcome cannot be altered
- The flood of intense emotion experienced during the illness process and reactions to it
- The defenses used to cope with the terminal illness and gradual loss of the loved one
- The intense separation anxiety experienced because of anticipation of parting from the loved one
- The contemplation of one's own death

The patient and family must labor under incredible stress:

> There is apprehension about the uncertainties of what to expect, the prospect of final separation, the altered life style, and the ability to cope with the changing family roles. The unpredictability of what each day will bring in the way of physical deterioration of the patient, the indefiniteness of his life expectance, and the stress of making decisions about such matters as treatment and care compound the anxiety. (Lebow, 1976, p. 459)

The inability to control the situation produces intensified frustration. At times the anxiety and uncertainty of the situation breeds ambivalence and there develops an increase in negative feelings or a reactivation of longstanding unresolved issues within and between family members.

Anger and hostility are frequent concomitants of terminal illness for everyone involved. They are derived not only from the potential death, over which no one has control, but also from the feelings of impotence, frustration, and helplessness generated by the continuing process of loss (which in itself will always prompt such responses). In addition there is the emotional and economic drain that is a consequence of terminal illness, and its impact upon lifestyle and standard of living. It is increasingly problematic as the resource drains become more severe and, despite the sacrifices, the patient declines anyway. Another source of anger is the failure of the loved one to fulfill the dependency needs of family members, due to decreased ability to function. The shifting of roles and responsibilities to other family members in order to cope with the reduced functioning of the terminally ill patient can be annoying and dissatisfying as well. The patient herself may contribute to the aggression felt by family members, either through personality changes due to the illness or previous personality traits. If the illness is perceived as being self-inflicted or caused by neglect, aggression is even more likely. Disappointment over unfulfilled ambitions, unfinished business, and expectations that will never be realized also serves as a catalyst to the anger and frustration of family members. These reactions should be identified and labeled in order to allow them to be therapeutically dealt with and to prevent their being projected onto caregivers or contributing to further family disruption or problems in relating to the dying person. Family members often need permission to appropriately express their anger at the patient (when it is legitimate and not a displacement of other feelings) and to be reassured of its normalcy. They require someone to help them get and maintain the proper perspective on their aggression. Family conferences are helpful in this regard. In addition, family members should be encouraged to find physical outlets for the release of their emotions. Especially when family members are confined with one another under one roof, the potential for explosion is quite high. Anything that can reduce individuals' level of aggression in this very aggression-provoking situation will be therapeutic.

Guilt is a common reaction of family members that occurs when they feel they have fallen short of their self-image. In the process of losing a loved one through a terminal illness there are numerous precipitants of guilty feelings. Guilt may accompany the recognition of anger and other hostile feelings towards the dying patient. Frequently it develops from the interpersonal conflicts that often arise during the terminal illness, when frustration, anxiety, and irritation are so much a part of the experience. Guilt may be caused if the family member believes that he was responsible for the illness in any way (e.g., as in hereditary diseases or as a result of neglect). It is not uncommon for individuals to feel guilty because they have failed to protect their loved one from the illness or because they will survive when the loved one will die. Guilt can also be stimulated by the repugnance family members may feel when confronting the ravages of the illness (e.g., the scars, the medication side effects). Wishing the end would come, even if for the benefit of the loved one, brings its own guilty sense of betrayal. Even normal reactions to loss may prompt guilt feelings. For example, a family member may sense a feeling of relief that she is not the one who has to suffer the terminal illness and face approaching death, but may be guiltily uncomfortable with the recognition of this feeling. Also, if the family member is not constantly preoccupied with the terminal illness and finds some time to enjoy other aspects of life, guilt can develop because of the unrealistic expectation that if he really loved the dying person he would only focus on her. Concern for the patient may cause family members to overextend themselves in numerous ways. This can lead to resentment of the dying person and then to guilt for feeling this way. Such overconcern may also be seen in those who want to compensate for preexisting guilt over the relationship with the dying individual. When such behaviors are recognized, the caregiver should speak to the family member about the need for rest and replenishment of energy. It should be explained that continuous neglect of one's own needs ultimately leads to resentment. The guilt itself should be referred to obliquely, since direct confrontation about the "resentment-guilt-restitution" pattern rarely falls on willing ears (Verwoerdt, 1966). By sending out appropriate verbal feelers, the caregiver can observe the person's reactions and encourage the expression of negative feelings whenever it seems appropriate. If some troubled thoughts are expressed, the caregiver can assure the person that hostile wishes towards sick individuals are human and that such thoughts are acceptable providing they do not prompt hostile actions. The caregiver may want to point out the positive feelings that may have been observed in the relationship between the family member and the dying patient; or remind him that angry feelings can coexist with loving ones. A little education about the normality of ambivalence, especially in this situation, can be very therapeutic. It may also be important to convey to the family member that in times of stress people sometimes fixate on the negative aspects of a relationship, forgetting the positive ones. All of this will assist the person to better tolerate negative or ambivalent thoughts, allowing them to coincide with positive and constructive ones without fear. Unrealistic and irrational expectations of the self and the situation can be identified and more appropriate ones offered. The family member will then be able to care for the patient with more realistic self-expectations, and consequently less guilt and self-reproach for failure to meet unrealistically high standards. Further relief or prevention of guilt can be provided by enlisting the person's appropriate participation in the overall treatment program. This gives them the opportunity to make restitution for any acts of omission or commission in the past, and provides them with experiences that illustrate to themselves and others their concern for the patient.

In dealing with family reactions it is important to keep in mind the "multiplier effect," the fact that individual family members' emotional responses will directly influence those of the others in the system. Be aware of this tendency, which can be both beneficial or detrimental. Working with the family as a system should help prevent overlooking this critical fact. It is also important to remember that family members' needs and reactions will change over the course of the illness, just as those of the dying patient do. They must be continually reevaluated. Changes will occur as the result of adaptation, fluctuations in the illness, or other alterations in the family system as a whole.

One situation that probably will effect a change in the intensity and experience of emotional responses is "the Lazarus syndrome." Named for the biblical character who returned from the dead, this syndrome occurs when the patient appears ready to die and family members prepare for the death, but the patient then experiences a remission. The family members must readjust themselves to the continued existence of the individual they had been prepared to lose permanently, and it is often difficult for them to be thankful for such a reprieve. They may have been as psychologically prepared as possible and would have wanted the painful loss to have occurred so that they could finally get it over with. Now the painful inevitability has been postponed and they still have to look forward to it happening. They have had to deal with all the suffering of the dying scene, and now they will have to go through it all again. Adding to this frustration is the fact that usually, although the patient still survives, she is not given a respite from her suffering and the family is still expected to expend its depleted emotional and financial resources. In many instances, when families have to endure the numerous relapses and remissions of a chronically ill patient, they end up detaching themselves from the dying patient. For them it is too painful to lose and regain the loved one repeatedly. This, coupled with anticipatory grief that has been too effective, may result in premature detachment from the dying patient while she is still alive.

The issue of decathexis and reinvestment is a delicate one for families of the chronically ill. It is not uncommon for some family members to wish that their loved one would die in order to terminate the up-and-down, unpredictable nature of the experience. In fact, many individuals get angry at the patient for not dying when she is supposed to and ending the anxiety and painful process of waiting. It is critical to recognize that this does not constitute a lack of love on the part of the family member. Rather, it reflects the intense depletion of that person's resources due to coping with the anxiety, uncertainty, and uncontrollability of the dying of a loved one.

As research has shown (Rando, 1983; Sanders, 1982-83), there appears to be an optimum length of time and amount of anticipatory grief in a terminal illness. If there is too little or too much of either, family members are less prepared for the death and evidence poorer adjustment afterward. Caregivers must understand the tremendous pressure and demands placed upon the families of terminally ill patients when these illnesses continue for too long or have courses that present the family members with the overwhelming task of facing the imminent death of their loved one many times over. It may be easy to criticize the reactions of family members who are exhausted and depleted after such experiences; but exquisite sensitivity to the dying person is a luxury that only those who are not completely drained and fatigued can afford.

A point must be made regarding how family members cope with the last days of the dying patient's life. As the illness winds on to its logical conclusion, they are put in what is sometimes a particularly pressured situation. The death has not yet occurred so, by definition, there still is hope. However, the person is deteriorating and there may be pressure on family members to experience as much as possible with the patient and/or try to change what they know in their hearts really cannot be changed. It is similar to the experience of watching the last few grains of sand slide through an hourglass. There is still some time remaining, yet it is going and nothing can stop it. Should they try for whatever can be possible in the few dwindling moments that remain, even if these are extremely painful because of the circumstances of deterioration, loss, and imminent death? Or should an eye be kept towards the future when the long wait will be over and at least "it" will have happened? Many times family members are greatly pressured by not knowing which perspective to take and feel riddled with guilt for putting anything, even their own needs, in front of their being with the dying person. There may be a rush to do as much as possible with the person in the time remaining. The intensity of trying to make all the last times memorable and meaningful can be an overwhelming burden; and, as if to add more fuel to the fire, family members know that at the time of the death the patient's troubles will end, but not those of the family. Caught between holding on and letting go, between experiencing and remembering, between pushing for as much meaning as possible in the time that is left and allowing nature to take its course, family members must make decisions that will profoundly affect them for the rest of their lives.

Finally, as the patient nears death, the family must give her permission to die. Despite their grief and pain, family members must convey to the dying patient that it is acceptable for her to go, and must refrain from attempting to bind her here on earth through guilt, responsibility, or unfinished business. This does not mean that the family is unmoved that the patient is dying; far from it. It signifies that, despite their wishes to the contrary, they love the patient enough to recognize that her death is natural and inevitable and do not act in ways that will meet their needs at the expense of the dying patient's need to let go. (See "Avoidance of Withdrawal From the Patient" in Chapter 11 for more on giving permission to die.)

FAMILY ASSESSMENT

To help the families of dying patients, we need to know what characteristics to assess and which ones are useful in coping with the illness and subsequent death.

Variables to Be Assessed

In order to develop effective interventions, a complete psychosocial assessment of each particular family must be made. The more specific the information gained, the more applicable and effective the interventions will be.

Since each family member profoundly affects the whole family system, it is important that we understand family members as well as possible. Knowledge of the following variables for each family member is critical in designing appropriate interventions:

- Personality
- Sex
- Age
- Coping styles and abilities
- Religion/philosophy of life
- Social, cultural, and ethnic background
- Previous experiences with loss and death
- Maturity
- Characteristics of relationship with dying person
- Amount of unfinished business with dying person
- Intelligence
- Mental health
- Lifestyle
- Fulfillments in life
- Timeliness of the death
- Specific fears about dying and death
- Previous experiences with and personal expectations about illness and death
- Knowledge of illness
- Personal meaning of specific illness

In addition to assessing individual members, we must assess the family as a system. Remembering that the whole is more than the sum of its parts, we must analyze variables describing the family constellation, its systematic functioning, and the impact of the dying patient and his terminal illness on the family.

FAMILY CONSTELLATION
- Makeup of family
- Developmental stage of family
- Subsystems (dyads, triangles, coalitions) within family
- Specific roles of family members and appropriateness of roles

CHARACTERISTICS OF FAMILY SYSTEM
- Degree of family flexibility/rigidity
- Communication style in family
- Family rules, norms, and expectations
- Family values and beliefs
- Quality of emotional relationships among family members

- Dependence, interdependence, and individual freedom of each family member
- Degree of enmeshment/disengagement of family
- Established patterns of transaction among members
- Socialization patterns of members in extrafamilial interactions
- Strengths and vulnerabilities of family
- Family leadership style and decision-making process
- Habitual methods used to resolve problems and conflicts or overcome crises
- Disciplinary patterns
- Family resources
- Cultural, religious/philosophical, and socioeconomic disposition of family
- Past experiences with illness or death
- Number, type, and effectiveness of family support systems
- Current problems identified by family
- Quality of communication with caregivers
- Anticipated immediate and long-range needs of family

THE DYING PATIENT AND THE ILLNESS

- Nature of patient's illness (death trajectory, problems of particular illness, treatment, amount of pain, degree of deterioration, rate of progression)
- Time passed since diagnosis
- Current family awareness of and understanding about illness and its implications
- Family members' specific feelings about particular illness
- Degree of strain illness puts on family system
- Number and type of patient's roles in family
- Degree of patient's knowledge of illness and its implications
- Patient's responses to illness
- Patient's subjective experience of illness (losses, pain, deterioration)
- Patient's acceptance/rejection of sick role
- Patient's striving for dependence/independence
- Patient's feelings and fears about illness
- Patient's comfort in expressing thoughts and feelings and extent of that expression
- Family's degree of participation in patient's care
- Location of patient (home, hospital, nursing home)
- Family members' fears and current emotional state pertaining to potential loss of patient
- Extent and quality of communication about illness
- Relationship of each family member with patient since diagnosis
- Family rules, norms, values, styles, and past experiences that

might inhibit grief or interfere with therapeutic relationship with dying patient

As in evaluating and planning for the treatment of the dying individual, the patient's family must be worked with at their current level of functioning. While caregivers may entertain differing notions as to how families should behave, and what types of rules and regulations they should live by, these personal preferences must be put aside in favor of the current status and functioning of the family as assessed when determining how to best intervene. The values, beliefs, norms, and priorities of the family must be appreciated if there is to be successful intervention in that system. When a family member is dying, family adaptation is usually highly related to previous familial adaptive capacity. For example, if family members have always been open and honest in communicating with one another, they probably will continue to be so during the crisis of the terminal illness of one of the family's members, although they will feel a strain. Conversely, families that have had chronic problems with disruptive communication and poor role assignments, and with inflexible boundaries and negative patterns of interaction, will tend to behave similarly when called upon to manage the catastrophe of terminal illness. We must recognize that we cannot radically change the long-standing patterns of the family in order to provide what we believe to be the best possible circumstances for the dying patient. For example, we might want to facilitate an appropriate death for the patient by bringing the family together to be warm and supportive of him; however, if this is not the style of the family it will be an inappropriate and unfair expectation to place upon them and will probably be doomed to failure from the start. Interventions, to be effective, must fit within the existing framework of the patient-family unit. Gross changes in behavior and patterns of relating and communicating rarely occur simply because one family member is dying, for these processes are usually so ingrained that they are highly resistant to change. This does not mean that some positive growth cannot be fostered, but we must maintain realistic expectations that are consistent with the family system as it exists. Interventions must be geared specifically to its unique needs and abilities.

Variables Associated With Positive Family Adjustment

Prior to deciding upon treatment goals and interventions, it is necessary to know which variables are associated with positive family adjustment. Vollman et al. (1971) believe that appropriate role assignment allows better functioning after the death of the terminally ill patient:

The resumption of adaptive functioning, following a death, is facilitated in a family where vital roles and functions have been apportioned among members in a just and equitable manner for optimal comfort and satisfaction in their performance. This type of apportionment occurs when roles are assumed according to individual need, ability, and potential. In such a case, role assumption is usually explicit and well understood by all family members. When a member of this type of family dies, the critical period of reorganization is not likely to be experienced as a crisis because the family already had a built-in process which allows it to reallocate the role functions of the decedent with minimal difficulty. (p. 104)

Cohen and Cohen (1981) describe what constitutes adaptive and maladaptive role changes. Since role changes are a necessary part of the readjustment process after the death of a family member, their findings are of interest here:

Adaptive role changes are alterations which are based on a realistic understanding of present and future realities, are fully supported by all family members, and are likely to have a positive effect on an individual's intra- and extrafamilial adjustment. Maladaptive role changes foster a denial of reality, placing an undue amount of stress on one or all of the family members. (p.182)

In addition to appropriate and adaptive role reassignment, there are several other variables characterizing the family that copes more effectively with the terminal illness of one of its members: open, direct communication in an open awareness context; appropriate family participation in the care of the dying patient; open emotional expression; flexibility in family rule patterns; awareness and empathy in relationships; appropriate and flexible boundaries; and flexibility in relationships. Characteristics found to be descriptive of the "energized family," the family that was most effective in protecting its members' health, include varied contacts with groups and organizations in the community in an active attempt to cope and master their lives; fluid internal organization, including flexible role relationships (i.e., sharing tasks such as housecleaning or caring for the ill); shared power, with each family member participating in decisions that affect him; and a high degree of autonomy within the family, with relationships among members that support personal growth (Pratt, 1976).

Four adaptational responses of family members of terminally ill patients have been described by McCollum and Schwartz (1972): information seeking, invoking emotional support, partialization or compartmentalization, and rehearsing death. In the first response, information seeking, three types of information are sought. Families want to know facts about the illness, the status of the patient vis-á-vis the illness, and the "search for meaning" to comprehend the reasons for this illness. Appropriate information seeking is a healthy process that, when guided correctly, can assist families and patients to come to grips with the illness, the treatment process, and their own feelings. The second type of adaptive behavior involves invoking emotional support. This can "reduce feelings of loneliness, temporarily satisfy heightened dependency needs, and afford some gratification experiences" (McCollum & Schwartz, 1972, p. 33). A third adaptive behavior, partialization, is the process of breaking down the mourning experience into component parts that can be assimilated and mastered in the present. It is a way of saying that families learn to take 1 day at a time, which allows them to obtain the most they can from life, especially when there is considerable uncertainty about the future of the patient (Adams, 1979). Finally, there is the rehearsal of death, a process that is part of the anticipatory grief and serves as a preparation for the patient's eventual death. If verbalization of fears, fantasies, and expectations about the death can be encouraged, distorted expectations can be corrected and painful emotions can be reduced. Caregivers can ascertain family members' concerns and respond to them, facilitating better coping and adjustment.

FAMILY TREATMENT INTERVENTIONS

After completing the assessment of the family, we have the information necessary to design appropriate interventions for before, during, and after the death.

Interventions Prior to the Death

There are several goals of intervention prior to the death of the loved one:

> Goals for families wherein a member is dying may be . . . devoted to support of adaptive functioning . . . The supports may be directed toward greater sharing and understanding: toward improving quality of communication and flexibility in family rule patterns, arousing awareness and empathy in relational conflicts, reducing patient-family alienation, and dealing with the pain and grief of feelings stirred-up around pending loss and abandonment. This is a time when the mourning process can begin for the family. The processes of grief, anger, remembering, longing, and identification can be worked with, in preparation for the final abandonment and decathexis of the patient that is required (Furman, 1974). (Orcutt, 1977, p. 25)

Three broad areas of intervention at this time are communication and awareness contexts; the anticipatory grief and unfinished business of the family; and clinical therapy intervention and clinical education and advocacy.

The key to family support and intervention is the communication process. Flexible, open communication is the hallmark of healthy families, while distorted, unclear, and disqualifying messages are associated with family disturbance. Variables such as family rules and decision-making processes, as well as the relative openness or closure of the family system, both affect and are revealed through communication processes. When a terminal illness afflicts a family member, patterns of communication may be strained by both the emotional content and the coping mechanisms that are employed by the family to deal with the impending loss. Consequently, the communication patterns in the family may be an indicator of how well the family is handling the loss.

In addition to verbal communication, nonverbal communication must be addressed. Distancing from the dying patient and changing the patterns of relating to him are obvious ways of communicating discomfort with the situation, if previous communication patterns were more open and flexible. Indeed, research has indicated that one of the most frequently reported problems for cancer patients is the absence of open communication within the family. It is mentioned as often as physical discomfort and more frequently than difficulties with medications or overall treatment (Gordon, Feidenberg, Diller, Rothman, Wolf, Ruckdeschel-Hibbard, Ezrachi, & Gerstman, Note 20). Many times, even in families with open communication patterns, the desire to protect the dying patient or other family members from the pain of the situation eventually restricts communication. The withholding of information results in closed awareness contexts, and the concealment of emotions often disrupts relationships and causes emotions to explode later on.

As discussed in an earlier chapter, Glaser and Strauss (1965) identified four types of awarenesses that can exist between dying patient and caregivers. These are applicable to dying patient and family interactions as well. In a closed awareness context the family is aware of the patient's condition, but attempts to keep this information from the patient. A suspicion awareness context occurs when the family knows the truth and the patient suspects that he is dying. He simultaneously wants to discover and avoid the truth. A mutual pretense awareness is one in which family and patient are aware of the illness and its implications, but pretend they are not. All three of these awareness contexts rob the dying individual of the intimacy of genuine communication. There must be a concealment of the truth, which precludes the closeness or further communication so desperately needed by the patient. Consequently, the patient will suffer additional losses as his relationships are compromised. An open awareness context is the optimal one, in which there is shared knowledge, information, and communication about the patient's dying.

As noted previously, while we might like to foster an open awareness context for all families in which they could share feelings, give and receive clear and congruent messages, and have flexible interactions with each other, many families have never had open and fluid relational patterns. Consequently, to expect them to communicate in an open and honest way about their feelings, fears, and thoughts during such an anxiety-provoking and stressful time is totally inappropriate. In such cases, we must strive to promote whatever amount of open communication the family system can tolerate. Orcutt (1977) offers a way to improve family communication through increased understanding of each other's feelings and motivations, creating "relational awareness with empathy":

> In this procedure the [caregiver] ... encourages the member's recollection and expression of feeling around a difficult life experience(s) that relates to the current family distress. The listening family members tend to be affectively moved as they grasp an awareness of the meaning and pain of these experiences and how they relate to a piece of current behavior. With this awareness, empathy and warm affect tend to flow, and the relationship begins to take on a different meaning. The spouse who has seen his partner as rejecting and uncaring can link these reactions to an earlier hurt or bitter experience rather than interpret them as directed solely to himself. He also achieves some awareness of how his own behavior can set off these reactions to the earlier hurt. Actually the family or the marital dyad perceives the reality more correctly and with empathy. This procedure can be useful to the family, particularly when there has been conflict or bitterness before the terminal illness. (p. 30)

This is very similar to Paul's (1969) building empathy through conjoint family therapy. In this strategy he attempts to stimulate unresolved grief and encourage the expression of intense feelings in one marital partner. He then solicits the feelings stimulated in the other marital partner by the expressed grief. Paul sees his ability to empathize with the individual expressing intense inner feelings about losses as a critical factor in allowing the spouse to react empathetically. He focuses on generating a reciprocating-empathic responsiveness in the couple. Our role with families of the terminally ill would be to stimulate this type of empathy so unexpressed feelings could be expressed and families could have the opportunity not only to finish unfinished business and say their good-byes, but also to relate to one another during the living-dying interval without inhibition due to unexpressed communication.

The second area of intervention is stimulating appropriate

amounts of anticipatory grief among family members and helping them finish unfinished business with the dying patient, while promoting whatever ongoing involvement remains possible. These processes, while seemingly in opposition, do not necessarily have to be so. Indeed, it is only by interacting with the dying patient that family members will be able to finish unfinished business, a crucial accompaniment to anticipatory grief. Conversely, only by preparing for the ultimate loss of the loved one will they become aware of unfinished business. In this regard anticipatory grief facilitates the identification of unfinished business and the development of ways to achieve closure. Although anticipatory grief does entail starting to decathect from the dying patient, it does not mean that he has to be abandoned. Some individuals actually feel that the terminal illness can intensify closeness between the patient and loved ones (Parkes & Weiss, 1983). Intervention should be guided by the principle of encouraging the anticipatory grief process and supplanting responses that would inhibit it. Those who cannot face the pain of confronting current and potential grief and trying to complete unfinished business will attempt to avoid dealing with their anticipatory grief or with the dying patient himself. Such individuals may have to be confronted in cases where time is limited and unfinished business will complicate their grief after the death. In some instances we may need to actually prompt family members to talk with the dying patient by saying such things as "You only have a limited amount of time left. Make sure that you say the things you need to so you won't feel guilty later on." At such times it is permissible to be more directive than normal with family members. While their desires must be respected, the deleterious consequences of leaving unfinished business undone must definitely be pointed out to them.

The third area of intervention involves clinical therapy interventions and clinical education and advocacy. It is assumed that the person intervening will possess the requisite knowledge on the following topics: the anticipatory grief process; the experience of the dying patient; family systems theory; children's reactions to death; and the problems accompanying illnesses in general and the patient's illness in particular. With this information as a background, the following clinical intervention recommendations are made:

• Because of the complexity of the family system, make sure that a comprehensive psychosocial assessment is conducted prior to undertaking work with the family and patient. Do not just ask questions. Listen to family members and find out what they know, imagine, fear, and feel. When communicating, always check to determine what was actually understood by them.

• Recognizing the properties of the family as a system, meet with the entire family together whenever possible.

- Try to establish a personal relationship with each family member when and if possible.
- Remember to always include the children. Educate the adults on how to most therapeutically deal with the children.
- Involve the whole family in the care and treatment of the dying patient, including children and others who are important to the patient. This will decrease their anxiety and render a sense of control, participation, and support; allow for atonement for past guilt; provide an expression of their sentiments; and help them finish unfinished business and appropriately grieve in anticipation of the death. Help them deal with their ambivalent feelings about being involved with illness and possibly performing unpleasant medical or palliative tasks such as suctioning or dressing a sore. When family members are not included in the planning of patient care, that care frequently fails.
- Recognize the importance to the dying patient of those who may not be related by blood. Friends and co-workers may be just as significant as relatives. Have the patient and family identify those individuals who are meaningful to them, and involve those individuals in the patient's care.
- At times there may be people important to the dying patient who are socially unacceptable. Be prepared to confront the delicate situation of finding ways for patients to spend time with illicit lovers or friends who are criminals, if these people are significant to them. Your personal and social value judgments should not interfere with your support of the dying patient.
- Within their limits, help the family to appropriately express their anticipatory grief, develop or maintain open communication, identify and finish unfinished business, and avoid distancing themselves from the patient.
- Recognize the individual strengths and weaknesses of family members and the family system as a whole. Capitalize on strengths and offer support in areas of weakness.
- Realizing the differences in families, be realistic about what you can expect, given each family's psychosocial history. Families may not meet your expectations; therefore, you must alter your treatment goals accordingly.
- Help the family identify and cope with the vicissitudes and demands of the living-dying interval. Educate them about its psychosocial and medical aspects as they relate to both the patient and themselves.
- Interpret the dying patient's responses for the family and educate them about his feelings. Help them understand what the dying patients experience—the intense anticipatory grief in which they are losing everything they have ever known, their specific fears, the emotional reactions and coping mechanisms stimulated by thinking about the oncoming death, the struggles with dependency

and independence. The family should come to appreciate the patient's fears of dying in pain and dying alone, and do what they can to assuage them. Explain to them the concept of social death and work with them to avoid its occurrence. Show them how to support the patient's self-esteem and sense of control. Give them guidance in helping the dying patient achieve an appropriate death.

• Support the patient and family in continuing normal functioning for as long as possible. Encourage the patient's continued participation in family matters and decision making as much as possible for as long as possible.

• While planning for certain events is therapeutic, help families see that they need to take the perspective of confronting a single day at a time.

• Help the family to see that they will not lose emotional control if they acknowledge and express their emotions. They need to understand that it is only those emotions that are not addressed that will cause them to lose control.

• Evaluate the expectations of the family with regard to each other, the dying patient, and the illness and death. Normalize the usual, but uncomfortable, feelings of guilt, resentment, and anger that occur when a family member is terminally ill, especially when many of the family's resources are being expended on him. Legitimize these feelings and point out that they do not supplant the more positive and affectionate ones.

• Assist the family not only in addressing painful feelings such as grief, anger, guilt, and disappointment, but also positive feelings such as affection, the desire for identification, and plans for remembering the dying patient.

• Educate the family members in how family systems function and adapt to change. Predict problems and assist the family in the stressful process of role reorganization and responsibility redistribution. Help them make sure that these new role assignments are fair, equitable, and appropriate to given individuals. Discourage scapegoating. Also identify future changes that will be necessary and work with the family to plan for them.

• Assist families in understanding that not only are they grieving for the dying patient, but also for themselves and the family as a whole. Facilitate grief work in these areas as well.

• Help the family cope with the competing tasks of remaining involved with the dying patient while simultaneously starting to decathect from him. Assist them in balancing appropriate anticipatory grief with enjoyment of the remaining satisfactions still available to them with the patient.

• Advise family members to prepare for the practical realities of the illness and the death. At times they may feel guilty about it because they feel that considering practical matters at this time, especially those involving money, is too mercenary or reflects a lack of sensitivity. However, dying patients are very concerned about practical matters and do not want their loved ones to be left behind without adequate resources. Discussing with the family plans for the time when the illness becomes more debilitating, preferences for burial, or future financial arrangements are ways that the dying patient can assert control and ensure that his preferences are honored. It also is a way that his anxiety about survivors can be minimized. (See "Assistance With the Practical Considerations of Dying" in Chapter 11 for more on this topic.)

• Encourage family members to let the dying patient know how he will be remembered. When said in the context of the meaningfulness of the relationship and the love that the family member will always have for him, it can be very comforting for the dying patient to hear "Every time I watch *Casablanca* I'll remember you" or "Whenever I see a sunset like this one I'll think of the times we've shared watching them." It is a way of transcending death.

• Intervene to reduce later problems. Primary prevention is a critical part of the caregiver's role. Work to prevent family fragmentation and disorganization during the illness and after the patient's death.

• Give family members permission and encouragement to take time out to replenish themselves and to meet the other ongoing needs of family members.

• Help the family maintain realistic hope. Even though they are greatly burdened, they can live with the illness and have some good times remaining. Encourage them to enjoy these remaining times as much as possible without constantly reflecting on what will be lost.

• Recognize that the time immediately after diagnosis is a critical period. Research has indicated that this is the most difficult time of the entire terminal illness experience for a majority of people. Be aware of the shock, despair, resentment, anxiety, and depression such news brings and remember that the reactions to it have not been processed, dealt with, or mellowed by the passage of time. Facilitate appropriate questioning, expression of feeling, and compliance with medical advice. While families understandably may try to distance themselves from the pain of loss through activities that numb their feelings or let them avoid acknowledging the illness, these activities must not be allowed to continue if they interfere with requisite family tasks, persist too long, or hamper medical treatment.

• Predict patient relapses and support the family when they occur. Normalize family members' frustration, anger, and helplessness, sometimes even their desire for the patient to die in order to end the painful process of dying.

• Alleviate the family's suffering by placing it in a context of meaning. Help them cope with their intense feelings of sorrow. (See "Emotional Responses of the Family" in this chapter for relevant interventions.)

• Explain to family members that the continued stress of the terminal illness will deplete their usual coping mechanisms. They can expect anxiety and other indications of the stress and anticipatory grief they are experiencing to show up in other areas of their lives (e.g., at work, in relationships with friends).

• Refer families to appropriate support groups as needed. There are now numerous national and local groups to assist families in coping with the stress of a terminally ill member, including Make Today Count, Can Surmount, and Candlelighters. Check with the national organization pertaining to the patient's disease (e.g., the American Cancer Society, the American Heart Association) for a listing of psychosocial support services, and seek out local hospital, organizational, or church-based groups that serve the same purpose.

• Encourage patient and family discussion about preferences for type and location of death.

Another form of intervention is clinical education and advocacy. This means providing practical information in such a way that it helps individuals cope. It supports strengths and offers alternatives for deficient skills and weaknesses.

• Teach family members about the illness and the medical treatment, and give them information pertinent to the institutions with which they must deal. Help them identify resources for answering questions that may arise in the future.

• Help the family identify, locate, and utilize material, financial, and social assistance. Work the family into existing support systems and explore all avenues of supportive assistance available to them (e.g., assistance from the American Cancer Society for equipment loans, transportation, and surgical dressings; assistance from church and community organizations for volunteer visitors and meal preparation).

• Assist the family in deciding how to explain the illness and its implications to others. Practice with them, if necessary, to make sure they are able to disseminate the requisite information. Educate them about how to communicate with children.

• Explain to the family what can be expected at the time of death and afterward. It will be especially important to dispel any unrealistic expectations they may have. Provide them with appropriate normative data.

• Discuss options with the family, encourage mutual discussion, and discourage unilateral decision-making.

• Refer those family members who evidence pathological responses to the illness to appropriate mental health resources.

• Recognize that dealing with families and patients in these crisis situations will cause confrontation with your own mortality and place you in situations where your own unresolved family issues may arise.

Interventions at the Time of the Death

The following suggestions are made for supporting the family at the time of the death of their loved one.

• Whenever possible, and to whatever extent is desirable, allow the family to be present at the time of death. For many it is critically important that they be in attendance. Individuals who have been keeping a vigil, and then are not present at the actual moment of death, often feel very guilty about this afterwards.

• Help the family to see that the withdrawal and detachment that often occurs immediately prior to the death of a terminally ill patient is not a rejection of them but a necessary part of the dying process. (See "Acceptance, Withdrawal and Detachment, and Hope" in Chapter 11 for more on this topic.) At this point they need to be supported, as they may feel acutely abandoned and need to understand that this is a normal part of the experience.

• Many times family members are frightened of what the death will be like, even if they have spent long months taking care of the terminally ill individual. At times they may be conflicted about what to do at the very end. This can occur when the dying patient appears to have an increase in pain and there is a decision to be made about abandoning previous noninvasive palliative approaches for acute care practices, or about attempting hospitalization if the patient is at home. The family can be helped at this time by discussion of what the patient would want. Many times, if they can talk over their concerns with a well-informed caregiver, the last-ditch effort to "rescue" their loved one can be seen as a normal response, but one that does not necessarily have to be carried out, since it would not reflect the wishes of the patient and family to achieve a natural death. By the same token, do not convey the expectation that the patient must die at home. Some families cannot deal with this and/ or need to hospitalize the patient at the end in order to feel that they have done all they could. Recognize that there is a big difference between planning to have a loved one die at home and actually being able to tolerate its occurrence, especially if caregivers are absent.

• Assure families that their presence is still important to the patient as he approaches the point of death. While it most probably is comforting to the patient to know that loved ones are in attendance at this point, decathexis may have been occurring and possibly will have limited the interactions between patient and family. Those who are the closest to the patient and who feel a desire to do so should be encouraged to be present at the death, despite a lack of responsiveness on the part of the patient. Even in times of coma, hearing is believed to be the last sense to deteriorate. Thus, although dying individuals may not respond, they may be comforted by the awareness that their loved ones are still present.

• Allow the family adequate time to be alone with the body, touch the body, and talk to it after death. Do not rush this time that they have with the corpse. This is a crucial part of the bereavement process during which the realization of the death can be made clearer. Encourage verbalization of feelings at this time.

• Occasionally individuals become frightened by the presence of the dead body. For some this will be frightening even though moments before it was the body of their loved one. In most cases this will not happen and individuals will relate to the corpse with great affection. However, in those cases where there is a fear because of the death, your supportive presence can be very helpful.

• Support the family (if you have not already done so) in undertaking and arranging those funerary and memorial rituals that would be the most meaningful to them in celebrating the life of their loved one and aiding their grief work.

• Encourage healthy expressions of grief.

• Assist families in the painful task of notifying appropriate medical and legal officials about the death.

• Refer grievers to support groups if these appear to be relevant and possibly helpful to them. If they seem to need more in-depth psychiatric intervention, refer them to appropriate mental health personnel.

Interventions After the Death

There is a series of tasks that must be completed following the death of a family member: allowing mourning to occur; relinquishing the memory of the deceased; realigning intrafamilial roles; and realigning extrafamilial roles (Goldberg, 1973). Permitting family members to mourn together in effect says "We are all hurting. Let us suffer our pain together" (Eliot, 1932). It only makes sense that individuals within the system are best able to understand the loss that other family members are experiencing, and also are able to stimulate those memories and review processes that will give rise to the necessary decathexis and expression of emotion. Relinquishing the memory of the deceased in a family is a process similar to individual decathexis. Goldberg (1973) offers this description of the criteria for successful completion of this task:

This task requires time. It is accomplished when the family, respecting and cherishing the memory of the departed, is able to make decisions based on what will best meet its present needs without continually invoking what the departed might have said or done. This task is also facilitated by the family's dealing successfully with its other tasks. (p. 401)

The realignment of intrafamilial roles springs up as a consequence of the roles that have been left vacant by the death of the loved one. The family must alter its relationships so that it can redistribute family responsibilities and needs. It seeks to return to a homeostatic balance. Realignment of extrafamilial roles involves changing relationships with those organizations and institutions that comprise the social system of the family. These also require realignment if a family member's status in the organization or institution changes as a consequence of the death. For example, after the death of his father, a son who had been on a father-son baseball team would either continue in his present activities with a substitute, perhaps his uncle, or withdraw from the organization or group and participate in something else more suited to his new status, such as a soccer team.

The family may have any of four possible responses to the demand for role changes caused by the death of a family member (Goldberg, 1973). One response is role reorganization. The degree of role reorganization that will be required is dependent upon the number and type of roles that had been held by the individual who died (Vollman et al., 1971). As noted previously from this study, families with good communication systems and prior equitable role allocation tend to be those who respond most adaptively after the crisis of death. The second response is increased solidarity in the family. It may result from the tendency for individuals to unite when in trouble and the need for family members to have emotional support at a crucial time. If the member who died had caused conflict in the family, his absence might also promote solidarity. Solidarity presupposes consensus regarding role reorganization. Family members must come to some agreement as to what roles should be filled and who should fill them; otherwise, roles are left unfulfilled, overlap, or conflict.

There may be several reasons for conflict: continuation of conflict regarding role definition prior to the death of the member, several persons able and willing to assume the same role, and lack of clarity as to what the role entails. Another possibility. . . is that the member who died fulfilled a socio-emotional role which kept hostilities and conflict dormant or at least under control. What was latent now becomes active. This reaction is seen in the family in which a child served to bind the parents into a tenuous relation-

ship; with the child's death, difficulties previously held in check
arise, and the spouses must confront a serious marital conflict.
(Goldberg, 1973, p. 403)

The third response to death is object replacement. This occurs
when partners remarry or when parents decide to have another
child to replace the deceased child. There are severe problems
inherent in forcing a new child to live in the image of the deceased
one (Cain & Cain, 1964). (See "Parenting of Remaining Children"
in Chapter 6 for more on this topic.) The final response is scapegoating. This is an unhealthy reaction in which the family seeks
to displace its guilt and anger, or unresolved issues over the death,
by creating the role of a scapegoat and placing a family member
in this role.
    After the death of the patient the normal interventions for
grievers described earlier in this book should be made. However,
in viewing the family as a system, and one whose members may
have been known to the caregiver prior to the death, the following
additional recommendations are made:
    • Any interaction between the family and yourself following
the death should support the appropriate addressing of grief work.
    • The family should be helped to mourn as a system, not just
a collection of individual mourners. There must be appropriate
grieving and decathexis for the entire family. Both individual members and the family as a whole must develop a new relationship
with the deceased and new identities for themselves. Additionally,
intrafamilial and extrafamilial role reorganizations must take
place. Make sure that the new role reassignments are appropriate
to the individuals involved and to the family as a system. Help the
family achieve a new functional balance.
    • If there has been a previous relationship, make follow-up
contacts with the family through phone calls, visits, or letters. It
is often very helpful to attend the funerary rituals, since it indicates
to the family that their loved one was more than just a case to you.
This can also be very helpful when processing your own feelings
and issues around loss.
    • Later on in grief, contact family members with an anniver-
sary note or call, or some indication that you appreciate that certain times may be difficult and foster brief upsurges of grief in the
family when the death of the loved one is recalled.
    • The family needs to know that, while their closeness may be
supportive in their grief, it can also make them vulnerable to dis-
placing blame, anger, and other hostile feelings onto one another.
Family members may ask one another unanswerable questions
about the death or place irrational demands on each other. There
must be a clear recognition of each other's differences in grieving

styles and these must be respected and accommodated. Family members may also painfully remind one another of the deceased by their presence. (See "Grief After the Death of a Child" in Chapter 6 for more on this topic.)

• Scapegoating should not be allowed to occur. Make sure family members do not align against the surviving member who had either the most closeness or difficulty with the deceased as a way of acting-out their feelings of grief.

CHAPTER 13

The Dying Child

The terminal illness of any loved one is a painful experience for all involved. The demands it makes and the changes it engenders are enormous. Witnessing the suffering of someone close is an arduous task that confronts people with the very meaning of life and death. When the dying loved one is a child, there is a host of additional factors that make the task even harder.

SOCIETAL REACTIONS
TO THE DEATH OF A CHILD

The death of a child causes immense social concern. For several reasons the death of a young child seems much worse than the death of an older person:

> The life of a child has great social value. He has not had a chance to live, and we feel he is entitled to this. Also, his general helplessness moves us . . . . Another factor is that we do not attribute the death of a child to "his own fault," to inevitability, or to a style of living of which we disapprove . . . . The child who dies in contemporary American society is not considered mature enough to be responsible for behavior leading to his death, and, unlike the elderly man, he cannot be considered to have died inevitably. (Kalish, 1969, p. 102)

Glaser and Strauss (1964) also believe that the death of a child is considered a greater loss because the child has not had the opportunity to live a full life as compared to the adult or aged individual. They indicate that such an evaluation may be responsible for the better quality of care and personal treatment given to children by health care personnel. However, in much of the thanatological literature the pediatric ward is cited as an example of the ultimate situation of frustration, anguish, and personal/professional stress for the caregiver. A dying child causes the greatest anguish for all involved.

Added to the child's plight is the agony of the parents, whose very roles of protecting and nurturing their child are usurped by an illness over which they have no control. They also need a caregiver's help to handle their feelings of helplessness, hopelessness, anger, frustration, and guilt.

Because of parents' needs, and the dependent status of the child, the patient and family must be treated as a complete unit. This multiplies the demands on the caregiver, as more people must be cared for when working with dying children.

Proof of society's difficulty in facing the death of children is the fact that there are relatively few pediatric hospices, despite the recent proliferation of hospices for adults. Even though hospices are as appropriate for children as they are for adults, the needs of terminally ill children and their families are not currently being met as well as they could be (Wilson, 1982).

THE CHANGING REALITY OF CHILDHOOD TERMINAL ILLNESS

Reflecting the medical experience of the time, literature in the 1950s and 60s devoted to the dying child and his family focused on helping the patient and family to prepare for what was an inevitable death. The key issues were the extent of the child's understanding and conceptualization of death. Under the erroneous assumption that children did not have an adult concept of death, theorists reasoned that children were not afraid of it. Discussion centered on whether or not to inform the child and how protective to be. Family members were assisted in coping with the numerous initial reactions to the diagnosis and in dealing with the painful experience of anticipatory grief. As recently as the late 60s and 70s, research questions were geared towards systematically ascertaining what children knew about their illness and possible death (Spinetta, 1981a).

However, as progress in medicine and research has resulted in increased chances of survival for the child patient, diagnoses of some serious illnesses are no longer inevitable death sentences. For example, the child with cancer now has an increased chance of long-term survival. This has created new issues in pediatric oncology for both the children, their families, and their caregivers. Today cancer can be viewed as a chronic, life-threatening illness with an uncertain outcome. The illness may extend over many years, if there is not an actual cure. Consequently, treatment, accompanied by remissions and relapses, becomes a way of life for an extended amount of time. This elongates the period of uncertainty and threat of death with which children and their families have to contend. The resulting emotional, social, and practical problems may become more troublesome and incapacitating than the illness itself.

Previously children did not survive long enough for researchers to analyze their illness experience. The change in survival time has resulted in the formation of different research questions that now focus on the quality of the child's remaining life, rather than his imminent demise. Consequently, the current literature is now addressing the child's problems in living with serious illness and coping with changes in body image, adolescent development, reintegration into school, treatment and its side effects, long-term uncertainty and its effects, and the unique problems that face "cured" pediatric cancer patients (Slavin, 1981). For the family, there is more investigation of the practical demands of long-term illness, such as how to create a normal home life or how to cope with extensive outpatient treatment, and the emotional demands, such as setting priorities and living with uncertainty (Slavin, 1981).

Recent advances in medicine have dramatically altered the experience of childhood terminal illness for both patient and family, as well as caregivers. It has changed from being a short-term event, followed inevitably by death, to a long-term chronic state that is both more demanding and more hopeful for all concerned.

BASIC PRINCIPLES OF CARE
FOR THE DYING CHILD

Coinciding with the changes in the treatment and experience of childhood terminal illness are the changes in attitudes and perspectives about the dying child. The literature shows a dramatic reversal of assumptions made about the child's knowledge of her death and the caregiver's behavior based on those assumptions. Prior to the 1970s the prevalent view was that the children should be protected from knowledge of the complete truth about their diagnosis and prognosis because (1) children under 10 were not capable of understanding death and therefore did not experience anxiety about death; (2) children did not want or need much information about their disease and should not be given more than they requested; and (3) children's immature ego defenses were inadequate to cope with the distress and anxiety that knowledge of a fatal illness would produce (Share, 1972). Vernick and Karon (1965) were among the first to indicate that such assumptions were unwarranted and that, in fact, fatally ill children's passivity and minimal questioning reflected their perceptions of and reactions to adults' fears and concerns about the topic. Once an atmosphere was provided in which children could comfortably ask questions and know that their questions would be answered honestly, they provided much evidence of their knowledge of the seriousness of their illness and the anxiety it precipitated. In the 1970s a host of research investigations demonstrated even more dramatically that children were aware of the seriousness of their illness and were significantly more anxious than either chronically ill children who did not sustain fatal diseases or healthy controls (Spinetta & Maloney, 1975; Spinetta, Rigler, & Karon, 1973; Waechter, 1971). Consequently, it has been concluded that children do experience grief and anxiety related to their illness and deserve support and help in coping with these feelings (Spinetta, 1974). Children have been found to be very responsive to the initiation of discussions about their fears and concerns relative to their illness and death (Drotar, 1977; Lansky, 1974; Vernick, 1973). Slavin (1981) outlines the new, open approach:

> To summarize, those who are critical of the protective approach and who advocate openness argue as follows. First, research on healthy children's concepts of death is not wholly relevant to fatally ill children; even very young children who are dying experience a great deal of fear about the seriousness of their illness. Second, the observed passivity and lack of questioning about death by these children simply indicates that adults' discomfort and silence make it difficult for children to raise the issue. Finally, since children do experience and cope with a great deal of anxiety about the illness, there is no reason to believe that their coping skills are inadequate, and there is evidence which suggests that discussing fears and fantasies about death can be supportive of good coping. In recent years, the open approach (Share, 1972) has been adopted by most professionals who treat child cancer patients. (p. 5)

Therefore, one of the basic principles by which most caregivers now operate is that children do have an awareness of the seriousness of their own condition and experience grief and anxiety as a consequence of it. It cannot be assumed that it is lacking merely because the child does not have the sophisticated adult terminology to discuss it verbally. Additional clinical research has further proven that children can sense the emotional distancing of the adults around them and often modify their behavior as a result (Spinetta, Rigler, & Karon, 1974).

Another current basic principle is that as much open communication as can be tolerated should be encouraged. As with any seriously ill individual, communication is a primary concern. Communication with children about serious illness has been a particularly thorny issue because of the concerns about age-related cognitive deficiencies and the societal desire to protect the child from painful information. However, recent evidence suggests that a terminally ill child's understanding of the seriousness of her terminal illness will be less dependent on age and intellectual ability, and more directly related to her capacity to integrate and synthesize the information, which has been found to be experience-related (Bluebond-Langner, 1977). This explains why terminally ill children can understand their dying in terms previously thought of as possible only in older children and why their concepts are more sophisticated than those of healthy children. "What children tell you about their view of death reflects their experiences, concerns, circumstances, and self-concept at the time of interview" (Bluebond-Langner, 1977, p. 52).

Often the terminally ill child's assimilation of information about the disease is a prolonged process involving changes over time. It develops over the course of the illness. There are five stages in children's acquisition of information about their illness (Bluebond-Langner, 1977). Following diagnosis the child first learns that "it" is a serious illness. In the second stage, the child knows the names of the drugs, how and when they are used, and what the side effects of them will be. The third stage is marked by an understanding of the purposes of treatment and the special procedures required to administer the drugs and ameliorate the drugs' side effects. At this point the child knows which symptoms will require which procedures and understands the relationship between a particular symptom and its procedure. Each procedure and each treatment are viewed as unique events. In the fourth stage the child is capable of putting the treatments, procedures, and symptoms into the larger perspective of the cycle of relapses and remissions. The child comprehends that it is possible to get ill repeatedly in the same way and that medicines do not always function as well or last as long as they are supposed to. It is not until the child passes to the final stage that there is recognition that the cycle is finite and at the end there is death. The child learns that there is a finite number of drugs and that when these are no longer effective death becomes imminent.

Paralleling the children's passage through these five stages in the acquisition of information is their movement through five different stages of definitions of themselves (Bluebond-Langner, 1977). Prior to diagnosis, the child conceives of herself as well. In the first stage the child views herself as seriously ill. There is a belief in the second stage that she is seriously ill but will get better. The child recognizes she is always ill in the third stage, but she still believes that she will get better. In the fourth stage there is a realization that she is always ill and will never get better. Finally the child recognizes that she is dying.

Certain significant events must take place in order for the child to pass through these stages of acquisition of information and changes in self-concept. The passage to the first stage occurs almost immediately after the parents learn the diagnosis. The child does not pass to the next one until she has been to the clinic several times, spoken with other ill children during these visits, and had her parents informed that she is in remission. The third stage is signaled by the first relapse. The child remains in this stage until several more relapses and remissions are experienced. After this the child passes to the fourth stage, where she remains until she learns of the death of an ill peer, which prompts her to move to the last stage. Bluebond-Langner asserts that if these events do not occur at the appropriate time, the child will not pass on to the next stage. For example, if a child is at the fourth stage and another child does not die, she will not move to the final stage. Stages also cannot be skipped: if a child is in the second stage and a peer dies, the child does not pass to the fifth stage.

> Information is cumulative; the child can integrate certain information only if he has the necessary requisite information. Without the requisite information, the child cannot integrate new information to come to a new conclusion . . . . age and intellectual ability have not been mentioned as factors in a child's coming to know that he or she is dying. They are not significant. What is significant is the ability to integrate and synthesize information—an ability which is not age-related, but experience-related. The role of experience in developing awareness and . . . in determining forms of communicating that awareness, also explains why age and intellectual ability are not related to the speed or completeness with which the child passes through the stages. There are 3- and 4-year-olds of average intelligence who know more about their prognosis than very intelligent 9-year-olds. The reason for this is that the 9-year-olds may still be in their first remission, have had fewer clinic visits, and hence less experience. They are only aware of the fact that they have a very serious illness. (Bluebond-Langner, 1977, p. 54)

Such research has made the question of whether or not children can comprehend their own dying a moot issue. It remains up to the adults around them to decide whether or not these children will be given adequate information and support in appropriately integrating this information in the least uncomfortable ways possible. A child, no less than an adult, can end up being isolated in a world of concerned others who are fearful of openly discussing the consequences of the illness or the impending death. Children often feign ignorance in order to protect their parents and caregivers, whom they correctly realize may have difficulty dealing with the situation, and to ensure that they will not become so anxiety-provoking to others that they will be left alone. Like the adult dying patient, they react to the cues of others. "While children want to express their awareness, they do not want to do so at the risk of being left alone. They know that direct expression of awareness could cost them the companionship of those they want near them, their parents. So to assure their continued presence, they practice mutual pretense" (Bluebond-Langner, 1977, p. 65). In their research on childhood leukemia, Binger, Ablin, Feuerstein, Kushner, Zoger, and Mikkelsen (1969) found such children "the loneliest of all," since they had no one to whom they could openly express their feelings of sadness, fear, and anxiety. A touching example of this is mentioned by Kavanaugh (1974), who describes one of his experiences as a priest:

> Of the many children I visited near death, Tildy affected me the most. Burned beyond repair, her obvious pain and severe disfigurement were instrumental in keeping many friends away. I am ashamed at how frequently *I* manufactured excuses until she shared with me in our huddled confession her perplexity about how to handle her parents. This lovable nine-year-old could not tell them how much she knew and they would not tell her. Together, Tildy and I kept her secret. Only days before she died, she took my hand and said with smiling pride: "We did it, Father, we did it! I don't think they know I know!" (p. 142)

The implications are clear. Children need to be provided the information that will allow them to understand, as much as they can, the experience they are undergoing. Of course, this must be couched in age-appropriate terms; for instance, a child can understand that she has "sick blood." Children, like all dying patients, need an atmosphere that lends itself to open communication and awareness. There must be recognition that although children may not be able to articulate their concerns, they recognize the seriousness of their illness and, if nothing else, their differences from other children. Also like the adult patient, children can be expected to vacillate between acceptance and denial of their illness. The cardinal rule is to listen to the child and take cues from her, while promoting and supporting the open discussion of concerns and feelings.

> I would suggest that the best approach to psychological management of terminally ill children would be one that allows a child to practice mutual pretense with those who feel most comfortable in that context, and open awareness with those who feel most confortable in that context. One should not use an either-or approach in these cases . . . .
>
> If you are the person with whom the child practices open awareness, listen to what he or she says. Take your cues from the child. Answer only what is asked, in the child's own terms. Remember, children will honor whatever rules you set up. They benefit most when questions are responded to in their own terms,

when they are helped to do what they want—reveal to some, conceal from others—and be what they are—children aware of themselves, their needs, and the needs of others. (Bluebond-Langner, 1977, p. 65)

Kavanaugh (1974) cautions against the child's needs being overlooked or denied because of adults' personal feelings about and resentment over the impending death of an allegedly innocent child. He points out that regardless of what has been said, children are aware of the nonverbal communication that indicates the seriousness of their condition: the doctor who comes around so much; the father who never hollers anymore; the mother who looks harried; and all the gifts. Because children will know something is wrong, whether they are told explicitly or not, Kavanaugh advises being honest with them: "When children have known the truth about their condition, and were allowed to talk about it openly, they have been as brave as any adult. Compacts can do the same job as Cadillacs" (p. 143).

Koocher (1980) believes that treatment should focus on direct supportive measures, including facilitating communication among family members, encouraging the expression of significant emotional concerns, assisting in the management of reactive behavior problems, and sensitizing clients to the emotional subtleties that are so easily overlooked. The usual mental health clinician's focus on uncovering and interpreting unrecognized or unconscious material is secondary in these situations. During initial contacts with the dying patient, questions such as these should be asked: What does the patient know? What surface concerns does the patient have? What sources of support are available? What sources of stress are anticipated?

Spinetta (1980) and Spinetta and Deasy-Spinetta (1981) suggest some factors that ideally should be understood by caregivers prior to discussing the illness or death with the dying child:

- *The parents' philosophical stance on death.* It is from the family's unique philosophy of life and death that the child will draw her own meaning. A basic understanding of it is an essential prerequisite to communication with the family.
- *The parents' emotional stance on death.* Clearly the parents' responses will influence the child's responses. Their feelings about death, often developed through previous experiences, will affect their responses in this situation.
- *The child's age, experience, and level of development.* These variables influence the nature and characteristics of communication with the child. They are important determinants of how well the child understands the experience, especially the concept of death. However, while developmental differences will affect the child's ability to conceptualize and un-

derstand many of the aspects of death, the experience of
terminal illness may make the child aware of her own impending demise at a much younger age than her healthy
peers.
- *The family's coping strategies.* An understanding of the family's usual manner of dealing with crisis will help determine
  how and what type of support the child will get from family
  members. It will also serve to indicate the repertoire of behaviors from which the child may adopt her own responses.
- *The child's perception of process over content.* The child will
  pick up on how something is said more than what is said.
  Adults must recognize and take into account that their nonverbal behavior is more revealing than their verbal behavior.

These, along with an awareness of one's personal attitudes towards
death, are critical factors that ought to be understood if there is
to be meaningful communication with children about their illness.
There must at least be some initial attempt at developing self-
awareness and resolving objections to talking about death with a
child before meaningful communication can take place.

Throughout the literature findings consistently illustrate that
open family communication and explicit confrontation of anxieties
surrounding the illness result in better adaptation to the illness by
the child and family and more successful reintegration and adaptation by the family after the death of the child (Spinetta &
Deasy-Spinetta, 1981). Families with more closed communication
styles have more unfinished business and regret following the death
of the child. The child will decide whether or not to discuss feelings
and concerns about the illness based upon the family's rules of
openness of communication about that illness.

The following topics,* suggested by Spinetta (1980), should be
raised in an age-appropriate manner at the child's own level of
readiness. The caregiver should be aware of the child's level of
concern, employ the child's own language, and raise points using
a tactful, process-oriented approach. The child's history and the
specific familial and institutional environment must be taken into
account. The first 11 points can be raised during the living-dying
interval, when the child may have months or years of valuable life
ahead. Points 12 through 14 should be reserved for when the child
is very close to actual death.

(1) Death is a part of the natural order of things.
(2) Death has a social significance. We have special feelings for
    the other persons we share our lives with, as they do for us.
(3) Death is a separation on both sides. Not only does the person

---

*From J. Kellerman (Ed.), *Psychological Aspects of Childhood Cancer*, 1980. Courtesy
of Charles C Thomas, Publisher, Springfield, Illinois.

who dies lose the people left behind, but they lose their child as well.

(4) The loss is never complete. The deceased lives on in some way. (Here the specific cosmological stance of the family is critical; some feel that the child will live on in spirit; others that the child will have passed on a legacy of the meaning of life to friends; others that the child will live on in both body and soul for eternity.)

(5) The child will not be alone at death and after. (What the child is looking for is parental presence and support throughout, both during the death process and after death. It is important to reassure these children that they will not be suffering death alone, and that the parents will remain with them even after death. This last point is critical, essential to the child, and of necessity to be phrased within the context of the parent's cosmological stance, as with point 4.)

(6) People at the point of death, whether adults or children, have the need to know that they have done all that they could with life. This is a universal human concern that is shared by children as well as by adults. Even young children can live fulfilled and happy lives before they die. It is not necessary to live to eighty-five to make a lasting contribution to the human condition. Young children can touch the minds and hearts of those they deal with at school, in the hospital, at home, in a manner that will live on in others' memories. If the child's life, manner of facing the illness, and death can help modify a parent's, sibling's, or professional's attitude in a manner that helps move the human condition one step further forward, that child will have contributed to humanity and will have led a highly effective life in a short period of time.

(7) It's all right to cry and to feel sad.

(8) It's all right to feel angry and resentful.

(9) It's all right not to want to talk to anyone anymore about it for a while.

(10) When the child is ready to talk about it, the adult will be there to listen and support. (This had better be true.)

(11) It is not necessary to express how you feel in words. Sometimes it's all right just to sit there and not have to talk. And if what you say when you want to talk sounds confused or silly, that's all right too. Adults don't always know what to say either.

(12) Death will not hurt. The dying process may be painful, and the doctor will do all that can be done to reduce the pain to a minimum, but death itself won't hurt. The pain will never return again. (Children are very concerned with having the pain finally end. It is important to reassure them that it will finally end.)

(13) When someone that you love dies, it is important for you to be able to say goodbye. People have a social custom of saying

their last goodbyes together, crying together, talking over what happened. Sometimes people do this in the privacy of their homes; sometimes they do it in church. These goodbye group-happenings are usually called funerals. Don't be scared of them. They are very important for your mother and father and your brothers and sisters.

(14) We grown-ups sometimes don't know very much about death either. If we talk to the doctor a lot, and cry afterwards, or if mother and dad talk about your illness and are teary-eyed, that's because we love you and don't want to lose you, and don't know how we're going to be able to get along without you. If someday you won't be here with us anymore, we will be very unhappy. But we will remember the happy times, and you will live on with us (in body, mind, spirit, memory, see #4 and #5 above). We will be happy knowing that you have been happy. And we will always be with you. (pp. 265-267)

Another basic principle now in use is the active involvement of the child as part of the treatment team. The noncompliance, rebelliousness, and fear that work against successful treatment can be avoided when the child is allowed to actively participate in treatment planning. It not only gives the child a critically needed sense of control, but also develops the trust needed for optimum treatment efficacy. Since terminal childhood illness has become a more long-term experience, it is even more essential that children be included. Now that it has been established that children are aware of the seriousness of their condition, and that open communication is a requirement for successful adaptation to the illness, it seems clear that children *must* participate in treatment planning to whatever extent possible.

While family members were previously only tolerated in the care of the dying child, they now also must be actively involved. As terminal illness becomes more chronic, the family must cope with problems that affect all aspects of family life over an extended period of time. The patient and family should be considered the unit of care, with more emphasis placed upon family dynamics and parent and sibling reactions.

The last basic principle in caring for dying children actually is a set of principles derived from the changes in the experience of terminal illness. As emphasis has shifted from coping with imminent death to handling chronic illness and enhancing the quality of the child's life, several intervention goals have emerged. Attention is now given to normalizing the patient's and family's lives, fostering as much open communication as possible, supporting the parents, and understanding and addressing the developmental needs and concerns of the patient and siblings.

ADJUSTMENT TO THE TERMINAL ILLNESS
OF A CHILD

The patient and family must readjust their lives to accommodate the demands of the illness starting from the day the diagnosis is pronounced. They will have to cope with the initial shock of hospitalization, the long-term task of pursuing treatment, the ongoing attempt to keep home and school life as normal as possible, and the vicissitudes of the patient's condition. Each of these areas has its own problems and elicits different reactions.

Diagnosis and Hospitalization

At the time of diagnosis, the sick child must be told as much about the illness as his age allows him to understand. He should be given the diagnosis no later than 24 hours after the parents have been informed, to avoid his hearing it from someone else and to minimize the opportunity for mutual pretense or other communication disorders to develop. The child can be told by parents, caregivers, or both together. (Parents should be present, regardless of who talks to the child.) If the parents volunteer to inform the child, it should be ascertained later whether or not this was actually done.

The diagnosis must be offered in a way that stresses positively combatting the illness, rather than overfocusing on mourning (although clearly permission for grieving must be provided). No diagnosis should be given without some degree of realistic hope. While the initial diagnosis is usually the time of heaviest emotional distress during the entire illness, it is also a time during which open discussion of concerns and feelings can begin among the patient, family members, and caregivers.

Regardless of the child's prognosis, it is imperative that parents and caregivers attend to the continuing needs of childhood development. The possibilities for maximizing positive, adaptive experiences for the child must not be overlooked, even if he is facing imminent death (Katz, 1980). This emphasis on living life and striving for growth will not only assure the child's well-being if treatment is successful, but will give parents a sense that their child lived as fully as possible with their help if death should occur (Kagen-Goodheart, 1977; Lucas, Note 21). There needs to be a philosophy of allowing the child to savor life as fully and as normally as possible up to the point of death. "The issue when a ten-year-old is diagnosed is just as much, if not more so, preparing him for adolescence as for a possible death" (Lucas, Note 21, p. 3).

Usually the child is immediately hospitalized following the diagnosis for the commencement of treatment. This is a difficult and confusing period of time, as both the child and family must accommodate themselves to the changes entailed in hospitalization. The patient must undergo painful and frightening treatment while family members watch helplessly, without any sense of control. Everyone is forced to acknowledge that the illness is serious.

For the child, withdrawal from his family and normal home environment brings on fears of separation and emphasizes his differences from his peers. Anxiety about bodily injury, mutilation, and loss of control is also aroused by hospitalization and treatment procedures. At this juncture, children may be angry and disillusioned by the fact that their parents cannot protect them from these experiences. Where previously parents were seen as omnipotent, they are now seen as powerless figures, unable to change what is happening. Some children come to believe that the illness and treatment are punishment for past wrongdoings or symptoms of parental rejection.

Parents and siblings also suffer from the jarring impact of diagnosis and commencement of treatment. For parents, the worst has been confirmed—they have been unable to protect their child. This sets off a whole host of reactions, making the initial confrontation with the diagnosis and threat of death particularly painful. Indeed, the experience is so unnerving that parents often require repeated communication about the diagnosis and the treatment implications before they adequately comprehend. Siblings need to be made aware that the illness is not contagious and that it was not caused by their wrongdoing or magical thinking. Both parents and siblings, as well as the patient, require as much information as possible in order to cope with the situation at hand. Treatment procedures should be explained in detail and all parties should be encouraged to tour hospital and treatment facilities to diminish their anxiety and develop some sense of predictability and control.

Treatment

The treatment process will demand a great deal from the child and family. There will be a complete disruption of life, which can leave permanent scars on every member of the family. For the rest of the child's life, or until the point when the child is recognizably cured (and even this is not without its difficulties), the family's life will revolve around the child's illness and treatment. The U.S. Department of Health and Human Services resource book for health professionals on coping with cancer describes it as follows:

> Consider what the process demands of the child and his family: acceptance of treatment without assurance that it will eradicate the disease, pain and fear, hospitalization, frequent clinic visits, possible financial problems, and disruption of family life. If the family lives in a city other than the one where the child receives

treatment, disruption and logistical problems are increased. Treatment is a lengthy process. For a period of years, the family's life will revolve around the child's cancer. (U.S. Department of Health and Human Services, Note 11, p. 55)

Previously children did not experience outpatient treatment because they died quickly. Consequently, the issues of living with chronic terminal illness are of relatively new concern to patients, families, and caregivers alike. Families may be somewhat anxious about taking children home after the initial hospitalization; it is often frightening to think that they have sole responsibility for the child, without the help of hospital staff. Their anxiety can be minimized by predicting situations that may occur, giving written instructions about medications, and telling them how to obtain information during and after regular working hours. Necessary phone calls can be encouraged and the family pediatrician's help can be enlisted in answering questions.

The routine of trips to the clinic may become stressful in and of itself. It often entails scheduling the family's life around appointments, arranging transportation to the clinic, waiting for long periods, and being reminded of the seriousness of the child's condition. For many it will involve absences from the home, as treatment centers may be located at a distance. Various researchers have found that there may be high anxiety in a tense and depressed atmosphere in clinic waiting rooms (Hoffman & Futterman, 1971; Spinetta & Maloney, 1975). Such conditions can be alleviated; Hoffman and Futterman (1971) reduced anxiety in a clinic waiting room setting by establishing a play group for the children and encouraging parents to talk with each other or a therapist about their concerns. Other suggestions for making waiting rooms more palatable include providing children with toys and scheduled activities, and opportunities for involvement with siblings, and also offering parents overnight accommodations during prolonged treatment and chances to socialize with other parents.

One of the new, dramatic stresses placed upon children and their families with the extension of survival time is the side effects of treatment. Many physical changes can take place. There can be unpleasant bodily reactions such as pain, weakness, nausea, and vomiting. Body changes may result: hair loss, skin discoloration, weight fluctuation, surgical scars, and distention or loss of body parts. Chemotherapy and radiation therapy may interfere with motor skills, neurological abilities, developmental skills, and cognitive functioning. Personality changes may even occur.

Besides these physical problems, there are the ensuing psychosocial difficulties. Body image and sense of self often become impaired. Loss chips away at the sense of integrity. There may be rejection by peers, increasing feelings about being unacceptable and different and restricting social contacts. These may in turn contribute to low self-esteem, anxiety, depression, withdrawal, despair, or acting-out behaviors.

These additional changes due to treatment are extremely difficult to cope with. For many of the terminally ill children, the concern about side effects becomes more important than the disease itself (Plumb & Holland, 1974). Especially with the older child and adolescent, these changes may become so unnerving that therapy is terminated.

Maintenance of Home and School Life

As increasing numbers of children are living with illness, attention has turned to fostering their normal development. It may not always be possible to pursue this goal during relapses, or times of acute illness, but it certainly must be attempted when the child is in remission or not severely symptomatic. For example, care of the child with cancer, according to van Eys (1977), should be directed at producing a "truly cured child," one who is "mentally healthy and who can function at an age-appropriate level in society." This requires acceptance of the child as he is, neither concentrating on the cancer nor pretending that it is not there. To ignore the cancer would be to deny a major aspect of the child's reality; but to focus solely on it would deny the child a normal world. Consequently, the environment must be one that allows the child "normal development during abnormal circumstances" (van Eys, 1977). This means treating the child as someone who might die, but who also might live. When a cure is not expected, subtle cues may retard the normal development of the child. Expecting the child to be cured may cause pain if the child in fact dies; however, if the child does not live with that expectation, he cannot be "truly cured."

One of the dilemmas in this regard is parental maintenance of discipline. Parents must guard against the tendency to both overprotect and overindulge. Overprotection springs from the parents' fear that their child will become more ill or be harmed further in some way. It may also stem from the parents' unconscious attempts to compensate for their anger about the disease and its effects. Overindulgence is easily recognized by children and is often quite frightening. Not only is the suspension of normal limits unpleasant in and of itself, but there is concern that the suspension means that they are even more seriously ill than previously believed. Parents must maintain appropriate limits in order to safeguard their child's sense of well-being and security.

A balance must be struck between trying not to overprotect the child and responding to real needs that have developed as a consequence of the illness. Because this can be confusing, parents need information on what can be reasonably expected of the child, given his illness and treatment effects. They also need support in finding ways to cope, sorting out responses to given situations, and maintaining appropriate discipline. This is based upon the need for the child to have as normal a development as possible.

Consistent with maintaining this normalcy, it is important to continue the child's education. This not only allows the further intellectual development of the child, but provides important emotional and social experiences with peers and authority figures. School is the child's "work" and, as childhood terminal illness becomes more of a chronic experience, children should be integrated back into the school whenever possible, as soon as possible.

During hospitalization, children may continue their schoolwork in hospital schools. Even in this setting the school experience gives children the opportunity to interact with peers and master new competencies. It also establishes an atmosphere of hope, giving children the secondary message that they are going to do well and that they still function in many of the same ways as their peers. Additionally, it provides a sense of continuity for those children who will be reintegrated back into the school as soon as the illness permits. This consistency may be helpful in the midst of all the other changes that must be endured.

For those children who are not hospitalized, but are still unable to attend school, homebound programs exist. The child's isolation at home can be minimized by having other children communicate with him and fostering the expectation of returning to regular school. At times homebound programs can be alternated with attendance at regular school for those children who cannot attend on a daily basis.

Although hospital schools and homebound programs should be used when necessary, they are not substitutes for regular schooling. The child should be encouraged to return to regular schooling as swiftly as possible, with the understanding that emotional and social problems secondary to the child's illness may emerge. Many children are concerned about returning to school because of their feelings about the side effects of the illness or its treatment. Physical changes or limitations may be viewed by the child as stigmas that differentiate or alienate him from peers, causing humiliation and rejection. The child will require as much support as possible from parents and caregivers in coping with these untoward results of the illness. Teachers can be especially effective in working with the class to help them understand the experience and treat the child as normally as possible.

Parents may interfere with the child's successful integration back into school. Those who feel that further education is useless, since the child will not live to reap its benefits, may want to keep the child at home. A desire to protect the child or to prevent any further separation may also contribute to parents' reluctance to send the child to school. Such parents need to learn to appreciate the critical emotional and social importance of school for the child and support the child as he copes with the school experience. Discussing potential problems with parents and children can assist them in anticipating and dealing with difficulties ahead of time. Schooling can be encouraged during clinic visits, reinforcing the idea of education as an essential part of the child's life (U.S. Department of Health and Human Services, Note 11).

When the child does return to the classroom it will probably be with a somewhat altered capability to function. Schooling will often be interrupted by treatment demands, physical problems, or reactions to treatment side effects. In some cases the disease or its treatment (irradiation, chemotherapy) will have a demonstrable effect upon central nervous system functioning and other intellectual processes. The child, family, and teacher need to be informed of these possibilities in advance and to work together to minimize any adverse consequences. In particular the child will require help in grieving over lost abilities and adjusting to lowered capacities. Interventions should be designed to strengthen the child's compensatory skills.

Working with the terminally ill child requires communication between the home, the hospital, and the school. For this reason it is suggested that a caregiver act as school liaison and contact the teacher prior to the child's returning to school. This person can provide information about the illness and the child's condition, the limitations imposed by the disease or its treatment, the schedule of treatment and clinic visits, and possible reactions to treatment. A liaison can anticipate certain problems, facilitating as smooth a transition as possible. It cannot be emphasized enough how critical it is that school officials and teachers understand the child's illness and limitations. Without adequate information, teachers often presuppose certain limitations and lack of abilities in the child. Realistic expectations need to be established. Teachers also need to be aware of probable changes in the child's physical appearance, moods, and abilities so they are prepared to deal with the reactions of other children in the classroom. They themselves may feel uneasy about handling the terminally ill child, and may require ongoing support. This is especially true in the area of discipline. Frequently, ill children are judged with a different set of standards than their peers, as teachers try to be supportive and understanding. But this only serves to increase the child's feelings of inadequacy and isolation. Again, the child with chronic life-threatening illness needs to be treated as normally as possible.

Caregivers serving as liaisons with the school system need to help teachers assess their own attitudes and feelings about terminal illness, since these will surely be conveyed to the child when he returns to school. Many misconceptions can be erased when there is open and ongoing communication between teachers and health care professionals. It is most helpful if one person can serve as a continuing consultant to the teachers should questions arise pertaining to the child's terminal illness.

Well-prepared teachers will be able to help the child reintegrate into the classroom and minimize the disruptive effects that negative peer reactions may have on the child. They will also be able to assist the parents in identifying which changes in the child's behavior may be the result of the illness and its treatment and which may be due to other causes, such as developmental issues normal to all children. Frequently parents of the sick child erroneously assume that all alterations in the child's behavior are a direct result of the illness.

The teachers of siblings of terminally ill children also must be made aware of the experiences those children are undergoing. They need to know how the patient's illness affects everyone in the entire family. They should be encouraged to be supportive to siblings, looking for behavioral changes that may indicate something is bothering those children and possibly answering questions the children may ask of themselves or their classmates. Appropriate information may also help other school staff members (e.g., the school nurse, administrators) deal effectively and supportively with the sick child and his siblings.

In summary, the cardinal goal for schooling is to approximate normalcy as much as possible.

> Whether or not a formal school liaison program is established, caregivers, parents, teachers—even classmates and siblings—must treat the child with cancer as if he will do well. The children and families who benefit from efforts to make patients' lives as normal as possible are not only those for whom treatment is successful and who are now cautiously labeled as being cured. Those whose lives are lengthened by treatment even though that treatment ultimately fails also benefit. For while they live, they are allowed to be with their families and peers, to experience, and to learn. (U.S. Department of Health and Human Services, Note 11, pp. 71-72)

Remission and Relapse

To put the disease into remission is the goal of treatment. When it is reached, it is ecstatic news for the patient, family, and caregivers. However, a remission also brings uncertainty. There is likely to be concern about how long it will last and fear of the illness' recurrence. For some parents, the thought that the child still has a potentially fatal illness is ever present in the back of their minds; for others, there will be a denial of this fact. Most parents will fall somewhere in between. During remissions family life ideally returns to a more normal routine, although it still will be one dictated by the child's medical treatment demands.

Perhaps one of the worst times in the course of the child's illness is the first relapse. This is especially difficult because in most cases all involved have been working to comply with the medical treatment regime and feel disappointed, helpless, and frustrated that their best attempts have been thwarted. Some children and families may feel that the pain and hard work have all been in vain. Those who felt that adherence to the treatment program would ensure health are forced to deal with anger, depression, and other responses. Although this time is very hard for everyone involved, it forces the patient and family to come to grips with the reality of the illness and its potential threat to life. Subsequent cycles of remission and relapse underscore this fact. The potential for family and caregivers to prematurely separate from the child may be heightened by these cycles, and careful monitoring will be required to ensure appropriate continued interaction with the child (see the Lazarus syndrome described in "Emotional Responses of the Family" in Chapter 12).

THE PSYCHOSOCIAL RESPONSES OF THE DYING CHILD

A host of variables influence the dying child's responses to illness and imminent death. Many of these are the same as those of the dying adult, but in terms that reflect a child's experience. The child's conception of death in particular is affected by her cognitive abilities and experiences, and that conception obviously will greatly determine the types of responses elicited by the illness. Kastenbaum and Aisenberg (1972) have illustrated that there is an intimate relationship between the young child's growing awareness of death and other cognitive schemata. Once it was erroneously thought that dying children were unaware of their condition unless they had attained an age at which the conception of death could be held at an adult level, and unless they had been explicitly informed of their diagnosis. Researchers have since made it very clear that children are well aware of the seriousness of their illness, even if they have not been directly informed, as they pick up the subtle cues from the environment and from their own bodies. Consequently, dying children experience death anxiety and need help in dealing with their concerns (Spinetta, 1974; Spinetta et al., 1973; Spinetta & Maloney, 1975; Waechter, 1971).

Responses at Different Ages

While almost all dying children have some awareness of impending death, children of varying ages demonstrate differing concerns when they become terminally ill. (See "Reactions to Death Across the Life Cycle" in Chapter 9 to look at an integration of the conceptions of death, the identity tasks of the individual at a given age, and the issues for the terminal patient.)

The Young Child

The following section is based on Easson's (1970) studies of dying children.

Infants. The infant has no awareness of or cognitive response to dying. The child reacts solely to the physical distress of the illness. She is barely aware of the people and environment outside herself and does not have the ability to use the love and support of caring people around her. Maximum physical relief and comfort should be provided, but the infant will still die in a solitary fashion. Parents and caregivers often need a great deal of support as they struggle with their real helplessness.

Toddlers. The toddler takes cues from significant others as to how to respond to the disease process. Personal death has meaning insofar as it affects the people around her. The feelings and responses of the parents become those of the child, as she has not yet successfully differentiated herself from others.

> The feelings of the parents and the family are communicated to the child and become the child's feelings also. The task of dying may thus become much more burdensome for the young child because he also bears this load of his parents' feelings. Young children will respond with fear as they die, not because they can appreciate the fearfulness of death but rather because their parents are upset and fearful. (Easson, 1970, p. 24)

Hospitalization is extremely stressful, as it means separation from significant others and the familiar environment, along with the added burden of being discomforted by pain. Therapeutic intervention should focus on minimizing the child's separation from parents as much as possible. If the child's parents are unavailable there should be a reliable, consistent parent substitute to facilitate constancy, closeness, and a sense of being.

Older preschool children. The older preschool child has become increasingly differentiated and self-sufficient from her parents; she enjoys making decisions, expressing herself, and asserting herself. She is developing a deepening understanding of her separate identity. At this point, everything is viewed in terms of black or white, good or bad. Magical thinking reigns, as there is an inability to separate personal thoughts from events in the external world. Consequently the pain of illness and the separation that must be endured may be perceived as punishment for bad thoughts or actions. Guilt and feelings of rejection are common to sick children at this age, and there may be feelings of anger or resentment directed towards the self and significant others.

The older preschool child may have more of an appreciation of what death could mean personally and consequently may try to deny these ideas and feelings. While these concerns may not be obvious, as the child may deny or hide them to avoid rejection or reproval by others, they may come out in symbolic ways in dreams and in play. Likewise, feelings of aggression and concerns about death-related matters may become apparent.

Just as the adult does, the child may regress to earlier modes of behavior that provided her with more security. Those who cannot appropriately regress may struggle to maintain their newly won independence, blaming their pain on those around them and becoming suspicious and untrusting of caregivers and family. Such children may be forced to withdraw into their own personal world of daydreams in order to tolerate the experience.

Therapeutic intervention should focus on assuring the child that she is not being punished because of thoughts, deeds, or omissions. Honest and rational explanations of the illness should be given. Separation from parents and significant others should be avoided when possible, and changes should be kept to a minimum. Outlets for normal childhood emotions and impulses, which may be intensified by the illness, should be provided.

Grade-school children. The grade-school child has started to strike out further from home. Peers are critically important in defining the child's identity. Rules and orders are internalized. There is a newly acquired ability to master and learn, and the child is constantly doing, acting, and experiencing. But although she is expanding her experiences, she still returns to the security of home and family, even at the end of grade school, when most of the family's attitudes, beliefs, and feelings are integrated into her own personality.

The child of this age is developing a deeper and more stable awareness of separateness from others. Her greater independence, self-confidence, and awareness of individuality also bring feelings of vulnerability and concern over nonexistence. As the child begins to appreciate the past and the future, there is a recognition that someday she will not be. Parents are reluctantly understood to be human beings with their own failings and foibles.

At this time the universe seems symmetrical to the child: every act has a punishment or reward; unpleasant experiences are a consequence of something bad. When such a child experiences hospitalization or other uncomfortable aspects of illness, there is a belief that it is a penalty for past wrongdoings. This may bring up concerns about abandonment, destruction, or body mutilation.

As the illness progresses, the body, which has performed those acts that have provided self-identity and a sense of mastery and control, now becomes disabled. This is an assault on the child's capacity to be a person. She may feel angry, resentful, bewildered, or depressed. Parents and caregivers may be held responsible for her suffering.

As the child at this age is more capable of understanding what is happening to her, there is a need for truthful, open communication about the illness. The child also needs concrete details about medical treatments, with reassurances that they do not constitute punishment. Illness threatens the child's ability to sustain active mastery, self-sufficient functioning, and peer relationships. To counteract this threat, the child must have opportunities to exercise remaining skills and develop alternative ones for those that are lost. A sense of achievement, mastery, and control is needed. Access to peers is also critical. Parents still need to be around as much as possible, as separation from them arouses anger, frustration, and anxiety. If at times the child does not focus on the illness, this should not be misconstrued as ignorance about the illness or inability to understand it. Children need respites from the threat of illness and death just as adults do.

It should be recognized that the grade-school child quickly learns from her hospitalization. She becomes knowledgeable about illnesses, develops a sensitivity to the anxieties on her unit, and comes to appreciate the nuances of behavior indicating the emotional responses of others to the illness and death of children. She wants to be involved and often feels happier when included in planning or carrying out treatment procedures, organization, and hospital routine.

The Adolescent

The psychosocial tasks and issues of adolescence make adolescents more psychologically vulnerable to potential fatal illness than any other age group (Kagan, 1976). Their reactions also cause more problems to family and caregivers than those of patients of other ages (Hamovitch, 1964), and their deaths are the most difficult for staff to cope with (Adams, 1979).

There are a number of developmental tasks adolescents must complete for successful maturation:

1. Development of a comfortable body-image and self-esteem.
2. Creation of identity through socialization.
3. Establishment of emotional and economic independence.
4. Sexual identity formation.
5. Future goal-orientation and career-development or employment. (Zeltzer, 1980, p. 71)

All five of these tasks are made tremendously difficult by the development of a terminal illness. Since adolescence is the time when such psychosocial issues are most sharply drawn, a chronic, potentially fatal illness seriously compromises the individual's functioning and development and poses Herculean demands for coping and adaptation.

In early adolescence children strive to separate and achieve independence from their families by associating with peers like themselves. There is often rebellion against the dictates of parents and their teachings. In an attempt to emancipate themselves (not without some degree of discomfort and guilt) they may overcompensate for the pull they feel back to the warmth of past childhood and the security of dependence. Consequently, the young adolescent who is dying may be in a difficult situation in which he cannot allow himself to accept the support and care of the family. Quite proud and attempting to maintain independence and control, the adolescent may struggle against natural regressive tendencies and may refuse to allow himself the support of others. At this time, too, the peer group often betrays the adolescent. Whereas in health they could be mutually supportive to one another, the threat of death strikes at their attempts to establish independence and self-sufficiency, increasing their vulnerability and discomfort. As a result, they often withdraw emotionally from peers who are facing death. This leaves young terminally ill adolescents feeling quite lonely, as they experience rejection and isolation from peers, and feel distant and alienated from parents. As the illness continues on, the dying adolescent may finally accept help if he becomes weak enough and can convince himself that surrendering to care is a forced choice, not one that was voluntarily made. This allows him to retain dignity and a sense of self-respect. The adolescent may respond to the comforting of family members as long as his dependency is not emphasized. Although no longer able to act like an independent teenager, he must still be respected as such. This respect must be shown in all interventions and communications. Association with peers can be encouraged; mutual support groups of terminally ill adolescents are very helpful.

In mid-adolescence, the teenager has developed more self-confidence and greater independence. There is no longer such a reliance on the peer group, although it clearly is still very important. He takes pride in himself as an individual and not merely as a member of the group. This maturing teenager now becomes an individual in his own right for the very first time. At a point when the adolescent is tasting the pleasures of personal mastery and self-achievement, and is first experiencing his sexuality, the threat of death is enormously cruel. The rage and bitterness is profound. At this age if the teenager has developed appropriate self-confidence and security, he will have less of a need to reject parents and family as death draws nearer. The adolescent at this age tends to direct anger more onto caregivers than parents and family.

The older adolescent devotes much time and energy to developing deep relationships and caring for others. He has come to learn that the greatest emotional gratification can come from caring for and being cared for by others. When this adolescent is faced with death, he focuses on the loss of the rich and meaningful relationships he has established. This young adult can allow himself to be cared for and continue to care for others as death approaches. He mourns and can usually accept the comfort of others.

Poised between childhood and adulthood, being neither fish nor fowl, the adolescent with a terminal illness is in a uniquely difficult situation. At no other point in time is the ego so busy, both reliving past conflicts and attending to new and stronger impulses and developmental tasks. Terminal illness ravages the body, threatening the adolescent's development and integration of a sexual identity. It creates emotional, cognitive, and physical changes that work against successful socialization and development of a secure sense of self-esteem that will facilitate the growth of important peer and sexual relationships. Absences from school and the numerous side effects of treatment isolate the adolescent at a time when association with others is a necessity. The achievement of emotional and economic independence is thwarted by the disease, which forces the individual to become dependent on others. Hospitalization, pain, relinquishing of control to caregivers, restrictions on normal emancipative activities—all rob the adolescent of the ability to successfully assert independence. Terminal illness strikes at the heart of the most critical tasks of adolescence.

Relationships with parents and caregivers may be excruciatingly tenuous. Although it is a time in life when appropriate distance should be encouraged, fatal illness requires close cooperation and communication between parties that would usually sustain respectful distance from one another. Conflicts with authority, so typical of this age group, become heightened when the adolescent is forced by illness to interact with not only his parents, but also with a number of caregivers.

Planning for career and life goals also is threatened by terminal illness. Uncertainty over the illness, and a lack of clarity about future possibilities and/or limitations, leave the adolescent unable to clearly plan for the life that remains.

Lack of communication about the prognosis and realistic expectations for the quality of life remaining will only hurt the adolescent. Clear, honest, and direct communication is needed if there is to be any relationship with the adolescent, who demands mutual respect and trust. Respect can also be shown by providing for the adolescent's need for privacy and by finding ways to recognize and support his unique identity (e.g., accepting his choices of friends, music). Opportunities should be offered to the adolescent for ventilating anger and working through losses. Appropriate development can be aided by providing access to peers, especially those closest to the patient, and allowing as much maintenance of control and independence as possible. At the end it will be important to help him achieve his own appropriate death.

The responses and needs of terminally ill adolescents really do not differ that much from those of their adult counterparts. Although they may exist in a different developmental and age-related context, and clearly are experience-related, they reflect many of the same concerns of adults in a more immature form. The developmental stage of adolescence may in fact make some of these responses and needs more intense than those of the adult, since they arise at a time when the individual is most vulnerable.

Needs and Reactions

The needs of the fatally ill child can be divided into three major areas: (1) overall emotional needs common to all children regardless of health status; (2) needs arising from the child's reaction to illness and hospitalization; and (3) needs arising from the child's conception of death (Green-Epner, 1976). Green-Epner asserts that it is imperative to not lose sight of the fact that the fatally ill patient is first of all a child. She requires assistance and support in meeting the normal needs of children—needs for love, achievement, belonging, self-respect, freedom from guilt, security, and self-understanding. This is especially true because of the difficulty the child may have in meeting them due to the illness, altered routines, and decreased contact with others who would normally assist her in satisfying these needs. The second group of needs arises from the child's reaction to illness and hospitalization. Feelings of guilt and worthlessness are not uncommon. In order to deal with these strong feelings the child requires "support, love, attention, understanding, approval, security, friendship, compassion, acknowledgment, empathy, behavioral limits . . . and discipline" (Green-Epner, 1976, p. 138). The third category of needs comes from the child's concept of death. Vernick and Karon (1965) contend that it is ludicrous to even entertain the thought that the child might not know that she is seriously ill. Such knowledge, whether derived from direct communication or from the subtle cues of significant others in the environment, brings on some type of death anxiety. Its form varies with the child's age, maturity, cognitive development, and other psychosocial variables. There may be numerous psychological reactions that occur as a result of this death anxiety: frustration, fear, anxiety, isolation, passivity, regression, and withdrawal (Green-Epner, 1976). In many cases the child is left to contend with these responses alone, since she may be isolated by participation in a mutual pretense designed to protect the parents from knowing that the child knows.

What are some of the specific emotional reactions evident in children as they contend with terminal illness? As with adults, anger is a primary one. Not only is anger stimulated by the experience of the illness and the deprivations it brings, but also by the child's recognition of the parents' inability to protect her from the illness. Depending on age and maturity, the child normally sustains some belief that parents are omnipotent. Indeed, in the child's life this has always been the case. However, when parents are unable to stop the pain of the illness or change its course, the child is often frustrated, disillusioned, and enraged. This is a very difficult experience for parents, who may be doing their best to be supportive and helpful to the child, and who may be perplexed as to why such hostility is directed at them. They need to understand where this rage comes from and how to put it in the appropriate context of the child's illness. Ironically, it is only those parents who have made the child secure enough to feel free to express herself who will bear the brunt of such anger. Those children who are insecure in expressing negative emotions will most usually withdraw, become depressed, or displace their anger in inappropriate ways.

Concern over regression and feelings of anxiety and depression are common among children. Even the very young child may be upset by the loss of functioning and the fact that earlier behaviors must be returned to. Children's anxiety, restlessness, and aggressiveness may be increased by the curtailment of motor activity secondary to hospitalization, treatment procedures, or physical limitations, as children typically require physical outlets for the release of their boundless energy. Fears of separation, abandonment, and mutilation may be seen in varying degrees in children of different ages. Depression over concurrent and future losses and anticipatory grief are not uncommon and are increasingly expectable in older children and adolescents.

Guilt is also frequently felt. It not only stems from the child's feeling that the illness may constitute a punishment for some wrong thought or action in the past, but also from the recognition that her illness causes pain and stress to significant others. Indeed, children often will be more distressed when they see the reactions of their parents than they would be on their own.

Shame is a frequent concomitant of the illness, as the child's ability to actively master the environment, attain competency, and socialize are all seriously compromised. Embarrassment over the gross changes caused by the illness or treatment (e.g., amputation, hair loss, weight gain, nausea, vomiting) further isolates the child.

Plumb and Holland (1974) astutely point out that the symptoms incurred in the illness are usually of greater concern to the adolescent (and, by implication, even to younger children as well) than the actual existential meaning of the illness itself. They are more preoccupied with the social effects of the illness and treatment than their broader ramifications.

Children and adolescents utilize many of the same defense mechanisms to cope with these feelings as adults. Geist (1979) describes a quartet of adaptive defenses: appropriate intellectualization; denial in the service of hope (differentiated from neurotic denial, which interferes with the ability to plan realistically and to care responsibly for needs); identification with medical staff; and idiosyncratic rituals (which serve to bind the staff and patient together in a shared, nonpathological ritual).

> The mechanisms of intellectualization, denial, identification with the medical staff, and ritualization, when used in concert, proved to be an adaptive and fruitful way for patients to maintain hope and faith both in caretaking adults and in the future. Only when such defenses become pathological, when denial in the service of hope yields to neurotic denial, when intellectualization interferes with human communication of affect, when identification with medical staff blends with overidentification with the aggressor, and when ritualistic behavior merges with pathological compulsion—only then must we consider the defensive functioning to be nonadaptive. (Geist, 1979, p. 19)

To this list must also be added appropriate regression in the service of treatment, displacement of emotions, withdrawal, and rebellion (Adams, 1979). Overcompensation may be another method of coping with the illness and is used to support the child's feeling of mastery over the threat and continued normalcy. The older child and adolescent may react to the enforced dependency of the illness with several defenses: regression; increased anxiety; high risk-taking behaviors; withdrawal from peers; and noncompliance with medical therapy (Zeltzer, 1980).

Children are just as vulnerable to social pressure to die in the "acceptable" way as adults are. The child or adolescent finds that expression of pain or discomfort may result in disapproval and rejection by significant others. She will learn not to talk too much, nor too openly, about her death because of the anxiety it generates in others. There will be a recognition that anger, anxiety, and separation will result if people fail to think they are being comforting or they are reminded of their powerlessness.

> A dying child will learn even at an early age that his family members are much more comfortable if he dies "a good death." His family would like to remember him as someone comfortable

rather than as someone who is constantly complaining and bitter—even though these complaints and this bitterness were reasonable and justifiable. The dying child will find that his parents,
his relatives and the people who treat him respond more readily
to his few fleeting smiles rather than to his repeated angry outbursts. Somewhat to his dismay, the child who is dying will find
that he cannot be too childish as he moves toward death. The
youngster who has always been open and outgoing learns that,
in death, he has to be more reticent and withdrawn. In death, the
young child finds he has an unavoidable part to play in his family
and his culture. He must play this social role from about the age
of five or six and frequently even younger. (Easson, 1970, p. 18)

Even more vulnerable than the dying adult, who may have other
resources to depend upon, the dying child is compelled by her
developmental needs to even more vigorously undertake the role
that society prescribes.

Communication

As with the dying adult, but even more so because of the lack
of adult intellectual ability and maturity, the dying child may
indicate his feelings, thoughts, and concerns in other than straightforward, verbal ways. Kübler-Ross (1974) believes that dying children use three "languages" to communicate their knowledge of
their impending death. The first of these is plain English, in which
the child verbally articulates his knowledge. Symbolic nonverbal
language, the second language, refers to those behaviors through
which the child indicates his feelings and thoughts. Kübler-Ross
gives the example of the child with failing kidneys who "shot"
critically ill little girls on his ward with his toy pistol. This little
boy never picked on other boys, but only on little girls who all had
good healthy kidneys. Through observation and discussion about
his behavior, Kübler-Ross determined that this little boy was symbolically wanting others to die so he could secure his needed kidney
transplant; his choice of little girls as "victims" reflected his anguish
that his mother had recently given birth to a baby girl and stopped
visiting him at the hospital. The third language that is utilized is
one most often used by the neediest patients. This is symbolic
verbal language. Kübler-Ross illustrates this with the 8-year-old
terminally ill girl who asked one night what would happen to her
should a fire break out in her oxygen tent. The nurse recognized
that there was a hidden message in this question and the little girl
later was asked to repeat her question and was comforted by the
presence of another caregiver. This allowed her to articulate in
more plain verbal language her fears about her impending death,
which had previously been symbolized by a concern about a cat-

astrophic destructive force bearing down upon her over which she had no control (the concept Kübler-Ross feels exemplifies the real fear of death.)

The one overriding need of fatally ill children is the need to find a way to communicate their emotions (Green-Epner, 1976). An overabundance of emotions is aroused by the illness, hospitalization, and impending death. The child often lacks the requisite maturity for dealing with anxieties and concerns that even adults have trouble with. Thus, the child should be helped to understand and cope with the vicissitudes of the illness as much as his age, maturity, previous experiences, and intellectual and social development allow. However, this can often not be done solely on an adult, verbal level. Intervention and support may have to be directed in symbolic, nonverbal ways.

> [Caregivers] must provide the child with a convenient and acceptable outlet for emotional release. This outlet must afford the child an opportunity for self-expression, direct or indirect. It must be a means through which the child can express all his emotions positive and negative. It must provide a feeling of safety and security, so that the child need not fear adult reprisal for the revelation of forceful, negativistic feelings. Once expressed, these feelings must be dealt with in a manner that is beneficial to the child. Trust, faith, relief, security, and happiness are to be promoted.
>
> Is there such a method, device, tool, or outlet available to the [caregiver]? Fortunately, yes. Play, especially therapeutic play, meets the stated requirements. (Green-Epner, 1976, p. 140)

Since play is the natural means of communication for children, it is only natural that it be a primary mode of communication with the child who is seriously ill. It also may provide an opportunity for the child to experience some control and mastery over the environment, which may be totally lacking due to the dependency enforced by the illness. Play can give insight into the child's thoughts, feelings, and needs, and provide supportive experiences for dealing with specific issues aroused by the illness.

It is clearly necessary to be observant of and responsive in several modes of communication when working with children. Although young patients struggle with many of the same issues as adult patients, they lack the more mature methods of communication and thought that would allow them to cope more successfully with the illness and threat of impending death. Consequently, it is imperative to assess and respond to the needs of terminally ill children in whatever "language" is most appropriate for each individual child.

FAMILY RESPONSES
TO THE TERMINAL ILLNESS OF A CHILD

The terminal illness of any family member throws the family system into severe disequilibrium, demanding many readjustments as they react to constantly changing events. The illness frequently becomes the central focus around which the family organizes itself and its activities. When the dying family member is a child, the innocence and helplessness of the victim and the unfairness of the situation combine with unique parental responses to the potential loss of a child to create a profoundly stressful experience that, due to advances in medicine, may continue on for years. During that time the child will be simultaneously growing and dying. The child's family must now respond to the new practical demands of living with an extended treatment regimen that dictates family life and creates continued stress for family members, while providing as normal a home life as possible (Slavin, 1981). There are also emotional demands, such as setting priorities so the ill child and the healthy family members all get their needs met and coping with uncertainty. Instead of preparing for imminent death, families now have to prepare themselves for continuing life despite the possibility of death:

> Literature on the family has emphasized the practical and emotional burdens imposed on parents by their child's cancer treatment. These burdens include the physical effort necessary for frequent outpatient cancer therapy; balancing the needs of the patient in the home with those of healthy siblings; fostering the patient's normal social and emotional development while coping with long-term uncertainty; and dealing with unresolved anticipatory grief if the child survives. (Slavin, 1981, p. 30)

Although this is a time of immense emotional and social upheaval for family members, it is important to remember that for the most part such individuals are normal people undergoing an extremely difficult time. They must not be approached from the typical mental health perspective of uncovering unconscious or unrecognized material. The situation must be recognized as one that prompts emotional problems in any family.

> It is unlikely that a clinician's first encounter with the child who has cancer will be in a relaxed setting or otherwise be typical of the youngster's "normal" behavior. The usual interaction cannot be predicated on the model of a professional helping emotionally troubled people to overcome long-standing maladaptive behavior patterns. Instead, one can expect to encounter basically sound families confronting inordinate amounts of stress which they are powerless to control. In the face of such events even the best adjusted families will be unable to escape reactive emotional difficulties linked to powerful reality events. (Koocher, 1980, p. 231)

Instead of traditional psychotherapeutic intervention, the situation calls for aiding the family members in adapting to stress and using appropriate coping mechanisms. They will also require support, resources, and information in order to handle reality-based problems.

It must be remembered that families will differ in their approaches to communication and support. Spinetta (1977, 1978) categorized families into three types. Supportive families talk openly about life's concerns and allow free expression of positive and negative feelings, supporting the needs of individual members. Quasi-supportive families may talk about the illness but do not allow the child and family members to openly discuss feelings. In these families there is often a nonmalicious, well-intentioned resistance to open communication, suggesting that support may be less than genuine. Noncommunicative families do not mention the word "cancer." They will not allow conversation about death or any other crisis. These families appear to need encouragement and assistance in reaching greater levels of communication, but their lack of experience in dealing openly with critical issues must be taken into account. Interventions must always be carried out within the context of families' specific needs, abilities, and levels of readiness.

Besides the strain on emotional resources that occurs as family life is centered around a child's terminal illness, there is a significant drain on financial resources. There are two major components of expenses for the family: medical costs and nonmedical, out-of-pocket costs. Medical costs are often fully covered by third-party carriers; if not, the remainder can be paid in installments. In contrast, out-of-pocket expenses, which often are not anticipated by the family, must be paid immediately and are usually not even tax deductible. Such expenses include transportation, food, clothing, family care, and lodging (Lansky, Cairns, Clark, Lowman, Miller, & Trueworthy, 1979), plus the loss of wages on the part of parents staying with the ill child. The combined costs generate a loss of family income that is economically catastrophic. Financial concerns create considerable psychological stress for the family, both by affecting the emotional, physical, and social quality of life and by causing practical problems. Thus, caregivers must be prepared to intervene or refer the family to appropriate resources. (See "Financial Issues" in Chapter 8 for more on this topic.

Parents' Responses

The loss of a child is a uniquely difficult loss with which to contend. The role of the parent appears to promote particularly severe grief. There is mourning not only for the child, but for the loss of parts of self and of immortality. The loss of the child threatens a basic function of parenthood—protection of the child. This, combined with the unnaturalness of the child's predeceasing the parent, contributes to the particularly intense grief experienced by parents who are losing or have lost their child. Additionally, the roles of provider, problem-solver, and advisor, and the qualities of being self-sufficient and in control—all major factors of the adult's identity—are taken from the parent when a child is dying or has died. (See "Grief After the Death of a Child" in Chapter 6 for more on this topic.)

Parents must combine the task of trying to establish normal development for the child with coping with the emotional shock of facing the possibility of the child's death, while shouldering the physical and financial burdens of outpatient treatment and attending to the heightened needs of spouse and siblings due to the illness as well as their basic ongoing needs. The integration of these tasks requires enormous emotional energy. Parents must recognize their own limitations, set priorities, conserve their energy for the long haul, and, very importantly, remember that "a 'normal' life for their child . . . does not mean a perfect life or a completely smooth childhood" (Slavin, 1981, p. 28).

There are 11 investigations in the literature that form the backbone of the research on the experience of parents of terminally ill children: Binger et al., 1969; Bozeman, Orbach, and Sutherland, 1955; Chodoff, Friedman, and Hamburg, 1964; Easson, 1970; Friedman, Chodoff, Mason, and Hamburg, 1963; Hamovitch, 1964; Knudson and Natterson, 1960; Natterson and Knudson, 1960; Orbach, Sutherland, and Bozeman, 1955; Richmond and Waisman, 1955; and Solnit and Green, 1959. However, these early investigations had inconsistent results, often based upon subjective clinical judgment without objective, valid, or reliable measures of adjustment. Moreover, they were generally conducted prior to the advances in the treatment of cancer, which now has become more of a chronic life-threatening illness. In recent years there have been some relatively more comprehensive studies of parental experience during and after the child's terminal illness that are more applicable to present clinical reality: Foster, O'Malley, and Koocher, 1981; Kemler, 1981; Kerner, Harvey, and Lewiston, 1979; Kreuger, Gyllensköld, Pehrsson, and Sjölin, 1981; Kupst, Schulman, Honig, Maurer, Morgan, and Fochtman, 1982; Rando, 1983; and Spinetta, Swarner, and Sheposh, 1981.

Initial Diagnosis

Parents routinely report that the period of diagnosis is the most stressful during the entire illness. Shock, denial, and disbelief are common reactions. Initially this denial may be helpful in allowing parents to avoid being overwhelmed by the catastrophic news they are receiving. Parents consistently report that it is critical to have some dimension of hope conveyed with the diagnosis. Although they want a realistic picture of their child's chances for survival, they also need some minimal hope to hang on to. Those parents who were satisfied with the deliverance of the diagnosis note that their physician gave them hope, was honest, offered information, and showed consideration by being supportive and tactful (Foster, O'Malley, & Koocher, 1981). The physician might also help by supporting parents in seeking second opinions to confirm the diagnosis (Easson, 1970). Parents must be convinced in their minds that they have not failed to obtain the most accurate diagnosis or the best treatment of their child. If the physician suggests that the family seek only one or two confirmatory opinions, he places some limits on their anxiety (by restricting how far the parents should go in seeking other opinions), while at the same time allowing them to ensure they have done the best they possibly could for their child. Of course, if immediate treatment is necessary, this option may not be open. One of the things that consistently comes across in the reflections of parents is that it is more important *how* the initial period is handled, rather than specifically *what* is done.

Due to their intense emotional responses, it is exceptionally difficult for parents to absorb the reality of the situation and take in all the information given at the time of initial diagnosis. This information may have to be disseminated several times following the first meeting. If at all possible, both parents should be present at the initial diagnosis so that one will not have to convey the information to the other. This ensures that both have heard the appropriate information. If necessary, subsequent meetings should be scheduled in order to review information relayed in the initial meeting and to assess the parents' understanding of the disease, its treatment, and its side effects. At this very difficult time it is crucial to be available to them, as well as to provide them with written information about the illness and the resources available to them. It is important to assist parents with successful coping at the time of diagnosis because these initial behaviors and attitudes may set the pattern for subsequent ones later in the illness.

Emotional Reactions

Some of the immediate emotional responses that parents experience following a diagnosis center around their feelings of guilt and failure at having been unable to protect their child from this catastrophe. Parents may look back to previous symptoms and berate themselves for failing to act upon them. When the disease may have been caused by some genetic flaw, parents may assume irrational guilt for passing the disease along to the child. Such guilt also may arise from previous unconscious death wishes harbored towards the child or from the belief that she may not have been cared for properly (Karon, 1975). Similar to bereaved individuals following the death of a loved one, parents will tend to reflect on the ambivalence in the parent-child relationship and feel guilty. The magical thinking of childhood is not restricted to children; parents may interpret the disease as a punishment for previous wrong thoughts or actions. Opportunities for appropriate ventilation of guilt should be offered before direct intervention is tried. As with the bereaved, guilt often dissipates once released. However, because of the unique role of the parent, psychological and social pressures for guilt are quite intense and parents will often require some intervention. The medical realities of the situation must be pointed out to them, to counter their irrational concerns over causation. They must also be helped to acknowledge their normal ambivalence and recognize the positive aspects of their feelings towards the child. This will hopefully put their more negative feelings in an appropriate perspective. Later in the course of the illness, parents and other family members will be susceptible to guilt as normal resentments and frustrations build up. These must be interpreted as normal reactions to an exceptionally stressful situation. Guilt may make parents tend to overindulge and overprotect the terminally ill child. Such attitudes should be discouraged, as they interfere with the child's normal development and convey to the child the frightening idea that something is horribly wrong. It is especially important to intervene when children sense their parents' guilt and use it to manipulate them or express anger towards them for failure to stop the painful process. It takes little to reinforce parental guilt, so parents need help in developing a reasonable perspective on this. (See "Grief After the Death of a Child" in Chapter 6 for more on the causes and treatment of parental guilt, and "Emotional Responses of the Family" in Chapter 12 for more on guilt generated by the terminal illness of a family member.)

The normal components of anticipatory grief will be part and parcel of the parents' experiences. Sadness, depression, anxiety, sorrow, and anger are all prevalent emotional responses. Separation anxiety is heightened by the child's hospitalization. Although there is now more support for parental rooming-in when the child is hospitalized, the obvious separation from the home environment and the altered family schedule indicate all too well the fact that there will someday be a permanent separation, despite togetherness at the present. Many times parents unwittingly reinforce separation anxiety by overprotecting the child in an attempt to reduce their own anxiety. School phobias and a reduction in the child's motivation to continue with other normal activities may result (Futterman & Hoffman, 1970; Lansky, Cairns, & Zwartjes, 1983; Lansky, Lowman, Vats, & Gyulay, 1975). As noted previously, children take on many of the feelings of their parents and anxiety is often transferred from parents to child. Parents must be helped to acknowledge feelings of anticipatory grief, recognize when those feelings have been displaced, and discharge the feelings through nondestructive channels that will not interfere with the child's development.

Another possible parental response to the illness of the child is overidentification, as the child's death foreshadows the parents' own death. This will prompt parents' concerns about their own vulnerability and mortality as they struggle to cope with that of their child. Katz (1980) reviewed the literature on parental anxiety and found that such anxiety influences children's responses to hospitalization and clinic appointments, and can increase the child's anxiety and maladaptive behavior. Additionally, parents who are themselves highly anxious appear to impose their perceptions of the child's illness onto the child, emphasizing symptoms and disabilities that had not previously disturbed the child. Again, parents need to learn to cope with these emotions in ways that will not be detrimental to the child.

One of the most difficult issues for parents to contend with is surrendering much of their authority and control over their child to caregivers. This not only escalates feelings of helplessness, lack of control, and separation anxiety, but also fuels additional parental guilt and concern over not being able to carry out the parental functions of nurturance and protection of the child. The illness of the child may force increased family dependency on caregivers, which can further undermine the parents' sense of competency. When the child expresses anger at the parents for not being able to control the situation and protect her from the pain of the experience, the parents are burdened with even more stress. Parents should be encouraged to participate in treatment care to the fullest extent possible and/or desirable. This will alleviate some of the parental concerns over loss of control and lack of involvement in the child's care. It will give them something to combat their sense of powerlessness because of their inability to protect the child. Previous research has indicated that participation in the care of the terminally ill child is related to parental adaptation during the illness and after the death (Friedman et al., 1963; Knudson & Natterson, 1960; Richmond & Waisman, 1955; Wiener, 1970; Willis, 1974). Such participation appears to be quite helpful to parents:

> We have found that the involvement of parents in the physical care of the child is extremely important in facilitating parental adaptation. First, this permits the parents to have a feeling that they personally have done everything possible for the child; second, feelings of guilt are somewhat relieved by the expenditure of personal effort in the care of the child; third, in retrospect

parents are very grateful for having had the opportunity to spend as much time with the child as is possible; and fourth, an opportunity to observe and to participate in measures directed to relieve pain and discomfort as much as possible is comforting to parents. (Richmond & Waisman, 1955, p. 45)

However, there is a caveat. Both Hamovitch (1964) and Rando (1983) found that too much participation can be detrimental to parental adjustment. There appears to be an optimum amount of participation in the child's treatment that engenders sound parental adjustment and ensures adequate attention to other family members at home. Rando (1983) also found that there were optimum amounts of anticipatory grief during the child's illness. As with participation in the child's treatment, too little or too much appears to compromise the parents' adjustment subsequent to the death of the child. Although there has long been an awareness of the negative affects of insufficient anticipatory grief and limited participation in the care of the child, there now needs to be a recognition of the undesirable consequences that may result from "too much of a good thing." Further research is necessary to clarify what constitutes "appropriate" and "optimum" amounts of these variables before it will be possible to identify, differentiate, and predict what will be the most therapeutic for different parents and situations. For now, the best course is to keep in mind the importance of balancing involvement with the terminally ill child with involvement in other ongoing aspects of life.

Parents may also prematurely decathect from the dying child, just as they might from an adult. The chances of this occurring must be minimized by encouraging appropriate interaction until death. The Lazarus syndrome (described in "Emotional Responses of the Family" in Chapter 12), along with the continued emotional and financial strain, can cause great resentment. The neglect of other family responsibilities and roles, due to the investment of resources in the dying child, will create the same types of pressures in the case of the terminally ill child as it does in the case of the terminally ill adult.

An aspect of the parental experience that is frequently overlooked is the parents' "search for meaning." Chodoff, Friedman, and Hamburg (1964) found that an important part of the parents' experience during the child's terminal illness was the "search for meaning," in which the parents urgently tried to make sense out of the tragedy. This search would take various forms such as seeking out some personal agency to be blamed for the disease or placing it within the realm of God's will. The loss of any loved one may stimulate such a quest for meaning. However, the violation of the natural order in the child's predeceasing the parent cries out for the assignment of meaning to an otherwise meaningless event. Several writers have pointed out that the search for meaning is an essential part of the grief work of bereaved parents in coming to some resolution of their child's death (Craig, 1977; Miles, Note 22).

Personal Adjustment

There have been conflicting reports as to how the experience of a child's terminal illness and death will affect the marital relationship. One study found that 3 months after the death of a child from leukemia 5% of the parents had divorced, 18% were separated, and 70% reported serious marital problems (Kaplan, Grobstein, & Smith, 1976). Later contact showed an increased number of divorces. This study supported the view of numerous writers who suggested that severe marital discord, even divorce, is an inevitable outcome of coping with a child's terminal illness. In contrast, a larger and more empirical study found that parents of children with cancer experienced more marital stress than a comparison group of couples with hemophiliac children, but not to the point that they resorted to divorce (Lansky, Cairns, Hassanein, Wehr, & Lowman, 1978). In fact, contrary to the prediction of a high divorce rate among these families, the divorce rate of parents of children with cancer was lower than the average divorce rate in the two states covered by the study. Other research investigations have found differing percentages of family disruption following the experience of childhood terminal illness. Whereas some of these investigations indicate that families cope fairly well, given the inordinate stress of the illness, others indicate that the rate of family disruption is extraordinarily high—88% in the Kaplan et al. study. Kupst et al. (1982) suggest that the difficulty in reconciling these viewpoints stems from the fact that studies focusing on the problems of families do not allow for positive indicators as well. In studies where it is possible to evaluate positive indicators, families came out looking relatively better. Also, early studies were not longitudinal, so that families were typically seen at the crisis period of diagnosis or asked for retrospective accounts after the death of the child. It was in these studies that family disruption was thought to be relatively higher than in more recent studies.

Interesting information has come from a study of parents whose children survived pediatric cancer. Foster, O'Malley, and Koocher (1981) report that the stress of the cancer experience did not appear to adversely affect the parents' marriages. Although a few couples reported a negative effect, most couples felt that the impact was positive over the long run, as they became sensitive to positive and negative aspects of the marital relationship. Those couples who had been in the process of separating or divorcing at the time of the diagnosis did not alter their decisions; but many couples were able to share their feelings from the beginning of the experience and felt that their marriages became stronger through reliance on each other's strengths and increasing respect for each other. For these people "family relationships became a conscious priority and they no longer took them for granted. They reported developing a much deeper sense of unity than they had been aware of before this experience" (p. 94). All of this illustrates that, while the stress of childhood illness is exceptionally high, it does not have to disrupt family relationships. Each family must be evaluated individually, so its strengths can be supported and its weaknesses can be compensated for.

Although its effects may vary, a child's terminal illness does put a great strain on the marital relationship. It may severely limit the amount of time parents can have together, and much of that time may be involved in discussing the child's condition. Previous areas of communication may be abandoned as efforts now are focused more directly on the child. In reaction to grief and distance from each other, the sexual relationship may deteriorate and cause further pain and loss. Parents need support in maintaining as much as possible their relationship with each other, as well as with other family members, and in understanding how the stress of a dying child can affect them. It is critical to bolster the marital relationship, the foundation of the family, with whatever interventions are possible.

One problem couples may face is that male and female roles sometimes predispose partners to experience their child's illness differently. Stereotypically, the father has had to continue to work, while the mother has been the one to be more involved in the treatment of the child. As society allows roles to become more androgenous, this can be expected to change. What must be recognized, however, is that different role expectations, economic pressures, and personality variables may combine to provide different experiences for each member of the marital dyad. As in parental bereavement, differing grieving styles may produce increased stress for partners if they misinterpret the meaning of their spouse's behaviors.

In an attempt to reduce marital distance and increase support for the child, stronger efforts are being made to involve fathers in the care of the child and to make contact with them as well as with mothers. Much of the criticism fathers have received has been quite inappropriate. Many are emotionally torn apart when economic responsibilities prevent them from interacting with their sick child. Although social conditioning often inhibits outward manifestations of grief, it is clear that large percentages of fathers experience the same feelings as mothers; some even experience more. Often fathers are overlooked by caregivers and society, and their anguish is relatively unrecognized as compared to that of mothers. They are asked how their wives are doing, while their status is unquestioned. This often means that they fail to receive the support they need to cope with their grief. It may also further reinforce the male role conditioning of avoidance of dealing with feelings. The experiences of fathers must be legitimized and attended to. Fathers should be included in treatment planning and care as much as possible. They may need help in balancing their role as provider with their desire to spend time with their dying child. In some cases obtaining a leave of absence or taking other steps to gain additional free time from work should be explored. The father-child relationship should be encouraged and supported, as should the father's relationships with other family members. Finally, fathers will need therapeutic assistance in processing their own grief.

Both parents can benefit from opportunities to discuss their experiences with parents of other terminally ill children. Frequently the support offered by other parents is cited as the most beneficial of all, for they are seen as the only other people who can truly empathize with the experience. Parent support groups, such as The Candlelighters Foundation or hospital-based self-help groups, can be utilized both before and after the child's death.

Such support is particularly invaluable because social expectations are often quite unfair to the parents of terminally ill children. They fail to recognize the need for parents, as well as other family members, to have respites from their anticipatory grief and outlets for their emotions (Easson, 1970). The parents who want to escape to a movie, the father who dares to laugh too freely, the mother who wears too colorful a dress—all may be socially condemned for insensitivity at a time when they need to be supported in their coping. Giving parents permission to take time out to replenish themselves can help ease the strain.

Of clinical note are the findings of Spinetta, Swarner, and Sheposh (1981) on the variables associated with parents who were most adjusted after the death of their child from cancer. Results suggest that the parents who were the best adjusted were those

> (a) who had a consistent philosophy of life during the course of the illness which helped the family accept the diagnosis and cope with its consequences, (b) who had a viable and ongoing support person to whom they could turn for help during the course of the illness, and (c) who gave their child the information and emotional support the child needed during the course of the illness at a level consistent with their child's questions, age, and level of development. (p. 251)

Effective interventions will support these variables in families of terminally ill children.

Foster, O'Malley, and Koocher (1981) found that parents whose

children had experienced long-term survival following cancer diagnosis and treatment reported that hope and honest communication, faith (not necessarily a formal religious affiliation), and the
support of other family members was very important. They noted
that trust that their child was getting the best and most up-to-date
medical care possible was essential in allowing parents to endure
the experience of a child with a potentially fatal illness. Interestingly, these parents also answered most emphatically that they
would have appreciated meeting with a staff person at the hospital
to talk about emotional issues while their child was in treatment.
They noted they would have liked the meeting to take place within
the first week or so after diagnosis and commencement of treatment. These parents thought the idea should be suggested by the
primary physician as a routine part of the system of care so that
parents would not feel stigmatized by referral to a mental health
professional. They felt the initial meeting should describe issues
that other parents have experienced in order to help them anticipate what they might undergo. They also wanted to be told that
the feeling of being in emotional shock would probably diminish
as they became accustomed to the hospital's system and routine.
Some parents thought one to three meetings would probably be
enough as long as they had the option to meet again when necessary. Most parents admitted they would have liked to have met
either individually or as a couple with a mental health professional
to discuss their own feelings. They felt that while they could talk
about their child to the hospital staff, they were reluctant to bring
up their own feelings since the staff's primary concern was for the
child. The parents did not want to "take up their time." All of this
indicates that parents do have needs that are not always articulated
and that most of them would like mental health supportive services
to be integrated into the overall care of the dying child and her
family.

Siblings' Responses

The siblings of a terminally ill child are in a very difficult
position. Not only do they face the loss of their sibling and the
family as they have known it, but also the loss of their parents'
attention as well. The heavy demands placed upon the parents to
care for the dying child often leave them without the time or financial and emotional resources that would normally be distributed equitably among siblings. In such situations, it is not uncommon for siblings to feel resentment towards the dying child. Such
children need empathy with and normalization of their resentful
feelings, and an explanation of the new priorities caused by the
illness. They also require recognition of their own worth to the
family. In addition, adults must make sure that siblings do not

harbor an unrealistic sense of responsibility for the illness. (See Chapter 6 for ways to help siblings cope with grief.)

The emotional and physical exhaustion of parents puts additional burdens on the siblings. Parents may be impatient, have unreasonable expectations, and give them increased responsibilities. Such demands may engender further resentment and may be taken as parental rejection. In addition, siblings may be left without the necessary support and guidance they require for normal development.

A series of recent investigations has proved what astute caregivers have recognized for many years: the siblings of dying children may suffer just as much, and at times even more, than the ill children themselves. Spinetta (1981b) reported on what happens to siblings of children with cancer. From the investigations of his team it was ascertained that families were able to meet the medical needs of the patient and the day-to-day needs of family members relatively well. There was more difficulty with meeting the emotional needs of the family members, however. The patient's emotional needs were met the most adequately, with the mother's and father's needs met slightly less well. The siblings' emotional needs were met at a level significantly less adequate than that of other family members. In terms of overall emotional adjustment to the cancer and its treatment, siblings showed less adjustment and greater need than did other family members (Spinetta, McLaren, Deasy-Spinetta, Kung, Schwartz, & Hartman, Note 23).

Spinetta et al. (1981) also reported on the findings of siblings relative to patients in three age levels. Compared to patients in the same age group, 4- to 6-year-old siblings had significantly lower self-concepts, a more negative attitude towards self, and greater sensitivity towards the patient than the patient towards the sibling; they also viewed their parents as more distanced psychologically from them. As the disease worsened, the siblings' decrease in self-concept was more drastic. In siblings aged 6 to 12 there was evidence of significantly less adaptation during the diagnosis period, during periods of relative stability of the disease, and when the disease was in a long-term remission. This is in contrast to patients, who scored at their poorest levels at points when the effects of the disease were more severe. These siblings manifested more anxiety, depression, and maladaptive responses in a story-telling test and viewed their parents as more distanced psychologically from them than did the patients. In measures of family relationships, young adolescent siblings aged 13 to 18 scored the family as significantly greater in conflict and lower in cohesion than did patients. Story-telling scores were higher for conflict and contained more elements of punishment and mutilation. The concerns of the teenage siblings appeared to surface in broad areas of life, whereas those of the patients were more directly disease-related. It was also indicated that when the patient was doing poorly, siblings of all ages tended to be left without attention and needed support; and when the patient was doing well, parental concerns shifted to other, nondisease-related matters. The siblings appeared to lose out on both ends. Spinetta (1981b) concludes:

> The results of the study lend support to the fundamental hypothesis that siblings suffer at least as much as and probably more than the patients in unattended emotional responses to the disease and the disease process. . . . All family members suffer when a child is diagnosed with cancer. In its attempts to keep marital relationships alive and vital and to help the children with cancer cope with and master their illness, the medical team should not ignore the needs and concerns of those persons who will in most cases live the longest with memories and concerns relative to the cancer—the siblings of children with cancer. (pp. 140-141)

Related findings have been reported by Cairns, Clark, Smith, and Lansky (1979). They found that siblings evidenced even greater distress than patients in the areas of perceived social isolation, perception of parents as overindulgent and overprotective, fear of confronting family members with negative feelings, and (for the older siblings) concern with failure. There were striking similarities between patients' and siblings' negative body image and high anxiety. Although the siblings did not directly experience any disease, apparently the sick child's illness had such a profound effect on them that they suffered severe anxiety about their own health. It was demonstrated that siblings felt very isolated from their parents and other family members and friends. There was a recognition that they were being neglected in favor of the ill child and that the parents' time, attention, and financial resources were directed towards the patient's needs rather than the siblings'. The siblings became concerned about their dependence on parents who had so little time and other resources for them. They often remained home alone, worried and cut off from emotional support and reassurance. Nevertheless, they were less likely than patients to express negative feelings towards other family members, which was seen to reflect their insecurity about their precarious position in the family.

Previous observations and reports pointed out that siblings often evidenced all manner of symptoms and maladjustment during their sibling's illness and after his death. Previously well-adjusted siblings developed symptoms such as enuresis, headaches, abdominal pain, school problems, depression, and separation anxiety, which increased in severity after the terminally ill child's death (Binger et al., 1969). Feelings of rejection, guilt, and fear were common. Children's disturbed reactions to the death of a sibling have included symptoms across all ranges of affect, cognition, belief systems, superego functioning, and object relationships, and have been evidenced on the intrapsychic, family, peer, neighborhood, school, and community levels (Cain, Fast, & Erickson, 1964). A developmental focus on siblings who were not psychiatrically disturbed was provided by Lindsay & MacCarthy (1974). They noted that infant siblings are at highest risk because the mother, preoccupied with the sick child, is unable to respond to their cues. Toddlers are unable to comprehend at a verbal level, and interpret family changes as parental rejection. These children may then feel unhappy about themselves and regress. School-age siblings are aware of the elevated level of family anxiety and may feel not only rejection, but resentment, anger, and guilt for these feelings. This may result in acting-out behaviors, withdrawal into daydreams, anxious thoughts, declining school performance, and psychosomatic symptoms. Accident proneness, school phobia, and separation anxiety may develop. Older siblings may take over the care of the patient in a reaction formation against the resentment they actually feel. It may also be an attempt to identify with parents in order to gain approval from them and to vicariously look after their own needs.

Several themes have emerged from Sourkes' (1980) psychotherapeutic work with pediatric cancer patients and their siblings. These can be applied to siblings of children with other life-threatening illnesses as well. She notes that these issues do not begin and end at specific points in the illness, but rather ebb and flow throughout the experience. Reactions can be expected to be intensified during the critical periods of diagnosis, exacerbation, and relapse of the illness.

• *Causation of the illness.* Siblings often sustain two views on the causation of their sibling's illness. One view stems from the medical information they have been given by their parents and the doctors. The second view is their own private version. This is often fraught with emotional and cognitive confusion. Magical thinking and intense fear or guilt may combine to provide siblings with a misunderstanding of the cause of illness. It is imperative to obtain siblings' views of the illness in order to correct misconceptions and eliminate reasons for guilt and inappropriate assumption of responsibility.

• *Visibility of the illness and the treatment process.* Illnesses that lead to dramatic physical change provide a visible focus for explanation. It is easier for siblings to grapple with something obviously wrong with their brother or sister, like an amputation, than with an illness that is invisible, for example, leukemia. Similarly, the visibility or invisibility of the treatment process affects the siblings' perception. They may perceive the hospital or clinic as a threatening place or as a special place with pleasurable activities. For this reason it is important for siblings to have the opportunity to visit the hospital or clinic in order to have a realistic understanding of what the dying child undergoes.

• *Identification with the illness.* Siblings naturally become concerned that they may develop the illness, for in the past what has affected one child has often affected the other. They need reassurance that there is little likelihood of their developing the same disease and that the disease is not contagious. They must be encouraged to pursue their own activities and relationships in order to avoid overidentification with the patient and to encourage their own independence.

• *Guilt and shame.* There are many causes of guilt and shame in siblings. Siblings may feel guilty that they escaped the disease or that the patient is restricted due to the illness. The recognition of ambivalent feelings in the relationship with the ill child also stimulates guilt. The times of anger, envy, frustration, and resentment at the loss and pain the ill child has caused combine with normal sibling rivalry, plus the resentment that develops as family resources become more exclusively devoted to the ill child, and contribute additionally to siblings' feelings of guilt and even responsibility for the illness. Shame is often experienced at having a brother or sister who is ill or disfigured, since he marks the family as "different." Siblings desperately need the opportunity to discuss these feelings and to have them explained to them and normalized. Adults must make sure siblings do not assume an inappropriate sense of responsibility for the dying child's illness, and do not constrict their own activities out of guilt that the patient cannot participate with them.

• *Siblings and their parents.* Siblings receive diminished attention and nurturance from parents. They often resent the attention that is focused on the ill child and the leniency accorded him as compared to their own restrictions. At times siblings may be angry at parents for not having better protected the patient from the illness; they may also perceive them as having played a role in causing the illness. In addition, it is frightening for siblings to recognize the limited ability of their parents to protect them from illness. Siblings require regular times alone with one or both parents in order to support and nourish their own normal development. They may require assurance that they will be protected by parents as much as is possible.

• *Academic and social functioning.* Performance in these areas may be compromised due to the preoccupation with the stress of the illness. Some siblings will focus on school because it will allow them a sense of competence in the face of stress. Peer relationships may be curtailed as siblings focus more on the family or increased in order to provide support and interpersonal contact. Since school and peer relationships are a normal part of children's lives, successful functioning in these areas should be encouraged.

• *Somatic reactions.* These include physical symptoms, sleep problems, and accident proneness. They may develop as an expression of psychological conflicts or grief, as a means of gaining parental attention or of identifying with the patient, or as a result of preoccupation with the patient or the distraction preoccupation causes. It is often helpful to clarify for siblings the psychological meaning behind the somatic concerns in order to relieve them of the necessity for the symptoms.

• *Bidirectionality of the sibling-patient relationship.* The relationship between sibling and patient is always a two-way street, despite the overemphasis on the dying child. While a sibling has feelings towards the patient, the patient also has feelings towards the sibling. Mutual anger/resentment and protectiveness/caring are common themes. These may occur simultaneously or may be expressed by one towards the other individually. For example, the patient may be angry at the siblings for being healthy (something that has often been overlooked) or the patient and siblings may take care of each other. Communication should be facilitated as much as is possible between the patient and siblings.

In 1981 Gogan and Slavin reported on the unique results of a study in which 101 siblings of former cancer patients were interviewed. They found that having a sibling with cancer had a sustained and profound impact on the lives of the siblings. Feelings of being left out, jealousy, resentment, and fears for their own health were relatively common in the siblings. Siblings aged 6 to 10 at the time of the cancer treatment were particularly vulnerable to problems with feelings of rivalry. It appeared that closed communication systems in families contributed to the development of behavioral and emotional problems among siblings. Many of these problems could apparently have been prevented or ameliorated if direct factual information had been provided at the time of diagnosis and during treatment. Some siblings reported positive aspects of the cancer experience, including feelings of enhanced closeness to the former patient or other family members and enhancement of their own emotional growth and development of personal coping skills. Most appeared to have resolved any anger towards the patient over time once the treatment had ended. Normal sibling relationships seem to have been restored in the majority of cases. It was very clear that the siblings should not be neglected by caregivers during the course of the child's illness.

TREATMENT INTERVENTIONS

The following interventions are based on the information given in this chapter. In addition to those suggested in Chapter 12, "The Family of the Dying Patient," these specific recommendations are made for the dying child, family members, and caregivers. They are to be utilized only after a complete psychosocial assessment has been made of the family.

The Patient

• Recognize that children are aware of the seriousness of their condition, although they may not be able to articulate it. Even very young children are capable of reading the cues of concerned, anxious adults.

• Remember that children may have adult fears, but be unable to articulate them in adult ways.

• Be honest with children in age-appropriate ways.

• See that the child is told of the initial diagnosis within 24 hours of the time the parents are informed in order to prevent the child from hearing it from someone else. The diagnosis should be given by either the parents or physician, or both. If parents assume the responsibility to convey the diagnosis, make sure they actually follow through on it.

• Introduce psychosocial intervention at the time of diagnosis. This allows time for primary prevention and development of a relationship that can serve as a basis for working on later problems.

• Remember that ill children and adolescents are working on forming an identity while experiencing a vicious attack on their efforts. Unlike the adult, who already has an identity and operates from this more secure foundation, the adolescent and child are more insecure and require more structure and support.

• Recognize that children use three languages for communicating their knowledge of their impending death: plain English, symbolic nonverbal language, and symbolic verbal language. Be prepared to listen and respond in all three modalities.

• Recognize the prevalence of magical thinking in children. Explore with them their understanding of the causality of the illness, its experience, and its prognosis. Vigorously correct any misconceptions.

• Help children and adolescents to conceptualize and understand the changes their illness has brought about. They need to comprehend the effects of the illness and treatment, the alterations in family life, and their own reactions to the experience. This will make what is happening seem more orderly and predictable.

• Recognize the critical role of the presence and support of parents, even with adolescents. Although the adolescent may need more privacy and time away from parents, they still are critical to her.

• Make it clear to everyone involved with the child that inappropriate limitations and lack of discipline are harmful to the child. Overprotection and overindulgence will hurt the child by indicating that she is not normal and retarding her appropriate growth and development.

• Recognizing that play is the child's medium, make toys and occupational therapy resources available to the child to provide diversion, stimulation, and a means of communication.

• Give children the right to speak to caregivers in their parents' absence, honoring their desire to protect their parents.

• Educate the child about treatment and surgical procedures. Demonstrations, tours, and advance warnings all allow the child to accommodate to stressful situations.

• Give children the opportunity to speak with others who have undergone the same treatments. For example, it may be useful for a child to speak to another child who has had an amputation. Also, changes that will result from treatment can be discussed and plans can be made and rehearsed to handle such events as informing friends about treatment or returning to school for the first time.

• Provide challenges as part of treatment intervention, as children and adolescents need them to achieve mastery and competency.

• Recognize that the child needs to move around, and try to avoid restriction of movement unless absolutely necessary.

• Provide ongoing contact with peers and groups. This is important for maintaining social development and connection with others.

• Make reintegration of the child into school a primary goal, since school is part of the normal life of any child. Assist teachers in planning for the smoothest possible transition of the child back into school.

• Recognize that the adolescent is half child and half adult. Do not treat her as too much of either one or the other.

• Remember that adolescence is a time of onslaught by impulses that must be defended against. Hospitalization and illness may intensify them. Offer adolescents opportunities for socially appropriate gratification and/or sublimation of impulses.

• Assist adolescents in dealing with the acutely painful issues that are a normal part of adolescence. Recognize that these make them particularly vulnerable to the stress of illness.

• Acknowledge that the older child or adolescent is intimately concerned with the social effects of treatment and side effects. These effects may concern her more than the illness and its broader ramifications.

• Recognize the issues of sexuality for older children and adolescents who are ill. To deny them their sexuality is to deny them a part of their lives that normally would be of primary concern at this time.

• Keep in mind that one of the acutely painful factors of terminal illness in adolescence is that there is both more to lose and less to fall back upon than in any other time in life.

• Remember that adolescents have difficulty communicating with adults in general, and take this into consideration when working with them. There must be a respect for their privacy and their need for honesty and independence.

• Attend to parents' needs, as the parents' feelings impact directly on the child.

Family Members

• Help parents to understand the child's need for honest communication. Make it clear that the child has an awareness of his condition whether or not he has been told officially.

• Support the parents as the fundamental dyad sustaining the family. Facilitate the most open communication possible, given their abilities. Predict sources of stress, and help them understand their unique situation as parents in danger of losing their child.

• Encourage siblings to participate as much as possible in the illness experience. They are vulnerable to stress, and require both education and emotional support if they are to successfully cope. Help them deal with their typical feelings of resentment and jealousy of the patient, and with their guilt over past hostility or their current concern that they may have caused the illness.

• Educate parents about the importance of taking care of ongoing family needs, especially the developmental ones of healthy siblings.

• Plan with parents to anticipate financial burdens. Provide guidance and information about financial resources.

• Encourage family visitation, and attempt to provide rooming-in facilities when possible. Friends of the child and of the family should be welcomed. Restricting access to only the immediate family will deprive the child and family of important social support.

• Help parents to understand the dying child's responses, especially if those responses are out of character for the child or if they reflect anger that the parents do not understand.

• Make parents aware of the stereotypical male and female role expectations for their situation. Historically fathers' participation and involvement in the dying child's care has been downplayed. Families must be evaluated individually so that family members can be supported in undertaking whichever roles are the most appropriate for them.

• Help parents realize that they cannot protect their child from everything. They need support in relinquishing some of their authority over the child to caregivers so that child can receive treatment.

• Point out the critical nature of appropriate parental discipline and limitations for the child.

• Explain to the parents how the entire family is affected by the child's illness and what dynamics are involved in families in which a member is terminally ill. (See Chapter 12 for more on this topic.)

• Use peer support groups. Parents report that parents of other dying children provide them with their greatest support and resources. Sibling and patient support groups can do the same.

Caregivers

• Be committed to the patient and family as the unit of care.

• To plan appropriate interventions, gain a comprehensive understanding of child development and parental and sibling reactions.

• Recognize that the life-threatening illness of a child will be exceptionally difficult for you as a caregiver. Be sure to take care of your own physical and emotional needs.

CHAPTER 14

The Caregiver's Personal Concerns

Caring for the dying inevitably brings situations of personal crisis. Families must be helped to make agonizing, potentially life-or-death choices in areas where there are no clear-cut criteria for right or wrong. Questions of personal morality arise and have to be resolved. There is also the toll that working with the dying and bereaved takes on those who provide care. Trying to do too much and not obtaining sufficient support and time out from duties can cause depression and burn-out in the most dedicated of caregivers. These problems are considered here.

ETHICAL ISSUES

Developments in medicine in this century have made it possible to prolong the lives of those who would have previously died more quickly. This, coupled with the fact that the population now has a higher percentage of aged individuals suffering from chronic illness, poses bioethical quandaries for those in medicine and the health care fields. The possibility of the extension of life with new technology creates dilemmas such as whether or not to issue "Do Not Resuscitate" orders; to discontinue artificial life and feeding supports; or to forego, withdraw, or terminate treatment. There are questions about self-determination, informed consent, duty, privacy, respect, even about the definition of death itself. Patients' demands for death with dignity further complicate the matter.

Before any specific ethical dilemmas can be considered, the process of decision making in ethical dilemmas must be examined. The following material is taken from Aroskar's (1980) analysis of ethical dilemmas and Robbins' model for decision making and isolating and defining ethical issues (Note 24).

A dilemma is a situation in which there are at least two equally disagreeable or favorable alternatives and it is not clear which alternative to adopt. To begin resolving a dilemma it helps to divide it into three parts: the data base (situational facts), the decision-making questions, and the underlying ethical theories (Aroskar, 1980). These parts can then be examined within the context of the caregiver's personal and professional value systems to whatever extent is possible within the amount of time available.

In order to have the information required for complete analysis, the following situational facts of the data base must first be identified as completely as possible (Aroskar, 1980):

- What is the alleged dilemma? (Robbins, Note 24)
- Who are the actors involved? What are their histories and roles in the situation?
- What is the proposed action?
- What is the setting or context of the proposed action?
- What is the intention or purpose of the proposed action?
- What other alternatives are available?
- What are the probable implications or consequences of the proposed action?

Next, the following questions taken from decision-making theory must be answered (Aroskar, 1980):

- Who should decide (the physician, nurse, patient, family, committee)? Why?
- For whom is the decision being made (self, proxy, other)?
- What criteria should be used (social, legal, physiological, economic, psychological, other)? Why?
- What degree of consent by the patient is needed (freely given, coerced, none)?
- How is consent to be nurtured? (Robbins, Note 24)
- What, if any, moral principles are adhered to or violated by a proposed course of action (self-determination, truthfulness, beneficence, justice as fairness, other)?

The third part of structuring an ethical dilemma involves deciding upon the moral approaches, ethical theories, or positions to be used in considering the alternatives for action in a given specific situation. They are used as frameworks for suggesting possible solutions.

Many ethicists divide all ethical theories into two fundamental types—*consequentionalism* or *non-consequentionalism*. Consequentionalism is based on the idea that consequences or results dictate the goodness or rightness of human action. Such expressions as "The end justifies the means," "It worked out just fine," "The greatest good for the greatest number," or "This is the best alternative" are examples of this form of ethical theory. The most widely discussed form of consequentionalism is Utilitarianism. Some have expressed it as "The greatest good for the greatest number with the least amount of harm for the most people" or in terms of alternatives, i.e., a given course of action is superior to any other alternative. Utilitarianism is a community-oriented theory in which each person counts equally. It is in conflict with the traditional medical ethic of doing all that can be done for a single patient.

Non-consequentionalism is based on a belief that consequences are not a factor in determining rightness or wrongness. The end does not justify the means. The focus in non-consequentionalism is that actions are determined to be good or right on the basis of such concerns as motive or duty or obligation, without regard to consequences. The most widely discussed notion of non-consequentionalism stems from Kant. It is often referred to as Formalism or Deontology. Kant argues that duty is the primary guiding principle, and also includes the notion that people should be treated as ends in themselves and not as means to an end.

Since health care professionals are motivated both by notions of duty and concerns about consequences, some blending of theory, sometimes referred to as ethical pluralism, is required. Insights from consequentionalism and non-consequentionalism are blended together to offer a more comprehensive view.

Some less-widely regarded theories also exist, as shown by the following examples:

- *Egoism.* Here the solution that is best for the person who is deciding is chosen. For example, the caregiver would choose the action that is most comfortable for himself. An action is deemed good when it best serves his interests.
- *Distributive justice.* Goodness and justice is determined by the distribution of the goods of society in an equitable way. The distribution of burdens and benefits is considered from the point of view of those who are least advantaged in society, with benefit to them becoming a fundamental criterion for decision making.
- *Divine command.* God says it, you do it. "The Bible says . . ."

Considering and applying these various theories highlights the ethical dimensions of the problems faced and the uncertainties they generate.

Following these three steps, all the information must be evaluated in light of the caregiver's personal and professional value systems. Some feel that the preservation of life is more important than the quality of it; some believe that the ends justify the means. These values will clearly influence the approaches taken and answers given to the questions asked in structuring a dilemma. The amount of time available before a decision becomes necessary also obviously influences this process.

A Decision-Making Model

Many of the problems that arise in health care have multi-faceted dimensions and require more sophisticated treatment than a facile application of personal values or beliefs. These problems are seldom neatly packaged as core issues; instead they are complicated by legal, policy, or systemic considerations. Thus, in order to focus on the central issues, some process of sifting or isolating the issues is required.

The following model, The Robbins Model for Decision Making and Isolating and Defining Ethical Issues,* is an organized format to assist in complex decision making. Since each problem is distinctive in terms of its degree of complexity, the format can be easily simplified or upgraded to adjust for individual ·circumstances. While this model in itself will not provide answers, it will serve as a framework for understanding issues and suggest possible decision options. Figure 1 is a flow chart outlining the basic steps of the model, and the following case example will demonstrate, step by step, how the model works.

> *Case Example:* Mr. Jones is a 56-year-old man who has come to the hospital for surgery. Because of complications in surgery he suffers severe anoxic depression, which renders him comatose. He has both signed the hospital consent form for this surgery and has informed his wife on various occasions that if any problems resulted he did not want to spend the rest of his life on the respirator and no extraordinary measures should be taken. The attending physician knows the family well, but has recently become very sensitive to the dangers of malpractice suits and wishes to insulate himself from potential liability. As a result he is somewhat reluctant to act in accordance with what he thinks are the patient's wishes. The wife is adamant that no measures be taken to extend her husband's life if he does suffer cardiac arrest. The patient's eldest son, an attorney, disagrees fervently and wants anything and everything to be done. There is intense family conflict as to what should or should not be done. Social services has attempted to resolve this with a family conference, without success. What should the physician do? What are his primary obligations? Should the family conflict or concerns about defensive medicine undermine the patient's wishes?

---

*This model and case example on pages 420–427 were developed by Dennis A. Robbins, PhD, MPH, Director of the Graduate Program in Health Services Administration, Salve Regina College, Newport, RI.

• *Step 1.* Identify the central ethical issues in general terms, based on the consensus of the members of the decision-making group if possible.

> The central ethical issues to be faced in this dilemma can be stated in such questions as these: What are the rights of this incompetent patient? What obligations do caregivers have to respond to and ensure those rights? Some discussion among the decision-making group on what rights or issues are at stake must occur before proceeding to the next step.

• *Step 2.* Identify the sub-issues, which are often confused with the central ethical issues. This minimizes confounding factors and provides early identification of other pertinent issues.

> Here there are legal, clinical, financial, and familial conflict sub-issues involved. Some legal issues are the patient's right of self-determination (either by his own volition or through a designated surrogate), the doctor's potential liability, and the institution's liability. The clinical issue involves what is feasible and appropriate from the medical perspective of prognosis, likelihood of reversibility of condition, and so forth. Financially, the family is of slender means and the wife does not want to exhaust what little is left. The familial conflict in itself constitutes another pertinent sub-issue to be treated later.

• *Step 3.* Temporarily refrain from considering or weighing all sub-issues and focus on the central ethical issues.
• *Step 4.* Distinguish and isolate the ethical component from other sub-issue components.

> Often the legal and ethical issues are confused and must be separated. Special care must be taken not to confound other pertinent sub-issues such as administrative or systemic issues with ethical issues. The ethical issues to be entertained in this case might include the following: (1) the right to refuse treatment; (2) the right of self-determination, that is, for the patient not to have his wishes compromised by external considerations and to have his autonomy assured; (3) the physician's duty to his patient; (4) the conflicts surrounding intent and insulation from liability; (5) the responsibility of the administration; (6) the question of clarifying patient intent when financial considerations are involved and ruling out any "foul play," such as a large life insurance settlement that might sway decision making on the part of the family.

• *Step 5.* Refine the ethical component by transforming it into an ethical dilemma: state it as a conflict between at least two existing alternatives where it is unclear which alternative to adopt.

> The central ethical conflicts here involve a potential compromise of patient rights, as well as the rights of the provider not to be placed in a compromising situation. The conflict is whether the

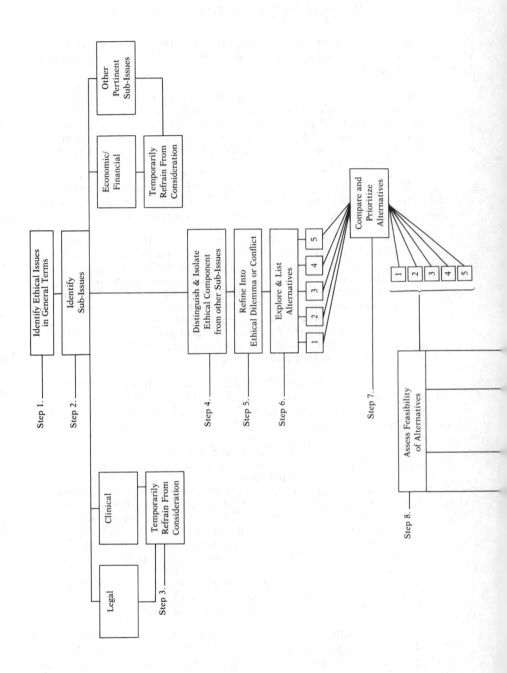

Step 1. Identify Ethical Issues in General Terms

Step 2. Identify Sub-Issues

Legal | Clinical | Economic/Financial | Other Pertinent Sub-Issues

Step 3. Temporarily Refrain From Consideration

Temporarily Refrain From Consideration

Step 4. Distinguish & Isolate Ethical Component from other Sub-Issues

Step 5. Refine Into Ethical Dilemma or Conflict

Step 6. Explore & List Alternatives
1 2 3 4 5

Step 7. Compare and Prioritize Alternatives
1 2 3 4 5

Step 8. Assess Feasibility of Alternatives

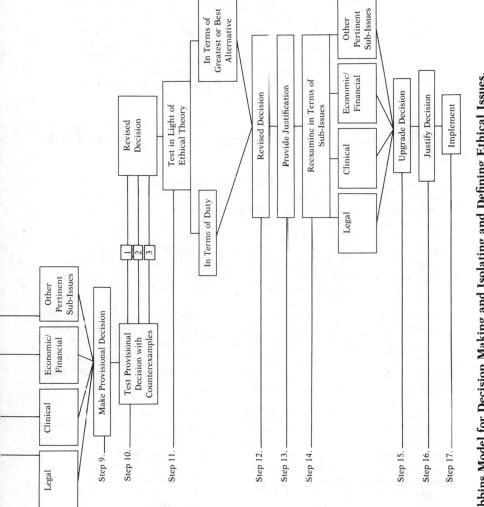

Figure 1. The Robbins Model for Decision Making and Isolating and Defining Ethical Issues.

physician should chart "Do Not Resuscitate" (DNR) orders in accordance with the wishes of the wife acting for her husband, risking the legal uncertainty of the son's suing him, or try to manipulate the wife to agree with the son to avoid potential litigation. The dilemma can also be characterized as a conflict between duty, as doing the best one can to serve one's patient's needs, or taking the least restrictive course, with less legal exposure for the physician and the hospital.

• *Step 6.* Explore and list alternatives for solution or resolution of the ethical dilemma in an attempt to develop a provisional decision.

Five possible alternatives for the physician are suggested. Possibility 1: Motivated by duty, provide the best possible care in accordance with the patient's wishes, remaining within the context of the law without compromising the wishes of the patient. Possibility 2: Lie to the son when DNR orders are performed. Possibility 3: Lie to the wife and do not tell her that her husband was ever coded. Possibility 4: Ignore both wife and son and do what is best medically. Possibility 5: Do what is possible to maximize protection from legal liability for both self and institution.

• *Step 7.* Compare, prioritize, or grade alternatives in terms of preferred choices. This step can be adjusted as the complexity of problems increases. In grading alternatives, consideration may be given to conflicts between sub-issue components to further clarify each component. Also at this stage some alternatives can be discarded and others can be revised or added.

Assume that in this particular case there is consensus that deceiving the wife or the son would not be the first choice and, in fact, is deemed unreasonable and unacceptable. Also assume that there is concurrence of opinion that the physician should act in the best interests of his patient and write the DNR orders. That would therefore be the first option. The second option would be that the physician act to insulate himself from liability, as long as it does not compromise the patient's wishes. Therefore the alternatives would be graded as follows: (1) physician's duty to patient; (2) protection from legal liability; (3) ignoring both wife and son and doing what is best medically; (4) deceiving the wife; and (5) deceiving the son.

In this case the only real alternative with which anyone is comfortable is the first option. Yet, the individual or group members making the decision may feel that a still better alternative might be available. And at this point he or they might choose to include that alternative, e.g., that an ethics committee at the hospital be empaneled to adjudicate the conflict that exists. For purposes of simplification, however, assume that the decision-making individual or group adopts the first option.

• *Step 8.* Assess the feasibility of the alternatives. This allows considerations of time, staffing, economics, legal constraints, and related issues to be integrated into the decision-making process.

Since in this case Number 1 is the obvious choice, it will not be necessary to assess the feasibility of each alternative. However, in other circumstances it may be appropriate to assess each alternative. Assessing feasibility includes focusing on clinical, legal, financial, and other pertinent components. For instance, is it medically feasible or appropriate to do this? Is this action consistent with legal standards or hospital policy or by-laws? There are also financial and economic considerations in this particular example, as in many, and they should be assessed if they have any bearing on the decision-making process at this stage.

• *Step 9.* Make a provisional decision on the basis of the assessment of earlier steps. This is a summarizing process.

Now an upgraded decision can be made incorporating the clinical, legal, financial, and policy perspectives. In this case the provisional decision will likely be that the physician act in the best interest of his patient and write the DNR order, but because of legal concerns and the financial consideration of the wife not wanting to exhaust all resources, contingency planning by bringing in a psychiatric consultant, changing to another caregiver, or implementing another family conference would be mechanisms to minimize the potential liability. These activities could be charted accordingly. This upgraded provisional decision allows for providing the best care for the patient, while at the same time includes a mechanism to minimize the threat of liability.

• *Step 10.* Test the provisional decision by constructing counterexamples. This is aimed at refining the provisional decision, upgrading it, or, in intense dilemmas, returning to earlier steps if the provisional decision does not withstand the challenges that the counterexamples pose.

The following counterexamples might be applied in this context: (1) Is it right to utilize caregivers and institutions and exhaust additional financial resources for the sole purpose of protecting against potential liability? (2) Does the introduction of non-medical issues compromise medical care? (3) Should the decision be taken to court to absolve caregivers of any decision making at all? Applying these counterexamples may result in further modification and revision of the decision.

• *Step 11.* Test the upgraded decision in light of ethical theory. Two examples of ethical theory, one stemming from duty, the other from the best alternative approach, are often sufficient. This is not a step to demonstrate how ethics can justify a given stance, but to understand what two or more ethical approaches offer as potential solutions. This step can also be the application of a given ethical posture that a particular institution has already adopted as part of its policy.

> Assume that only two ethical theories will be used to test the provisional decision: a non-consequentionalist and a consequentionalist approach. The non-consequentionalist approach will be testing in terms of duty or professional responsibility; the consequentionalist approach will be testing in terms of identifying the best alternative from a range of options. In this example duty brings up the question of why a patient comes to a physician in the first place. The patient comes to the physician in order to receive care and assumes that the physician will do whatever lies in the best interests of the patient and not compromise that with external considerations, e.g., protection against potential legal liability. The physician has a duty, as do other caregivers, to act in accordance with the wishes and intents of the patient, and when that is unclear, to rely upon the family as surrogates for decision making. Since the physician knows the family, and since the wife has been clear about her husband's intent, the physician's major responsibility lies with the patient, not with the survivors, even though survivors are generally the ones who sue. To act in opposition to the patient's wishes, consent, or intent is a violation of duty.
>
> The physician does also have a duty to be aware of potential malpractice liability to the institution and to take steps to minimize it. This may involve contacting the hospital risk manager or an attorney to find out how to use the patient chart to protect against liability and minimize future conflict. However, the previously mentioned duty of providing the best care to the patient overrides this duty.
>
> To examine the decision from the consequentionalist approach, those making the decision would try to imaginatively construct and list viable options other than the provisional one to determine whether, in fact, the provisional decision is the best alternative. The results of the assessment of both ethical theories would then be considered and the decision revised accordingly. In this situation it will be assumed that it will not be necessary to revise the decision significantly.

• *Step 12.* Make a revised decision as a result of the previous step.

• *Step 13.* Provide justification in terms of why one option was chosen over another or why the decision is an acceptable one.

> The way in which this decision would be justified is that it has been tested both in the light of counterexamples and ethical theory, and it has held up with minimal modification.

• *Step 14.* Reexamine the decision in terms of sub-issues. Consider each sub-issue component separately, then all components jointly. This is a refinement that addresses the subtleties of a particular case.

In this case modifications are not necessary.

• *Step 15*. Upgrade the decision. This is a redefinition of the provisional decision after the sub-issues have been considered.

If there had been modifications in Step 14, the decision would have been modified here; since there were none in this example, this step can be omitted.

• *Step 16*. Again provide justification of the decision, this time including the sub-issues, some of which may be so significant that they modify the earlier decision radically. Test with theory and give counterexamples.

In this case the earlier justification in Step 13 will suffice, since Steps 14 and 15 did not modify 13. If they had, a justification of the refined decision would have been attempted using theory and counterexamples.

• *Step 17*. Once justified, apply and implement the decision in the clinical context.

Specific Issues

Many torturous questions surround the care of terminally ill patients: "What ought the dying patient be told?" "When is a patient *in extremis* really dead?" "When, if ever, is it acceptable to allow or to assist a dying patient to die?" "What are the limits of human freedom in choosing, for oneself or for those for whom one is responsible, to change the natural course of the dying process?" (Veatch, 1977). The following is a brief outline of some issues pertinent to the patient and family, caregivers, institutions, and society. Of course, in clinical practice the distinctions between these people and institutions are arbitrary, and the questions pertaining to a specific patient entail a dynamic interplay among all the parties involved. Note how the issues of control and prerogative cut across all categories.

Ethical Issues
Pertaining to the Patient and Family
Patient
- What are the patient's rights?
- What right does the patient have to know the truthful diagnosis and implications of it?
- Does a patient have "the right to die" (the right to refuse or terminate treatment)?

- What, if any, are the limits of choice of the patient?
- Does the patient have the right to freely choose to actively end her life in the face of debilitating terminal illness, i.e., to commit suicide?
- How much legal/ethical/moral weight can be put on an individual's statement of preference, e.g., "The Living Will," the statement of "The Christian Affirmation of Life," the Natural Death Act, and other documents limiting treatment?

Family
- In what circumstances are family members to be considered responsible for making treatment choices for the patient?
- What happens if family choices conflict with those of the patient?
- How moral is it to put families in the position to make decisions about termination of treatment, setting them up for possible ensuing guilt?
- In what case is the parental responsibility towards tragic newborns (severely deformed newborns with limited capacities to survive or live a life with quality) overridden in authority by the doctrine of *parens patriae* (society's attempt to protect the weak and incompetent)?

Ethical Issues Pertaining to Caregivers
- How involved should caregivers be in the patient/family's decision to continue or terminate treatment?
- If the patient/family opts for euthanasia, should caregivers become involved in the process passively or actively?
- When, and on what basis, do caregivers make the decision not to treat an individual (withholding treatment) in order to forestall having to make decisions about termination of the treatment later on?
- What does the caregiver do when medical orders, e.g., "Do Not Resuscitate" orders, violate personal religious/moral convictions?
- What does the caregiver do when institutional and societal guidelines conspire to make existence more painful and inhumane for the dying patient?
- What is their role in relation to the patient at this time? Patient advocate? Maintainer of the status quo?

There are five major issues that impede therapeutic care of the dying in the modern hospital setting (Hamric, 1977): (1) hospital system pressures; (2) conflicting expectations placed upon the caregiver; (3) the caregiver's lack of adequate training in caring for dying persons and their families; (4) problems of teamwork among health professionals; and (5) difficulties in conveying and exchanging diagnostic information. The first issue—the hospital system itself—has the greatest impact. It creates problems because of time pressures and the hospital milieu. In hospital systems, basic physical aspects of care are given priority. These are time consuming, often leaving dying patients, whose needs for psychological assistance may be greater than their physical demands, without adequate intervention. Many caregivers may also tend to receive more acknowledgment and get more satisfaction out of the accomplishment of specific tasks, while talking with patients and ministering to their psychosocial needs may be less structured and less tangibly rewarded. In many cases caregivers, especially nurses, are admonished for spending too much time talking with patients and not enough time tending to physical care tasks. In addition to time pressures, the hospital environment interferes because of things such as lack of privacy, limited visiting hours, and hospital routine. All of these problems can prevent caregivers from establishing an environment that maximally meets the dying patient's psychosocial needs.

Ethical Issues Pertaining to the Institution
- What are the institutional responsibilities for maintaining dignity for the terminally ill patient?
- What are the institutional responsibilities for acceding to the wishes of the terminally ill patient in regard to refusal of treatment and euthanasia?
- How does the institution prioritize its allocation of monies and services for the terminally ill?
- How is it decided which patients will be given lifesaving treatment and which will be refused (e.g., terminal care committees)?
- What institutional safeguards exist to protect caregivers in their inevitable confrontation with decisions regarding life and death?

Ethical Issues Pertaining to Society
- What are the bases for societal rules and regulations pertaining to the terminally ill? Are they based on moral/religious/philosophical determinants? Are they politically based or motivated?
- How much does the issue of finances influence societal regulation of such things as determination of death?
- Society has to wrestle with legal definitions and advocacy. When does society take away the rights of its individual members to self-determination?

- How will one's desire to terminate her life be viewed in the context of mental competency to make such a decision?
- When can an individual being kept alive artificially be declared "legally dead" in order to facilitate organ donation for transplant?
- What ethical/legal responsibilities will be left to caregivers and family as far as making decisions about transplant procedures?

This has been only a brief survey of the many complex ethical questions that arise in the treatment of terminally ill patients. It is wise to contemplate these issues prior to direct personal confrontation with them in the case of an actual patient, although intellectual consideration of them is a far cry from facing them in real life. Whether our ethics are situationally based or founded in more structured theory or belief, they will necessarily have to be reviewed in the practice of caring for the terminally ill.

THE STRESS OF THE CAREGIVER'S GRIEF

In caring for dying and bereaved individuals we are subject to experiences that will demand a grief response of our own. Whenever we lose something or someone in whom we have invested ourselves emotionally, we have a need for a grief response. Whether this grief response is legitimized or given expression is another issue, but it does exist. By the very nature of their characteristics as a population, dying and bereaved individuals force our own confrontations with loss: that which is presently being dealt with by our patients or clients, that which will result after they die or terminate therapy, and that which is resurrected from our own past experiences. Dealing with the bereaved and dying usually requires a moderate to large amount of emotional investment, resulting in the type of cathexis that will demand grief and decathexis at a later time.

Fulton (1979) noted some of the sociological trends that are contributing to the development of a role for the caregiver as a "surrogate griever." With the faltering of traditional kinship networks, the disengagement of family members from the dying, and the absence of family due to social mobility or the segregation of the dying in institutions, professional caregivers find themselves participating in the emotional and social care of the patients. This results in caregivers taking emotional risks and forming bonds that will demand a grief response when terminated by death. When this is experienced intensely in serial fashion, without adequate processing, caregivers become subject to *bereavement overload* (Kastenbaum, 1969). In its original sense the term referred to the multiple bereavements experienced by the elderly as they lose a succession of loved ones and acquaintances, and as other psychosocial losses impinge upon them due to the aging process. This results in the elderly experiencing grief responses that sap their enfeebled energy. In the case of the caregiver, her occupation may set her up to be in a similar position. Indeed, when the determinants of an individual's failure to grieve are examined (Lazare, 1979), it is easy to see how they operate for the professional caregiver as well. Among the social factors influencing a failure to grieve are the following: the social negation of the loss, as the loss of a patient is not usually defined as an appropriate loss to be grieved; social isolation from social support, which is often experienced by individuals in visiting nurse services and in institutions where opportunities for peer support and debriefing sessions are nonexistent; assumption of the role of the strong one, which is fostered by professionalism; ambivalence and guilt towards the lost person, which is often exacerbated by the conflicting wish to cure the individual as well as to see him relieved of his suffering through death; the need to be strong and in control, which is often a personal as well as a professional expectation; a feeling of being overwhelmed by multiple loss, which is a professional hazard of the occupation; and the reawakening of an old loss, which is always a possibility for anyone.

If her accumulated grief is not worked through, the caregiver is every bit as vulnerable to all the malignant sequelae of unresolved grief as is any other individual who has suffered a loss but failed to complete his grief work. Additionally, working with such patients and issues often resurrects many of the caregiver's own feelings, thoughts, memories, and fantasies about loss-related experiences in her own life. Raphael (1980) points out that working in this area heightens mutual empathy and identification, which frequently develop in crisis situations. This occurs because the loss experience is so universal that we have all experienced its impact and inability to be controlled. It makes it difficult not to over-identify and causes the caregiver to be quite vulnerable to countertransference phenomena. Consequently, Raphael stresses that the need for self-awareness cannot be overemphasized. She advocates that the caregiver be involved in some continuing support systems (e.g., peer support groups, supervision, case discussion meetings). It is not a matter of simply resolving the issue once and for all and suddenly needing no further guidance. In addressing how to deal with the caregiver's personal issues Raphael proposes the following:

> A useful construct to facilitate this may be "the bereaved child in each of us." Those feelings that are aroused, but do not often

come to conscious perception when working in loss/separation/ death situations, are most frequently related to childhood experiences of separation, loss, and death or to fantasies thereof. When emotional pain, anxiety, depression, helplessness, anger, and guilt arise during bereavement counseling [or when working with the dying] and when blocks or other countertransference manifestations occur, it is well to seek the internal bereaved child. Then the counselor can attempt to get in touch with some of those feelings, separate from those of the client's, and slowly come to terms with both. (p. 161)

The need for us to attend to our own emotional responses to ministering to the dying patient was well articulated in an editorial in *Nursing Outlook* entitled "What Man Shall Live and Not See Death?" (1964). Although speaking of nurses specifically, the same issues apply to all caregivers:

A nurse faces two very grave responsibilities when her patient is dying. She must give life measures—including emotional support—to the patient as long as possible; she must reassure, understand, and, in a sense, share the grief of those who love the patient. Before she can do justice to either, she needs to resolve her own feelings. Her spiritual convictions may need support; her sense of failure must be alleviated; her reservoir of emotional strength should be replenished. (p. 23)

Working with the bereaved touches us personally in at least three ways (Worden, 1982):
- It may make us painfully aware of our own losses.
- It may contribute to our own apprehension regarding our own potential and feared losses.
- It may arouse existential anxiety in our personal death awareness.

It can be added that working with patients who are on an irreversible trajectory towards death is a threat to our senses of power, mastery, and control. We may feel that we can have no impact on the experience regardless of what we do. Seligman (1975) has noted that such "learned helplessness" can lead to debilitation, depression, and even death. This dovetails perfectly with the recent writings on professional burn-out. For instance, Maslach and Jackson (1979) describe burn-out as a syndrome of emotional, physical, and occupational exhaustion and cynicism frequently occurring among individuals who do "people work" and spend considerable time in close encounters with others under conditions of chronic tension and stress. Clearly this describes the situation of many caregivers of dying patients. The work conditions alone can predispose them to burn-out.

Those who care for dying patients may be particularly susceptible to certain issues that make them more vulnerable to unresolved personal stress from their work. Many caregivers enter their respective professions because they are "rescuers" who want to save people from distress. Being a rescuer may set a caregiver up for the unrealistic goal of rescuing the dying patient, when there needs to be acceptance of the inevitability of death and of the fact that it ultimately vanquishes us all. In some cases caregivers will pay lip service to the goal of palliation, but continue to be task-oriented, searching for a cure. It is important for both patients and caregivers that the rescue fantasy be relinquished. Otherwise patients lose the emotional support they need from caregivers, and caregivers continually frustrate themselves by trying to accomplish tasks that can't be done.

Caregivers also are set up for intense disenchantment by the myth that death is romantic. In describing how stress increases dramatically as caregivers discover the reality about dying patients, Vachon (1978) talks about the disillusionment secondary to recognizing that dying patients are not "all young, beautiful, and articulate people who are longing to spend their dying months talking about their philosophy of life and death" (p. 117).

These emotional responses and expectations of caregivers can also damage the caregiver-patient relationship. Just as patients can tell when caregivers are using defenses to distance themselves emotionally and physically, they also can sense when caregivers have unrealistic expectations that cause disappointment.

Coping With Stress From Caring for the Dying

In 1977 Harper developed the Schematic Growth and Development Scale in Coping With Professional Anxieties in Terminal Illness. This is the adaptation process that health care professionals go through in order to become comfortable in working with patients who are facing death. The stages in the model represent the normative sequence of emotional and psychological progress. Growth is reflected as a professional "gains understanding, knowledge, strength, and works through conflicts, internal and external, thus adding a new human caring dimension to his existing capacity to be helpful. In other words, this is the maturing of the health professional" (p. 21).

Stage 1. Intellectualization: Knowledge and Anxiety. During the initial confrontation with death and dying caregivers are very intellectualized. They focus on professional knowledge and factual, even philosophical, issues. However, conversations with the patients are not personal. This stage is marked by periods of brisk activity, as though caregivers are trying to manage latent anxieties by complete understanding of the environment, policies, and procedures. Ineffective means of coping with and managing anxiety may result in withdrawal from the patients and their families. While caregivers continually feel concerned, they are uncomfortable. At this point death is unacceptable.

Stage 2. Emotional Survival: Trauma. At this stage professionals experience trauma, often accompanied by guilt and frustration. As they confront the reality of patients' impending deaths they must confront simultaneously the reality of their own eventual death. The process of mourning and grieving for self becomes salient. Death is felt on an emotional level. Genuine pity for patients leads to feelings of guilt and frustration as caregivers feel uncomfortable with the contrast between their own health and that of their patients. The caregivers realize that patients' death and suffering are unavoidable and feel traumatized as they experience the reality of death. This often fosters extreme hostility within caregivers as they try to fight back. This emotional experience constitutes passing from Stage 1 to Stage 2—being jolted out of the inertia of intellectualization and into the activity of emotional involvement.

Stage 3. Depression: Pain, Mourning, Grieving. This is the most crucial of all stages, the "grow or go" stage. In this period mastery of self is a challenge; such mastery requires a growing acceptance of death and an orientation to the reality of death and dying. Caregivers are able to accept the fact that death does exist, and that their frustration cannot make their patients well. They may experience pain, mourning, and grief as they regress into not accepting the loss, then move forward into an acceptance of death and dying. Caregivers either accept the reality of death and the dying process or leave the field.

Stage 4. Emotional Arrival: Moderation, Mitigation, Accommodation. This stage is marked by a sense of freedom from the debilitating effects of the previous stages of the process. Caregivers are largely free from identifying with patients' symptoms and are no longer preoccupied with their own death and dying. They have no guilt feelings about their own good health, and are not incapacitated by depression. This does not mean that caregivers no longer experience pain when working with dying patients. Actually, their sensitivities have been sharpened rather than dulled. But even though they feel the pain, they are free from its incapacitating effects. Their emotional responses are very appropriate. They now have the sensitivity to grieve and also the resilience to recover.

Stage 5. Deep Compassion: Self-Realization, Self-Awareness, Self-Actualization. This stage is the culminating point of all previous growth and development. Caregivers are able to relate compassionately to the dying patient, in full acceptance of the impending death. Their behavior and performance are enhanced by the dignity and self-respect they afford themselves, enabling them to give dignity and respect to the dying patient. The ability to serve another human being and to give of themselves manifests the caregivers' humanity to others. They now know, understand, and accept that, in some instances, living can be more painful than dying. Their concern for the dying patient is translated into constructive and appropriate activities based on a humane and professional assessment of the needs of the dying patient and the family. The caregivers have matured both personally and professionally.

Harper's model is presented here to help us to reflect on our own emotional progress. We need to achieve a state of realistic acceptance of the impact of death and dying upon patients and families, and an appropriate expectation for our own performance as caregivers.

Coping With Stress From Organizational Sources

In addition to the psychosocial causes of stress generated by caring for dying patients, there are a number of organizational issues that increase the stress on those who care for the dying. These generally require system-wide intervention to create an environment conducive to healthy communication, interaction, and discharge of stress.

Problems with group support and communication are primary sources of stress. They were among those problems most perceived by the staff working on a newly opened palliative care unit (PCU) for advanced cancer patients studied by Vachon, Lyall, and Freeman (1978). Indeed, major problems with the work situation and with staff communications mentioned were cited just as often as problems in watching patients suffer and die. These problems tended to be exacerbated by the unrealistic expectations some of the staff maintained:

1. The nurses had been well socialized to know that the "good nurse" never had "bad" feelings As a result they were working in relative isolation with each one feeling she was the only "bad" nurse and the only one who at times felt angry, depressed, frustrated, helpless and hopeless.
2. This led to mistrust among the nurses who were hesitant to be open with one another for fear of criticism. As a result there was very little operative group support.
3. The lack of understanding and acceptance of their own feelings led to a lack of understanding and acceptance of the feelings of patients. In addition, the nurses were divided with respect to their feelings regarding the impact of cancer and the effectiveness of its treatment. The attitude ranged from: "Why do they bother taking treatment, they're only going to die anyway," to "Why should people be so upset just because they

have cancer?" Conflict was compounded when patients were dying, because the hospital was seen as an active treatment center and not a place where people came to die.

4. Because of the lack of insight into their situation nurses were unable to function in their accepted role of maintaining smooth interpersonal relationships and this led to anxiety which the omnipotent, omniscient physician was expected to resolve.

5. When the physicians failed to perform the expected magic and intervene to improve the situation, problems erupted, staff discord increased, and patient care deteriorated.

6. These problems all became particularly acute when patients in whom the staff had a significant personal investment were dying. In these situations the feelings of individual nurses were aroused and they were unable to share them with one another, therefore, they had trouble dealing with the patient and expected the doctor to help. He was often impotent, however, because of his own difficulties with dying patients. The nurses could not understand this because of the power and competence they projected onto the doctor. (Vachon, Lyall, & Rogers, 1976, pp. 180-181)

On the Goldberg General Health Questionnaire, the stress among nurses on another new PCU was only slightly lower than that of new widows and considerably higher than that of women beginning radiation treatment for breast cancer (Vachon, Lyall, & Freeman, 1978). These nurses also had considerably higher initial scores than other occupational groups that had been studied. The authors point out that, while stress declined considerably over the year following the opening of the PCU, the extremely disturbing stress of the initial period was significant enough to call attention to corresponding initial periods of other new hospice units. It illustrates that staff are at considerable risk during that time.

Caregivers may experience a form of culture shock as they move from an acute care environment to a palliative or hospice care environment. Their roles, responsibilities, orientation, and emphasis are different in this environment. Different values and behaviors are expected from them. For example, prolongation of life is not the goal here, as it may be in acute care settings; rather, the quality of life is paramount in importance. Caregivers are also expected to have a greater understanding of and ability to deal with psychosocial issues than was ever possible or even tolerable in the acute care setting. Many caregivers must go through a reorientation process to accommodate themselves to the care of the dying in an environment so different from traditional medical care settings.

Often caregivers are poorly prepared or educated for their redefined role of caring for dying patients. Providing care as opposed to cure demands the internalization of certain values and principles of treatment that may not have been dealt with previously. Additionally, they may be ill equipped for their duties, lacking the requisite knowledge about dying and grieving individuals, family dynamics, stages of grief and mourning, reactions to impending death, or the use of self in relationship to the patient. To expect traditionally trained caregivers, who have been taught to focus on the medical and technological aspects of intervention, to be able to automatically respond to the psychosocial needs of patients and families without training and practice is quite unfair. It predisposes them to feelings of failure, frustration, anger, and ultimately, burn-out. For example, Vachon, Lyle, and Freeman (1978) have found that nurses frequently feel impotent because their training has led them to believe that there should be answers where often there are none. Consequently, caregivers are vulnerable to stress if they have not been provided the appropriate training for their new positions.

Since the care of the terminally ill is different than traditional medical care, there are often unclear expectations for those who are working with the dying. A lack of clarity about and understanding of what is expected from them in their professional roles makes caregivers more open to stress because they are unable to ascertain the criteria against which they will be assessed. In many cases appropriate limits are not specifically delineated and responsibilities are worded too vaguely, e.g., "Pay attention to the psychosocial needs of the patient." There is a lack of the behavioral operationalization that is always needed in ambiguous circumstances. In addition, when there is a lack of understanding of the necessary mourning and grieving that occur when patients die, caregivers may feel that they have somehow failed by experiencing such reactions, when in fact these are completely normal and expected. If expectations and job descriptions are not clearly specified, there is also an increased possibility of role conflict, role overload, and lack of adequate feedback. The ambiguity and confusion only serves to exacerbate caregivers' stress.

There are a host of political problems that currently beset hospices, palliative programs, and other projects devoted to care of the dying. These occur both on an organizational level (e.g., difficulties with federal regulations and third-party reimbursement) and an individual level (e.g., how much of an advocacy role is the caregiver to take when there is a conflict between patient and family, or patient and physician) These also can be expected to stress the individuals working within the system.

Another source of stress is the lack of organizational support that frequently occurs in human service systems: no opportunities for emotional debriefing; unrealistic expectations for support from

other staff members, especially those in key roles; no explicit recognition of the need to incorporate meeting staff needs into the
schedule (e.g., provision of mental health days, recognition of the
importance of time outs, opportunities for spending time discussing emotional reactions to patients, or reassignment of duties in
order to attend a funeral); no support when there is a conflict with
physicians; and so forth. It is still the case that while many organizations devoted to care of the dying claim to recognize the
emotional needs of their staffs, there is rarely a translation of this
recognition into policies that assist caregivers to continue to cope
with the stress of their positions in the most healthy ways possible.

In many organizations devoted to care of the dying there develops a "we-they" mentality. In a field still struggling to define
itself, those devoted to care of the dying must fight to keep their
spirit, philosophy, and idealism alive in situations where psychosocial and physical distress are high and outside support is low.
Frequently these organizations can become like closed family systems: isolated, with rigid boundaries, strict ideologies, a lack of
open communication, little tolerance of differences in viewpoints,
and stringent expectations for the behavior of its members. There
can be an enmeshment of members, with diffuse boundaries among
themselves and rigid boundaries between them and the rest of the
world (not only other organizations, but even family members and
friends!). There can develop an unrealistic expectation that all
needs will be fulfilled in the service of working with the dying and
with the other individuals involved in the closed system. Such an
environment is conducive to staff burn-out, dissension, and insu-
lation from much-needed outside contact, with a consequent decrease in flexibility.

Those who are employed primarily in home-care or visiting
nurse agencies tend to be isolated from their peers and consequently are relatively more vulnerable to the accumulation of
stress, since they lack the necessary opportunities for interaction
with others that afford them not only replenishment, but the important processing of feelings that develop in the context of working with the dying. Constant adjustment to diverse settings puts
even more stress on this type of caregiver.

Like families, hospice and palliative care organizations benefit
from the promotion of open and fluid communication styles, appropriate role assignments, flexibility within the system, and
healthy, flexible boundaries. Duties and functions must be equitably
distributed, rules must be clearly stated and flexible, and there must
be appropriate differentiation among members and balanced subsystems allowing appropriate interaction and open emotional
expression. Other organizational responses to stress should include
the following:

- Support during the transition time for the caregiver moving from an acute care environment to a palliative or hospice care environment.
- Training and education appropriate to the individual's role responsibilities, and continued opportunities for education and training in ongoing developments in the care of the dying.
- Clear delineation of all expectations and job responsibilities.
- Training for staff on caring for themselves in the vulnerable role of caregiver, focusing not only on intrapsychic aspects of their own personalities, but also on family, social, and work relationships. It must include training in stress management.
- Employment of the interdisciplinary team to provide peer support, facilitate open communication, reduce the risk of overextension of individual caregivers, and promote debriefing and healthy grieving.
- Appropriate supervision to provide supervisory input and the necessary contact for assessment and evaluation of the individual's work performance and psychosocial responses to the work.
- Immediate, specific, behaviorally oriented, nonjudgmental, and respectful feedback to the staff, both positive and negative.
- Confrontation of the first signs of stress with early intervention to prevent the exacerbation of stress overload.
- Promotion on the individual, social, and organizational levels of the appropriate processing of grief. This includes encouraging caregivers to address their emotional issues, having supervisors meet personally with individual caregivers, and utilizing staff meetings to ventilate and debrief about stressful situations and to model effective stress reduction techniques.
- Alteration of conditions in the environment that may increase stress. For example, recognize the isolation of home-care and visiting nurses and find ways to integrate them with other staff and provide them opportunities for ventilation and replenishment. This applies to the physical environment as well, which, for example, may need restructuring in order to provide safe and private places for caregivers to debrief and adequate space for the performance of duties.
- Organizational structures that provide support for caregivers in this high-stress environment, such as rotating days off, ways to transfer when necessary, or procedures for taking time off without guilt or retribution.
- Avoidance of the "we-they" mentality that may engender

closed systems and isolate caregivers from others outside of the system.

Stress Management Strategies

All of us have different vulnerabilities to the stress of working with the dying. White (1981b) has determined some factors that account for hospice nurses' vulnerabilities to stress, which can be extrapolated to other caregivers dealing with dying patients. They include the caregiver's unique genetic and developmental history; prior history of stress management; professional training; values and beliefs; unique loss and death history; family and social support network; particular developmental period in life; number and intensity of life changes at any given time; and personal motivation for working with the dying.

When stress is prolonged, a person may fall into a state of deep disillusionment and withdrawal known as *burn-out*, discussed in Kalish (1981), Shubin (1978), Vachon (1978), and Worden (1982). Burn-out can be insidious because we may not recognize when it is happening to us. Feelings of emotional and physical exhaustion, occupational fatigue, cynical attitudes, and withdrawal from patients can all be attributed to outside circumstances or temporary lapses in effort. To prevent burn-out we must first be aware of what we're feeling and be honest about it. If we feel anger or disgust, we need to admit it, for only with honest appraisal can we figure out what is bothering us and how to cope with it.

Our feelings are the warning signs that our mental and/or physical limits have been exceeded. This often happens with caregivers, who may believe it is selfish to think of themselves while surrounded by people who are much worse off than they are. There is a tendency to want to be a "superperson," someone who can take on any task and be everything to everyone; but this is unrealistic and ultimately impossible. It is necessary to learn to request assistance when it is needed, without any guilt. We must master the skills of appropriate assertiveness in order to successfully advocate for ourselves, as well as for our patients. In fact, the earlier the warning signs can be recognized, the better. In this way potential problems can be headed off before they escalate and require more in-depth intervention.

We must develop an awareness of our own energy levels. Every person has her own characteristic requirements for rest and activity (Selye, 1956), and her own emotional limitations. We must avoid comparing our needs to others, both for our own sakes and to prevent dissension with co-workers. Our requirements will also vary over time, depending on the degrees of stress we are under. When we are overburdened, we need to realize that we deserve and need breaks, or "time outs," from the stressful parts of our work. This can mean simply arranging for free time during the day or days off for relaxation. It can also mean varying time between stressful and less stressful patients, either on a daily basis or over longer periods of time. Vacations are important and must be given a high priority.

When working with the dying, it is important for us to understand our own feelings if we are to avoid burn-out. We must be aware of our personal feelings about death and dying, as well as our attitudes towards the dying. These issues do not have to be totally worked through, but if we do not try to understand them, our anxieties and denials will hamper us in our work. Actually, by addressing them, we can often be strengthened by finding values and meanings that make sense to us and give us comfort and sustenance as we grapple with life and death on a daily basis. These may come from organized religion or philosophies, or from our own personal insights.

We also each need to identify those specific stresses in working with the dying that are the most troublesome for us individually, so that we may anticipate and counteract them. For example, for some caregivers it is more stressful to work with younger patients than it is to work with patients closer to one's own age. Some are comfortable talking with a dying patient about his impending death, but are unable to tolerate a similar conversation with that patient's spouse. Therefore, as part of learning to deal with the stress of caring for dying patients, we must discover those stressors that affect us the most intensely and develop appropriate responses to them.

There is also the question of how much of ourselves we are willing or able to give to others. We must acknowledge the fact that sometimes we must only "be, not do"; we must be realistic about how much we are truly capable of accomplishing for the patient; and we must realize that we can only be usefully involved with a certain number of patients at any one time. If we are not honest about it, we will find ourselves building up resentment towards patients and their families. It is better to acknowledge our limits and be able to provide as much care as we can willingly.

We are susceptible to all the emotions of grief—frustration, sadness, guilt, anxiety, depression, helplessness, anger—as we inevitably form bonds with those we work with. Active grieving over the losses of patients and their families is continuously necessary. Thus, we need to do for ourselves what we do for patients to help them with their grief work—provide an environment that facilitates healthy grieving. Peer support and the opportunity to share our feelings of loss, anger, frustration, or disillusionment with others in the same situation are crucial. This is why group work situations, such as being part of a team, are so helpful. Although our loved ones may want to help us deal with these feelings, they may not be able to fully appreciate the situation. Sometimes only a co-worker can totally understand the stresses inherent in taking care of the dying, working in an emergency room, or supervising a dialysis unit. Some friends and families even prefer not to discuss our work, and, in this case, there is even more of a need for a system of support.

There are two types of conferences that can meet the need for support: the support conference and the closure conference. In contrast to the team conference, which is patient-care focused, the support conference is caregiver focused. It is designed for caregivers to address their feelings about working in an area in general (e.g., on the pediatrics ward); with a specific individual and/or family (e.g., dealing with the dying man who is your own age); or with a particular issue (e.g., ethical dilemmas). Such a conference can occur on a scheduled or as needed basis. A closure conference is held after the death or relocation of a patient with whom the caregivers have had a long or intense involvement. It is similar to both a funeral and a therapy session: an occasion for reviewing the loss, remembering the person who is gone, dealing with the feelings the loss engenders, and confronting unresolved questions and concerns. Of course, there are informal ways to work out losses. The shared frustration over a cup of coffee in the ward kitchen can be most effective as well. The main issue is giving attention to the continuous demand for working out grief.

Gaps in our knowledge or job skills can add stress to our daily work. Becoming more aware of the thanatological research and literature that is available can alleviate some of these problems. We also should develop our own plans for continued growth in professional skills and knowledge, in order to meet new challenges requiring novel skills and information.

Our physical needs, as well as our mental ones, must be taken care of. To avoid depletion, adequate exercise, nutrition, and sleep are required and cannot be overestimated in terms of importance in stress reduction. Use of relaxation techniques is most therapeutic. Additionally, physical gratification from others, in caring and sexual ways, can help support us.

Those people who deal with burn-out most successfully seem to have "decompression routines." These are activities that come between leaving work and settling in at home, something that lets them relax and forget about their jobs. A good one is physical activity, although competitive sports are not recommended. Another outlet is meditative activities. A walk through the park, a hot bath, or any form of quiet relaxation alone will help in breaking away from the stresses of the day.

Besides trying to keep our personal and professional lives separate, it helps to clarify what our priorities are between our responsibilities to our work and to ourselves and loved ones. First, we need to know under what conditions one area takes priority over the other. For instance, there may well be a time when a weekend conference must be missed in order to spend time at home with the children. Second, we need to know when to ask for help from those at home. Again, instead of trying to be a "superperson," it is permissible, even desirable, to ask for help with chores or to look for emotional support without feeling guilty. In fact, it is healthier to have support from people both in and outside of work than to rely solely on a work-oriented network of people.

Finally, we need to be sure we allow ourselves time for doing those things we really enjoy. It is important to escape our responsibilities and give ourselves a chance to play, either alone or with others. Despite our interest in death, we need to engage in life-affirming activities. Social and emotional replenishment is a necessary requirement: we need to be given to, as well as to give. In fact, we need to be nurtured by others if we are to continue being caring ourselves.

The role of caregiver to the dying and bereaved is filled with experiences that bring grief and stress. We must attend to our own needs for relief from these demands; if we don't, we will hurt ourselves and diminish our capability to help others.

EXERCISE IX

Professional and Personal Expectations of Yourself

What expectations do you have about yourself in caring for the dying and the bereaved?

What would define success to you in your work?

What are the three most difficult aspects of your work with the dying and the bereaved?

What are you doing to help yourself cope with these?

How do you debrief after the death or relocation of a patient with whom you have had either long-term or emotional involvement? Does this afford you sufficient release and closure? If not, what can you do to achieve more of this?

Look at the different ways of experiencing stress. Which ones affect you most? What are your warning signs indicating that you are overstressed? What can you do to more efficiently manage your stress?

How do you nurture and replenish yourself to avoid becoming overstressed by your work? Are these ways succeeding? In what areas do you need to make changes to more effectively avoid becoming too stressed?

Reference Notes

1. Knott, J. E. Personal communication, February 6, 1984.

2. Parkes, C. M. *Unexpected and untimely bereavement—A statistical study of young Boston widows and widowers.* Paper presented at the Conference on Bereavement, Columbia University, New York, November 1973.

3. Breslin, M. *Unresolved grief in psychosomatic disorders.* Unpublished manuscript, Duke University Medical Center, 1977.

4. Weigert, A. J., & Hastings, R. *The family as a matrix of tragedy.* Paper presented at the Child Development and Family Relations Meetings, Toronto, October 16-20, 1973.

5. Healy, J. Bereavement issues and anticipatory grief. In *Symposium on Dying and Death: The Role of the Financial and Estate Planner; A New Compensable Service.* Symposium presented by The Foundation of Thanatology, New York, September 20, 1983.

6. Rickaroy, G. A., Single, T., & Raphael, B. *The development of rebonding therapy.* Unpublished manuscript, 1982.

7. Montgomery, R. *A study of stillbirth.* Unpublished manuscript, 1978.

8. Berardo, F. *Family, dying and bereavement.* Paper presented at the Conference on Death and Dying: Education, Counseling, and Care, Orlando, Florida, December 1-3, 1976.

9. Polumbo, J. *Parent loss and childhood bereavement.* Paper presented at a conference on Children and Death, University of Chicago, Chicago, March 17-19, 1978.

10. Cassell, E. Psychosocial aspects of terminal care: The *suffering* of the patient, the family, the staff. In *Symposium on Dying and Death: The Role of the Financial and Estate Planner; A New Compensable Service.* Symposium presented by The Foundation of Thanatology, New York, September 20, 1983.

11. U.S. Department of Health and Human Services. *Coping with cancer: A resource for the health professional* (U.S. Public Health Service Publication No. 80-2080). Bethesda, Md.: National Institute of Health, Public Health Service, September 1980.

12. Counts, S., Rodov, M. H., & Wilson, M. T. *Attitudes of employers and cancer patients towards patients' work ability: Two surveys and an action plan* (Rehabilitation Program, National Cancer Institute Contract No. N01-CN-55070). Pittsburgh: Center for Health Systems Studies, November 1976. (Available from Center for Health Systems Studies, The Fairfax, 4614 Fifth Avenue, Pittsburgh, Pa. 15213).

13. Krant, M. *Presentation on the dying patient.* Medical Grand Rounds, University of Massachusetts Medical School, Worcester, Massachusetts, February 3, 1977.

14. Doka, K. *Comments made in response to keynote address.* Presented at the Sixth Annual Conference of the Forum for Death Education and Counseling, Chicago, October 21-23, 1983.

15. Hyland, J. M. *The role of denial in the patient with cancer.* Paper presented at the First National Conference of the Forum for Death Education and Counseling, Washington, D.C., September 1978.

16. Humphrey, M. Personal communication, April 1980.

17. Knott, J. E. *Presentation on loss and death.* University of Rhode Island, Kingston, Rhode Island, February 10, 1975.

18. International Work Group on Death, Dying and Bereavement, *Assumptions and principles underlying standards for terminal care.* Unpublished manuscript, 1978. (Available from Jeanne Quint-Benoliel, Chairwoman, School of Nursing, University of Washington, Seattle, Wash. 98195).

19. Leimberg, S. Sensitizing financial and estate planners: Issues of coping with death and interacting with others involved (Reinforcing the image and role of financial counselors). In *Symposium on Dying and Death: The Role of the Financial and Estate Planner; A New Compensable Service.* Symposium presented by The Foundation of Thanatology, New York, September 20, 1983.

20. Gordon, W., Feidenberg, I., Diller, L., Rothman, L., Wolf, C., Ruckdeschel-Hibbard, M., Ezrachi, O., & Gerstman, L. *The psychosocial problems of cancer patients: A retrospective study.* Paper presented at the meeting of the American Psychological Association, San Francisco, September 1977.

21. Lucas, R. H. *Children with cancer: Denying death or denying life?* Paper presented at the meeting of the American Psychological Association, San Francisco, August 1977.

22. Miles, M. S. *The grief of parents: A model for assessment and intervention.* Paper presented at the Second Annual Conference of the Forum for Death Education and Counseling, Orlando, Florida, December 1979.

23. Spinetta, J. J., McLaren, H. H., Deasy-Spinetta, P. M., Kung, F., Schwartz, D. B., & Hartman, G. A. *Responses of siblings to their brother's or sister's cancer treatment: A three-year study.* Unpublished manuscript, San Diego State University, 1981.

24. Robbins, D. A. Personal communication, February 26-28, 1984.

References

Abraham, K. A short study of the development of the libido, viewed in the light of mental disorders. In *Selected Papers on Psycho-Analysis*. London: Hogarth Press, 1927.

Adams, D. W. *Childhood malignancy: The psychosocial care of the child and his family*. Springfield, Ill.: Charles C Thomas, 1979.

Aldrich, C. K. Some dynamics of anticipatory grief. In B. Schoenberg, A. Carr, A. Kutscher, D. Peretz, & I. Goldberg (Eds.), *Anticipatory grief*. New York: Columbia University Press, 1974.

Alexy, W. D. Dimensions of psychological counseling that facilitate the grieving process of bereaved parents. *Journal of Counseling Psychology*, 1982, *29*, 498-507.

American Cancer Society, California Division. Is there equal opportunity for cancer patients? *The American Cancer Society Volunteer*, 1976, *22*, 2-7.

Arndt, H. C. M., & Gruber, M. Helping families cope with acute and anticipatory grief. In E. R. Prichard, J. Collard, B. A. Orcutt, A. H. Kutscher, I. Seeland, & N. Lefkowitz (Eds.), *Social work with the dying patient and the family*. New York Columbia University Press, 1977.

Aroskar, M. A. Anatomy of an ethical dilemma. *American Journal of Nursing*, 1980, *80*, 658-663.

Arteberry, J. K. Distance and the dying patient. In *Current concepts in clinical nursing*. St. Louis: C. V. Mosby, 1967.

Attig, T. Respecting the dying and the bereaved as believers. *Newsletter of the Forum for Death Education and Counseling*, 1983, *6*, 10-11.

Averill, J. R. Grief: Its nature and significance. *Psychological Bulletin*, 1968, *70*, 721-748.

Averill, J. R., & Wisocki, P. A. Some observations on behavioral approaches to the treatment of grief among the elderly. In H. J. Sobel (Ed.), *Behavior therapy in terminal care: A humanistic approach*. Cambridge, Mass.: Ballinger, 1981.

Barton, D. The family of the dying person. In D. Barton (Ed.), *Dying and death: A clinical guide for caregivers*. Baltimore: Williams & Wilkins, 1977.

Bartrop, R. W., Lazarus, L., Luckherst, E., Kiloh, L. G., & Penny, R. Depressed lymphocyte function after bereavement. *Lancet*, 1977, *1*, 834-836.

Beeson, P., & McDermott, W. *Textbook of medicine*. Philadelphia: W. B. Saunders, 1975.

Bendiksen, R., & Fulton, R. Death and the child: An anterospective test of the childhood bereavement and later behavior disorder hypothesis. *Omega*, 1975, *6*, 45-59.

Benoliel, J. Q., & Crowley, D. M. The patient in pain: New concepts. In *Proceedings of the National Conference on Cancer Nursing*. New York: American Cancer Society, 1974.

Berardo, F. Widowhood status in the United States: Perspective on a neglected aspect of the family life cycle. *The Family Coordinator*, 1968, *17*, 191-203.

Berlinsky, E. B., & Biller, H. B. *Parental death and psychological development*. Lexington. Mass.: D. C. Heath, Lexington Books, 1982.

447

Bibring, E. The mechanisms of depression. In P. Greenacre (Ed.), *Affective disorders*. New York: International Universities Press, 1953.

Binger, C. M., Ablin, A. R., Feuerstein, R. C., Kushner, J. H., Zoger, S., & Mikkelsen, C. Childhood leukemia: Emotional impact on patient and family. *New England Journal of Medicine*, 1969, *280*, 414-418.

Blauner, R. Death and social structure. *Psychiatry*, 1966, *29*, 378-394.

Bluebond-Langner, M. Meanings of death to children. In H. Feifel (Ed.), *New meanings of death*. New York: McGraw-Hill, 1977.

Bornstein, P., Clayton, P., Halikas, J., Maurice, W., & Robbins, E. The depression of widowhood at 13 months. *British Journal of Psychiatry*, 1973, *122*, 561-566.

Bowen, M. Family reaction to death. In P. Guerin (Ed.), *Family therapy: Theory and practice*. New York: Gardner, 1976.

Bowlby, J. Grief and mourning in infancy and early childhood. In *Psychoanalytic study of the child* (Vol. 15). New York: International Universities Press, 1960.

Bowlby, J. Processes of mourning. *International Journal of Psycho-Analysis*, 1961, *42*, 317-340.

Bowlby, J. *Attachment and loss: Attachment* (Vol. I). New York: Basic Books, 1969.

Bowlby, J. *Attachment and loss: Separation: Anxiety and anger* (Vol. II). New York: Basic Books, 1973.

Bowlby, J. *Attachment and loss: Loss, sadness and depression* (Vol. III). New York: Basic Books, 1980.

Bozeman, M. F., Orbach, C. E., & Sutherland, A. M. Psychological impacts of cancer and its treatment. III. The adaptation of mothers to the threatened loss of their children through leukemia. Part I. *Cancer*, 1955, *8*, 1-19.

Bugen, L. Human grief: A model for prediction and intervention. In L. Bugen (Ed.), *Death and dying: Theory, research, practice*. Dubuque, Iowa: William C. Brown, 1979.

Cain, A. C., & Cain, B. S. On replacing a child. *Journal of the American Academy of Child Psychiatry*, 1964, *3*, 443-456.

Cain, A. C., Fast, I., & Erickson, M. E. Children's disturbed reactions to the death of a sibling. *American Journal of Orthopsychiatry*, 1964, *34*, 741-752.

Cairns, N. U., Clark, G. M., Smith, S. D., & Lansky, S. B. Adaptation of siblings to childhood malignancy. *Journal of Pediatrics*, 1979, *95*, 484-487.

Cannon, W. B. Voodoo death. *American Anthropologist*, 1942, *44*, 169-181.

Caplan, G. Foreword to *The first year of bereavement*, by I. O. Glick, R. S. Weiss, & C. M. Parkes. New York: Wiley, 1974.

Caplan, G. *Principles of preventive psychiatry*. New York: Basic Books, 1964.

Cassem, N. H. Pastoral care and the dying patient. *Pastoral Psychology*, 1972, *23*, 52-63.

Cassem, N. H. The first three steps beyond the grave. In V. R. Pine, A. Kutscher, D. Peretz, R. Slater, R. DeBellis, R. Volk, & D. Cherico (Eds.), *Acute grief and the funeral*. Springfield, Ill.: Charles C Thomas, 1976.

Cautela, J. R., & Wisocki, P. A. The thought stopping procedure: Description, application, and learning theory interpretations. *Psychological Record*, 1977, *27*, 255-264.

Chodoff, P., Friedman, S. B., & Hamburg, D. A. Stress, defenses and coping behavior: Observations in parents of children with malignant disease. *American Journal of Psychiatry*, 1964, *120*, 743-749.

Church, M. J., Chazin, H., & McBeath, K. When a baby dies. Reprinted in *The Compassionate Friends Newsletter*, Fall 1980.

Clark, A. Grief and Gestalt therapy. *The Gestalt Journal*, 1982, *5*, 49-63.

Clayton, P. J. The sequelae and non-sequelae of conjugal bereavement. *Psychiatry*, 1979, *136*, 1530-1534.

Clayton, P. J., Desmarais, L., & Winokur, G. A study of normal bereavement. *American Journal of Psychiatry*, 1968, *125*, 64-74.

Clayton, P. J., Halikas, J. A., Maurice, W. H., & Robbins, E. Anticipatory grief and widowhood. *British Journal of Psychiatry*. 1973, *122*, 47-51.

Clebsch, W. A., & Jaekle, C. R. *Pastoral care in historical perspective.* New York: Harper & Row, 1967.

Clinebell, H. J., Jr. *Basic types of pastoral counseling.* Nashville: Abingdon Press, 1966.

Cohen, M. S., & Cohen, E. K. Behavioral family systems intervention in terminal care. In H. J. Sobel (Ed.), *Behavior therapy in terminal care: A humanistic approach.* Cambridge, Mass.: Ballinger, 1981.

Coleman, J. C. *Abnormal psychology and modern life.* Glenview, Ill.: Scott, Foresman and Company, 1972.

Cornwell, J., Nurcombe, B., & Stevens, L. Family response to loss of a child by sudden infant death syndrome. *Medical Journal of Australia,* April 30, 1977, pp. 656-658.

Cox, P., & Ford, J. R. The mortality of widows shortly after widowhood. *Lancet,* 1964, *1*, 163-164.

Craig, Y. The bereavement of parents and their search for meaning. *British Journal of Social Work,* 1977, 7, 41-54.

Davidson, G. W. Death of the wished-for child: A case study. *Death Education,* 1977, *1*, 265-275.

Davidson, R. P. To give care in terminal illness. *American Journal of Nursing,* 1966, *66*, 74-75.

Derogatis, L., Abeloff, M., & Melisaratos, N. Psychological coping mechanisms and survival time in metastatic breast cancer. *Journal of the American Medical Association,* 1979, *242*, 1504-1508.

Dick-Read, G. *Childbirth without fear.* New York: Harper, 1944.

Dietz, J. H. How doctors can help solve cancer patients' employment problems. *Legal Aspects of Medical Practice,* April 1978, pp. 25-29.

Diggory, J. C., & Rothman, D. Z. Values destroyed by death. *Journal of Abnormal and Social Psychology,* 1961, *63*, 205-210.

Doka, K. J. The spiritual needs of the dying patient. *Newsletter of the Forum for Death Education and Counseling,* 1983, *6*, 2-3.

Donovan, M., Burns, D., Daley, M., Dietz, K., Faut, M., Gardenhire, J., Ivantic, E., McGuire, L., Steinweg, C., Wangler, N., Wright, Z., & Yuska, C. Pain and symptom management (Facilitator Manual). In U.S. Department of Health and Human Services, *Hospice education program for nurses* (Publication No. HRA 81-27). Washington, D.C.: U.S. Government Printing Office, 1981.

Dorpat, T. L. Suicide, loss, and mourning. *Life-Threatening Behavior,* 1973, *3*, 213-224.

Doyle, P. *Grief counseling and sudden death: A manual and guide.* Springfield, Ill.: Charles C Thomas, 1980.

Drotar, D. Family oriented intervention with the dying adolescent. *Journal of Pediatric Psychology*, 1977, *2*, 68-71.

Dyk, R. B., & Sutherland, A. M. Adaptation of the spouse and other family members to the colostomy patient. *Cancer*, 1956, *9*, 123-138.

Easson, W. M. *The dying child: The management of the child or adolescent who is dying*. Springfield, Ill.: Charles C Thomas, 1970.

Egbert, L. D., Battit, G. E., Welch, C. E., & Bartlett, M. K. Reduction of postoperative pain by encouragement and instruction of patients: A study of doctor-patient rapport. *New England Journal of Medicine*, 1964, *270*, 825-827.

Eliot, T. D. The bereaved family. *The Annals of the American Academy of Political and Social Science*, 1932, *160*, 188-190.

Ellis, A. The rational-emotive approach to thanatology. In H. J. Sobel (Ed.), *Behavior therapy in terminal care: A humanistic approach*. Cambridge, Mass.: Ballinger, 1981.

Enelow, A. J., & Adler, L. M. Basic interviewing. In A. J. Enelow & S. N. Swisher, *Interviewing and patient care* (2nd ed.). New York: Oxford University Press, 1979.

Engel, G. Anxiety and depression-withdrawal: The primary affects of unpleasure. *International Journal of Psycho-Analysis*, 1962, *43*, 89-97. (a)

Engel, G. *Psychological development in health and disease*. Philadelphia: W. B. Saunders, 1962. (b)

Engel, G. Grief and grieving. *American Journal of Nursing*, 1964, *64*, 93-98.

Erikson, E. H. *Childhood and society*. New York: Norton, 1950.

Feifel, H. The meaning of death in American Society: Implications for education. In B. Green & D. Irish (Eds.), *Death education: Preparation for living*. Cambridge, Mass.: Schenkman, 1971.

Feigenberg, L., & Shneidman, E. S. Clinical thanatology and psychotherapy: Some reflections on caring for the dying person. *Omega*, 1979, *10*, 1-8.

Feldman, F. L. *Work and cancer health histories: A study of the experiences of recovered patients. Findings and implications*. San Francisco: American Cancer Society, California Division, 1976.

Fenichel, O. *The psychoanalytic theory of neurosis*. New York: Norton, 1945.

Firth, R. *Elements of social organization*. Boston: Beacon Press, 1964.

Fitchett, G. Pastoral care of the bereaved. *Newsletter of the Forum for Death Education and Counseling*, 1983, *6*, 4-5.

Fleck, S. The family and psychiatry. In A. M. Freedman, H. I. Kaplan, & B. J. Sadock (Eds.), *The comprehensive textbook of psychiatry* (Vol. I, 2nd ed.). Baltimore: Williams & Wilkins, 1975.

Flesch, R. The clergy on the firing line. In V. R. Pine, A. Kutscher, D. Peretz, R. Slater, R. DeBellis, R. Volk, & D. Cherico (Eds.), *Acute grief and the funeral*. Springfield, Ill.: Charles C Thomas, 1976.

Flexner, J. M. Dying, death, and the "front-line" physician. In D. Barton (Ed.), *Dying and death: A clinical guide for caregivers*. Baltimore: Williams & Wilkins, 1977.

Fordyce, W. E. *Behavioral methods for chronic pain and illness*. St. Louis: C. V. Mosby, 1976.

Foster, D. J., O'Malley, J. E., & Koocher, G. P. The parent interviews. In G. P. Koocher & J. E. O'Malley (Eds.), *The Damocles syndrome: Psychosocial consequences of surviving childhood cancer*. New York: McGraw-Hill, 1981.

Frankl, V. E. *Man's search for meaning: An introduction to logotherapy.* New York: Washington Square Press, 1963.

Fredrick, J. F. Grief as a disease process. *Omega,* 1976-77, *7,* 297-305.

Fredrick, J. F. The biochemistry of bereavement: Possible basis for chemotherapy? *Omega,* 1982-83, *13,* 295-303.

Freud, A. Discussion of Dr. John Bowlby's paper. In *Psychoanalytic study of the child* (Vol. 15). New York: International Universities Press, 1960.

Freud, S. Totem and taboo (1913). In *Standard Edition of the Complete Psychological Works of Sigmund Freud* (Vol. 13). London: Hogarth Press, 1955.

Freud, S. Mourning and melancholia (1917). In *Standard Edition of the Complete Psychological Works of Sigmund Freud* (Vol. 14). London: Hogarth Press, 1957.

Freud, S. Letter to Binswanger (1929). In E. L. Freud (Ed.), *Letters of Sigmund Freud.* London: Hogarth, 1961.

Freund, J. When should the clergyman be called? In E. R. Prichard, J. Collard, B. A. Orcutt, A. H. Kutscher, I. Seeland, & N. Lefkowitz (Eds.), *Social work with the dying patient and the family.* New York: Columbia University Press, 1977.

Friedman, S. B., Chodoff, P., Mason, J. W. & Hamburg, D. A. Behavioral observations on parents anticipating the death of a child. *Pediatrics,* 1963, *32,* 610-625.

Fulton, R. On the dying death. In E. Grollman (Ed.), *Explaining death to children.* Boston: Beacon Press, 1967.

Fulton, R. The traditional funeral and contemporary society. In V. R. Pine, A. Kutscher, D. Peretz, R. Slater, R. DeBellis, R. Volk, & D. Cherico (Eds.), *Acute grief and the funeral.* Springfield, Ill.: Charles C Thomas, 1976. (a)

Fulton, R. The sacred and the secular: Attitudes of the American public toward death, funerals, and funeral directors. In R. Fulton (Ed.), *Death and identity* (Rev. ed.). Bowie, Md.: The Charles Press, 1976. (b)

Fulton, R. Anticipatory grief, stress, and the surrogate griever. In J. Taché, H. Selye, & S. Day (Eds.), *Cancer, stress, and death.* New York: Plenum, 1979.

Fulton, R., & Fulton, J. A psychosocial aspect of terminal care: Anticipatory grief. *Omega,* 1971, *2,* 91-99.

Fulton, R., & Gottesman, D. J. Anticipatory grief: A psychosocial concept reconsidered. *British Journal of Psychiatry,* 1980, *137,* 45-54.

Furman, E. *A child's parent dies: Studies in childhood bereavement.* New Haven: Yale University Press, 1974.

Furman, E. Comment on J. Kennell and M. Klaus "Caring for the parents of an infant who dies." In M. Klaus & J. Kennell (Eds.), *Maternal-infant bonding.* St. Louis: C. V. Mosby, 1976.

Furman, R. A. The child's reaction to death in the family. In B. Schoenberg, A. C. Carr, D. Peretz, & A. H. Kutscher (Eds.), *Loss and grief: Psychological management in medical practice.* New York: Columbia University Press, 1970.

Futterman, E. H., & Hoffman, I. Transient school phobia in a leukemic child. *Journal of the American Academy of Child Psychiatry,* 1970, *9,* 477-493.

Futterman, E. H., Hoffman, I., & Sabshin, M. Parental anticipatory mourning. In B. Schoenberg, A. C. Carr, D. Peretz, & A. H. Kutscher (Eds.), *Psychosocial aspects of terminal care.* New York: Columbia University Press, 1972.

Gauthier, J., & Marshall, W. Grief: A cognitive-behavioral analysis. *Cognitive Therapy and Research,* 1977, *1,* 39-44.

Gauthier, J., & Pye, C. Graduated self-exposure in the management of grief. *Behaviour Analysis and Modification*, 1979, *3*, 202-208.

Geist, R.A. Onset of chronic illness in children and adolescents: Psychotherapeutic and consultative intervention. *American Journal of Orthopsychiatry*, 1979, *49*, 4-23.

Gerber, I., Rusalem, R., Hannon, N., Battin, D., & Arkin, A. Anticipatory grief and aged widows and widowers. *Journal of Gerontology*, 1975, *30*, 225-229.

Glaser, B. G., & Strauss, A. L. The social loss of dying patients. *American Journal of Nursing*, 1964, *63*, 119-121.

Glaser, B. G., & Strauss, A. L. *Awareness of dying*. Chicago: Aldine, 1965.

Glaser, B. G., & Strauss, A. L. *A time for dying*. Chicago: Aldine, 1968.

Glick, I. O., Weiss, R. S., & Parkes, C. M. *The first year of bereavement*. New York: Wiley, 1974.

Gogan, J. L., & Slavin, L. A. Interviews with brothers and sisters. In G. P. Koocher & J. E. O'Malley (Eds.), *The Damocles syndrome: Psychosocial consequences of surviving childhood cancer*. New York: McGraw-Hill, 1981.

Goldberg, D. P. The detection of psychiatric illness by questionnaire: A technique for the identification of non-psychotic psychiatric illness. *Institute of Psychiatry, Maudsley Monographs 21*. London: Oxford University Press, 1972.

Goldberg, S. G. Family tasks and reactions in the crisis of death. *Social Casework*, 1973, *54*, 398-405.

Gorer, G. *Death, grief, and mourning*. London: Cresset Press, 1965.

Green, B., & Irish, D. (Eds.), *Death education: Preparation for living*. Cambridge, Mass.: Schenkman, 1971.

Green-Epner, C. S. The dying child. In R.E. Caughill (Ed.), *The dying patient: A supportive approach*. Boston: Little, Brown and Company, 1976.

Grollman, E. Children and death. In E. Grollman (Ed.), *Concerning death: A practical guide for the living*. Boston: Beacon Press, 1974.

Hackett, T. P. Pain and prejudice: Why do we doubt that the patient is in pain? *Medical Times*, 1971, *99*, 130-141.

Hamovitch, M. B. *The parent and the fatally ill child*. Los Angeles: Delmar, 1964.

Hamric, A. B. Deterrents to therapeutic care of the dying person: A nurse's perspective. In D. Barton (Ed.), *Dying and death: A clinical guide for caregivers*. Baltimore: Williams & Wilkins, 1977.

Hardt, D. V. An investigation of the stages of bereavement. *Omega*, 1978-79, *9*, 279-285.

Harper, B. C. *Death: The coping mechanism of the health professional*. Greenville, S. C.: Southeastern University Press, 1977.

Hartman, L. M., & Ainsworth, K. D. Self-regulation of chronic pain. *Canadian Journal of Psychiatry*, 1980, *25*, 38-43.

Hinton, J. *Dying*. Middlesex, England: Penguin Books, 1967.

Hofer, M. A., Wolff, C. T., Friedman, S. B., & Mason, J. W. A psychoendocrine study of bereavement. *Psychosomatic Medicine*, 1972, *34*, 481-504.

Hoffman, I., & Futterman, E. H. Coping with waiting: Psychiatric intervention and study in the waiting room of a pediatric oncology clinic. *Comprehensive Psychiatry*, 1971, *12*, 67-81.

Hogan, N. Commitment to survival (Part Two). *The Compassionate Friends Newsletter*, 1983, *6*, 5-6.

Hogshead, H. P. The art of delivering bad news. *Journal of the Florida Medical Association*, 1976, *63*, 807.

Holden, C. Cancer and the mind: How are they connected? *Science*, 1978, *200*, 1363-1369.

Horowitz, M. J., Wilner, N., Marmar, C., & Krupnick, J. Pathological grief and the activation of latent self-images. *American Journal of Psychiatry*, 1980, *137*, 1157-1162.

Irion, P. *The funeral—Vestige or value?* Nashville: Parthenon Press, 1966.

Irion, P. To cremate or not. In E. Grollman (Ed.), *Concerning death: A practical guide for the living.* Boston: Beacon Press, 1974.

Irion, P. The funeral and the bereaved. In V. R. Pine, A. Kutscher, D. Peretz, R. Slater, R. DeBellis, R. Volk, & D. Cherico (Eds.), *Acute grief and the funeral.* Springfield, Ill.: Charles C Thomas, 1976.

Ivey, A. E., & Gluckstern, N. B. *Basic attending skills: Participant manual.* North Amherst, Mass.: Microtraining Associates, 1974.

Ivey, A. E., & Gluckstern, N. B. *Basic influencing skills: Participant manual.* North Amherst, Mass.: Microtraining Associates, 1976.

Jackson, E. N. *Understanding grief: Its roots, dynamics, and treatment.* Nashville: Abingdon Press, 1957.

Jackson, E. N. Grief and religion. In H. Feifel (Ed.), *The meaning of death.* New York: McGraw-Hill, 1959.

Jackson, E. N. *For the living.* Des Moines, Iowa: Channel Press, 1963.

Jackson, E. N. *Telling a child about death.* New York: Hawthorn Books, 1965.

Jackson, E. N. Comment in section on "The Parents." In N. Linzer (Ed.), *Understanding bereavement and grief.* New York: Yeshiva University Press, 1977.

Jacobs, S., & Ostfeld, A. An epidemiological review of the mortality of bereavement. *Psychosomatic Medicine*, 1977, *39*, 344-357.

Janis, I. L. *Psychological stress.* New York: Wiley, 1958.

Kagan, B. Use of denial in adolescents with bone cancer. *Health and Social Work*, 1976, *1*, 71-87.

Kagen-Goodheart, L. Re-entry: Living with childhood cancer. *American Journal of Orthopsychiatry*, 1977, *47*, 651-658.

Kalish, R. A. The effects of death upon the family. In L. Pearson (Ed.), *Death and dying: Current issues in the treatment of the dying person.* Cleveland: The Press of Case Western Reserve University, 1969.

Kalish, R. A. The onset of the dying process. *Omega*, 1970, *1*, 57-69.

Kalish, R. A. *Death, grief, and caring relationships.* Monterey, Calif.: Brooks/Cole, 1981.

Kalish, R. A., & Reynolds, D. K. *Death and ethnicity: A psychocultural study.* Los Angeles: University of Southern California Press, 1976.

Kaplan, D. M., Grobstein, R., & Smith, A. Predicting the impact of severe illness in families: A study of the variety of responses to fatal illness. *Health and Social Work*, 1976, *1*, 71-82.

Karon, M. Acute leukemia in childhood. In H. F. Conn (Ed.), *Current therapy, 1975.* Philadelphia: W. B. Saunders, 1975.

Kastenbaum, R. J. Death and bereavement in later life. In A. H. Kutscher (Ed.), *Death and bereavement.* Springfield, Ill.: Charles C Thomas, 1969.

Kastenbaum, R. J. Toward standards of care for the terminally ill part II. What standards exist today? *Omega*, 1975, *6*, 289-290.

Kastenbaum, R. J. *Death, society, and human experience*. St. Louis: C. V. Mosby, 1977.

Kastenbaum, R. J. In control. In C. A. Garfield (Ed.), *Psychosocial care of the dying patient*. New York: McGraw-Hill, 1978.

Kastenbaum, R. J., & Aisenberg, R. *The psychology of death*. New York: Springer, 1972.

Katz, E. R. Illness impact and social reintegration. In J. Kellerman (Ed.), *Psychological aspects of childhood cancer*. Springfield, Ill.: Charles C Thomas, 1980.

Kavanaugh, R. *Facing death*. Baltimore: Penguin Books, 1974.

Keith, R. Some observations on grief and the funeral. In V. R. Pine, A. Kutscher, D. Peretz, R. Slater, R. DeBellis, R. Volk, & D. Cherico (Eds.), *Acute grief and the funeral*. Springfield, Ill.: Charles C Thomas, 1976.

Kellner, K., Best, E., Chesborough, S., Donnelly, W., & Green, M. Perinatal mortality counseling program for families who experience a stillbirth. *Death Education*, 1981, *5*, 29-35.

Kelly, G. *The psychology of personal constructs*. New York: Norton, 1955.

Kemler, B. Anticipatory grief and survival. In G. P. Koocher & J. E. O'Malley (Eds.), *The Damocles syndrome: Psychosocial consequences of surviving childhood cancer*. New York: McGraw-Hill, 1981.

Kerner, J., Harvey, B., & Lewiston, N. The impact of grief: A retrospective study of family function following the loss of a child with cystic fibrosis. *Journal of Chronic Diseases*, 1979, *32*, 221-225.

Klass, D. Self-help groups for the bereaved: Theory, theology, and practice. *Journal of Religion and Health*, 1982, *21*, 307-324.

Klerman, G. L., & Izen, J. E. The effects of bereavement and grief on physical health and general well-being. *Advances in Psychosomatic Medicine*, 1977, *9*, 63-68.

Kliman, A. S. Comment in section on "The Parents." In N. Linzer (Ed.), *Understanding bereavement and grief*. New York: Yeshiva University Press, 1977.

Knudson, A. G., & Natterson, J. M. Participation of parents in the hospital care of fatally ill children. *Pediatrics*, 1960, *26*, 482-490.

Koenig, R. R. Fatal illness: A survey of social service needs. *Social Work*, 1968, *13*, 85-90.

Koestenbaum, P. *Is there an answer to death?* New Jersey: Prentice-Hall, 1976.

Koocher, G. P. Initial consultations with the pediatric cancer patient. In J. Kellerman (Ed.), *Psychological aspects of childhood cancer*. Springfield, Ill.: Charles C Thomas, 1980.

Koocher, G. P., & O'Malley, J. E. (Eds.), *The Damocles syndrome: Psychosocial consequences of surviving childhood cancer*. New York: McGraw-Hill, 1981.

Koocher, G. P., O'Malley, J. E., & Foster, D. J. The special problems of survivors. In G. P. Koocher & J. E. O'Malley (Eds.), *The Damocles syndrome: Psychosocial consequences of surviving childhood cancer*. New York: McGraw-Hill, 1981.

Koocher, G. P., & Sallen, S. E. Psychological issues in pediatric oncology. In P. R. Magrab (Ed.), *Psychological management of pediatric problems* (Vol. I). Baltimore: University Park Press, 1978.

Kraus, A. S., & Lilienfield, A. M. Some epidemiological aspects of the high mortality rate in the young widowed group. *Journal of Chronic Diseases*, 1959, *10*, 207.

Kreuger, A., Gyllensköld, K., Pehrsson, G., & Sjölin, S. Parent reactions to childhood malignant diseases. *The American Journal of Pediatric Hematology/Oncology*, 1981, *3*, 233-238.

Kübler-Ross, E. *On death and dying*. New York: Macmillan, 1969.

Kübler-Ross, E. The languages of dying. *Journal of Clinical Child Psychology*, 1974, *3*, 22-24.

Kupst, M. J., Schulman, J. L., Honig, G., Maurer, H., Morgan, E., & Fochtman, D. Family coping with childhood leukemia: One year after diagnosis. *Journal of Pediatric Psychology*, 1982, *7*, 157-174.

LaGrand, L. E. Loss reactions of college students: A descriptive analysis. *Death Education*, 1981, *5*, 235-248.

Lamaze, F. *Painless childbirth: Psychoprophylactic method*. Chicago: Regnery, 1970.

Lansky, S. B. Childhood leukemia: The child psychiatrist as a member of the oncology team. *Journal of the American Academy of Child Psychiatry*, 1974, *13*, 499-508.

Lansky, S. B., Cairns, N. U., Clark, G. M., Lowman, J. T., Miller, L., & Trueworthy, R. C. Childhood cancer: Non-medical costs of the illness. *Cancer*, 1979, *43*, 403-408.

Lansky, S. B., Cairns, N. U., Hassanein, R., Wehr, J., & Lowman, J. T. Childhood cancer: Parental discord and divorce. *Pediatrics*, 1978, *62*, 184-188.

Lansky, S. B., Cairns, N. U., & Zwartjes, W. School attendance among children with cancer: A report from two centers. *Journal of Psychosocial Oncology*, 1983, *1*, 75-82.

Lansky, S. B., Lowman, J. T., Vats, T., & Gyulay, J. School phobias in children with malignant neoplasms. *American Journal of Diseases of Children*, 1975, *129*, 42-46.

Lazare, A. Unresolved grief. In A. Lazare (Ed.). *Outpatient psychiatry: Diagnosis and treatment*. Baltimore: Williams & Wilkins, 1979.

Lazarus, R. S. The costs and benefits of denial. In J. J. Spinetta & P. Deasy-Spinetta (Eds.), *Living with childhood cancer*. St. Louis: C.V. Mosby, 1981.

Lebow, G. H. Facilitating adaptation in anticipatory mourning. *Social Casework*, 1976, *57*, 458-465.

Leiber, L., Plumb, M. M., Gerstenzang, M. L., & Holland, J. The communication of affection between cancer patients and their spouses. *Psychosomatic Medicine*, 1976, *38*, 379-389.

Lemon, H. M. Control of pain in metastatic cancer. *Journal of Chronic Diseases*, 1956, *4*, 84-95.

LeShan, L. Psychotherapy and the dying patient. In L. Pearson (Ed.), *Death and dying: Current issues in the treatment of the dying person*. Cleveland: The Press of Case Western Reserve University, 1969.

Leveton, A. Time, death, and the ego-chill. *Journal of Existentialism*, 1965, *6*, 69-80.

Leviton, D. The significance of sexuality as a deterrent to suicide among the aged. *Omega*, 1973, *4*, 163-174.

Levitz, I. N. Comment in section on "The Parents." In N. Linzer (Ed.), *Understanding bereavement and grief*. New York: Yeshiva University Press, 1977.

Lewis, C. S. *A grief observed*. London: Faber, 1961.

Lewis, E., & Page, A. Failure to mourn a stillbirth: An overlooked catastrophe. *British Journal of Medical Psychology*, 1978, *51*, 237-241.

Lidz, R. Emotional factors in hyperthyroidism. *Psychosomatic Medicine*, 1949, *11*, 2-9.

Lieberman, S. Nineteen cases of morbid grief. *British Journal of Psychiatry*, 1978, *132*, 159-163.

Lifton, R. J. *Death in life: Survivors of Hiroshima*. New York: Random House, 1968.

Lifton, R. J. The sense of immortality: On death and the continuity of life. *American Journal of Psychoanalysis*, 1973, *33*, 3-15.

Lindemann, E. Symptomatology and management of acute grief. *American Journal of Psychiatry*, 1944, *101*, 141-148.

Lindsay, M., & MacCarthy, D. Caring for the brothers and sisters of a dying child. In L. Burton (Ed.), *Care of the child facing death*. London: Routledge & Kegan Paul, 1974.

Lipman, A. Drug therapy in cancer pain. *Cancer Nursing*, 1980, *3*, 39-46.

Lopata, H. Z. The social involvement of American widows. *American Behavioral Scientist*, 1970, *14*, 41-57.

Lopata, H. Z. *Widowhood in an American city*. Cambridge, Mass.: Schenkman, 1972.

Lopata, H. Z. Loneliness: Forms and components. In R. S. Weiss (Ed.), *Loneliness: The experience of emotional and social isolation*. Cambridge, Mass.: The MIT Press, 1973. (a) (First published in *Social Problems*, 1969, *17*, 248-261.)

Lopata, H. Z. Self-identity in marriage and widowhood. *The Sociological Quarterly*, 1973, *14*, 407-418. (b)

Maddison, D. The relevance of conjugal bereavement for preventive psychiatry. *British Journal of Medical Psychology*, 1968, *41*, 223-233.

Maddison, D. The consequences of conjugal bereavement. *Nursing Times*, 1969, *65*, 50-52.

Maddison, D., & Raphael, B. The family of the dying patient. In B. Schoenberg, A. C. Carr, D. Peretz, & A. H. Kutscher (Eds.), *Psychosocial aspects of terminal care*. New York: Columbia University Press, 1972.

Maddison, D., & Viola, A. The health of widows in the year following bereavement. *Journal of Psychosomatic Research*, 1968, *12*, 297-306.

Maddison, D., & Walker, W. Factors affecting the outcome of conjugal bereavement. *British Journal of Medical Psychology*, 1967, *113*, 1057-1067.

Malinowski, B. *Magic, science and religion*. New York: Doubleday, 1948.

Mandelbaum, D. G. Social uses of funeral rites. In H. Feifel (Ed.), *The meaning of death*. New York: McGraw-Hill, 1959.

Mandell, F., McAnulty, E., & Reece, R. Observations of paternal response to sudden unanticipated infant death. *Pediatrics*, 1980, *65*, 221-225.

Mandell, F., & Wolfe, L. C. Sudden infant death syndrome and subsequent pregnancy. *Pediatrics*, 1975, *56*, 774-776.

Markusen, E., Owen, G., Fulton, R., & Bendiksen, R. SIDS: The survivor as victim. *Omega*, 1977-78, *8*, 277-284.

Marris, P. Comment on grief. In N. Linzer (Ed.), *Understanding bereavement and grief*. New York: Yeshiva University Press, 1977.

Maslach, C., & Jackson, S. Burned-out cops and their families. *Psychology Today*, May 1979, p. 59.

Mawson, D., Marks, I. M., Ramm, L., & Stern, R. S. Guided mourning for morbid grief: A controlled study. *British Journal of Psychiatry*, 1981, *138*, 185-193.

May, H. J., & Breme, F. J. SIDS family adjustment scale: A method of assessing family adjustment to sudden infant death syndrome. *Omega*, 1982-83, *13*, 59-74.

Mayo Clinic Rehabilitation Program. *A study of discrimination toward cancer patients by insurers, employers and vocational rehabilitation agencies.* Rochester, Minn.: Mayo Clinic Rehabilitation Program, The Vocational Insurance Committee, October 1977.

McCaffery, M. *Nursing management of the patient with pain.* Philadelphia: Lippincott, 1979.

McCollum, A. T., & Schwartz, A. H. Social work and the mourning parent. *Social Work,* 1972, *17*, 25-36.

McDermott, N., & Cobb, S. A psychiatric survey of 50 cases of bronchial asthma. *Psychosomatic Medicine,* 1939, *1*, 201-204.

McGrory, A. *A well model approach to care of the dying client.* New York: McGraw-Hill, 1978.

Meerloo, J. A. M. The reflex of surrender and capitulation. *Psychiatry, Neurology and Neuropsychology,* 1962, *65*, 225-232.

Meichenbaum, D., & Turk, D. The cognitive-behavioral management of anxiety, anger, and pain. In P. O. Davidson (Ed.), *The behavioral management of anxiety, depression, and pain.* New York: Brunner/Mazel, 1976.

Melges, F. T., & DeMaso, D. R. Grief-resolution therapy: Reliving, revising, and revisiting. *American Journal of Psychotherapy,* 1980, *34*, 51-61.

Melzack, R., & Perry, C. Self-regulation of pain: The use of alpha-feedback and hypnotic training for the control of chronic pain. *Experimental Neurology,* 1975, *46*, 452-469.

Melzack, R., & Wall, P. D. *The challenge of pain.* New York: Basic Books, 1983.

Miles, M. S., & Crandall, E. K. B. The search for meaning and its potential for affecting growth in bereaved parents. *Health values: Achieving high level wellness,* 1983, *7*, 19-23.

Miles, M. S., & Demi, A. S. Guilt in bereaved parents. In T. A. Rando (Ed.), *Parental loss of a child: Clinical and research considerations.* Springfield, Ill.: Charles C Thomas, in press.

Mills, L. O. Issues for clergy in the care of the dying and bereaved. In D. Barton (Ed.), *Dying and death: A clinical guide for caregivers.* Baltimore: Williams & Wilkins, 1977.

Minuchin, S. *Families and family therapy.* Cambridge, Mass.: Harvard University Press, 1974.

Mitford, J. *The American way of death.* New York: Simon and Schuster, 1963.

Montgomery, P. Grief in couples. Reprinted in *The Compassionate Friends Newsletter,* 1980 *3*, 1, 5.

Moos, R. H., & Tsu, V. D. The crisis of physical illness: An overview. In R. H. Moos (Ed.), *Coping with physical illness.* New York: Plenum, 1977.

Morgan, E. *A manual of death education and simple burial* (7th ed.). Burnsville, N.C.: The Celo Press, 1975.

Morrissey, J. R. A note on interviews with children facing imminent death. *Social Casework,* 1963, *44*, 343-345.

Morrissey, J. R. Death anxiety in children with a fatal illness. In H. J. Parad (Ed.), *Crisis intervention: Selected readings.* New York: Family Service Association of America, 1965.

Moss, S. A. Acute grief, Aesculapian authority and the clergyman. In V. R. Pine, A. Kutscher, D. Peretz, R. Slater, R. DeBellis, R. Volk, & D. Cherico (Eds.), *Acute grief and the funeral.* Springfield, Ill.: Charles C Thomas, 1976.

Nagera, H. Children's reactions to the death of important objects: A developmental approach. *Psychoanalytic Study of the Child*, 1970, *25*, 360-400.

The National Cancer Foundation, Cancer Care, Inc., *The impact, costs, and consequences of catastrophic illness on patients and families.* New York: Cancer Care, Inc., 1973.

National Hospice Organization. *Standards of a hospice program of care.* Arlington, Va.: Author, 1981.

Natterson, J. M., & Knudson, A. G. Observations concerning fear of death in fatally ill children and their mothers. *Psychosomatic Medicine*, 1960, *22*, 456-465.

Nichols, R. V. Professionals and the funeral: Do we help or hinder? *Newsletter of the Forum for Death Education and Counseling*, 1983, *6*, 6-7.

Opler, M. An interpretation of ambivalence in two American Indian tribes. *Journal of Social Psychology*, 1936, *7*, 82-116.

Orbach, C. E., Sutherland, A. M., & Bozeman, M. F. Psychological impact of cancer and its treatment. III. The adaptation of mothers to the threatened loss of their children through leukemia. Part II. *Cancer*, 1955, *8*, 20-33.

Orcutt, B. A. Stress in family interaction when a member is dying: A special case for family interviews. In E. R. Prichard, J. Collard, B. A. Orcutt, A. H. Kutscher, I. Seeland, & N. Lefkowitz (Eds.), *Social work with the dying patient and the family.* New York: Columbia University Press, 1977.

Parad, H. J., & Caplan, G. A framework for studying families in crisis. *Social Work*, 1960, *5*, 3-15.

Parkes, C. M. Effects of bereavement on physical and mental health—A study of the case records of widows. *British Medical Journal*, 1964, *2*, 274-279.

Parkes, C. M. Bereavement and mental illness: Part I—A clinical study of the grief of bereaved psychiatric patients. *British Journal of Medical Psychology*, 1965, *38*, 1-12.

Parkes, C. M. Bereavement and mental illness: Part II—A classification of bereavement reactions. *British Journal of Medical Psychology*, 1965, *38*, 13-26.

Parkes, C. M. The first year of bereavement. *Psychiatry*, 1970, *33*, 444-467.

Parkes, C. M. Psycho-social transitions: A field of study. *Social Science and Medicine*, 1971, *5*, 101-115.

Parkes, C. M. *Bereavement: Studies of grief in adult life.* New York: International Universities Press, 1972.

Parkes, C. M. "Seeking" and "finding" a lost object: Evidence from recent studies of the reaction to bereavement. In *Normal and pathological responses to bereavement* (Series on Attitudes Toward Death). New York: MSS Information Corporation, 1974. (First published in *Social Science and Medicine*, 1970, *4*, 187-201.)

Parkes, C. M. Determinants of outcome following bereavement. *Omega*, 1975, *6*, 303-323.

Parkes, C. M. Bereavement counseling: Does it work? *British Medical Journal*, 1980, *281*, 3-6.

Parkes, C. M., Benjamin, B., & Fitzgerald, R. G. Broken heart: A statistical study of increased mortality among widowers. *British Medical Journal*, 1969, *1*, 740-743.

Parkes, C. M., & Brown, R. J. Health after bereavement: A controlled study of young Boston widows and widowers. *Psychosomatic Medicine*, 1972, *34*, 449-461.

Parkes, C. M., & Weiss, R. S. *Recovery from bereavement*. New York: Basic Books, 1983.

Pattison, E. M. Help in the dying process. *Voices: The Art and Science of Psychotherapy*, 1969, *5*, 6-14.

Pattison, E. M. (Ed.), *The experience of dying*. Englewood Cliffs, N. J.: Prentice-Hall, 1977.

Pattison, E. M. The living-dying process. In C. A. Garfield (Ed.), *Psychosocial care of the dying patient*. New York: McGraw-Hill, 1978.

Paul, N. The role of mourning and empathy in conjoint marital therapy. In G. H. Zuk & I. Boszormenyi-Nagy (Eds.), *Family therapy and disturbed families*. Palo Alto, Calif.: Science and Behavior Books, 1969.

Peppers, L. G., & Knapp, R. J. Maternal reactions to involuntary fetal/infant death. *Psychiatry*, 1980, *43*, 155-159.

Peretz, D. Reactions to loss. In B. Schoenberg, A. C. Carr, D. Peretz, & A. H. Kutscher (Eds.), *Loss and grief: Psychological management in medical practice*. New York: Columbia University Press, 1970.

Pine, V. R. Comparative funeral practices. *Practical Anthropology*, 1969, *16*, 49-62.

Pine, V. R. Social organization and death. *Omega*, 1972, *3*, 149-153.

Pine, V. R. *Caretaker of the dead: The American funeral director*. New York: Irvington, 1975.

Pine, V. R. Grief, bereavement, and mourning. In V. R. Pine, A. Kutscher, D. Peretz, R. Slater, R. DeBellis, R. Volk, & D. Cherico (Eds.), *Acute grief and the funeral*. Springfield, Ill.: Charles C Thomas, 1976. (a)

Pine, V. R. Social meanings of the funeral. In V. R. Pine, A. Kutscher, D. Peretz, R. Slater, R. DeBellis, R. Volk, & D. Cherico (Eds.), *Acute grief and the funeral*. Springfield, Ill.: Charles C Thomas, 1976. (b)

Pine, V. R., & Phillips, D. The cost of dying: A sociological analysis of funeral expenditure. *Social Problems*, 1970, *17*, 405-417.

Plumb, M. M., & Holland, J. Cancer in adolescents: The symptom is the thing. In B. Schoenberg, A. C. Carr, A. H. Kutscher, D. Peretz, & I. Goldberg (Eds.), *Anticipatory grief*. New York: Columbia University Press, 1974.

Poznanski, E. O. The "replacement child": A saga of unresolved parental grief. *Journal of Pediatrics*, 1972, *81*, 1190-1193.

Pratt, L. *Family structure and effective health behavior: The energized family*. Boston: Houghton Mifflin, 1976.

Raether, H. C., & Slater, R. C. The funeral and the funeral director. In E. Grollman (Ed.), *Concerning death: A practical guide for the living*. Boston: Beacon Press, 1974.

Raether, H. C., & Slater, R. C. Immediate postdeath activities in the United States. In H. Feifel (Ed.), *New meanings of death*. New York: McGraw-Hill, 1977.

Ramsay, R. W. Behavioural approaches to bereavement. *Behaviour Research and Therapy*, 1977, *15*, 131-135.

Ramsay, R. W. Bereavement: A behavioral treatment of pathological grief. In P. O. Sjöden, S. Bates, & W. S. Dockins (Eds.), *Trends in behavior therapy*. New York: Academic Press, 1979.

Ramsay, R. W., & Happée, J. A. The stress of bereavement: Components and treatment. In C. D. Spielberger & I. G. Sarason (Eds.), *Stress and anxiety* (Vol. 4). New York: Wiley, 1977.

Rando, T. A. An investigation of grief and adaptation in parents whose children have died from cancer. *Journal of Pediatric Psychology*, 1983, *8*, 3-20.

Rando, T. A. Creating therapeutic rituals in the psychotherapy of the bereaved. *Psychotherapy: Theory, Research and Practice*, in press. (a)

Rando, T. A. Bereaved parents: Particular difficulties, unique factors, and treatment issues. *Social Work*, in press. (b)

Raphael, B. Preventive intervention with the recently bereaved. *Archives of General Psychiatry*, 1977, *34*, 1450-1454.

Raphael, B. A psychiatric model for bereavement counseling. In B. Mark Schoenberg (Ed.), *Bereavement counseling: A multidisciplinary handbook*. Westport, Conn.: Greenwood Press, 1980.

Raphael, B. The young child and the death of a parent. In C. M. Parkes & J. Stevenson-Hinde (Eds.), *The place of attachment in human behavior*. New York: Basic Books, 1982.

Raphael, B. *The anatomy of bereavement*. New York: Basic Books, 1983.

Raphael, B., Field, J., & Kvelde, H. Childhood bereavement: A prospective study as a possible prelude to future preventive intervention. In E. J. Anthony & C. Chiland (Eds.), *Preventive psychiatry in an age of transition* (Yearbook of the International Association for Child and Adolescent Psychiatry and Allied Professions, Vol. 6). New York: Wiley, 1980.

Raphael, B., & Maddison, D. The care of bereaved adults. In O. W. Hill (Ed.), *Modern trends in psychosomatic medicine*. London: Butterworth, 1976.

Rees, W. D., & Lutkins, S. G. Mortality of bereavement. *British Medical Journal*, 1967, *4*, 13-16.

Reeves, R. B., Jr. The pastor's problem with his own discomfort. In V. R. Pine, A. Kutscher, D. Peretz, R. Slater, R. DeBellis, R. Volk, & D. Cherico (Eds.), *Acute grief and the funeral*. Springfield, Ill.: Charles C Thomas, 1976.

Reissman, F. The "helper" therapy principle. *Social Work*, 1965, *10*, 27-32.

Richmond, J. B., & Waisman, H. A. Psychologic aspects of management of children with malignant diseases. *American Journal of Diseases in Children*, 1955, *89*, 42-47.

Richter, C. P. The phenomenon of unexplained sudden death in animals and man. In H. Feifel (Ed.), *The meaning of death*. New York: McGraw-Hill, 1959.

Rosenblatt, P. C., Jackson, D. A., & Walsh, R. P. Coping with anger and aggression in mourning. *Omega*, 1972, *3*, 271-284.

Rothstein, S. *Aging and personalization of death in the young and middle adult years*. Unpublished doctoral dissertation, University of Chicago, 1967.

Rotman, M., Rogow, L., DeLeon, G., & Heskel, N. Supportive therapy in radiation oncology. *Cancer*, 1977, *39*, 744-750.

Rowe, D. Constructing life and death. *Death Education*, 1983, *7*, 97-113.

Rudestam, K. E., & Imbroll, D. Societal reactions to a child's death by suicide. *Journal of Consulting and Clinical Psychology*, 1983, *51*, 461-462.

Ryan, D. Value of religious support for the bereaved. *Newsletter of the Forum for Death Education and Counseling*, 1983, *6*, 6-7.

Sadoughi, W., Leshner, M., & Fine, H. Sexual adjustment in a chronically ill and physically disabled population: A pilot study. *Archives of Physical Medicine and Rehabilitation*, 1971, *52*, 311-317.

Sanders, C. M. A comparison of adult bereavement in the death of a spouse, child, and parent. *Omega*, 1979-80, *10*, 303-322.

Sanders, C. M. Effects of sudden vs. chronic illness death on bereavement outcome. *Omega*, 1982-83, *13*, 227-241.

Satir, V. *Peoplemaking*. Palo Alto, Cal.: Science and Behavior Books, 1972.

Saunders, C. M. S. Terminal care. In K. D. Bagshawe (Ed.), *Medical oncology: Medical aspects of malignant disease*. Oxford, England: Blackwell Scientific Publications, 1975.

Scheff, T. The distancing of emotion in ritual. *Current Anthropology*, 1977, *18*, 483-490.

Schiff, H. S. *The bereaved parent*. New York: Crown Publishers, 1977.

Schleifer, S. J., Keller, S. E., Camerino, M., Thorton, J. C., & Stein, M. Suppression of lymphocyte stimulation following bereavement. *Journal of the American Medical Association*, 1983, *250*, 374-377.

Schmale, A. H. Psychological reactions to recurrences, metastases or disseminated cancer. *Radiation Oncology • Biology • Physics*, 1976, *1*, 515-520.

Schoenberg, B. Management of the dying patient. In B. Schoenberg, A. C. Carr, D. Peretz, & A. H. Kutscher (Eds.), *Loss and grief: Psychological management in medical practice*. New York: Columbia University Press, 1970.

Schoenberg, B., & Senescu, R. A. The patient's reaction to fatal illness. In B. Schoenberg. A. C. Carr, D. Peretz, & A. H. Kutscher (Eds.), *Loss and grief: Psychological management in medical practice*. New York: Columbia University Press, 1970.

Schulz, R. *The psychology of death, dying and bereavement*. Reading, Mass.: Addison-Wesley, 1978.

Schuyler, D. Counseling suicide survivors: Issues and answers. *Omega*, 1973, *4*, 313-321.

Schwab, J. J., Chalmers, J. M., Conroy, S. J., Farris, P. B., & Markush, R. E. Studies in grief: A preliminary report. In B Schoenberg, I. Gerber, A. Wiener, A. H. Kutscher, D. Peretz, & A. C. Carr (Eds.) *Bereavement: Its psychosocial aspects*. New York: Columbia University Press, 1975.

Schwab, J. J., Farris, P. B., Conroy, S. J., & Markush, R. E. Funeral behavior and unresolved grief. In V. R. Pine, A. Kutscher, D. Peretz, R. Slater, R. DeBellis, R. Volk, & D. Cherico (Eds.), *Acute grief and the funeral*. Springfield, Ill.: Charles C Thomas, 1976.

Schwartz, A. M. Comment in section on "The Parents." In N. Linzer (Ed.), *Understanding bereavement and grief*. New York: Yeshiva University Press, 1977.

Scotto, J., & Chiazze, L., Jr. Cancer prevalence and hospital payments. *Journal of the National Cancer Institute*, 1977, *59*, 345-349.

Seibel, M., & Graves, W. L. The psychological implications of spontaneous abortions. *Reproductive Medicine*, 1980, *24*, 161-165.

Seligman, M. E. P. *Helplessness: On depression, development, and death*. San Francisco: Freeman, 1975.

Selye, H. *Stress of life*. New York: McGraw-Hill, 1956.

Senescu, R. A. The development of emotional complications in the patient with cancer. *Journal of Chronic Diseases*, 1963, *16*, 813-832.

Severo, R. Cancer: More than a disease, for many a silent stigma. *New York Times*, May 4, 1977.

Share, L. Family communication in the crisis of a child's fatal illness: A literature review and analysis. *Omega*, 1972, *3*, 187-201.

Shaw, C. T. Grief over fetal loss. *Family Practice Recertification*, 1983, *5*, 129-145.

Sheldon, A. R., Cochrane, J., Vachon, M. L., Lyall, W. A., Rogers, J., & Freeman, S. J. A psychosocial analysis of risk of psychological impairment following bereavement. *Journal of Nervous and Mental Disease*, 1981, *169*, 253-255.

Shneidman, E. S. You and death. *Psychology Today*, June 1971, pp. 43-45; 74-80.

Shneidman, E. S. *Deaths of man*. New York: The New York Times Book Company, Quadrangle, 1973.

Shneidman, E. S. Some aspects of psychotherapy with dying persons. In C. A. Garfield (Ed.), *Psychosocial care of the dying patient*. New York: McGraw-Hill, 1978.

Shubin, S. Burnout: The professional hazard you face in nursing. *Nursing 78*, 1978, *8*, 22-27.

Shuchter, S. R. How the family physician can help patients adjust to the death of a spouse. *Medical Aspects of Human Sexuality*, 1984, *18*, 30-32; 36; 41-44; 49; 54.

Siegel, K., & Weinstein, L. Anticipatory grief reconsidered. *Journal of Psychosocial Oncology*, 1983, *1*, 61-73.

Siggins, L. Mourning: A critical survey of the literature. *International Journal of Psycho-Analysis*, 1966, *47*, 14.

Slavin, L. Evolving psychosocial issues in the treatment of childhood cancer: A review. In G. P. Koocher & J. E. O'Malley (Eds.), *The Damocles syndrome: Psychosocial consequences of surviving childhood cancer*. New York: McGraw-Hill, 1981.

Sobel, H. J., & Worden, J. W. *Helping cancer patients cope: A problem-solving intervention program for health care professionals*. New York: BMA Audio Cassette Publications, 1982.

Solnit, A. J., & Green, M. Psychological considerations in the management of deaths on pediatric hospital services. I. The doctor and the child's family. *Pediatrics*, 1959, *24*, 106-112.

Sourkes, B. M. Siblings of the pediatric cancer patient. In J. Kellerman (Ed.), *Psychological aspects of childhood cancer*. Springfield, Ill.: Charles C Thomas, 1980.

Spiegel, D., & Yalom, I. A support group for dying patients. *International Journal of Group Psychotherapy*, 1978, *28*, 233-245.

Spinetta, J. J. The dying child's awareness of death: A review. *Psychological Bulletin*, 1974, *81*, 256-260.

Spinetta, J. J. Adjustment in children with cancer. *Journal of Pediatric Psychology*, 1977, *2*, 49-51.

Spinetta, J. J. Communication patterns in families dealing with life-threatening illness. In O. J. Z. Sahler (Ed.), *The child and death*. St. Louis: C. V. Mosby, 1978.

Spinetta, J. J. Disease-related communication: How to tell. In J. Kellerman (Ed.), *Psychological aspects of childhood cancer*. Springfield, Ill.: Charles C Thomas, 1980.

Spinetta, J. J. Adjustment and adaptation in children with cancer: A three-year study. In J. J. Spinetta & P. Deasy-Spinetta (Eds.), *Living with childhood cancer*. St. Louis: C. V. Mosby, 1981. (a)

Spinetta, J. J. The sibling of the child with cancer. In J. J. Spinetta & P. Deasy-Spinetta (Eds.), *Living with childhood cancer*. St. Louis: C. V. Mosby, 1981. (b)

Spinetta, J. J., & Deasy-Spinetta, P. Talking with children who have a life-threatening illness. In J. J. Spinetta & P. Deasy-Spinetta (Eds.), *Living with childhood cancer*. St. Louis: C. V. Mosby, 1981.

Spinetta, J. J., Deasy-Spinetta, P. D., Kung, F., & Schwartz, D. B. *Emotional aspects of childhood cancer and leukemia: A handbook for parents.* San Diego: Leukemia Society of America, San Diego Chapter, 1976.

Spinetta, J. J., & Maloney, L. J. Death anxiety in the outpatient leukemic child. *Pediatrics,* 1975, *65,* 1034-1037.

Spinetta, J. J., Rigler, D., & Karon, M. Anxiety in the dying child. *Pediatrics,* 1973, *52,* 841-845.

Spinetta J. J., Rigler, D., & Karon, M. Personal space as a measure of the dying child's sense of isolation. *Journal of Consulting and Clinical Psychology,* 1974, *42,* 751-756.

Spinetta J. J., Swarner, J. A., & Sheposh, J. P. Effective parental coping following the death of a child from cancer. *Journal of Pediatric Psychology,* 1981, *6,* 251-263.

Stack, J. M. Spontaneous abortion and grieving. *American Family Physician,* 1980, *21,* 99-102.

Stein, Z., & Susser, M. W. Widowhood and mental illness. *British Journal of Preventive and Social Medicine,* 1969, *23,* 106-110.

Stephens, S. Bereavement and the rebuilding of family life. In L. Burton (Ed.), *Care of the child facing death.* London: Routledge and Kegan Paul, 1974.

Stone, R. W. Employing the recovered cancer patient. *Cancer,* 1975, *36,* 285-286.

Stroebe, M. S., & Stroebe, W. Who suffers more? Sex differences in health risks of the widowed. *Psychological Bulletin,* 1983, *93,* 279-301.

Stroebe, M. S., Stroebe, W., Gergen, K., & Gergen, M. The broken heart: Reality or myth? *Omega,* 1981-82, *12,* 87-105.

Sudnow, D. *Passing on: The social organization of dying.* Englewood Cliffs, N. J.: Prentice-Hall, 1967.

Szasz, T. S., & Hollender, M. H. A contribution to the philosophy of medicine— The basic models of the doctor-patient relationship. *A. M. A. Archives of Internal Medicine,* 1956, *97,* 585.

Tan, S. *Acute pain in a clinical setting: Effects of cognitive-behavioral skills in training.* Unpublished doctoral dissertation, McGill University, 1980.

Taylor, D. A. Views of death from sufferers of early loss. *Omega,* 1983-84, *14,* 77-82.

Travis, G. *The experience of chronic illness in childhood.* Stanford, Calif: Stanford University Press, 1976.

Tucker, M. A. Effect of heavy medical expenditures on low income families. *Public Health Report,* 1970, *85,* 419-425.

Vachon, M. L. S. Grief and bereavement following the death of a spouse. *Canadian Psychiatric Association Journal,* 1976, *21,* 35-44.

Vachon, M. L. S. Motivation and stress experienced by staff working with the terminally ill. *Death Education,* 1978, *2,* 113-122.

Vachon, M. L. S., Formo, A., Freedman, K., Lyall, W. A., Rogers, J., & Freeman, S. J. Stress reactions to bereavement. *Essence,* 1976, *1,* 23-33.

Vachon, M. L. S., Lyall, W. A. L., & Freeman, S. J. J. Measurement and management of stress in health professionals working with advanced cancer patients. *Death Education,* 1978, *1,* 365-375.

Vachon, M. L. S., Lyall, W. A. L., & Rogers, J. The nurse in thanatology: What she can learn from the women's liberation movement. In A. Earle, N. Argondizzo, & A. Kutscher (Eds.), *The nurse as caregiver for the terminal patient and his family.* New York: Columbia University Press, 1976.

Vachon, M. L. S., Lyall, W. A. L., Rogers, J., Freedman-Letofsky, K., & Freeman, S. J. J. A controlled study of self-help intervention for widows. *American Journal of Psychiatry*, 1980, *137*, 1380-1384.

Vachon, M. L. S., Rogers, J., Lyall, W. A., Lancee, W. J., Sheldon, A. R., & Freeman, S. J. Predictors and correlates of high distress in adaptation to conjugal bereavement. *American Journal of Psychiatry*, 1982, *139*, 998-1002.

Vachon, M. L. S., Sheldon, A. R., Lancee, W. J., Lyall, W. A., Rogers, J., & Freeman, S. Correlates of enduring stress patterns following bereavement: Social network, life situation, and personality. *Psychological Medicine*, 1982, *12*, 783-788.

van der Hart, O. *Rituals in psychotherapy: Transition and continuity.* New York: Irvington, 1983.

van Eys, J. What do we mean by "the truly cured child"? In J. van Eys (Ed.), *The truly cured child: The new challenge in pediatric cancer care.* Baltimore: University Park Press, 1977.

van Gennep, A. *The rites of passage.* Chicago: University of Chicago Press, 1960.

Veatch, R. M. Caring for the dying person: Ethical issues at stake. In D. Barton (Ed.), *Dying and death: A clinical guide for caregivers.* Baltimore: Williams & Wilkins, 1977.

Vernick, J. Meaningful communication with the fatally ill child. In E. J. Anthony & C. Koupernik (Eds.), *The child in his family: The impact of disease and death.* New York: Wiley, 1973.

Vernick, J., & Karon, M. Who's afraid of death on a leukemia ward? *American Journal of Diseases of Children*, 1965, *109*, 393-397.

Verwoerdt, A. Communication with the fatally ill. *Southern Medical Journal*, 1964, *57*, 787-793.

Verwoerdt, A. *Communication with the fatally ill.* Springfield, Ill.: Charles C Thomas, 1966.

Videka-Sherman, L. Coping with the death of a child: A study over time. *American Journal of Orthopsychiatry*, 1982, *52*, 688-698.

Volkan, V. A study of a patient's "re-grief work" through dreams, psychological tests and psychoanalysis. *Psychiatric Quarterly*, 1971, *45*, 225-273.

Volkan, V. "Re-grief" therapy. In B. Schoenberg, I. Gerber, A. Wiener, A. H. Kutscher, D. Peretz, & A. C. Carr (Eds.), *Bereavement: Its psychosocial aspects.* New York: Columbia University Press, 1975.

Volkan, V., & Showalter, C. Known object loss, disturbance in reality testing, and "re-grief" work as a method of brief psychotherapy. *Psychiatric Quarterly*, 1968, *42*, 358-374.

Volkart, E. H. (with collaboration of S. T. Michael). Bereavement and mental health. In A. Leighton, J. Clausen, & R. Wilson (Eds.), *Explorations in social psychiatry.* New York: Basic Books, 1957.

Vollman, R. R., Ganzert, A., Picher, L., & Williams, W. V. The reactions of family systems to sudden and unexpected death. *Omega*, 1971, *2*, 101-106.

Waechter, E. H. Children's awareness of fatal illness. *American Journal of Nursing*, 1971, *7*, 1168-1172.

Wallace, J. Comment on "Family Functioning" in panel discussion on "Care of the Child with Cancer." *Pediatrics*, 1967, *40*, 512-519.

Warner, W. L. *A black civilization.* New York: Harper, 1937.

Warner, W. L. *The living and the dead.* New Haven, Conn.: Yale University Press, 1959.

Wasow, M. Human sexuality and serious illness. In C. A. Garfield (Ed.), *Psychosocial care of the dying patient*. New York: McGraw-Hill, 1978.

Weisman, A. D. *On dying and denying: A psychiatric study of terminality*. New York: Behavioral Publications, 1972. (a)

Weisman, A. D. Psychosocial considerations in terminal care. In B. Schoenberg, A. C. Carr, D. Peretz, & A. H. Kutscher (Eds.), *Psychosocial aspects of terminal care*. New York: Columbia University Press, 1972. (b)

Weisman. A. D. Thanatology. In A. M. Freedman, H. I. Kaplan, & B. J. Sadock (Eds.), *Comprehensive textbook of psychiatry* (Vol. 2, 2nd ed.). Baltimore: Williams & Wilkins, 1975.

Weisman. A. D. The psychiatrist and the inexorable. In H. Feifel (Ed.), *New meanings of death*. New York: McGraw-Hill, 1977.

Weisman, A. D. Special attention for the terminally ill. *Physician and Patient*, 1982, *1*, 28-34.

Weisman, A. D., & Hackett, T. Predilection to death. *Psychosomatic Medicine*, 1961, *23*, 231-255.

Weisman, A. D., & Sobel, H. J. Coping with cancer through self-instruction: A hypothesis. *Journal of Human Stress*, 1979, *5*, 3-8.

Weisman, A. D., & Worden, J. W. Psychosocial analysis of cancer deaths. *Omega*, 1975, *6*, 61-75.

What man shall live and not see death? *Nursing Outlook*, January 1964, p. 23.

White, W. Family dynamics and family counseling (Participant Manual). In U.S. Department of Health and Human Services, *Hospice education program for nurses* (Publication No. HRA 81-27). Washington, D.C.: U.S. Government Printing Office, 1981. (a)

White, W. Managing personal and organizational stress in the care of the dying (Participant Manual). In U.S. Department of Health and Human Services, *Hospice education program for nurses* (Publication No. HRA 81-27). Washington, D.C.: U.S. Government Printing Office, 1981. (b)

White, W., Kunz, C., & Hogan, J. Communication skills (Participant Manual). In U.S. Department of Health and Human Services, *Hospice education program for nurses* (Publication No. HRA 81-27). Washington, D.C.: U.S. Government Printing Office, 1981.

Wiener, J. M. Reaction of the family to the fatal illness of the child. In B. Schoenberg, A. C. Carr, D. Peretz, & A. H. Kutscher (Eds.), *Loss and grief: Psychological management in medical practice*. New York: Columbia University Press, 1970.

Willis, D. The families of terminally ill children: Symptomatology and management. *Journal of Clinical Child Psychology*, 1974, *3*, 32-33.

Wilson, A. L., & Soule, D. J. The role of a self-help group in working with parents of a stillborn baby. *Death Education*, 1981, *5*, 175-186.

Wilson, D. C. The viability of pediatric hospices: A case study. *Death Education*, 1982, *6*, 205-212.

Wolff, J. R., Nielson, P. E., & Schiller, P. The emotional reaction to a stillbirth. *American Journal of Obstetrics and Gynecology*, 1970, *108*, 73-76.

Woodfield, R. L., & Viney, L. L. A personal construct approach to bereavement. *Omega*, in press.

Woods, N. F. *Human sexuality in health and illness*. St. Louis: C. V. Mosby, 1975.

Woodson, R. Hospice care in terminal illness. In C. A. Garfield (Ed.), *Psychosocial care of the dying patient*. New York: McGraw-Hill, 1978.

Worden, J. W. Pastoral care workshop. In B. Schoenberg, A. C. Carr, D. Peretz, & A. H. Kutscher (Eds.), *Psychosocial aspects of terminal care.* New York: Columbia University Press, 1972.

Worden, J. W. *Grief counseling and grief therapy: A handbook for the mental health practitioner.* New York: Springer, 1982.

Yalom, I. *The theory and practice of group psychotherapy.* New York: Basic Books, 1975.

Young, M., Benjamin, B., & Wallis, C. Mortality of widowers. *Lancet,* 1963, *2,* 454-456.

Zeltzer, L. K. The adolescent with cancer. In J. Kellerman (Ed.), *Psychological aspects of childhood cancer.* Springfield, Ill.: Charles C Thomas, 1980.

Index

About the Author

THERESE A. RANDO, PhD, is a clinical psychologist in private practice in North Scituate, Rhode Island. She is the Clinical Director of Therese A. Rando Associates, Ltd., a multi-disciplinary team providing psychotherapy, training, and consultation in the area of mental health, specializing in loss and grief and the psychosocial care of the chronically and terminally ill. In addition she has consulted, conducted research, provided therapy, written, and lectured nationally in areas related to grief and death since 1970.

Dr. Rando holds a doctorate in clinical psychology from the University of Rhode Island and has received advanced training in psychotherapy and in medical consultation-liaison psychiatry at Case Western Reserve University Medical School and University Hospitals of Cleveland. A former consultant to the U.S. Department of Health and Human Services' Hospice Education Program for Nurses, she developed their program for training hospice nurses to cope with loss, grief, and terminal illness. Her current research interests focus on the long-term processes and effects of grief, the experience of bereaved parents, and the emotional reactions of rescue workers. She has recently edited the book *Parental Loss of a Child: Clinical and Research Considerations.*

477